THE REAL WORLDS OF
CANADIAN
POLITICS

THE REAL WORLDS OF
CANADIAN POLITICS

CASES IN PROCESS
AND POLICY

Robert M. Campbell
and Leslie A. Pal

broadview press

Canadian Cataloguing in Publication Data

Campbell, Robert Malcolm
  The real worlds of Canadian politics: Cases in process and policy
ISBN 0-921149-40-9

1. Canada — Politics and Government — 1984 —
I.Pal, Leslie Alexander, 1954-. II. Title.
FC630.P34 1989   971.064'7   C89-093696-X
F1034.2.P34 1989

In Canada: In the U.S.:
broadview press   broadview press
P.O. Box 1243   421 Center St.,
Peterborough, Ont., K9J 7H5   Lewiston, NY 14092

Printed and bound in Canada by Gagné Ltd.

Cover photograph: Doug Sadler

TABLE OF CONTENTS

List of Insets and Appendices

PREFACE

Readers should not be misled by this book's title. We do not presume to have the key to understanding the 'real worlds' of Canadian politics. We do hope, however, that our chapters tap aspects of Canadian political reality that demand attention, and that they will stimulate the reader's intellectual curiosity. We gladly shoulder, of course, the usual burden of full responsibility for everything in this book, even though there was of necessity was a division of labour. (Pal wrote the chapters on the CF-18 affair, abortion and free trade, while Campbell penned those on the drug patents case, pornography and Meech Lake.)

We wrote this book with several purposes in mind. First, while both of us are attracted to grand theory, we are acutely aware of the inability of such theory to fully capture the complexity and colour of actual politics. As teachers, we are constantly reminded that our students initially develop their interest in political science through a fascination with policy issues and political personalities. It struck us that there might be a way, through a case study approach, to provide a better balance between the intrinsic interest of the political spectacle and the bloodless analysis of the discipline. Second, both of us are persuaded that policy areas, to an extent, generate specific configurations of politics. Interest groups, for example, operate very differently in the contexts of free trade and abortion. Fruitful analysis of the role of groups and the larger configurations of power they express must be built upon 'sectoral' studies of the state and public policy. Third, we wanted to write a book that could supplement the more traditional texts by blending a journalistic style with analysis. We wanted the chapters of this book to be more than merely readable; we wanted to produce narratives that reflected the drama and the passion of the issues, without losing perspective and judgment.

Whatever success we have achieved would have been much diminished without the help of kind and careful colleagues. Donald Smiley and G. Bruce Doern each read the entire manuscript with characteristic perspicacity. Other who helped with selected chapters include John Allett, Rob Beamish, Bill Coleman, Carmen Emmott, Lyle Emmott, Vaughan Lyon, Ted Morton and David Taras. Don LePan of Broadview Press offered us a stimulating blend of entrepreneurship, good sense, amity and intellectual curiosity.

We are also grateful to Catherine Bailey, Carolyn Bassett and Joelle Favreau for the energetic research assistance they provided. The University of Calgary and Trent University (Trent Committee on Research and the Frost Centre for Canadian Heritage and Development Studies) provided generous financial assistance so that we might complete this project.

Mary Pal and Christl Verduyn were true partners in our enterprise: firm but forgiving critics, careful and caring readers, they sustained us with loving resolution as we tried to bridle our truant pens. Our children were firm, careful and resolved as well: they insisted that we keep ourselves rooted as well in the real worlds of play and laughter.

Leslie Pal
Robert Campbell

INTRODUCTION

There are by now many good books on Canadian politics, and several interesting collections of cases on political processes and public policy. While no one should ever apologize for writing a book, some explanation of why we thought it would be useful to add to the groaning shelves is in order.

Most undergraduate courses in Canadian politics rely on traditional texts to cast light on the particular subject at hand: federalism, political leadership, parties, and so on. These courses, for which this book has been designed, have at their disposal several large and learned tomes that embrace virtually every detail of the political process in this country. In talking to colleagues (some, the authors of these tomes) and in our own teaching, we have noticed that the virtues of large and exhaustive texts can simultaneously become liabilities. It is difficult, for one thing, to write with passion and style when the purpose of the enterprise is analytical. And yet most students *take* introductory courses in politics because they are excited or agitated about what they perceive to be "real politics": fire and blood, strife and conflict, the quest for peace and the chilling disciplines of power.

Even the best introductory texts on Canadian politics sometimes have the character of an autopsy. The system is stretched out on the unyielding slab, and readers are given a catalogue of limbs and organs, skeletal features, sinews and nerves, and even blemishes and congenital deformations. As useful as pathology is, however, no student of medicine would ever concentrate exclusively on cadavers. In politics, this means some exposure to the political process, to institutions and forces as they combine in complex and marvelous ways to produce odd or exciting results.

Most of the main texts presently used across the country recognize this, of course, and have incorporated a case study to illustrate the ways in which the various parts of the system combine and clash in real life. This book is nothing more than an extended version of this stratagem; instead of a single, short, case study, we provide six extensive ones. This book tries to open a small window into the real world of Canadian politics; not a world of clean charts and straight arrows that tidily delineate the flows of power, but a complex and shifting world of issues, personalities, forces, and institutions as they combine in process.

The use of the plural *Worlds* in our title is deliberate. We want to show that beneath the canopy of a single political system there can be tremendous variety in political processes and public policy. Not all elements or ingredients of the system carry the same weight in each and every case. Sometimes the fact that Canada is a federal system is critical and determining, sometimes it is not. The executive does not always dominate the legislature. The judiciary plays bit parts in some political dramas, leading roles in others. The cases chosen for this book not only illustrate how the different components of the political system interact, but also why certain features are operative in certain circumstances and not in others. The key political institutions and players vary enormously from case to case in the many worlds of Canadian politics. It is useful to consider politics in terms of "issue networks" or "subgovernments": processes, actors, institutions, and even political discourse will vary across these networks. In economic policy, for example, producer groups such as manufacturers, labour unions, and agriculture are clear players, and the terms of debate are for better or worse set within the limits of modern economic theory. The politics of abortion or pornography are entirely different: the actors change, the issues mutate, and the language shifts. Business organizations, for example, have little to do with abortion, and none of the main players in the abortion policy arena rely on economic concepts in making their claims.

Cases have their limits, of course, chief among which is their limited representativeness if they are not carefully selected. They have a prime virtue, however, in that they can delineate the complex elements of a process in narrative rather than analytical form. This is the other contribution that we hope to make with this volume. To take *process* and *policy outcomes* seriously means taking a unique sequence of events and understanding it from the perspective of the actors. Why did they do what they did, what structural constraints did they face, and how did these combine to produce (or not produce) policy? Indeed, most people, when they think of politics, think in terms of "stories" and issues and personalities, of "what happened." It is easy to dismiss this as uninformed and superficial, but it captures something that academic analyses often miss: politics as the engagement of living wills, of real persons with interests and passions, visions and mad dreams. Politics at this level — perhaps the primordial level — demands a narrative voice rather than an exclusively analytical one. That is why, in the cases that follow, we have tried to blend the analysis of larger forces with an appreciation of the situation as seen by political actors themselves. We have tried to tell "the story," weaving in as best we can the elements of personality and circumstance, irony and comedy.

We chose six cases: the CF–18 maintenance contract affair of 1986; the revisions to the drug patent act in 1986–1987; the attempt to introduce new legislation on pornography in 1987; the Supreme Court's 1988 decision to strike down Canada's 1969 abortion legislation in the Morgentaler case; the Meech Lake Accord of 1987; and the Free Trade Agreement with the United

States, signed in January 1988. All six are relatively recent, and all reached their policy crescendo during the first Mulroney government (1984–88). While together they cast an interesting light on the federal Conservative government in this period, each case study takes pains to develop the background specific to the issue. The chapter on abortion, for example, examines the legacy of 19th century British law for Canada's treatment of abortion and contraception in the 1969 legislative changes. The chapter on the drug patent act goes back to the Liberal governments of the 1950s and 1960s to show why they created the legislative provisions on pharmaceutical patents that made Canada unique in the industrialized world.

The cases were not randomly selected. In keeping with our theme of "many worlds," we deliberately chose cases that would sharpen contrasts and illustrate differences. We were also guided, however, by some convictions about the nature of politics in the modern state. New kinds of political issues have arisen on Canada's agenda in the last decade, as they have for many other industrialized nations. Ideological currents have been swirling and the old-style consensus politics has been undermined if not destroyed. The rise of neo-conservative tendencies has generated new policy approaches to economic problems (e.g., free trade) and morality (e.g., tougher pornography laws). The triumph of provincialism has elevated regional concerns to matters of critical national importance (e.g., the CF–18 decision and the Meech Lake Accord). The adoption of the Charter of Rights in Canada has further constrained parliamentary sovereignty (e.g., the Morgentaler decision). Technological change has transformed our perception of economic policy and economic priorities (e.g., the drug patent case). In each of these areas, profound changes have created new political issues, which in turn affect the Canadian political process and its capacity to deal with these issues. Free trade raises questions about national sovereignty; Meech Lake may transform the nature of the Canadian political system; regionalism affects national politics; an evolving political role for the courts in the context of the Charter makes politics far less predictable; technological change has harrowing economic and political consequences; interest group politics compete with party and electoral politics; women's issues literally change the conceptualization of politics itself.

Looking for contrasts is not in itself a method. Each of the six cases contained in this book, while emphasizing one or two key themes, also touches on several others that we consider important to anyone trying to grasp the realities of Canadian politics. These themes comprise the ones outlined above concerning the new politics of the 1980s and 1990s, as well as more enduring ones about the nature of political institutions and policy processes. Synoptic Table I summarizes the thematic orientations of each of the cases, explained in somewhat greater detail below. Synoptic Table II, which accompanies the final section of this introduction, reverses the axes and shows how the cases bear on different dimensions of the political process.

Synoptic Table I

Chapter	Principal Themes	Sub Themes
CF-18 Affair	- regionalism - politics vs. technical considerations	- political symbols - premiers as provincial spokesmen - party tensions
Drug Patents	- new economics - role of Senate	- interest groups - regionalism
Pornography	- designing laws - role of courts vs. legislature	- feminism - new morality
Abortion	- role of courts - Charter of Rights	- feminist politics - reproductive rights
Meech Lake	- intergovernmental bargaining - constitution making	- interest groups - unpredictability of politics
Free Trade	- politics of international trade - political symbols	- party competition - role of Senate

THE CASES: AN OVERVIEW

The CF–18 Affair

Ottawa's decision in the early 1980s to select the F–18A Hornet as Canada's new fighter aircraft led directly to the struggle over the multi-million dollar maintenance contract for the plane. By 1986 there were only two real competitors, a consortium led by Bristol Aerospace based in Winnipeg, and a consortium led by Canadair Ltd. based in Montreal. A special committee of government experts recommended that the contract go to Bristol, on grounds of superior technical merit and a lower bid on the contract. Fierce lobbying by politicians from both cities and provinces succeeded in propelling the issue from a simple one about fixing airplanes to a complex test of national unity, industrial policy, historical justice and rational decision making. In the fall of 1986, the federal cabinet decided to ignore the recommendations of its expert committee, and handed the contract over to Canadair. This enraged not only Manitobans, but most westerners, and the CF–18 decision quickly joined the 1980 National Energy Program as a symbol of regional resentment and injustice.

The CF–18 Affair is a sublime illustration of two powerful and persistent themes in Canadian politics. The first is the extraordinary grip of regional resentments and jealousies. A government decision of this type, which delivers concentrated benefits in a well-defined region of the country, is a dagger twisted in the heart of federalism. The stakes were high in the CF–18 maintenance contract: jobs, millions of dollars of work stretching ahead for twenty years, and ultimately several technological benefits that might further stimulate the fledgling Canadian aerospace sector. Westerners were initially confident about the contract competition, since for the first time in decades there was a Conservative government in Ottawa, and the West had been electing Conservatives (though not governments) since Diefenbaker. But the Tories had a debt to pay in Quebec as well, since that province had given them a majority of seats in the 1984 election. Moreover, in Quebec the issue was not West v. East, but Quebec's right to industrial development after what it saw as decades of favouritism to Ontario.

The second pre-eminent theme of this story is the tension between rational decision-making and political calculation. Almost everyone recognizes that these categories are absurd, at least in the sense that real policy decisions could ever be based purely on value-free, technical, expert knowledge. There is no geometry of politics, no ultimate calculus that can reduce political questions to mere matters of measurement. In the real worlds of Canadian politics, however, there remains the assumption that politicians will strive to apply uniform standards fairly and with an eye to the common good of the community. It was this loose standard that seemed to be violated by the CF–18 decision: federal politicians ignored the advice of their officials. Indeed, they seemed in the end to base their decision on criteria that had never been part of the original competition among the firms. On the other hand, it is true that some of the key considerations in awarding the contract had to be based on hunches rather than expert knowledge (e.g., the possible spin-offs the contract might have in the aerospace sector). In a democratic polity, the responsibility for decisions of this sort — ones that rely in the end on sheer judgment — ultimately *must* rest with politicians.

Other themes surface in the case as well. For example, the CF–18 affair demonstrated the importance of political symbols in policy-making. Very early in the debate, the maintenance contract became burdened with powerfully charged political symbols: the belief in both Quebec and the West that federal governments always ultimately bow to "Eastern" interests (defined as the interests of Quebec by Manitobans, of Ontario by Quebecers). The case also demonstrates the way in which regional politicians act as spokespersons for interests within their jurisdiction. Premiers Robert Bourassa of Quebec and Howard Pawley of Manitoba both lobbied Ottawa to award the contract to the consortium located in their province. When the decision to give the contract to Quebec was finally announced, Premier Pawley went so far as to run ads in local papers urging people to contact their federal MPs and demand justice for the "people of Manitoba." In cases like these, premiers are not just political leaders, they are societal leaders as well. Of course, the Manitoba federal MPs also felt the heat, and so the case reveals the tensions that sometimes arise between being an elected member of a political party, bound to support the policies of that party, and a representative of a particular region. If the region is hurt by the policy, MPs and especially cabinet ministers walk a razor blade of expectations. Losing their balance can be distinctly uncomfortable.

The Pharmaceutical Patent Case

Economic markets depend on protection of property, since what one owns is essential to making profits, and profits themselves are property. This concept of property has had to be extended in recent decades as the economies of advanced industrial societies depend more and more on technological innovation. If the research done by a company to produce a new product were not protected in some way — if, in other words, as soon as the product came onto market some other company copied it — then costly, innovative research might not be done at all. On the other hand, society has partially underwritten the research done by companies (not least by administering an educational system that produces a highly skilled workforce) and so may after some time demand a return on that investment by reducing the protection for innovations and allowing lower cost copies to come onto market.

This is the nub of the problem of patents. All countries provide legal protection for the research that goes into the production of an original product. Patents are a form of legal monopoly granted to an inventor for a limited period of time, and are especially important in areas like pharmaceuticals. In the 1960s Canada passed one of the most liberal pharmaceutical patent acts in the world, giving very limited protection to the manufacturers of new drugs and forcing them to license their discoveries to other manufacturers for a small fee. This gave rise to the growth of a "generic" drug industry in Canada, consisting of small Canadian-owned firms who did little research on their own but who could purchase the rights, under license, to produce clones of name-brand drugs. The result over the years has been that Canadians enjoy some of the lowest pharmaceutical prices in the industrial world. In 1987 the federal Conservative government passed legislation to revise the patent act and increase the protection given to original drugs produced in Canada.

The battle over the pharmaceutical patents act was bitter and long, and revealed yet another world of Canadian politics. In this case, a central theme was the new economic philosophy of the federal Tories. They were inclined to accept the arguments made by the powerful Pharmaceutical Manufacturers Association of Canada (PMAC), representing mostly large foreign (American) drug companies, that Canada's patent legislation had had a chilling effect on innovative research. The backdrop for the legislation and for PMAC's lobbying was the "new economic reality" of global markets and international competition. If Canada were to have a pharmaceutical industry in the 1990s, that industry would have to be internationally competitive. It could not be competitive unless it did research on new products that could capture niches in international markets. The industry could not and would not do the research unless it could earn a return on its investments that it deemed acceptable. Canada's security in the global economy and the new, more market-oriented economic policies that are allegedly necessary to achieve this security are the prime themes of this case.

Another major theme in the case is the role of the Senate, especially under conditions where the Senate majority party is different from the government. The drug patent legislation bounced back and forth between the Senate and the Commons until all constitutional options were exhausted and the legislation could be thwarted no more. The Liberals controlled the Senate, and saw the legislation as a heaven-sent opportunity to embarrass the government. It thus strengthened Opposition leader John Turner's hand in the Commons, and forced a much longer review and examination of the bill than might have happened under any other circumstance.

The patents case also illustrates several sub-themes. Because PMAC represents foreign firms, and the Canadian Drug Manufacturers Association represents the Canadian-owned generic drug industry, the conflict between the organizations is a classic case of interest group politics. The bubbling stew of their antagonisms was spiced by the fact that the debate was largely between foreign-owned and Canadian-owned firms. This allowed the opposition parties to excoriate the government for passing legislation favouring non-Canadian interests. The government's admission that the legislation would lead to an increase in drug prices only raised the decibels of outrage. The mobilization of groups against the legislation was fascinating, and showed the power of appeals to nationalism, low domestic prices, and the fear of job losses. A complicating factor in this mobilization, one capitalized at every opportunity by the Prime Minister, was that Quebec favoured the changes in the hope of attracting more pharmaceutical research to the province. Mulroney was thus able to portray opposition to the patent changes as opposition to Quebec.

Thus another sub-theme was the regional impact of the changes. With Premier Bourassa behind him, Mulroney had a powerful ally, one, incidentally, who as a Liberal premier, could create discomfort for his federal counterparts who attacked the bill. The regional dynamics in this case played out much the same way as they did in the CF-18 case: federal MPs (from Quebec this time) were torn between what they knew was a popular policy (outside of Quebec) of opposing the drug patent changes, and a widespread sentiment in Quebec favouring the bill.

Pornography

Canada does not have special legislation governing the production and dissemination of pornography. At the federal level, the regulations concerning obscene materials are contained in sections of the Criminal Code. These provisions have been under official scrutiny for over two decades, and there has been a long series of attempts to provide better definitions of obscenity and pornography and better mechanisms of enforcement. The latest attempt came in 1987–88, with the introduction of amendments to the Criminal Code that would have provided for very broad definitions of pornography and very stiff punishments against transgressors.

With this case the book shifts to an area of public policy and a world of politics often ignored or underplayed in textbooks but obviously critical in real life: morality and moral regulation. The case reveals some of the contortions that the political system undergoes, in a pluralistic and democratic society, in trying to come to grips with universal and enforceable definitions of evil. The problem has several levels. First, there is the simple question of relativism. Modern societies like Canada have loosened many of the traditional bonds of church and family that used to provide an unspoken and widely accepted pattern of values. Today, it is much more likely that people will disagree over what constitutes an unacceptable degree of explicitness in sexual depictions. For some, any nudity is unacceptable, for others, graphic depictions of intercourse are merely erotic. In these circumstances, it is difficult to achieve a broad consensus on what constitutes pornography.

Second, beyond the somewhat superficial issue of relativism, is the tension in a liberal society between freedom of expression and freedom of conscience. Any attempt to control pornography can be seen as an attempt to control speech, publication, and even conscience. If consenting adults wish to produce pornography that other consenting adults would like to purchase, what place does the state have in forbidding it? But freedom of conscience cuts both ways: should people who object to pornography be placed in a position where they might inadvertently come across it while looking for their *Maclean's* magazine at the local store? The easy answer to these tensions is that the state should not interfere with the actions of consenting adults, except to control the display of pornographic products so that they do not accidentally become an affront to others.

This formulation forces consideration of the issue on yet another, deeper level. Can legislation of this type look only to what individuals do? Does individual behaviour, even among consenting adults, affect some broader community mores? Are there, in short, community standards that must be maintained if a community is to exist at all, at least as a moral community? Canada's efforts at dealing with pornography have consistently assumed that there is more to the question than individual taste, that there must be a sense of what the community as a whole is willing to tolerate.

This background to the pornography question helps explain why the legislative record in this area has been such a dismal failure. Virtually every federal government since 1970 that has tried to deal with pornography has failed. The failures were sometimes due to bad timing, accidents of politics such as elections that caused legislation to die on the parliamentary order paper, and vigorous interest group reactions. But just as often the underlying cause of parliamentary paralysis was the sheer difficulty of designing legislation that would balance the delicate principles and interests that frame the policy field. The last attempt by the Tory government went further than any before it in providing an explicit statement of what was to be considered pornographic, but the proposals were so sweeping that civil libertarians as well as feminists objected strongly.

Thus a main theme that emerges from this study is how difficult it is to design a good law, especially in a field as fraught with dangerous emotions as this one. Another key theme is the role of courts in filling the legislative vacuum. Since obscenity and pornography were governed by the Criminal

Code, violations were eventually brought to the courts. The vagueness of the legislation forced the courts to apply legal principles and rationales to decide specific cases. But in doing this, of course, judges often went far beyond anything ever envisaged by legislators.

Two other themes surface in the case study. The first is the growing importance over the last twenty years of feminist political discourse. In the 1960s there was virtually no feminist voice speaking on the question of pornography; indeed the debate was wholly determined by the traditional philosophical approaches of liberalism and conservatism. Throughout the 1970s the feminist voice grew stronger, and with it the feminist analysis of the meaning and import of pornography. Interestingly, though, in contrast to the strong consensus in the feminist movement over economic issues like equity employment, there are disagreements among feminists about the nature of pornography. Despite these disagreements, contemporary debates on the issue are completely different from what they were twenty years ago: that difference in large part comes from feminist interventions and perspectives.

The second sub-theme is a counterpoint to the feminist discourse on pornography and sexuality: the rise of the "new morality." The outlines of this new morality are obscure and contradictory, but there seem to be clear connections to the rise of the new right thinking in economic matters. The "neo-conservatism" of Ronald Reagan and Margaret Thatcher, it has been noted, is an odd amalgam of economic *liberalism* (as much freedom as possible) and moral *conservatism* (a return to traditional values). The new morality, as a consequence, is not new at all, but is simply a re-assertion of traditional "community" values regarding sexual behaviour. The Conservative government's attempt to deal with pornography was widely criticized for its broad definition of pornography and its harsh, punitive approach to even mild transgressions. To this extent, the politics of Canada's pornography legislation mirrored the politics of the new morality.

Abortion

Despite, or perhaps because of, a Supreme Court decision in January 1988, abortion remains one of the most divisive and explosive issues in Canadian public life. The January court decision struck down the law that had prohibited abortion in Canada (except under certain narrow conditions) since 1969. Parliament wrestled with the issue through the summer of 1988, and in an extraordinary Commons debate completely failed to reach consensus on even a direction in which a new law should go.

This case study once again delves into the contested zone between politics and morality. Its main theme is the role of the courts, especially after the Charter of Rights and Freedoms, in the modern political process. In 1969, after a debate the terms of which have not changed that much in recent years, Parliament passed amendments to the Criminal Code that prohibited abortion except when the mother's life and health were in danger and the procedure was approved by a hospital committee. In one of those jests of fate that confound virtually every political theory based on "grand forces" and "structural constraints," a single man, Henry Morgentaler, decided to fight the law through the courts and have it changed. The story of Morgentaler's battle is virtually synonymous with the story of Canada's abortion policy, since it was through Morgentaler's efforts that the law was finally struck down by the Supreme Court in January 1988. It is both a fascinating and disturbing saga of deliberate disobedience that forced authorities to raid illegal clinics, lay charges, and go through court arguments on the law's validity. The role of courts was critical in this case, since Morgentaler and the pro-abortion lobby early decided that getting legislative change through Parliament was virtually impossible: abortion was *so* contested that politicians wished to avoid dealing with it at all costs. Moreover, while the forces on both sides of the issue were committed and well organized, it was difficult to generate widespread popular support for either of the extreme options (complete, unfettered choice v. complete prohibition against abortion).

This strategy of litigation was enhanced after 1982 with the adoption of the Charter of Rights and Freedoms. Section 7 of the Charter protects the liberty of the person, and the Charter as a whole has precedence over legislation passed by federal and provincial governments. Interpretation of the Charter is up to the courts, particularly the Supreme Court, and this has changed the relationship of the legislature to the courts in the Canadian political system. Legislation may now be struck down by the courts if they deem it to be inconsistent with the Charter. Henry Morgentaler began his crusade well before the Charter, but his last assault, which led finally to the Supreme Court, incorporated the argument that Canada's 1969 abortion law was inconsistent with the Charter because it interfered with the liberty of the (female) person. It is expensive and difficult to use the courts as an avenue of political protest, but with the Charter now in play, many interest groups will at least consider the litigation route since it favours rights-based, minoritarian claims over the majoritarian logic of legislatures.

The abortion case also bears on several other themes of contemporary Canadian politics. It provides a perspective on feminist politics in Canada, since so much of the contemporary Canadian feminist movement has been bound up with the fight for abortion choice. Indeed, the early feminist movement in Canada was almost synonymous with the fight for "free abortion on demand" (as the slogan then was), as many radical women drifted out of the student and peace movements into feminist organizing. Other, primarily economic, issues eventually eclipsed abortion as the central focus of the women's movement, but ironically, as the decade of the 1980s closes, abortion has once more been propelled to forefront of the feminist agenda. Anti-abortion forces are better organized than ever before, and the Supreme Court's decision created the opportunity to lobby for even more restrictive legislation.

The Meech Lake Accord

The CF–18 affair and the pharmaceutical patent case cast a sharp light on regionalism in Canadian politics. The study of the Meech Lake Accord turns up the wattage and focuses carefully on the dynamics of intergovernmental bargaining and constitution making in Canada. It also explores what turned out to be a central priority on the Conservative government agenda in the latter half of its mandate.

Prime Minister Trudeau's legacy to the country was his patriation of the constitution and the entrenchment of a Charter of Rights and Freedoms. The legacy was soured, however, by Quebec's refusal to sign the agreement in 1981. Premier Lévesque, though the leader of a separatist government, broadly reflected Quebec's sentiments that the province had been betrayed. Even while the Charter and the new constitution had the effect of law in Quebec, the province was not a willing participant, and so almost one-third of the country's population could be viewed as reluctant partners in confederation. Flags flew at half mast throughout the province. Clearly the situation was intolerable.

Brian Mulroney vowed to initiate a new round of constitutional talks to bring Quebec back in to the constitutional fold. These talks culminated in two extraordinary sessions in 1987, one at a government retreat at Meech Lake and another in the Langevin block of Parliament in Ottawa. The result was what has come to be called the Meech Lake Accord, a short statement that gave Quebec the designation of a "distinct society" in the constitution, and extended some powers and prerogatives for the other provinces. Premier Bourassa proclaimed himself well satisfied with the Accord, and immediately had it passed in the Quebec National Assembly. All but two provinces followed suit over the next year, and the Accord looked as though it was on its way to becoming part of Canada's constitutional fabric. The Supreme Court's December 1988 decision against prohibition of English signs and Quebec's swift reaction in Bill-178 to circumvent that decision caused such an anti-Quebec backlash that the Accord was once more thrown into doubt.

No case could more perfectly illustrate the dynamics of modern Canadian intergovernmental negotiations. The Meech Lake process was, for instance, a closed process. The Prime Minister and ten premiers sat together in a stuffy room through the small hours of the night, trading and arguing, playing their cards and seeking their advantages. Public participation in the process came afterwards, and even then it was largely a charade. The Prime Minister stated before any hearings began that the Accord could not be reopened; to do so would start the bargaining process all over again. So, eleven men forged a far-reaching constitutional amendment. Intergovernmental politics was ever thus, a matter of deals and debates among a very closed circle of policy makers.

The case also demonstrates the bargaining strategies and tactics of the players. Premier Bourassa emerges from this vignette as a master of the intergovernmental poker game, but the other premiers also played their hands with aplomb. In this world of Canadian politics, the stakes are about governmental power and jurisdiction. The winners are those who can claim that they have enhanced their powers; the losers let power slither from their grasp. Of course, part of the game is never to admit losing, and so the comedy of Meech Lake was played out in the aftermath of the agreement, as groups and individuals pondered the ultimate effects of the Accord on the federal–provincial balance of power. A strong sentiment arose that Mulroney had sold out the national government in what Pierre Trudeau called a "gutless" manoeuvre.

The reactions to Meech Lake form a sub-theme of the case study. Few political issues manage to stimulate such a broad response from the political community (free trade is another example); the committee rooms of Parliament echoed with the impassioned pleas of groups both favouring and condemning the agreement. Interestingly, the sides were fairly balanced, which reflects the ambiguity of the Accord and its open texture. Just as in the pornography debate, the issue comes down to the meaning of the words in the text, so the proof of Meech Lake will be in the way in which its vague phrases are conceived in practice.

Another sub-theme is the role of accident and personality in real politics. The Meech Lake Accord was propelled, it is true, by certain broad forces. Quebec's absence from the national constitutional framework would have compelled action no matter which government was in power or who was at its helm. Nonetheless, the case shows how the Meech Lake Accord is the result of a specific political and personal chemistry. Brian Mulroney shaped the negotiations by his style and approach, learned as a labour negotiator. David Peterson of Ontario was a reluctant participant, Don Getty of Alberta wanted to discuss Senate reform, and Robert Bourassa of Quebec came in with a minimal package that skillfully capitalized on a situation where most provinces, whatever their reluctance to give up powers, felt that Quebec had to become a full constitutional partner. The fortunes of Meech Lake also show that affairs of state are just as often the creatures of fate as of men. Mulroney could go nowhere in his constitutional initiative with René Lévesque and the Parti québécois: in 1986 they were conveniently defeated by Bourassa and the provincial Liberals. Howard Pawley of Manitoba signed the agreement and then shortly afterwards was forced into a provincial election by one disgruntled backbencher. The Manitoba Liberals held the balance of power, and did not support the Meech Lake Accord. Without their support, the provincial Conservatives could not pass the necessary legislation. Finally, Richard Hatfield of New Brunswick was defeated by Frank McKenna's Liberals, who also opposed the Accord. The real world of politics is unpredictable and quixotic.

Finally, the case throws some light on the politics of constitution making in Canada. It reveals that process to be closed, dominated by governments with their own agendas and interests, and relatively unaffected by popular pressures.

The Free Trade Deal

At one level the Free Trade Agreement (FTA) was merely a component of Canada's international trading policy, an aspect of economic strategy. In the end it was much more than that; it quickly swelled to almost impossible proportions. It was an economic policy, a cultural policy, a daring gambit, a drastic error, a key to Canada's future in the global economy, the tight coffin of our national aspirations. It became virtually the only issue of the 21 November 1988 federal election. The Prime Minister launched the initiative in 1985 with the promise that an FTA would stimulate industry and jobs across the country, provide guaranteed access to American markets, and immunize Canada evermore from capricious and irrational spasms of U.S. trade protectionism. Opponents claimed that everything from crime to dangerously flawed blood tests would result from the FTA with the United States.

Free trade is to Canadian public policy what Ithaca was to Ulysses: a dream to pursue through all trials, a goal, however unrealistic, to strain for. So, almost every generation since Confederation has tried its hand at free trade with the United States, and even Pierre Trudeau's Liberal government in 1983 thought that some limited version of it might be worth negotiating. Ironically, Brian Mulroney, the man who finally signed a deal more comprehensive than anything previously contemplated by a Canadian prime minister (indeed, the most comprehensive trade deal in history), rejected the idea in 1983. The rise of protectionism in the United States, the lack of American interest in sectoral trade, and ultimately the possibility that a good deal would be the crowning glory of Tory economic promises to produce more jobs everywhere and especially in the regions, pushed an uncertain cabinet and government into the talks. The case shows how, far from being clear about their goals, federal politicians were confused, evasive, and even faint-hearted. After two years of negotiations, weeks before the deadline, the deal looked dead. Frantic eleventh hour interventions at the highest political levels yielded an agreement barely minutes before the legal time limit ran out. The following year saw an extraordinarily wide-ranging debate on the FTA as the government produced legislation to implement the deal and, in November 1988, fought an election campaign around it.

The FTA case shows another world of Canadian politics, the world of international and bilateral negotiations. Not all negotiations are like the one that produced the FTA, but most contain at least some of the features that made the FTA talks especially difficult. In talks like these, position is everything, and Canada walked into the talks in a position of weakness. The Americans neither needed nor especially wanted a deal with Canada; this was evident from the initial reluctance in Congress to permit the talks at all, and the trade sanctions Canada suffered in softwood lumber and shakes and shingles while the talks were underway. As well, there has to be clarity of purpose if negotiations are to succeed. The cabinet was not at all clear about what it wanted, and was even more confused about what it might have to concede in order to attain its vaporous aspirations. This indecision might not have been an impediment had the Canadian position been consistent from the beginning, but it was not. It was in fact hopelessly inconsistent. Canada wanted a free trade deal with the United States, but simultaneously wanted to exempt certain things (culture, the Auto Pact, social programs) from the discussions. In this the American position was at least logical: if there were to be talks at all, they had to start by putting everything on the table. This structural weakness on the Canadian side created some of the difficulties in the final days of the negotiations.

Like the CF–18 affair and to some extent the debate over abortion policy, the FTA carried a heavy burden of political symbolism. It had few ardent supporters, but those who opposed it were adamant about what it could and would do to the country. The FTA, as important as it was substantively, came to be seen as an attack on the fundamental nature of the country. Canada, it was said in various quarters, was unique because of its more collectivist traditions as compared to the U.S., because of its social programs that showed a commitment to community caring, because of its spirit of public and not just private enterprise, because of its cultural forms in theatre and prose and painting and broadcasting. The FTA would threaten all of that, by insidiously injecting foreign microbes into the Canadian body politic. Indeed, one critic did compare the FTA to AIDS: the effects of the virus would take decades to become visible, but when they did, that would be the end of Canada.

The supplementary themes of this case are numerous. It illustrates the power of party competition, for example, in the way that the Liberals and the NDP decided to stake out their opposition to the deal. It provides a bit part to the Senate, which in a dramatic move in August 1988, agreed to John Turner's request not to pass the enabling legislation until a federal election had permitted the people to vote on free trade. It even touches on intergovernmental bargaining, since in the early stages of the talks the provinces insisted that they be consulted, and everyone thought that any trade deal would have to include provincial jurisdiction. The final deal did not, perhaps because Ottawa knew that it would have difficulty in enforcing provincial compliance. Finally, it exposes some of the drama and the strategies of election campaigns: the FTA was forced onto the election agenda through deliberate Liberal tactics, and almost succeeded in burying the Conservatives.

CASES AND THE STUDY OF CANADIAN POLITICS

These six cases illustrate a few of the real worlds of Canadian politics. Other cases might have dealt more directly with issues like the media's effect on politics, or with provincial and municipal politics. But any volume, even with different cases, would eventually arrive at the same portrait of our political life: not the tepid perfection of a cubist drawing, but the raw, riotous colour of passions and principle, structure and symbol.

This book may be used in several ways. It should provide some enjoyment, and its narrative structure should permit a more vigorous and engaged reading than is typical of texts in the field. We have given each essay, inconspicuously we hope, an analytical framework, so that the reader will be introduced to the necessary background on international pharmaceutical markets, trade negotiations, or contraception, as needed. Each essay also ends with several discussion questions. These questions can be used in several ways. One way is to read the questions before plunging into the case, thereby using them as signposts for what is important in the story. Another way is to use the list of questions as a basis for reflecting on or discussing the case. This introduction and its Synoptic Tables provide a guide to some of the themes expressed in each of the cases, but readers should also take note of other aspects of politics that are revealed, even if only briefly, in the narrative. The essay on the FTA, for example, mentions in passing several characteristics of the American political system that sharply contrast with the Canadian practice. The drug patent case raises interesting questions about interest group politics, and most of the cases should stimulate some reflection on the role of political leadership in Canadian government.

Finally, the cases should not be treated separately. One of our purposes in writing them was to distinguish the different styles of politics that develop around different types of political issues. Readers should think about how the politics of moral regulation (e.g., abortion and pornography) differ from the politics of economic policy. How does capitalism affect policy making, and how do governments respond to different interests? What is the balance of power between different institutions of Canadian government, such as the legislature, the judiciary, and the executive? How do party politics affect this institutional balance?

Synoptic Table II

Aspect of System	Principal Chapters	Cognate Chapters
Institutions		
Cabinet	2, 5, 6	1
Legislature	3, 4	2
Senate	2, 5	6
Judiciary	3, 4	5
Bureaucracy	1, 2	5
Actors		
Parties	2, 5, 6	1
Interest Groups	2, 5, 6	3, 4
Experts	1, 2, 6	3
Processes		
Political Symbols	1, 4, 6	3
Intergovernmental relations	1, 5	2, 6
Regionalism	1, 2, 5	6

Chapter 1: CF-18; Ch. 2: Drug Patents;
Ch. 3: Pornography; Ch. 4: Abortion;
Ch. 5: Meech Lake; Ch. 6: Free Trade

Synoptic Table II may be used as a guide to exploring some of the broader aspects of the Canadian political system. The cases show how similar elements of the system get combined in different ways around different policy issues. Those interested in regionalism, for example, will find that theme developed principally in the chapters on the CF–18, drug patents, and Meech Lake. Other, cognate chapters may also treat the same theme, though in more muted tones. In the case of regionalism, Chapter 6 on the Free Trade Agreement addresses the tensions between the provincial governments and Ottawa during the negotiations.

A key point to bear in mind is that the cases allow the examination of different aspects of the same processes or institutions in different political worlds. Parties, for instance, may be examined from the perspective of the differing policy proposals they put forward (in the case of drug patents legislation), the tensions generated between national and provincial wings (the Liberals and Meech Lake), their strategies and tactics during election campaigns (the 1988 election over free trade), or the way that they deal with patronage (the CF–18 contract). The same might be said of political symbols and political language: the cases allow comparisons between the use of "region" as a symbol in the case of the CF–18 and "rights" in the case of abortion. Comparison of the role of the courts in the pornography and abortion cases can also provide fruitful perspectives on how these institutions operate in the contemporary Canadian state. These cases, if read creatively both for the contrasts they provide and the generalizations they might stimulate, should help develop an analytical appreciation of the policy process as well as a sharp sense of politics as it is lived and felt.

THE CF–18 AFFAIR

Ottawa announced its long-awaited decision on the CF–18 maintenance contract on 31 October 1986. Even though the bid by Winnipeg's Bristol Aerospace was cheaper than and technically superior to Montreal's Canadair bid, Canadair received the billion dollar contract. Manitoba reacted with bitter incredulity and a resentment so strong that Prime Minister Brian Mulroney called the issue a "challenge to national unity." Manitoba MPs and ministers were pressured to resign, western separatist parties rallied, and observers decried what they saw as rank political opportunism designed to bolster sagging Tory popularity in Quebec.

    The affair illustrated the real and often raucous world of Canadian regional politics, and some of the dilemmas of contemporary economic policy making. Both Quebec and Manitoba nursed historical grudges against Ontario's industrial success, and both demanded that Ottawa act "fairly." For Quebec, this meant strengthening the province's aerospace industry and "giving it a share" of industrial benefits that seem normally to flow to Ontario. To Manitobans, "fairness" meant making a decision on technical, rather than political merit. And that was precisely Ottawa's dilemma: how to balance technical considerations such as cost and efficiency against political considerations such as lasting regional resentment and possible electoral retribution.

Halloween 1986: At a press conference on the morning of 31 October, Treasury Board President Robert de Cotret announced the biggest trick-and-treat in Canadian history. A consortium led by Montreal-based Canadair Ltd. was awarded the sweet prize of a billion dollar maintenance contract on Canada's newly purchased fighter aircraft, the CF–18. Canadair's rival in the two-year bidding war was a consortium led by Bristol Aerospace Ltd., based in Winnipeg. Had Bristol lost because of inferior technical merit or high price there may have been sighs of regret, but no outrage. And yet outrage there was, crackling with cries of betrayal and whipped by indignant fury. Why?

Because *Bristol had won the technical battle, even while it lost the political war.* A federally appointed committee of 75 experts studied each of the bids and found Bristol's superior in technical merit as well as about $3.5 million cheaper. (In January 1988 the Toronto *Globe and Mail* reported that, on the basis of documents it had received under the Access to Information Act, the Bristol bid was actually cheaper by as much as $65 million.) Manitoba could be excused for thinking that there was a razor in its Halloween apple.

The issue hinged on the CF–18 and who would get the twenty-year contract to service it. The CF–18 Hornet is a mix of *Star Wars* and *Top Gun*, of sleek steel, weapons and computers that make it, in the words of its pilots, the "Cadillac of the skies." A "Cadillac" with some added features: twin General Electric F404 engines, Hughes APG-65 radar, 20 mm cannon, a top speed of Mach 1.8, and integrated on-board systems linked by over 25 computers.[1] On 10 April 1980 the Cabinet decided to buy 137 F–18A Hornets from the McDonnell Douglas corporation to replace Canada's aging fleet of fighter aircraft: the CF–104 Starfighter, the CF– 101 Voodoo, and the CF–5 Freedom Fighter. The Hornet was to be a multi-role aircraft, capable of serving in air-to-air as well as air-to-ground missions. In an age when fighter aircraft are often highly specialized, Canada wanted a plane to cover its European NATO obligations, patrol the Canadian Arctic, and act as an interceptor in case of air space violations. The Canadian Armed Forces rate the Hornet highly: in 1986 a team of five CF–18 pilots came second in the William Tell fighter competition held in Florida; in 1987 a pair of Hornets flew 5,800 kilometres from Iqaluit, NWT to the North Pole, with three refuellings en route.[2] A machine this complex and this expensive (almost $5 billion for 137 planes) needs complex and expensive maintenance. But the 1980 decision to select the Hornet was more than just the logical antecedent to the need for a maintenance contract: the way in which cabinet decided and the context of that decision came back in October 1986 to dramatically inflame regional tensions and historical resentments.

The CF–18 affair illustrates several features of Canadian political life that are unique to the problems of industrial policy-making. Modern governments in Canada and throughout the industrial world are not mere collectors of taxes; they are generators of economic growth in their own right. They spend vast sums of money on everything from office equipment to advertising. A key spending category is defence, because modern weapons are both very expensive to produce and require high levels of technology and skill. If a country can afford it, and if its has the industrial potential, it is tempting to try to produce those weapons domestically. The money thus stays in the country and has the added benefit of generating jobs and industry. These economic benefits are often bought at a price however, since the same equipment might be purchased more cheaply from foreign suppliers. Governments have to decide what premium they are prepared to pay to have the work done domestically. In Canada's case, most large defence procurements from foreign suppliers require that the company build some proportion of the weaponry in Canada, so that there will be "industrial benefits." But once politics enters the decision-making, it is difficult to remove it. If it makes sense to pay slightly more to generate jobs in the country as a whole, does it not also make sense to locate those jobs in high unemployment regions? If the government has the choice of building a munitions factory, for example, where should that factory be located? There are several "technical" criteria that might apply, such as proximity to a trained labour force or to other such plants. A political criterion, however, might be to locate the plant in a depressed region so that it could provide jobs and growth. Another political criterion might be to locate the plant in a politician's riding.

Decisions like the one Ottawa had to make with the CF–18 maintenance contract lay bare some of the dilemmas and tensions in public policy decision making. Which criteria should apply? Since the CF–18 maintenance contract was a "locational" decision (only one contract to a specific region), from the start it threatened to inflame regional rivalries. This case was particularly interesting and divisive because it pitted against each other two regions that have historically *both* felt deprived and discriminated against. The government, the first Tory majority since Diefenbaker's, faced an excruciating dilemma, since it wanted to hold Quebec's allegiance (newly and gingerly given in the 1984 election) as well as to reward its traditional support in the West.

BACKGROUND TO THE DECISION

The CF–18 story began on 17 March 1977, when the federal cabinet approved the New Fighter Aircraft Program. The program was to replace Canada's aging fleet of fighters with a new, state-of-the-art war plane. With cabinet approval of the purchase, the next complex decision was what kind of plane to buy, for what role? A New Fighter Aircraft Program Office (NFA/PO) was established and staffed by officials from the Departments of National Defence (DND), Supply and Services (DSS), and Industry, Trade and Commerce (DITC).[3] The need for DND's involvement was obvious, but the other departments were there for several reasons. DSS handles all of the federal government's major purchases of capital and equipment and provides expertise on contract negotiations. DITC was involved because, even though the cabinet had decided to purchase an American plane the successful bid would hinge on its industrial benefits to Canada country. These benefits are called "offsets," because the initial purchase price to a foreign supplier may be "offset" to the extent that the supplier agrees to build some components in Canada, transfer technology to affiliated Canadian firms, or buy equipment from Canadian companies. For example, if the government decided to pay $1 billion for something produced in the United States, it could demand that the supplier spend one-third of that amount in Canada, perhaps in assembly or production. If the supplier wanted the contract badly enough, it would think of a way to accommodate the government. The Defence people were the experts on what the plane had to do; the other departments were experts at negotiating offsets and deciding what package would provide the greatest industrial benefit to Canada.

In September 1977 the NFA/PO sent a detailed Request for Proposal (an invitation by the government to submit a bid) to six companies: Grumman, General Dynamics, McDonnell Douglas, Northrop, Panavia, and Dassault-Breguet. This Request specified how much the government was prepared to spend, and what it was looking for in a new fighter plane. The first five companies were able to submit proposals by the 1 February 1978 deadline.[4] These proposals went to cabinet in June, but the companies were given additional time to refine their bids. On 23 November 1978 the cabinet shortlisted two of the bids: the General Dynamics F–16 and the McDonnell Douglas F–18A Hornet. Six months passed as draft contracts were drawn up with each firm. Officials needed another six months to evaluate the contractual details. The experts chose the McDonnell Douglas F–18A Hornet and forwarded their recommendation to the new Clark government in December 1979. The inner cabinet was to have decided the issue on 14 December. The government was defeated in the Commons on 13 December, and the New Fighter Aircraft decision was frozen.[5]

By now rumours were widespread that the bureaucrats favoured the Hornet, and the election hiatus gave General Dynamics the time and the opportunity to lobby in favour of its own bid. With the Quebec referendum campaign under way in March 1980, the newly elected Trudeau government wanted to minimize any political damage from the fighter aircraft decision. On 28 March, René Lévesque and the Parti québécois proclaimed their support for the General Dynamics F–16 bid because, in their judgment, it offered greater industrial benefits to Quebec. Lévesque said "It's not a favor we're asking for,...it is an absolute right of Quebec to have its fair share."[6] Montreal MPs and the Quebec Liberal caucus as a whole lobbied hard to tip the balance, and succeeded in persuading McDonnell Douglas to increase its transfer of industrial benefits to the province. Six years later, in the middle of the CF–18 maintenance affair, Lévesque, claimed that Ottawa had promised the maintenance work on the new fighter to Quebec as a trade-off for choosing the F–18A Hornet. "We were promised very solemnly, during a tense period, at least 48 per cent of the economic fallout of the F–18 would come to Montreal."[7] Lévesque claimed that the original F–16 bid would have given all of the fighter maintenance work to Montreal firms. In his view, this accorded perfectly with established regional concentrations of different industries. "Traditionally, the air industry centre in Canada was, and in great part still is, in Montreal....Automobiles go to Ontario or elsewhere, but our share was aerospace. This is a memory a lot of people are bringing back, saying if we don't get some reasonable fallout on the maintenance job on that same bloody plane, the fat will be in the fire again."[8]

Lévesque, in his colourful way, was echoing the reality of modern politics, and in particular of modern Canadian politics. Industries do not locate in some purely "natural" way: they respond to government incentives as well as to market forces. If certain industries are located in certain parts of the country, this is due in part to political will, and not merely economic logic. Of course, the obverse is also true: if industries are *not* located in certain parts of the country, this too is shaped by political choice. The fighter decision was, from Léevesque's point of view, as much about regional justice in the political distribution of wealth as it was about defence.

The cabinet chose the McDonnell Douglas F–18A Hornet (the Canadian version known simply as the CF–18 Hornet) on 10 April 1980, and the contract was signed on 16 April. The agreement called for 137 planes costing US$2.369 billion, and McDonnell Douglas agreed to invest CAN$2.453 billion in industrial benefits in Canada.[9] The planes were to be built and delivered over an eight year period. In the interim, McDonnell Douglas would maintain the planes at its St. Louis, Missouri plant. The warranty would expire in 1988, and a new, specific maintenance contract would have to be written. While Ottawa had decided to save money by having the plane built in the United States, it wanted the twenty-year, multi-billion dollar maintenance contract to go to Canadian firms. Thus, the stage was set for the struggle between Bristol and Canadair six years later.

THE MAINTENANCE CONTRACT DECISION

Maintaining a multi-million dollar modern jet fighter requires technological wizardry and tight corporate coordination. At least two highly specialized tasks need attention: the engineering and overhaul of the plane's structural components, and the maintenance of "avionics" (the aviation electrical system) and computer software. The CF–18's advanced and integrated data systems presented new challenges to potential bidders. Very few companies are singly capable of handling these different tasks, and so consortia are the preferred arrangement. In the CF–18 affair, three consortia eventually submitted proposals: the Canadair group comprising Canadair Ltd. (Montreal), CAE Electronics (Montreal), and Northwest Industries (Edmonton); the Bristol group comprising Bristol Aerospace Ltd. (Winnipeg), Litton Systems of Canada Ltd. (Toronto), Bendix Avelex Inc. (Montreal), Garrett Manufacturing Ltd. (Toronto), and Leigh Instruments Ltd. (Ottawa); and the IMP group comprising IMP Aerospace Ltd. (Dartmouth), Canadian Marconi Co. (Montreal), Canadian Astronautics Ltd. (Ottawa), Spar Aerospace Ltd. (Toronto), and Fleet Industries (Fort Erie, Ontario).

The CF–18 maintenance contract was especially valuable to the competing companies because of its revenue (estimated at between $1.2 and $1.8 billion) and its stability (the initial contract was valued at $104 million over 3.5 years, but if renewed would extend over the twenty year life of the plane). The Canadian aerospace industry is notoriously volatile, and a stable, long-term contract could be an anchor in stormy international markets. Hundreds of jobs were at stake, most of them in what governments deem to be the most desirable areas of high technology industry with export potential.

The three competing bids were submitted on 29 November 1985, with a final decision due by 1 April 1986. The bidding process was controversial from the beginning, for several reasons. First, the Mulroney government had put Canadair, then a crown corporation, on the auction bloc in October 1984. In mid-August 1986, in the middle of the CF–18 maintenance decision, Canadair was sold to Bombardier Inc. of Montreal. It was rumoured that Bombardier, as part of its bid for Canadair, insisted that it get the CF–18 contract.[10] The contract was specifically mentioned in the Canadair purchase agreement, and Ottawa must have considered the boost that it would give to the newly privatized company.

The second complication was rooted in the 1984 federal election, in which the Tories surged to power after twenty years of opposition, on a platform of national reconciliation, of healing what they saw as the inter-regional wounds caused by Pierre Trudeau's confrontational style. The Prairies had voted Tory throughout the Trudeau years, electing oppositions and once, with Joe Clark, a government. Thus westerners have been in almost perpetual opposition to Ottawa, many of them resentful at what they perceive to be a perverse combination of indifference to them and favouritism towards Ontario and especially Quebec. The election of the first majority Tory government since Diefenbaker's augured a reorientation of policy: no longer would Ottawa skim the cream — in the form of government spending on contracts as well as in other policy areas — for the East and save the dregs for the West. The Mulroney Tories were a federal government with large numbers of western members, good western representation in the cabinet, and a debt of loyalty to repay. The CF–18 decision process, in pitting Winnipeg against Montreal, placed enormous pressure on the Tories to come to the aid of western industry. But the Tories had another problem: they had won the government primarily because they had won Quebec. For the first time since Diefenbaker, the Progressive Conservatives had won the majority of Quebec seats. Brian Mulroney, himself a Quebecer, had convinced the party that its fortunes depended on not just winning Quebec but keeping it. The Liberals and Conservatives were evenly balanced in Ontario and the East, but Quebec had so many seats compared to the West that no amount of Tory dominance in the Prairies would be enough to win power.

The third factor relates to the decline in Tory fortunes in Quebec. Mulroney carried Quebec in 1984 by winning 58 out of 75 seats, and Quebecers also seemed to think that they should be "rewarded" for their loyalty. Instead, one month after the submission of the CF–18 maintenance bids, the Tories announced that, as part of the complex sale and purchase of Gulf Canada by various interests, British-owned Ultramar Canada Ltd. would be allowed to buy a Montreal Gulf refinery. Ultramar planned to close the Montreal refinery and terminate 450 jobs. The issue was hotly debated in Quebec, and provoked one Montreal cabinet minister, Suzanne Blais-Grenier, to resign.[11] Some Quebecers saw the Ultramar decision as the result of collusion between Pat Carney (Energy Minister) and Sinclair Stevens (Regional Industrial Expansion Minister) to promote the interests of the West and Ontario against Quebec.

After being submitted in November 1985, the three competing bids sank into the murk of the bureaucratic review process. An evaluation team was established within DSS to assess the responses to "Request for Bid Repair 2795354 (BQ02), CF–18 System Engineering Support," as the contract was affectionately known in official Ottawa circles. The assessment process would be complex, since in a sense the experts had to assess not only the quality of the work, but the company's ability to do it. The evaluation team worked on a points system, awarding points on such diverse qualifications as avionics and software engineering, management functions, and airframe and associated systems engineering. These points were awarded in four broad areas: project requirements (engineering functions), financial requirements (cost effectiveness), contractual requirements (special terms of contract), and socio-economic benefits area (percentage of Canadian content and employment on the project). Although housed in DSS, the evaluation team had military advisors on it. The maintenance contract decision, however, was less a military one than an engineering and economic one, and so DSS officials had the upper hand. Since the evaluation team's role was to award points on technical merit in the four areas, it did not have to consider the thornier political aspects of the bidding process.

The first rumblings of an imminent decision were heard in February 1986, shortly after the evaluation team had completed its initial review. All three bids were re-opened in mid-February for what was called "bid repair," or clarification of selected aspects of the highly complex proposals. Rumours flew that Canadair (and hence Quebec) had the edge at this stage of the bidding, but Jake Epp, Minister of National Health and Welfare and Manitoba's key cabinet representative, assured Manitobans that the race was still open and that Bristol could win.[12] The evaluation team decided to drop IMP's bid at this point because it was technically inferior to Bristol's and Canadair's.[13] IMP claimed, however, that it had presented the lowest bid of the three. In fact, it said, technical expertise or competence should not in themselves be a basis of awarding the contract, because any successful bidder would have to learn the relevant techniques from McDonnell Douglas.[14] IMP fought back in March 1986, in part by successfully lobbying Stewart McInnes, the Minister of Supply and Services and a Haligonian. The consortium was reinstated, all three bids were reviewed, and a final recommendation was submitted to cabinet in June.[15]

A thundering silence ensued, partly because of the parliamentary summer recess, which normally slows down government business, but also because the issue was political gelignite. Federal by-elections were scheduled in Alberta and Quebec for late September, and so the government decided to delay the decision at least until they were over. The Tory party was paralysed by its own electoral success: with strong representation from the West, Quebec, and the Maritimes, it was a microcosm of the very rivalries that were starting to poison the bidding process. MPs from the respective regions knew very well how their constituents would feel if the contract went to a rival firm and another region. With the formal bidding process over and the government immobilized by the fear of offending regional interests, the only course left open was for those interests to make their feelings clear should they lose. Teetering on a precipice, the government needed a nudge.

First and most vigorous into the fray was Canadair and various Montreal interests. In mid August the Chambre de commerce de Montréal wired the Prime Minister urging that the CF–18 maintenance contract be awarded to Canadair. The Chambre had the support of the City of Montreal, the Montreal Urban Community, and the Montreal Board of Trade.[16] Marcel Laurin, mayor of St. Laurent (the suburb of Montreal in which both Canadair and CAE Electronics are located) said that he would increase his efforts to help Canadair get the contract.[17] The business representatives aggressively claimed that Montreal had a right to the contract. Manon Vennat, President of the Montreal Board of Trade, said that in 1980 "the federal government promised since the Montreal area was not obtaining the contract itself, that we should be given offsets...and important subcontracts. And we have seen little." Yvon Marcoux, President of the Chambre de commerce de Montréal, argued that "Ontario has the automobile industry and we want the aerospace industry consolidated here."[18]

These Montreal business interests, and Canadair itself, were joined by a group that had originally been established to promote the sale of Canadair to Bombardier, the Committee for Survival of Canadair. The group's president was Normand Cherry, who also happened to be the president of the Canadair local of the International Association of Machinists. All Canadair employees were members of the Committee, which saw itself as a formal lobby group devoted to ensuring that Ottawa did not make a "political decision" and award the contract to anyone other than Canadair.[19] Cherry injected a new note into the debate by criticizing the Bristol group as "foreign-owned." CAE Electronics and Canadair were 100 per cent Canadian, whereas Bristol was a subsidiary of Rolls-Royce of Britain. Litton was owned by an American firm of the same name.

Prominent Quebec politicians came on side as well. Liberal Premier Robert Bourassa had more than the ordinary desire to see his province prosper: his provincial riding included the suburb of St. Laurent. At a press conference with the CAE factory for a backdrop, Bourassa claimed that if the CF–18 contract went to Bristol, 60 per cent of the work would go to Ontario rather than to Winnipeg. He went on to argue that Ontario's economy was faring better than Quebec's, with almost twice the level of investment. Indeed, the desire to get the CF–18 contract for Montreal overrode normal partisan differences: Progressive Conservative Gerry Weiner, the federal minister of state for immigration and a Montreal MP, joined Bourassa in hoping that the maintenance contract would come to Canadair.[20] The Premier met Brian Mulroney in Montreal that same day, ostensibly to discuss constitutional strategy and broad economic matters. Instead, they spent almost the entire 75 minute meeting at the Premier's Outremont home discussing the CF–18. Bourassa, speaking to reporters later in his driveway, played on Mulroney's earlier promises of a new regional diversification strategy. Giving the CF–18 contract to Canadair would be "a good way to start a new policy of regional economic development."[21] Sensing that high expectations could create deep and dangerous disappointments in the event of failure, Mulroney tried to minimize the contract's potential economic impact: "It's one contract, not the salvation of Quebec." [22]

Just as this manoeuvering was underway, Bombardier raised the stakes by offering a "rebate" to Ottawa should it get the contract. Interestingly, the rebate was for $4 million, just slightly more than the difference of $3.5 million between the Bristol and Canadair bids later reported by Treasury Board President Robert de Cotret. The first reports of the rebate surfaced in early September. Bombardier was offering the federal government an immediate $4 million rebate on the CF–18 contract in lieu of a one per cent royalty it had agreed to pay in its original purchase agreement for Canadair should Canadair get the contract.[23] The royalty clause had been inserted into the original purchase agreement at Bombardier's insistence, and simply reflected the fact that the bids on the CF–18 contract had been closed for several months and Bombardier itself had no opportunity to shape Canadair's original proposal. The move to offer a $4 million rebate, however, came dangerously close to being a new bid and had the unfortunate appearance of a bribe.[24] IMP President Ken Rowe said the offer was "ridiculous, amateurish, and borders on the grey area of inducement. It's not helping them and it's embarrassing the government. Now everyone is wondering if they [the government] can be bought." Greg Walker, director of product support for Bendix Avelex, part of the Bristol consortium, also attacked the Bombardier offer: "It's not the way to do business in a major defence contract."[25]

Oddly, this flurry of Quebec lobbying was not matched by Winnipeg or Manitoba interests. Jake Epp hinted in early September that the CF–18 contract should be linked to another maintenance contract for the older, Canadair-built CF–5. "There's also...the CF–5. That is a plane that is built by Canadair and...would make a lot of sense to go to Canadair."[26] Epp was clearly implying that if the CF–18 contract went to Winnipeg, the CF–5 contract would be Canadair's consolation prize. In the first five years, the two contracts would be broadly similar in terms of jobs created and monies spent. Perhaps sensing this, Canadair officials began early in September to highlight technological benefits: the CF–18 contract would not merely create jobs but would transfer sophisticated technology. Canadair was playing the "nationalist card" in this argument, since if technology were transferred through the contract, it would come (in Canadair's case) to a Canadian firm that would then be able to use it to stimulate Canadian industry.

Apart from Epp's sporadic interventions and periodic assurances that the contract race was still open, other Manitoba politicians and leaders kept silent. In large part this was due to Bristol's request that there be no political lobbying on its behalf. Bill Norrie, the mayor of Winnipeg, explained that his city's silence on the issue was due to Bristol: "They wanted to make it a business approach. I think they are wise to realize that if they make it a political issue, then Manitoba likely would not get the contract, because the political weight of the country is in Quebec. In the broad sense, I think they are correct...We don't have the political clout in Ottawa and that has always been a major problem in the West."[27] Premier Howard Pawley of Manitoba also agreed that the CF–18 contract could not be won by "a war of words." This silence, while in one sense peculiar, made some sense. Quebec did have the seats and a strong political voice in cabinet. If Manitoba and Bristol were to fight their battle on that terrain, they would lose before joining arms. It was widely known that Bristol's bid had the approval of the expert committee, and so a strategy of focusing on technical rather than political merit seemed prudent. But as one Winnipeg observer noted, it was also risky: "Bristol may be the favored bidder as far as the armed forces are concerned, but in any battle where logic is pitted against political advantage, logic has an uphill fight on its hands. The icing on Quebec's cake is the declining popularity of the federal government in that province."[28] This assessment of Quebec's strategic advantage was echoed by Normand Cherry two weeks later, when he claimed that the CF–18 contract had become a symbol of Ottawa's presence in the province. "If Mr. Mulroney does not decide in our favor, we'll make sure that he and his Government will never forget the decision he's made."[29] Indeed, any hint that the contract would not go to Montreal caused anxiety and redoubled lobbying effort. On 1 October 1986, federal Minister of Supply and Services Monique Vézina (replacing Stewart McInnes) let some innocuous remarks on the CF–18 slip into a luncheon address on Export Trade Month. Manon Vennat, President of the Montreal Board of Trade, was taken aback: "It certainly reminds us that we must not let up on our efforts to persuade Ottawa of Montreal's importance to obtain this CF–18 contract."[30]

Though Bristol had kept silent and asked others to do so as well, it was not above some public relations. On 3 October 1986, Vézina received a final briefing from her officials and planned to present a report to the cabinet committee on priorities and planning the following Tuesday. (This committee is a sub-committee of cabinet, chaired by the Prime Minister, and acts unofficially as an "inner cabinet" of the most powerful ministers, the government's key decision-makers.) On 6 October, the Bristol consortium paid for full page colour advertisements in the Toronto *Globe and Mail* and the *Ottawa Citizen*, proclaiming that "Canada and the CF–18 deserve the very best." The ads kept to Bristol's theme of technical superiority, highlighting its record in aircraft maintenance, but were intended, as one Bristol executive put it, "to make sure our name was in there when cabinet meets."[31] The ads had little effect: the cabinet committee met on Tuesday, 7 October, but Vézina emerged to say that no decision had been made.[32]

While it was widely agreed that the IMP bid was dead, neither Canadair nor Bristol could be sure of cinching the contract. As hopes were dashed on the rocks of cabinet indecision, the war of words intensified. Canadair opened its assault on two fronts. The first was to concentrate on an issue that had, at best, been given minor consideration in the earlier stages of the debate: technology transfer. Canadair began to emphasize the importance of the spin-offs associated with the contract. Maintaining the CF–18 would require technology and skills not currently being used in Canada, most of which would be transferred from McDonnell Douglas. The issue of technology transfer was to become a decisive one and so Canadair's assumptions in the argument were important. Canadair claimed that by getting the CF–18 contract it would effect a transfer of high technology from a foreign (American) firm to a wholly-owned Canadian one. It would "Canadianize" this technology, and then use it to strengthen its abilities on other projects (such as the Canadair-built Challenger business jet.[33] Normand Cherry had, in fact, been at some pains to emphasize this in early September.[34]

The second front was also opened by Normand Cherry. At a packed news conference in Montreal, Cherry charged that the bidding process had been abused by the Bristol group and federal officials. Cherry claimed that Canadair had been the low bidder when the competition closed on 29 November 1985. Canadair's bid was 10 percent lower than Bristol's, but an "unsolicited price reduction" from Bristol was accepted two months later by the evaluation team. This new Bristol bid, according to Cherry, was 13 percent lower than the original, and "it is evident that it obtained privileged and confidential information."[35] Federal officials and politicians denied the charges. While Cherry offered no evidence for his accusations, the issue was further inflamed on 17 October, when Monique Vézina admitted that the final CF–18 decision would be a political one. Facing a meeting of the Treasury Board (which reviews government spending practices) to discuss the issue and recommend to cabinet, Vézina said that "civil servants are there to serve us...and help us with our technical operations and we, the politicians, are in there to make the political decisions, and that is what we will do."[36] She denied, however, that there had been any meddling in the bidding process. Her point simply was that as elected politicians, the cabinet would have to place the technical recommendations of the evaluation team report in the broad context of the national interest. This might mean *not* awarding the contract to the lowest or even the most competent bidder, in a purely technical sense. Assuming that all the bidders could do the job within reasonable cost, how much tolerance should be applied to cost differentials, and to socio-economic benefits? Vézina's point was that these questions called for political and value judgments, and ultimately could only be made by elected politicians.

With the Treasury Board meeting imminent, Bristol decided to once again break its silence. Its first sally was to publicly express its concerns about the possible politicization of the bidding process. A Bristol spokesperson said on 19 October that "I think the power of the Quebec lobby is a real threat to us. I'm concerned not only for the contract, but for the whole system."[37] A few days later Frank Hinings, Bristol's secretary, played the regional card for the first time, arguing that even on that basis the Bristol consortium deserved the contract. If Canadair won, most of the work would go to Montreal; if Bristol won, he said, about 50 percent of the contract money and 187 jobs would go to Manitoba, 35 percent and 99 jobs would go to Ontario, and 15 percent and 29 jobs would end up in Montreal. Hinings regretted the company's earlier refusal to lobby: "We still think the best way to win a government contract is to be the best company, but it is obvious that a lobby effort is needed to keep attention where we want it to be."[38]

Bristol also tried to recruit its workers in the attempt to pressure the government. The Bristol local of the Canadian Association of Industrial, Mechanical and Allied Workers was prepared to support the company, though some union officials were worried about the apparent sense of panic among management. The poisonous atmosphere that now enveloped the bidding war was reflected in the comments of one Bristol worker: "This whole thing has really gotten out of hand. We [the workers] told them [the company] months ago that when you're dealing with a bunch of Frenchmen in Quebec, you're starting three steps behind. It's stupid to think you can compete on an equal footing when it's Quebec you're fighting. Mulroney and the rest of them are just covering their asses."[39]

Having decided to enter the political fray, Bristol provided the signal to Manitoba politicians to start lobbying for the contract. Premier Pawley, who had been silent on the CF–18 affair, suddenly raised the flag on the issue from London, England. At a dinner with Sir Francis Tombs, chairman of Rolls-Royce Ltd. (Bristol Aerospace's owner), he detected concerns about political meddling in the CF–18 contract. Pawley tried to call Mulroney from London to "plead with the Prime Minister to make sure the contract is awarded on technical merits rather than political considerations. I want a specific assurance...that the award is not being given on the basis of politics and political pressure, but on the basis of the recommendation of the federal technical officials. If he did that, the contract must be Bristol's."[40] Pawley finally reached the Prime Minister from Europe a few days later, and was assured that the decision would be made fairly. Pawley explained that "fairness to me indicates the contract will go to the company that submits the best product at the best price and which most closely meets the specifications of the contract. From all accounts Bristol of Winnipeg has done that."[41] Pawley knew that high noon was approaching: the decision would have to be made within a week, since all three bids expired on 31 October. The companies knew it too: in the last weeks before the deadline, both Bristol and Canadair ran ads extolling the merits of their bids.

The last days before the decision were marked by both drama and farce. The drama came on 30 October, one day before the final decision was announced, when Mulroney presented the case for Canadair to the Tory caucus. Sources said that though he personally supported Canadair, Mulroney still claimed that the final decision would be up to cabinet. Mulroney said that Canadair deserved consideration for four reasons: (1) Ottawa had already helped the west with $1 billion in aid for grain farmers, (2) Canadair was a Canadian firm, (3) Edmonton would get some of the maintenance work if Canadair won the contract, and (4) the Manitoba NDP government had recently used political discretion in awarding some contracts.[42] Both Premier Pawley and his Minister of Industry, Vic Schroeder, reacted angrily to the report. They knew how important Mulroney was in the game: with the cabinet and the caucus split on the issue, Mulroney could tip the balance. Schroeder showed his anger by cancelling scheduled meetings with federal officials, while Pawley said that if Canadair did win the bid, he would lead a province-wide lobby to get the contract back for Bristol. Pawley's frustration had been mounting for weeks, ever since he had difficulties in reaching the Prime Minister from Europe. In a final effort to rally regional forces, he telexed the other three western premiers to ask for their support. Only William Vander Zalm, the premier of British Columbia, agreed. The other two premiers, both Tories, did not respond to their NDP colleague's pleas.[43] Premier Grant Devine's silence was explained by the favour he owed Mulroney for delaying the contract announcement. Devine was fighting a provincial election in October, and Michel Gratton, Mulroney's press secretary, recalls that the delay was a "little favour we did for Grant Devine" since even though the contract affected only Manitoba "the bad reaction was bound to overflow into neighbouring Saskatchewan. Devine, as the results showed, was in a close race, and any negative gesture by Ottawa at this point could be devastating. Devine won his election on October 20."[44]

For many Manitobans, 31 October 1986 was a black day in Canadian regional politics. That morning, Robert de Cotret, president of the Treasury Board, announced that the cabinet had decided to give the maintenance contract to Canadair. The key to the decision, he argued, was technology transfer. Canadair would benefit more from the new technology than Bristol would. De Cotret admitted that Bristol's bid had been superior in technical capability and price. On the former, Bristol scored 926 out of 1000 points to Canadair's 843. Bristol's bid was also $3 million lower. Howard Pawley heard the news over the radio and called it a "royal shaft." In Ottawa, de Cotret put the point tersely: "We had a choice, we made a choice."[45]

THE REACTION

By 31 October 1986 the CF–18 contract was no longer about servicing a jet plane. It was no longer about jobs, money or even technology. It had through long delay and tension become a question of deep political passion, a symbol of deeply held resentments, memories, hopes, and aspirations. It is impossible to understand the West's reaction without understanding the contract's symbolic importance. Canadians across the Prairies, not just in Winnipeg, were exasperated and insulted by what they perceived as a traitorous decision in Ottawa. Even as far away as Vancouver, a B.C. minister said that the decision "will prove once again that western Canada has been ignored.... It is very disappointing to the western provinces when they see federal national policy directed in this way."[46]

Howard Pawley echoed and amplified this sentiment. The decision "flies in the face of all that is fair and equitable and that we expect in respect to integrity from a federal government."[47] Pawley called the decision cynical and callous, claimed that he could never trust the Prime Minister again, and demanded a meeting with Mulroney for the following Monday. The premier was not alone among Manitoba politicians: irrespective of party stripe, they universally condemned the decision. Winnipeg Liberal Lloyd Axworthy said that it was a "clear message to Western Canadians that we should be hewers of wood and drawers of water."[48] Winnipeg NDP Cyril Keeper grilled de Cotret in the House of Commons on the issue of technology transfer.

> Mr. Cyril Keeper (Winnipeg North Centre): Mr. Speaker, my question is for the President of the Treasury Board. If technology transfer was the basis for the decision with regard to the CF–18 contract, why was it not part of the original 75-member panel process? Why were the rules of the game changed at the end of the game in the ninth inning? How does the Minister square his claim that technology transfer was the basis for the decision with the fact that the technology transfer was left out of the original panel process?

> Hon. Robert de Cotret (President of the Treasury Board): Mr. Speaker, first, I have already answered the question. It is a little dif-

ficult to enhance my previous answer. Perhaps we should have said that in the original bids. I have instructed my officials to talk with the officials of the Department of Supply and Services to ensure that we might mention that type of thing. However, technology transfer is not something that is within the purview of the bidding firm. It is something that is within its own composition.

When we saw that the final offers were very close to each other, we had a choice. We had a choice to look at how the technology would be transferred.[49]

De Cotret's admission that the question of technology transfer had never been explicit in the original tender enraged Manitobans and the other bidders. The government, in short, had based its decision on a criterion never advertised to bidders. From the point of view of IMP and Bristol Aerospace, their efforts had from the beginning been a complete waste of time. Bristol had spent over $5 million in preparing its bid, and IMP had spent approximately $1 million. On hearing the announcement, IMP said that it might try to recoup this money from Ottawa.[50] Equally galling was the government's preference for a Canadian-owned firm. Not only had this also been absent from the original tender, but it flew in the face of the Mulroney government's commitment to open investment, symbolized by its replacement of the Foreign Investment Review Agency with Investment Canada. In establishing Investment Canada, the government had proclaimed that "Canada is open for business" and would no longer look suspiciously at foreign investors. Now, with the CF–18 maintenance contract, it seemed to be saying that being Canadian-owned was important for companies seeking federal contracts.

Winnipeg mayor Bill Norrie challenged all Manitoban Conservative MPs to resign in protest over the decision, and John Malow, president of Local 5 of the Canadian Association of Industrial, Mechanical and Allied Workers at the Bristol plant, called the decision a "dirty trick."[51] These reactions placed Manitoban Progressive Conservative MPs in a delicate position. As Tory members, if they protested too strongly they would call their own party loyalty into question; as Manitobans, if they kept quiet they would be branded as traitors. Several Manitoba Tory MPs spoke out. George Minaker, whose riding of Winnipeg-St. James embraced the Bristol plant, publicly said that the decision should have been made on the merits of the tender, and that he would raise this with the Prime Minister as soon as possible. Leo Duguay, Tory MP for St. Boniface, took the interesting position that while he disagreed with the cabinet's decision, he nonetheless accepted it. Dan MacKenzie (Winnipeg-Assiniboine) pleaded ignorance: since only the cabinet had access to the full documentation on the issue, he could not criticize the decision, as much as he disliked it. Mackenzie sagely looked to the future for Winnipeg's reward. Brian White (Dauphin-Swan River) was more direct:

"It's a political decision and they should have had the courage to come out and say so."[52]

Jake Epp faced the greatest heat over the decision. As a cabinet minister he was directly implicated in it. As a member from Manitoba, he had fought hard to bring the contract to Bristol. As senior minister from Manitoba (one of only two), Epp's influence was tested throughout the CF–18 decision. The principle of cabinet solidarity made the situation especially acute for him: if he remained in cabinet he would have to openly, and with some degree of enthusiasm, defend the decision, all the while knowing that Manitobans hated that decision. Epp handled the issue well, considering the potential for political damage. His defence was that there would be other contracts in the future, and that while he had lost over the CF–18, he could help win the others. "I think Canadians know the system and they have a decision to take at the next election. That's fair ball.... I think it is important to take note that when I look at other defence contracts, which I've done, I see money equal to or greater than this contract over 20 to 25 years. While that may not be satisfactory to some, obviously not to the bidder, the decision today does not exclude the fact that there is other work I want to get to Winnipeg and, quite frankly, in view of what's happened today I think that work must come to Winnipeg."[53] Epp was true to his word: within two months Cabinet would decide in Winnipeg's favour on the CF–5 maintenance contract. To anticipate, two years later, on the eve of the 1988 federal election, more goodies would be announced.

For the next few days, Manitoban commentators focused on three issues, apart from their own emotional outrage. The first was the logic behind the decision itself. De Cotret had defended the decision almost entirely in terms of technology transfer, since he had already admitted that Bristol had won on technical merit and price. His announcement made it clear that technology transfer had been the critical consideration.

> In making its decision, the government considered a wide variety of factors: the technical merits of each bid, price, technological transfers arising from the contract and the state of the aerospace industry in Canada.... The compelling arguments which ultimately determined the outcome are centred on a highly valuable feature of the contract - a transfer of technology from the CF–18 U.S. manufacturer, the Mc-Donnell Douglas Corporation. Unlike its competitors for this contract, Canadair is a Canadian company that builds as well as repairs aircraft. The government believes that the benefits to Canada as a whole, in terms of the technology transfer, have greater potential in the hands of Canadair....[54]

Apart from the complaints about the absence of technology transfer in the original tender, commentators wondered if, in fact, Canadair could use the technology it gained for the CF–18 for other, unrelated projects. All of the technology would be transferred from McDonnell Douglas, and Bristol spokespersons argued that the giant American aerospace company would only licence the technology for specific use on the CF–18. Bristol also claimed that its partners already had access to much of the technology through their parent companies. Bristol, for example, had been servicing the engines on the F–18 for several years, the same engines used on the CF–18.[55]

A second theme in the early commentary concerned the exact timing of the decision. After Michel Gratton's revelations in 1987, it was clear that the decision to award the CF–18 contract to Canadair had been made at the highest levels sometime in the late summer or early fall of 1986, but the announcement was deliberately delayed until Grant Devine won his October election. At the time the announcement was made, however, no one knew this. There were suspicious signals though, such as Mulroney's caucus intervention in the week before the decision. The day after the announcement, the *Winnipeg Free Press* quoted sources as saying that the decision had been known for weeks. The mechanics of the final decision and the announcement aroused suspicions as well. The cabinet meeting was scheduled for Friday morning but a press conference had already been set for 10:30 am. This left no time for full discussion. The news releases circulated afterwards had been printed a week earlier.[56]

The third and most anguished theme in the flurry of Manitoban commentary that followed the announcement dealt with its political effects. In 1985 the contract had been about jobs; by 1986 it was about the nature of Canada. The decision engendered a depth of bitterness not seen in the West since the energy wars over the National Energy Program. Life-time party members tore up their cards[57] and Frank Lawson, a former Manitoba Tory youth president, erected a sign outside his Winnipeg store that read: "A letter to the Prime Minister Mullooney [sic]...Take your politics. Take your contract. Take your B.S. & shove it."[58] The Manitoba Progressive Conservative party, led by (future premier) Gary Filmon, felt the heat and responded in the only politically viable way it could. It denounced the decision, and within a week had voted to consider a formal party resolution condemning its federal counterpart. For a while, the party even thought of changing its name. Fundraising was affected, and some former Tories took the step of switching to the Liberal Party. In fine entrepreneurial spirit, the Manitoba Liberal Party offered half-price memberships to any Tories who would come to its office and tear up their Conservative cards.[59] More worrisome was the possibility that disaffected Manitobans would reject the federal system in its entirety and begin to support either provincial rights movements or separatist parties. The possibility seemed genuine: the Western Canada Concept, in announcing plans to form a federal political party, cited the C-18 decision as "just one of many insults to the West which cannot be effectively answered by the present federal political parties which are directed from central Canada."[60]

In a display of collective memory rivalling Quebec's recollection of promises in 1980, the following slights to Manitoba were resurrected to prove that the CF–18 was just the latest example of a long tradition of federal abuse and neglect:

§   the removal of Air Canada's overhaul base from Winnipeg to Montreal in the late 1950s;

§   the "killing" of a $36 million science and technology research institute on Winnipeg's Ellice Avenue in 1984-85;

§   the discontinuation of Canertech, a crown corporation created by the Liberals, with an annual budget of $30 million and headquarters in Winnipeg;

§   the termination of the VIA Rail maintenance centre to be located in Winnipeg and costing $28 million.[61]

The CF–18 decision would be added to this roster of perfidious treatment, so that future generations of Manitobans could warm their feelings of regional alienation against the fire of this memory.

The morning of 3 November found Premier Pawley in Ottawa with a small delegation representing Manitoban business and labour interests. They were there to meet with the Prime Minister and plead one last time for a reconsideration of the contract decision. Such a reconsideration after the events of the last six months would have been extraordinary, so it is unlikely that Pawley thought his intervention could change anything. He knew, though, that the home crowd demanded some action, however futile; he had to perform the rituals of outrage and supplication. After an hour with the Prime Minister, Pawley emerged "empty-handed and angry," vowing to continue his fight for the contract at the First Ministers' Conference in Vancouver on 20-21 November. Brian Mulroney seemed philosophical about the premier's reactions, saying that he expected them and that they simply reflected the nature of regional politics in Canada. "It has always been the case and it ever shall. The decision must be taken in the national interest as best we perceive it. That is what we have done."[62] Mulroney argued that the CF–18 decision had to be set against previous, beneficial policies for the West. Pawley resisted any tally of wins and losses, preferring to focus exclusively on the issue of fairness.

Pawley's room to manoeuvre was severely restricted. He had no leverage over Ottawa in the sense of programs that he could terminate or monies that he could cut off. Intergovernmental money in Canada flows from Ottawa to the provinces, at least to provinces like Manitoba. The province had neither the population nor the federal seats to threaten real trouble in the next federal election. With only fourteen seats, the Tories could lose them all and still easily win a majority government. (As things turned out, the Tories lost two Winnipeg seats to the Liberals in November 1988.) Pawley was further weakened by his inability to rally western premiers against the CF–18 decision. Premier Vander Zalm of British Columbia, heading a Social Credit government, had been happy to attack Tories, but both Don Getty and Grant Devine refused to support Pawley's call to arms. In fact, Devine undercut Pawley by defending the CF–18 decision and the federal government, arguing that the latter had, on the whole, been good for the West. He cited drought relief, flood relief, agricultural deficiency payments, and the termination of the hated NEP's petroleum and gas revenue tax as evidence that the West had prospered under Mulroney.[63]

Under these circumstances, Pawley's retaliatory strategy boiled down to three tactics. The first was to attack the rationale of the decision itself. It might be too late to reverse the decision, but if it could be shown that the decision was either stupid or sneaky, then Manitoba would have won the moral point if not the jobs. This had already been done to some degree by industry and Bristol spokespersons in criticizing the idea of technology transfer. Within days of the announcement, the Manitoba government took this argument one step further. It issued a report claiming to show that the decision to award the contract to Canadair would cost the taxpayer an additional $30 million. This was the cost of the royalty payments Manitoba alleged that Canadair would have to pay for use of McDonnell Douglas technology. Ottawa had argued that the technology would be transferred without cost, and could be applied to unrelated projects. Manitoba disputed this, and attached a price tag.[64] The province's position was confirmed the next day by the McDonnell Douglas corporation. A spokesperson said that any technology or data transferred by McDonnell Douglas would have to be purchased, and could not be applied or used on projects other than the CF–18.[65]

In the face of these stories, Robert de Cotret admitted that, contrary to what he and other government officials had implied only a few days earlier, the technology would in fact have to be bought by Canadair. He still argued that this would not involve any increased cost over the Bristol bid, since all three bids had been adjusted upwards by $30 million to account for the need to pay royalties on the technology. De Cotret claimed Bristol had never indicated that it could get access to McDonnell Douglas technology for free or at reduced cost, and so this had not been considered in the bid assessment. Bristol and anonymous Ottawa sources immediately denied this, pointing to a 4 March 1986 meeting where Bristol informed federal officials that the technology to which it had access could be conservatively valued at $20 million.[66]

Pawley's second tactic was to threaten non-cooperation in inter-governmental affairs. One of the Mulroney government's highest priorities in 1984 had been to bring Quebec into the Constitution. Any realistic attempt would require substantial if not unanimous provincial approval of federal proposals to Quebec. Pawley threatened to not cooperate and thus to stall the constitutional talks. In fact, he did attend the Vancouver First Ministers Conference on 20-21 November, and tried to use it as a platform to attack the federal government's treatment of the West. Mulroney was ready for him, however, and expected this attack on his "sense of fairness." He reminded the Premier that he had no criticisms of Mulroney's sense of fairness when the Prime Minister had defended Pawley's bilingualism policy during a heated provincial debate on the issue. Mulroney had decided weeks earlier to play hardball with Pawley. After their 3 November meeting he issued instructions that all federal business in Manitoba would bypass Pawley, and that the premier would share none of the credit when good news was announced.[67]

Pawley's third and last tactic was to appeal to the people of Manitoba. Again, it was not clear what such an appeal would accomplish, except to tarnish the federal government's image. But in war of this type, public opinion is the crucial hostage: capture it and moral victory is almost assured. Pawley reached out in the form of an open letter published in the Saturday edition of the *Winnipeg Free Press*, urging Manitobans to write to the Prime Minister and the fourteen MPs representing the province in Ottawa. The letter also cast Pawley as the protector of provincial rights. It read, in part, as follows:

To the People of Manitoba:

Manitobans are a proud people. We play by the rules and, when we do so, we expect to be treated fairly. There is deeply-felt and well-founded resentment throughout Manitoba at the recent CF–18 maintenance contract decision. Trust in the fairness of our national government has been shaken. When such federal decisions as this fly in the face of reason, they do harm to Canada.

Manitoba and other small provinces insist not on special treatment, but fair treatment.... That is the case I presented when I headed a delegation which met recently with the Prime Minister and other federal ministers.... We were unanimous in emphasizing the serious damage that Ottawa has done to confidence in the fairness of federal tendering practices. I regret to advise you that federal ministers appear unwilling to review their decision on the CF–18 contract....

At this difficult time, the people of Manitoba are understandably angered by the unfairness of recent federal actions. I am calling on Manitobans to use their anger constructively to improve Ottawa's understanding of the need for fairness in contract tendering, equalization payments and regional development.

I urge you to let your Member of Parliament know where you stand on these important issues.[68]

The ad sparked a controversy between Pawley and the two provincial opposition parties. For more than a month, all three parties had to swallow their partisan differences in favour of maintaining a united front on the CF–18 affair. The ad finally allowed the opposition parties to attack; this was particularly important to the provincial Tories, since the CF–18 decision, made by their federal brethren, had been the kiss of death. Gary Filmon, leader of the provincial Progressive Conservatives, and Sharon Carstairs, leader of the provincial Liberals, called the ad self-serving and redundant, since everyone in Manitoba knew about the contract and hated its outcome.[69] While the critics themselves were criticized,[70] the more important result of the campaign was the first emergence of a spirit of resignation. Some of Pawley's critics went beyond saying that the ad was redundant; they argued that the CF–18 decision was history, and that Manitoba should heal the rift with Ottawa.

If the reaction in Manitoba was two weeks of white hot rage, what was the reaction in Quebec? In a word, elation. The response was less complex than Manitoba's because the result was so much more congenial. No possibilities were foreclosed, no futures denied, no resentments fanned by anger: the newspapers showed photos of a beaming Normand Cherry hugging a co-worker, and his sparkling, cherubic grin was the perfect symbol of Montreal's triumph. That triumph would have been shallow and self-deceiving had Montrealers believed that the CF–18 decision was based on politics. In a strange transmutation of every key Manitoban grievance. Montrealers felt that giving the CF–18 maintenance contract to Bristol would have been a "political decision." In their view, Montreal was the site of 50 percent of Canada's aerospace industry, Montreal had been given promises in 1980, Montreal was competing with British- and American-owned firms who would do the work in Ontario, and Montreal, through Canadair, had played by the rules while Bristol submitted unsolicited bids to undercut its competitors.[71]

In a somewhat more sober, almost melancholic, assessment, the respected Montreal newspaper *Le Devoir* noted that "dans ce pays impossible, le bonheur des uns fait souvent le malheur des autres. Pendant que Canadair célèbre la victoire et esquisse déjà de nouveaux plans pour l'avenir, le groupe Bristol et les gens de Winnipeg ne cachent pas leur mécontentement devant ce qu'ils qualifient de 'favoritisme politique'." Noting that in fact all of the three consortia bidding for the contract were competent to do the work, the editorial argued that the decision had been taken in terms of "critères plus globaux, prenant en considération non seulement les facteurs proprement économiques mais aussi politiques."[72]

By November, the first, intense chapter of the CF–18 saga was over. For Manitobans, there had never been a Halloween quite like the one of 1986, with its witch's brew of politics, jobs, and votes. Weeks passed, and thoughts turned to Christmas. The federal Tories had one more surprise, however. The cabinet changed from Halloween goblin to jolly St. Nick, reached into its bag of goodies, and hinted just before Christmas that the CF–5 maintenance contract would go to Bristol.[73] Valued at $350 million over ten years, the CF–5 contract was more labour intensive and would therefore create 500 jobs compared to the estimate of 300 for the CF–18 work. While arguing that the CF–5 work was better suited to Canadair and that the CF–18 work should have gone to Bristol,[74] Premier Pawley was prepared to accept the *untendered* award to Bristol as compensation for earlier injustice.[75]

Bristol got the contract, fences were mended, and the affair was almost forgotten until January 1988, when the *Globe and Mail*, after a fifteen month battle, finally received access to the documents outlining the bids for the CF–18. The documents showed that the Bristol bid would have been 13 percent cheaper in the first four years of the contract, and 1.8 percent cheaper for the remainder of the contract.[76] Bristol had been given a "significantly higher technical assessment" than Canadair by the evaluation committee. Premier Pawley claimed that the real difference between the bids was not $30 million, as he had originally estimated, but $65 million (this included the original value of technology transfer at $30 million, plus an extra $35 million in lower contract costs over 20 years).

This last flare of CF–18 passion was not sustained, even though it briefly rekindled old memories. The federal opposition parties managed to fabricate some outrage for a few days, but then turned their attention to fresh scandals. In a final attempt to put the government's case, Robert de Cotret (now Minister of Industrial Regional Expansion) reiterated that according to the government's figures, the bids had only been $3.5 million apart. Bristol had scored 926 out of a possible 1000 points; Canadair had scored 841. De Cotret pointed out again that in "our system of government, it is up to the elected representatives of the Canadian people to weigh officials' advice".[77]

That should have been the end of the matter, but the CF–18 affair had by now entered into the province's political folklore, and moreover provided a convenient weapon for Liberals and the NDP against the Tories. Days before the 26 April 1988 provincial election, during a televised debate among the three party leaders, Liberal leader Sharon Carstairs attacked Tory leader Gary Filmon for his party's passivity in dealing with Ottawa over aerospace contracts. This barely veiled reference to the CF–18 may have helped gain some of the Liberals' 20 provincial seats, and certainly eroded what to that point had looked like a clear Tory victory, reducing it to a minority government. And there was no doubt of the CF–18 affair's importance in the November 1988 federal election. Lloyd Axworthy, to that point the only federal Liberal MP from Winnipeg, remarked that the local campaign would focus on two issues: free trade and the CF–18. The federal Tories responded, days before the election was called, with several promises for Manitoba: two laboratories ($93 million), a centre for environmental research ($100 million), a national park for Churchill, in northern Manitoba, and the contract to maintain Air Canada's new Airbus jets. As Conservative MP Leo Duguay observed, "We'll take the blame for the CF–18 if we get credit for all the other things we've done in Manitoba."[78]

DISCUSSION

The CF–18 decision illustrates the extraordinary power of symbols in everyday politics. The contract, while lucrative, involved only a few hundred jobs. Prime Minister Mulroney was surely right in cautioning that it did not mean the salvation of Quebec, but he could not have been blind to the way that regional aspirations and memories took wing with the CF–18. The plane and the issues surrounding it became transformed into powerful condensations of emotions and expectations, so much so that to say "CF–18" on the streets of Winnipeg or Montreal in October 1986 would evoke a set of almost unconscious political reflexes.

In Quebec the CF–18 was a dense fusion of rich and provocative feelings and ideas. Primary among these one was the importance of Quebec's regional industrial advantage vis-àa-vis Ontario. In what to a Winnipeger would have seemed a bizarre twist, the majority of Quebecers placed the CF–18 decision on a Quebec v. Ontario axis of conflict. This idea was grounded in two assumptions. The first was that many of the CF–18 jobs would in fact go to Ontario if Bristol got the contract. The second was wholly unrelated to the specifics of the contract. It had to do with the industrial rivalry between Ontario's automotive sector and Quebec's aerospace sector. If Ottawa gave the CF–18 contract to Winnipeg, it would be undermining this delicate provincial balance in Ontario's favour. Ottawa had to recognize and ratify the traditional concentration of aerospace industries in Montreal. Ontario's prosperity at the time only piqued Quebec's sensibilities further. Interestingly, this is precisely the sort of rivalry that exacerbated the debate over the pharmaceutical patent case (see chapter 2).

Entwined with these considerations was a pervasive sense of provincial alienation, once again vis-à-vis Ontario but also more generally against the rest of the country. In what to a Winnipeger would again have seemed curious logic, much of the Quebec debate over the CF–18 assumed that Quebec had historically been neglected or deliberately undermined by Ottawa. The

Ultramar episode and recollections of the choice of the F–18 over the F–16 fed this preoccupation. Accordingly, the CF–18 decision quickly came to be seen as a test of Ottawa's true intentions with respect to Quebec's place in the national economy, and a test of federal veracity. That it had been Trudeau and not Mulroney who had promised the CF–18 maintenance contract in lieu of the F–16 did not seem to matter. "Ottawa," and not a specific government, was the antagonist.

The view from Manitoba was merely a complex mirror image of these grievances. Manitobans also condensed a variety of symbols and images into the CF–18 so that it became much more than a maintenance contract. For Winnipegers, the contract reflected on the nature of political power in this country and the fidelity of politicians to a "rational" decision-making process. To Canadians living west of the Lakehead, the fundamental reality of confederation seems to be their subjugation to "eastern" interests. Ontario - and, it is thought, Quebec - have the industry, the diversified base that allows them to ride out the international economic storms that wreak so much havoc in the resource-dependent provinces. They have the population and the federal seats that seem to ensure their will on virtually any issue. From the vantage point of Portage and Main, the western provinces will be perpetual losers in the federal bargain if the only things that count are votes and seats.

That is why the CF–18 so rapidly became a test of the nature of the Canadian confederation. No country can afford to ignore the aspirations of its minorities, and regional alienation is so strong in parts of western Canada that citizens there have no difficulty in thinking of themselves as "minorities." What would Ottawa do in the face of a report that recommended that the "minority" be given the contract? The Winnipeg view of the matter was that David had vanquished Goliath in single combat. Would Ottawa ignore this outcome and respond to the crude calculus of political power? In addition, of course, the government in power in Ottawa had explicity championed the interests of minority regions through years of political opposition. Now the opportunity presented itself for that government and that party to make good its promises.

Whereas Quebec had demanded that the CF–18 decision recognize the country's traditional concentrations of industry, Manitoban opinion demanded a decision that would explicitly release that province from the chains of past patterns of economic growth. The western provinces have for years tried to diversify their economies, knowing that excessive reliance on a single resource whose price is set in international markets can be disastrous. But the very concentration of industry and investment in central Canada makes it economically rational to continue to concentrate industrial investment there. Breaking the pattern is as much a matter of political will as it is of economic forces, and so Winnipegers looked to Ottawa for a policy that would acknowledge that not all industry or high technology would be contained in Ontario and Quebec.

A crucial aspect of the CF–18 affair was the expert committee's recommendation that Bristol be given the contract on the grounds of technical merit and price. Had Bristol lost the competition, the issue would have evolved very differently. None of the allegations made by Normand Cherry were ever substantiated, though it is true that Bristol enjoyed fairly close ties to the Canadian military, as did all of its partners. It must be assumed, therefore, that Bristol did win the competition. The technology transfer argument was dismissed in Manitoba, and so the only conclusion could be that the Tories had looked at their sagging popularity in Quebec and decided to give the contract to Montreal to improve their election chances.

It is not entirely clear that this was, in fact, the rationale that guided the government. A federal election was at least two years away, and the Tories had been in power long enough to realize that one contract was not going to win or lose their position in Quebec. Even if this were granted, the negative impact of awarding the contract to Canadair would be felt not just in Winnipeg but throughout the western provinces. It is possible that the government worried about the loyalty of Quebec voters more than it did about the West, which had supported the Tories for a generation.

The government's decision was widely pilloried outside Quebec as "political." It was assumed that somehow the decision could have been taken by simply adding the points or assessing technical merit. This is unlikely. De Cotret and Vézina before him were right: the job of officials is to advise; the job of politicians is to decide. A decision is only "technical" if people agree in advance to the criteria and standards they will apply, as well as to the weight that those criteria and standards will have. But in the real worlds of Canadian politics, this is rarely if ever the case. Indeed, politics is precisely about defining what the criteria of decision should be. "Experts" can help, of course, in providing factual information about any given criterion, but they cannot resolve the really tricky questions about political values that ultimately determine a decision. Who was to say whether socio-economic factors should weigh more than technical merit? Who would weigh the importance of regional resentment? What experts could measure the long-term effects of helping a Canadian-based firm? These were precisely the issues that cabinet had to grapple with, issues that no one else was competent to decide, and more importantly, issues no one else had the final responsibility to decide.

It is nonetheless true that Canadair and Montreal mounted a much more concerted lobbying effort than Manitoba did, but this is not to say that their arguments were without any rational basis. Two of these arguments may have had more force than Manitobans were willing to allow. The issue of technology transfer, for example, was addressed almost exclusively in monetary terms in Winnipeg, but the issue was about more than the licencing costs of using certain data. Even if we assume that Canadair paid a premium for the technology in excess of what Bristol would have charged, it might still be true that Canadair's workers and engineers could gain various benefits that could be applied to other projects. How is one to assess the intangible benefits of exposure to new technology and ideas? Though this must be speculative, since the cabinet never put its defence of technology transfer quite this way, Ottawa might have concluded that since Canadair was in the business of building planes, its exposure to CF–18 technology might create a synergy that would manifest itself in unpredictable but beneficial ways in other areas.

No decision of this type will be without controversy. This is in part, as the politicians themselves recognized, because of the regional tensions that characterize the bidding process in many cases. The symbolic importance attached to any decision of this sort often completely eclipses the pragmatic effect of the decision itself, because public policies are not only about solving problems. They are not just about more jobs, economic growth, technology transfer, or any other of the host of goals that were proclaimed in the CF–18 affair. Policies are also an expression of a political community, in the same way that one's use of language is not just a means of communication but a measure of one's culture and appreciation of the world. In the abortion debate, for example, the issue is about how we, as Canadians, want our society to respect either life or the rights of women. Child care policy expresses our views of the family; immigration policy is a signal of the way we feel about races and cultures and the rest of the world. In the CF–18 case, the maintenance contract was seen as a symbol of how Canada's regional communities co-exist.

Another factor also intensifies the conflict inherent in decisions of this nature. The CF–18 decision was a prime example of the increasingly large role that governments play in determining the level and location of economic activity. The weight and influence of government in everyday affairs is undeniable, but the extent to which governments, through their decisions to purchase equipment or services, influence the economy is sometimes only dimly understood. It is obvious, of course, that governments have been doing this for a very long time indeed. The idea of a perfect free market with only minimal government interference is mythical at best. Governments under advanced capitalism are involved in regulating virtually every aspect of economic activity. So intimate is this relationship that it is usually more fruitful to speak of a "political economy" than simply an economy. Why, then, should decisions like the CF–18 occasion any comment? Because for much of the postwar period governments were able to rationalize their economic interventions in minimalist terms. They had their hands on the large levers of economic policy, such as interest rates or the budgetary balance, and could claim that they were aiming their efforts at the macro-economic level. They were addressing the "general economic climate" rather than specific regions or firms. In the 1960s that policy approach began to be supplemented by much more direct efforts to generate regional growth, to pick winners and

Inset I

Cast of Characters:
the CF–18 Affair

1. The Companies

Canadair Group:
Canadair Ltd. (Montreal)
CAE Electronics (Montreal)
Northwest Industries (Edmonton)
Bristol Group (CAST-18):
Bristol Aerospace (Winnipeg)
Litton Systems of Canada (Toronto)
Bendix Avelex Inc. (Montreal)
Garrett Manufacturing Ltd.(Toronto)
Leigh Instruments Ltd. (Ottawa)

IMP Group:
IMP Aerospace (Dartmouth)
Canadian Marconi Co. (Montreal)
Canadian Astronautics Ltd.(Ottawa)
Spar Aerospace Ltd. (Toronto)
Fleet Industries (Fort Erie)

2. Politicians

Brian Mulroney, Prime Minister
René Lévesque, Premier of Quebec
Robert Bourassa
Howard Pawley, Premier of Manitoba
Grant Devine, Premier of Saskatchewan
Jake Epp, Minister (Health and Welfare)
Stewart McInnes, Minister (Supply and
Services
Monique Vézina, Minister (Supply and
Services)
Gerry Weiner, Minister of State
(Immigration)

Robert de Cotret, Minister (Treasury
Board)
Vic Schroeder, Manitoba Minister of
Industry
Lloyd Axworthy, MP (Liberal, Winnipeg
South Centre)
Cyril Keeper, MP (NDP, Winnipeg
North)
George Minaker, MP (Cons.,
Winnipeg-St. James)
Leo Duguay, MP (Cons., St. Boniface)
Dan Mackenzie, MP (Cons., Winnipeg-
Assiniboine)
Brian White, MP (Cons., Dauphin-Swan
River)
Marcel Laurin, Mayor, St. Laurent
Bill Norrie, Mayor, Winnipeg

3. Private Sector

Ken Rowe, President, IMP
Frank Hinings, Secretary, Bristol
Aerospace
Greg Walker, Director of Product
Support, Bendix Avelex
Manon Vennat, President, Montreal
Board of Trade
Normand Cherry, President, Canadair
Local of the International Association of
Machinists
John Marlow, President, Local 5 (Bristol
Plant) of Canadian Association of
Industrial, Mechanical and Allied
Workers

losers among industries and firms, and to deliberately encourage Canadian ownership. The downside of efforts as visible and minute as these is that losers and winners are much more easily identified. Decisions like the CF–18 one reflect this. Here the state becomes the arbiter of investments and industries. The process is explicitly politicized, and the losers cannot simply shrug and ascribe their bad fortune to the vagaries of the market. They know (or think they know) that they lost because of power, their lack of it or its superior use by someone else. This is especially critical in defence procurements, since the companies that supply arms for the most part have no other customers apart from governments. In the United States, this has led to a military-industrial complex, wherein billions are spent each year by the American federal government on products produced by firms scattered throughout the country. Canada does not have a large defence budget, or an extensive arms industry similar to the United States, but there are "procurement whirlpools" where regions, industries, and government departments swirl in spirals of self-interest.[79]

Finally, the CF–18 decision casts some light on the nature of regionalism in Canada. Of the many types of political processes in Canada, regional politics is perhaps the most pervasive and puzzling. It is a "real world" for all federal and provincial politicians, with its own rules, dynamics and forces, symbols and rituals. In a peculiar way, Manitobans and Quebecers shared more similarities than differences. They used the same logic to make their claims; these arguments were simply mirror images of each other. This is an important observation, for it undermines the notion that Canada has regional tension because the people in regions differ so much from each other either socially or culturally. There were no visible social or cultural differences between Manitoba and Quebec: their agendas were almost precisely the same, and the fact that they expressed their demands in different languages had absolutely nothing to do with the outcome. Even the animosity shown by the Bristol worker in ranting against "Frenchmen" was less a racial slur than an assessment of the balance of political power.

If sentiments of regionalism are not due primarily to the existence of distinct socio-cultural regions, to what do they owe their existence? Is there such a thing, as Premier Pawley suggested in his *Winnipeg Free Press* advertisement, as a "Manitoba people," or just people that happen to live in Manitoba? In the case of the CF–18 decision, political mobilization in favour of the pursuit of material interests seems to have been a critical factor. In other words, it is not that these sentiments exist in themselves; they lie dormant in the form of collective memory, to be revived as needed in the heat of competition for scarce resources. Decisions like the CF–18, decisions of location, emphasize the geographical dimension and so exacerbate regional tensions in ways that other, equally momentous decisions, do not. They *invite* people to think in regional terms, since the decision itself will have uniquely regional results. They also provide arguments that can be used strategically in making claims. That is why the CF–18 posed the dramatic challenge that it did to the Mulroney Tories: no matter how they played it, one or another region would see itself as the victim and absorb the memory of defeat as part of its legacy of domination.

DISCUSSION QUESTIONS

1. What is the balance between political responsibility and "rational" or expert decision making? If the cabinet had simply accepted the official recommendation on the CF–18, would it have reneged on its democratic responsibility to make decisions in the "national interest"?

2. What is the nature of "regionalism" in Canada? If it is not based on socio-cultural differences, how does it get processed in the political system?

3. Would an elected Senate have helped Manitoba in the CF–18 decision?

4. Consider the nature of party allegiances during the CF–18 affair. How did provincial parties relate to each other, and how did they position themselves with regard to their federal counterparts?

5. What arguments could one devise to support the practice of giving contracts on a rotating basis first to one region and then another and then another, until every region has had some plum?

6. Review the importance of symbols in the CF–18 affair. Make a list of the key symbols on the Quebec side, the Manitoba side, and the federal government's side.

7. Consider the Prime Minister's role in the CF–18 affair, in terms both of the fact that he is a Quebec MP and that the caucus was seriously divided on the issue.

8. Reflect on the problems that Manitoba Tory MPs faced when the decision was announced. What does this say about party discipline

in a parliamentary regime?

9.   Review the electoral considerations that the federal government may have faced in the CF–18 affair. Be sure to think about both regions and ridings.

10.   Compare the regional aspects of the CF–18 decision with those that arose in the pharmaceuticals patents case (see chapter 2). How were they similar? How did they differ?

CHRONOLOGY

17 March 1977   Cabinet approves New Fighter Aircraft Program.

September 1977   Request for Proposal goes out to aircraft companies.

1 February 1978   Bids for fighter aircraft submitted.

June 1978   Bids are reviewed and go to cabinet.

23 November 1978   Cabinet shortlists General Dynamics F–16 and Mc-Donnell Douglas F–18A Hornet.

13 December 1979   Clark government defeated; was to have decided on the recommendation to accept F–18A on 14 December.

28 March 1980   Renée Lévesque and Parti québécois declare support for General Dynamics bid.

10 April 1980   Federal cabinet chooses McDonnell Douglas F–18A Hornet as Canada's new fighter jet.

29 November 1985   Three competing maintenance contract bids submitted. Final decision due 1 April 1986.

mid-February 1986   All three bids re-opened for "bid clarification" (inclusion of new considerations indicated by evaluation team). The evaluation team drops IMP from race.

March-April 1986	IMP fights to get reinstated, and is.
June 1986	Final recommendation from evaluation team goes to cabinet: Bristol Group is the preferred bidder from technical and cost perspective.
15 August 1986	Chambre de commerce de Montréal wires Prime Minister urging that maintenance contract be awarded to Canadair.
3 September 1986	Premier Bourassa and federal Minister of State Gerry Weiner join to demand contract for Canadair. Bourassa meets with the Prime Minister the same day and presses his case.
September 1986	Bombardier offers a "rebate" to Ottawa should its new subsidiary, Canadair, get the CF–18 contract.
3 October 1986	Monique Vézina, Minister of Supply and Services, receives final briefing from officials on CF–18. Cabinet meeting scheduled for the next week to decide.
7 October 1986	Cabinet fails to make decision.
late October 1986	Bristol spokespersons for the first time speak publicly about the issue. Acts as a signal for Manitoba politicians to increase pressure.
21 October 1986	Premier Pawley tries to call the Prime Minister from London, England, where he has talked to owners of Bristol.
30 October 1986	Day before deadline for decision; the Prime Minister makes case for Canadair to Tory caucus. Pawley outraged at reports, and telexes other western premiers for their support.
31 October 1986	Robert de Cotret (President of the Treasury Board) announces that the CF–18 maintenance contract will go to Canadair.

| 3 November 1986 | Premier Pawley heads delegation to see Prime Minister about the decision. |
| January 1988 | New revelations about the bidding process prompt Premier Pawley to claim that Tories made political decision. |

NOTES

1   Brig.-Gen. P. D. Mason, "The CF–18 Hornet: Canada's New Fighter Aircraft," *Canadian Defence Quarterly* 10 (Summer 1980): 16.

2   *Globe and Mail*, 9 January 1988.

3   Michael M. Atkinson and Kim Richard Nossal, "Bureaucratic Politics and the New Fighter Aircraft Decisions," *Canadian Public Administration 24* (Winter 1981): 536.

4   Ibid., 537.

5   Ibid., 538.

6   *Globe and Mail*, 28 March 1980.

7   *Winnipeg Free Press*, 28 October 1986.

8   *Winnipeg Free Press*, 28 October 1986.

9   Atkinson and Nossal, "Bureaucratic Politics and the New Fighter Aircraft Decisions," 539.

10 *Globe and Mail*, 4 September 1986.

11 *Globe and Mail*, 31 December 1985. See also *Globe and Mail*, 1 January 1986. Ms. Blais-Grenier's resignation, while dramatic, was prudent, since she was probably going to be dropped from the cabinet in any event for reasons unrelated to the Ultramar refinery issue.

12 *Winnipeg Free Press*, 13 February 1986.

13 *Financial Post*, 18 October 1986.

14 *Winnipeg Free Press*, 9 September 1986.

15 *Financial Post*, 18 October 1986.

16 *Globe and Mail*, 16 August 1986.

17 *The Gazette*, 22 August 1986.

18 *The Gazette*, 22 August 1986.

19 *Globe and Mail*, 3 September 1986.

20 *The Gazette*, 4 September 1986.

21 *The Gazette*, 4 September 1986.

22 *Winnipeg Free Press*, 4 September 1986.

23 For details on the Canadair privatization and its links to the CF–18, see G. Bruce Doern and John Atherton, "The Tories and the Crowns: Restraining and Privatizing in a Political Minefield," in *How Ottawa Spends 1987–1988: Restraining the State* ed. Michael J. Prince (Toronto: Methuen, 1987), 129–75.

24 *Globe and Mail*, 4 September 1986.

25 *The Gazette*, 5 September 1986.

26 *Winnipeg Free Press*, 4 September 1986.

27 *Winnipeg Free Press*, 13 September 1986.

28 *Winnipeg Free Press*, 8 September 1986.

29 *Globe and Mail*, 22 September 1986.

30 *The Gazette*, 2 October 1986.

31 *Winnipeg Free Press*, 7 October 1986.

32 There were conflicting reports on whether the issue had in fact been on the committee's agenda. *The Gazette*, 10 October 1986.

33 *The Gazette*, 9 October 1986.

34 *Le Devoir*, 3 September 1986.

35 *The Gazette*, 15 October 1986.

36 *Globe and Mail*, 18 October 1986.

37 *Winnipeg Free Press*, 19 October 1986.

38 *Winnipeg Free Press*, 22 October 1986.

39 *Winnipeg Free Press*, 22 October 1986.

40 *Winnipeg Free Press*, 22 October 1986.

41 *Winnipeg Free Press*, 24 October 1986.

42 *Winnipeg Free Press*, 30 October 1986.

43 *Globe and Mail*, 31 October 1986.

44 Michel Gratton, *"So, What Are the Boys Saying?": An Insider Look at Brian Mulroney in Power* (Toronto: McGraw-Hill Ryerson, 1987), 194.

45 *Winnipeg Free Press*, 31 October 1986.

46 Vancouver Sun, 1 November 1986.

47 *The Gazette*, 1 November 1986.

48 *Globe and Mail*, 1 November 1986.

49 House of Commons, *Debates*, 31 October 1986, 949.

50 *Globe and Mail*, 1 November 1986.

51 *Winnipeg Free Press*, 1 November 1986.

52 *Winnipeg Free Press*, 1 November 1986.

53 *Winnipeg Free Press*, 1 November 1986.

54 Press Release, Robert de Cotret, President of the Treasury Board. Reprinted in part in *Winnipeg Free Press*, 2 November 1986.

55 *Winnipeg Free Press*, 1 November 1986.

56 *Winnipeg Free Press*, 2 November 1986.

57 *Winnipeg Free Press*, 3 November 1986.

58 *Winnipeg Free Press*, 4 November 1986.

59 *Winnipeg Free Press*, 7 November 1986; *Winnipeg Free Press*, 6 November 1986.

60 *Globe and Mail*, 3 November 1986.

61 *Winnipeg Free Press*, 2 November 1986; 3 November, 1986.

62 *Globe and Mail*, 4 November 1986.

63 *Globe and Mail*, 3 November 1986.

64 *Winnipeg Free Press*, 4 November 1986.

65 *Winnipeg Free Press*, 5 November 1986.

66 *Winnipeg Free Press*, 6 November 1986.

67 Gratton, *"So What Are the Boys Saying?"*, 195.

68 *Winnipeg Free Press*, 15 November 1986.

69 *Winnipeg Free Press*, 16 November 1986.

70 *Winnipeg Free Press*, 17 November 1986.

71 *Le Devoir*, 4 November 1986.

72 *Le Devoir*, 1 November 1986.

73 *Winnipeg Free Press*, 21 December 1986.

74 *Globe and Mail*, 23 December 1986.

76 *Globe and Mail*, 7 January 1988.

77 Letter to the *Globe and Mail*, 9 March 1988.

78 *Globe and Mail*. 4 October 1988.

79 See Edgar Dosman, "The Department of National Defence: The Steady Drummer," in *How Ottawa Spends 1988/89: The Conservatives Heading into the Stretch*, ed. Katherine Graham (Ottawa: Carleton University Press, 1988), 165–94.

THE LONG AND WINDING ROAD: BILL C-22 AND THE POLITICS OF DRUG PATENTS

The passage of Bill C-22 — an Act to Amend the Patent Act — was one of the more bizarre political incidents in recent Canadian history. Despite having Canada's largest ever electoral majority, the Conservative government took an extraordinary amount of time and energy to pass this legislation, which gave the pharmaceutical industry increased patent protection for its products. The Senate finally passed the bill in November 1987, but not before the government had sent it Bill C-22 for an unprecedented third time. What appeared to be a relatively 'technical' matter — the issue of patent protection for the drug industry — raised a variety of sensitive political and ideological matters that the government could not contain. As it lost political control over the issue, the question of patent protection was eclipsed by other symbolic issues, such as the free trade debate, Quebec's place in confederation, the power of multinational corporations, the role of the Senate, and the question of the state's place in social and economic life. As the legislative process ground on and on, the issue ultimately became a test of the government's credibility. Bill C-22's odyssey revealed many of the worlds of Canadian politics, including the role of experts and studies, regional and interest group pressures, bureaucratic influences, a suddenly operative bicameral legislature, and the ultimate dominance of the executive.

"An Act to Amend the Patent Act". This is not exactly a catchy phrase or a title that might set political hearts aflutter. Indeed, it is hard to imagine that the subject of patent protection for pharmaceutical products could generate passionate debate or divisive controversy, yet this is exactly what was wrought by Bill C-22. First introduced in June 1986, the bill was not passed until November 1987. During this time, the legislation held a central place on the political agenda and paralysed the legislative process for extended periods of time. The ordeal caused the government considerable political grief and embarrassment, and forced it to expend an extraordinary amount of time and effort in order to pass the legislation.

Bill C–22 was designed to give increased patent protection for the pharmaceutical industry. Since the last legislative initiative in this area in 1969, multinational drug companies had complained that the Patent Act provided poor protection for intellectual property and meagre incentives for investment. The Conservative government was ideologically disposed to private enterprise and so was alive to this complaint. The government was also keen to increase Canadian involvement in the emerging field of biotechnology, a branch of the 'new technology' that appeared to offer the promise of jobs and economic growth. Bill C–22 was designed as an investment incentive for the pharmaceutical industry to increase its research and development in this area.

A government with the largest electoral majority in Canadian history should have had little difficulty passing this legislation. Despite having legislative and political priority, the bill was not passed until three years after the election; the government struggled on and off to pass the bill over an eighteen-month period. In the process, it lost control of the issue. Everything that could go wrong for the government, did. In the end the bill was passed, but it was a topsy-turvy process: viewing the proceedings is a bit like visiting Wonderland with Alice.

The story of Bill C–22 is a classic illustration of how a majority government in the Canadian political system can change the political agenda, create new political priorities, and pass legislation expressing these priorities — without a specific political mandate or a substantial degree of popular support for that legislation. At the same time, this case sheds light on the difficulties and constraints faced by a majority government in pursuing its priorities. Even with its unprecedented electoral mandate, the government confronted political, bureaucratic, and social conditions and issues outside of its control. In the process the bill took on a life of its own. The substance of the bill — how much patent protection should be given to those who invent new drugs and medicines — became submerged into peripheral but controversial and politically damaging issues.

Foremost amongst these issues was the question of Canadian-American relations. The Canadian pharmaceutical industry is dominated by multinational corporations, many of them American. Opponents of the bill were able to transform the issue into the broader question of Canada's economic relations with the United States. The debate over Bill C–22 foreshadowed the free trade debate, and was just as intense and divisive.

Bill C–22 ultimately became a regional issue as well. The multinational pharmaceutical companies are concentrated in the province of Quebec. As the debate over the legislation dragged on, the government itself transformed the issue into a 'Quebec' issue, by maintaining that opponents of the bill were hampering Quebec's economic development.

The debate over Bill C–22 was also underpinned by the tension between the ostensible financial needs of multinational corporations (for profits) and the budgetary needs of the sick and the elderly (for access to inexpensive medicine). What was perhaps most unanticipated was how Bill C–22 generated a constitutional controversy about the role of the Senate. Given the huge Conservative majority, opposition to the bill in the House of Commons was weak and ineffective. The Liberal majority in the Senate in effect took on the role of opposition to the government, and managed to delay passage of Bill C–22 for six months. It ultimately passed the bill, but only after the government had sent it the legislation for an unheard-of three times. All the while, the substance of the bill was smothered in the debate over the role of the Senate.

The case demonstrates the extent to which issues or policies cannot be treated as 'technical' matters. Patent protection appears to be a relatively technical matter open to 'non-political' analysis and approach. Indeed, the issue was examined extensively by a variety of departments, studies, and commissions. Regardless of 'expert' advice, the government was incapable of insulating the legislation from a variety of political and ideological issues. And in the final analysis, the Conservative government rejected the expert advice of a Royal Commission and simply pushed ahead with an approach that reflected its political goals. The case also illustrates how difficult it can be to change what might be termed the 'framework' laws under which economic activity takes place.[1] Finally, the case suggests how important 'credibility' is for a government. As time went on, the political costs of Bill C–22 became greater and greater. Nonetheless, the government gritted its teeth and pushed ahead. The legislation came to symbolize the government's approach to economic, scientific and technological policy as well as its capacity to govern. This legislation was not as critical or far-reaching as, say, the Free Trade Agreement or Meech Lake. But the government acted as if this were the case — in order to salvage its credibility. There is a serpentine quality to this case, so an extensive chronology has been appended to this chapter as a reader's guide. Before tracking Bill C–22's passage through Parliament, the chapter will first set the stage by discussing the question of patents, the nature of the pharmaceutical industry in Canada, and the evolution of patent legislation in Canada prior to the advent of the Mulroney government.

PATENTS AND THE CANADIAN
PHARMACEUTICAL INDUSTRY

The debate over Bill C–22 revolved around one basic policy choice: to what extent should public policy treat drugs and medicines as an 'economic' as opposed to a 'social' issue? That is, should government policy be directed primarily to ensuring that the economic benefits or profits of the (essentially oligopolistic) pharmaceutical industry are used to promote innovation and economic growth? Or should government policy be mainly concerned with guaranteeing that all Canadians — regardless of income — have access to the drugs and medicines that can restore health? What makes the pharmaceutical industry a 'special' case (unlike, say, the soft drink or cosmetic industries) is the fact that its products touch on the primary issue of illness and health. But the choice between 'economic' and 'social' goals was not purely an 'either/or' dilemma; policy decisions tend to reflect a combination of goals. Rather, the debate was over the re-positioning of these goals, and whether economic or social goals should be emphasized.

The discovery of a new drug is an expensive business. The pharmaceutical industry has exceptionally high research and development costs. The material costs of a drug are marginal, compared to the costs of maintaining a large, highly skilled research team that uses 'intellectual resources' to develop a new product. Research is a hit and miss affair, and it takes a long time and substantial investment to make a 'hit'. It seems reasonable, then, that those who incur the costs and risks of discovery should be paid back. Over and above the fact that investors should be allowed a fair rate of return, adequate incentives should be allowed, to ensure that creators and inventors continue to do this work. To realize these two goals, a patent is assigned to a new discovery. This patent affords a monopoly over the use of the discovery for a fixed period of time during which the new product can be sold in a market without competitors. Since anything unique bears a high price tag, the producer will reap monopoly profits. In the process, investment costs are recouped and profits are made, which stimulates further research and discovery. In economic terms, a patent is the means of closing the gap between 'public' benefits (to those who benefit from the use of the new product) and 'private' returns (to the inventor who has taken the risk).

On the other hand, new drugs and medicines offer immense potential benefits for the treatment of illness, so one would like these products to be accessible to everyone, irrespective of income. At monopoly prices, though, it is unlikely that the product will be within reach of low income earners, which is why patent protection should not be indefinite. Once the patented period ends, companies other than the patent-holding one can enter the market and offer the new product. In a competitive situation, the price will fall and the new product will have wider use.

There is a second reason why patent protection should not be indefinite or lengthy: if the creator of the new product continues to reap high, monopoly-based rewards, there is no incentive for the inventor to go back to the drawing board and do it again. Moreover, other companies will be attracted by these high profits, and will be stimulated to create marginally different products that will avoid the patent protection but offer no new benefit. This is called 'product differentiation'.

These two perspectives on the issue — price and investment — mirror a broader tension that informs all economic policy issues, between 'stability' and 'equity' on the one hand and 'change' and 'efficiency' on the other . Of course, one would like to devise policies which 'balance' the supply-side interests of producers and the demand-side interests of consumers — but this is a delicate balance to realize. Investors want a policy that maximizes their returns, while consumers want a policy that minimizes their costs. Governments correspondingly want to construct policies that simultaneously encourage economic development and growth as well as public health. Drug patent policy is a complex area in which to legislate, and no matter how hard politicians attempt to create a balanced policy, the perception will be that one side or the other is being favoured. This is particularly the case because policy is devised neither from scratch nor in a vacuum, but in response to an already existing situation, which may be satisfactory to one group but not to another. Policy is also constructed in a world of ad hoc pressures and expectations and idiosyncratic situations.

As will be seen, drug patents policy in Canada shifted to the investment side after the war, and to the price side in the 1960s and 1970s. In the 1980s revived concern over investment produced Bill C–22. These shifts in policy have mirrored the two waves of change in the drug industry over the past 50 years. The first involved a decline during the 1930s and 1940s in the importance of 'plant' or natural drugs and the advent of organic synthetics (antibiotics such as penicillin and tetracycline are the best-known examples). There was then an explosion of new drugs such as antihistamines and antidepressants in the 1950s and 1960s. These involved extensive applications of the discoveries made in earlier decades. More recently, a new wave of basic innovations has begun, generally associated with the emerging field of biotechnology. This promises to produce a new generation of drugs, medicines and techniques for the treatment of illness.

Drug patents policy in Canada has been shaped to a significant extent by the character of the process by which these drugs are produced, and by the industrial structure that has developed as a result.[2] There are basically two stages in the production of prescription drugs. The first stage is chemical synthesis, in which fine chemicals are produced. This stage is technically demanding, and involves a series of research and development steps over an extended period of time. The costs involved are high, and the skill requirements and scientific needs are intensive. Economies of scale are possible. That is, it makes economic sense to concentrate these scientific and research efforts and to bring scientists together in a research facility, rather than to spread them out in countless small laboratories. The result is that this stage of production is concentrated and centralized. The second stage involves the mixing of these chemicals into the appropriate pharmaceutical preparation. This stage is far less demanding, with little research and development required. It is easier to decentralize this operation and the process is geared to local markets.

The logic of this industrial division of labour has had pronounced results for Canada. The pharmaceutical industry is organized on a world scale, with 25 multinational companies dominating the market, none of which is Canadian. These companies carry out research and manufacture the raw chemical materials in a limited number of locations, usually in the home country. The multinationals follow global investment strategies; countries like Canada (with small domestic markets) have attracted little investment capital in the first stage of production. Canada has instead specialized in importing these raw materials for pharmaceutical preparation, packaging and marketing. None of these activities allows for independent research initiative or innovation. The independent research that exists in Canada comprises 'efficacy' research, which aims at establishing whether a drug is effective (actually does what it claims to do). This is necessary if the product is to be approved for sale in Canada. Profits in the Canadian pharmaceutical industry are high but so too is foreign ownership. The high costs of research and development act as a formidable barrier to the entry of new, Canadian participants in the industry.

Canadian policy with respect to the pharmaceutical sector has confronted an industrial world of a very specific sort. The industry has been dominated by multinational drug companies with the Canadian industry functioning as a branch-plant operation. This has affected the political discourse surrounding drug patents policy.

THE ROAD TO COMPULSORY LICENSING AND SECTION 41(4): DRUG PRICES AS THE PRIORITY

Bill C–22 was designed to nullify its predecessor, Bill C–190. This earlier legislation had been the culmination of an extended and heated battle from the late 1950s to the late 1960s over the *price* of drugs, which took place against the backdrop of the apparently endless postwar economic boom and appearance of new drugs. A series of studies and commissions (see Inset I, pp. 60-61) documented the strength, profitability, and foreign domination of the pharmaceutical industry. They vindicated the public feeling that drug prices were too high and created considerable political momentum for changing drug patent legislation. Not only did the reports bring equity and price considerations to the attention of policy-makers; they also presented the policy tactics appropriate to realizing these objectives.

These studies suggested that there were two policy options open to the government, if it wanted to realize equity and price goals. It could follow the recommendation of the Restrictive Trades Practices Commission and abolish patent protection. Or it could introduce *compulsory licensing*. This is a less drastic policy measure, but it is a coercive measure nonetheless. The idea is to *compel* a patent holder to allow another individual or company to use the patented process in return for a fee (usually a percentage of the retail selling price of the product). The rationale is that the competition engendered by increasing the number of producers will produce lower prices. The patent holder is in effect forced to trade away the benefits of monopoly prices in return for a royalty on the sales of the licensed products of his competitors.

Oddly enough, Chapters 2 and 3 of the Canadian Patent Act already provided for compulsory licensing (Section 41(3)) but companies had not acted on the opportunity. Why not? Section 41(3) only allowed the licencee the right to make, sell and vend the patented process — in short, it allowed the licencee to use the patented process and to sell the result. This licence was more or less useless, because the patented *process* could not be used in the absence of the *active chemical ingredient*. Section 41(3) did not force the patent holder to provide the licence for this active ingredient, whose only source was foreign. There was no 'right to import.' Hence, the policy tactic suggested was not compulsory licensing *per se* but, more specifically, the principle of *compulsory licensing to import* either the active ingredient or the finished product itself.

In 1967 the Liberal government decided to introduce compulsory licensing. Bill C–190 was the first piece of legislation introduced by the newly formed Department of Consumer and Corporate Affairs. The purpose of the bill was to "allow compulsory licensing to import prescription drugs, having the effect of injecting more competition at the manufacturer's level in the drug industry, and beneficially affecting the price of drugs." The bill was introduced by John Turner, who took care not to blame the industry for high drug prices:

> The drug industry operates within a given economic framework, and members of the drug industry have responded to the profit opportunities produced by that framework...There is no issue between myself and spokesmen for the drug industry about the great benefits that...the Canadian industry has conferred on Canadians....What we do not wish to see is great benefits flowing from the availability of modern drugs being persistently overshadowed by their high cost to the consumer.[9]

He articulated the tension between the price and investment dimensions of the issue:

> The patent right is not an absolute right. It is a right that has to be weighted in the balance of economic convenience. In this case, it is the objective of the bill to weigh the legitimate rights of the Canadian consumer against the legitimate rights of the investor and the drug industry...The relevant argument is free trade against protection. I

EXPERT STUDIES IN THE 1950s AND 1960s

D.H.W. HENRY'S 'GREEN BOOK' REPORT[3] : In 1961 D.H.W. Henry, the director of investigation and research, Combines Investigation Act, submitted to the Restrictive Trades Practices Commission (RTPC) a statement relating to the manufacture, distribution and sale of drugs in Canada. The 'Green Book' charged that:

§ drug prices were excessively high in relation to industry's costs;
§ there was little price competition at the retail level;
§ drug companies were essentially acting under American laws;
§ patents were used to inhibit competition.

RESTRICTIVE TRADE PRACTICES COMMISSION:REPORT CONCERNING THE MANUFACTURE, DISTRIBUTION AND SALE OF DRUGS[4] : Between 1958 and 1962, the commission carried out research and held public hearings, and issued a report in January 1963. Its report echoed the Green Book view that patents in the industry eliminated price competition. It demonstrated that:

§ profits in the pharmaceutical industry averaged 17 per cent;
§ profits were higher than any sector save paper products;
§ in the 1950s profits were on average 71 per cent higher than in the manufacturing sector as a whole;
§ Canadian drug prices were much higher than American prices and amongst the highest in the world. It conclusion was that "the abolition of patents relating to drugs is...the only effective remedy for the undesirable consequences arising out of the control of drugs in Canada."

ROYAL COMMISSION ON PATENTS, COPYRIGHTS AND INDUSTRIAL DESIGNS[5] : In 1960, the Ilsley commission argued that drug prices and corporate rates of return were too high. It recommended that these be moderated by adopting a policy similar to Section 41 of the United Kingdom Patents Act. This section provided for compulsory licensing.

ROYAL COMMISSION ON HEALTH SERVICES[6] : The Hall commission studied Canada's health services in the early 1960s. It discovered high drug prices and an exceptionally profitable pharmaceutical industry. The tone of its report can be gathered from in the following passage:

> Although we accept that the manufacture and distribution of drugs in this country is a private venture, we have no hesitation in stating that the public interest is dominant. Either the industry will make these drugs available at the lowest possible cost, or it will be necessary for agencies and devices of government to do so.

The Hall commission suggested a five year delay in the RTPC recommendation for the abolition of patents, during which time Section 41(3) be expanded to include compulsory licensing to import.[7]

HOUSE OF COMMONS SPECIAL COMMITTEE ON DRUG COSTS AND PRICES[8]: In 1967, the Harley committee issued its final report. The committee had been established to inquire into and report on the cost of drugs, and to consider and recommend a program to reduce the price of drugs. It met 63 times, and heard dozens of witnesses, including government, industry, and consumer and special interest groups. It produced an exhaustive study of the pharmaceutical industry, showing that:

§   there was little production of active chemicals in Canada;
§   Canadian firms imported the basic raw materials and prepared and mixed them;
§   the pharmaceutical sector was concentrated and foreign-dominated;
§   Canadian firms did little or no research and did not export;
§   Canadians paid up to 75 percent more for drugs than in other countries, because of the high cost of the imported chemical ingredients (transfer pricing), high promotion costs in brand-name 'competition', and the impact of patents.

It concluded that compulsory licensing had had little to no impact upon drug firms' monopoly position, because few firms were able to take out licenses; they were either tied up in court cases or did not have access to the active chemical ingredients (80 percent of which had to be imported). It concluded that "price competition, not product competition...will lower prices...promot[ing] lower costs through increased efficiency and cut[ting] through extravagant promotional costs". To this end, it endorsed the principle of compulsory licensing to import.

think that this country...must always weigh the balance of having free trade for the benefit of consumers, and a certain amount of protection for the benefit of a viable domestic industry.[10]

In this case, the government opted to tilt the balance in favour of price over investment concerns, and chose what Turner described as 'free trade' for consumers over protection for the pharmaceutical industry. As it turned out, Bill C–190 died in adjournment, but was re-introduced in late 1968 as Bill C–102 by the new Minister, Ron Basford, and passed in March 1968. Throughout this legislative process, the organized arm of the industry, the Pharmaceutical Manufacturers Association of Canada (PMAC), fought a furious battle against the policy change. It was unsuccessful in its efforts for a number of reasons. Its case was not perceived to be legitimate, because the studies cited above had created a solid public perception of high drug prices and profits generated by a foreign dominated sector. Moreover, its political strategy was American-inspired and, as a result, inept. It lobbied the wrong people (committees and MPs rather than permanent officials). [11]

Section 41(4) of the Patent Act had its intended effects over the ensuing decade. Various firms — many of which were Canadian — came into existence to take advantage of compulsory licensing to produce products essentially the same as the patent- holders' products. They paid a moderate 4% royalty on the net price of these products. These firms were called *generic companies* and their products known as *generic drugs*. Generic products were commercially popular given their low price. Canadians had access to cheaper drugs as a result of 41(4). In 1983, the price of generic drugs was half the market price of the patented products, and this resulted in $211 million in savings to consumers. Moreover, it is estimated that the prices of patented products would have been 15-20% higher in the absence of this price competition from the generics. In sum, it is estimated that the effect of 41(4) was to reduce the price of compulsorily licensed drugs from 86% of the US price in 1968 to 45% in 1980. [12]

During the regime of 41(4) the multinational drug companies battled to undo the patent change. They threatened to pull out of Canada, or to discontinue research here. This was a hollow threat as they were doing very little research and development in Canada to begin with. Despite their complaints, their market position was not irreparably harmed as a result of compulsory licensing. The fact remained that it took a considerable period of time for a generic company to produce a copy of the patented drug. In the first instance, it had to wait and see if a new drug was a commercial success. Then, it would have to apply for a license, research the chemical principles, produce and test the drug, and market it. Depending on market and other conditions, as well as bureaucratic alacrity, this could take years, during which time the patent-holder remained in a monopoly position. If desperate to delay competition, the patent-holder could always resort to a lawsuit. Or it could attempt to destroy competition through price-cutting (Hoffman-La-Roche was actually convicted for pursuing this strategy).[13]

Moreover, compulsorily licensed drugs comprise only a portion of the prescription drug market — about 20% of total sales — and the generic companies had but a 21 percent share of this market. In sum, generic firms had only 3 percent of the pharmaceutical market in 1983.[14] Nonetheless, the multinational drug companies remained hostile to compulsory licensing, and PMAC displayed single-minded resolve in a ceaseless attempt to undo 41(4). To the industry, the Canadian approach set a 'bad example' to other countries, especially in the emerging Third World markets, who might be influenced by this example of lowering drug prices.

In 1976, the Department of Consumer and Corporate Affairs issued a study of how 41(4) was working, concluding that no changes were required in Canada's drug patents policy. In 1981, an Economic Council of Canada study concluded that compulsory licensing should be retained. [15]

THE ROAD TO C-22: THE LIBERAL PRELUDE

Save for the multinationals, there was widespread if implicit support given to 41(4) over the next decade. Drug prices were low, which was welcomed by the public as well as by politicians increasingly concerned about inflation. The price orientation tilted, however, toward an investment orientation in the late 1970s and early 1980s. The postwar boom tailed off and investment conditions became less buoyant. Price, equity, and welfare concerns were replaced by the goals of investment, growth, and efficiency. It appeared that the economy was undergoing far-reaching and fundamental technological changes whose encouragement and management required new types of economic policies in general, and a new drug patents policy in particular.

Even before the advent of the Conservative government, 41(4) came under political scrutiny from the Trudeau government. The pharmaceutical industry appeared to be undergoing a transformation from a chemistry- to a biology-based industry. Biotechnology was a fashionable word, and the Liberal government was concerned about the low level of investment in this sector. Concern was intensified in the early 1980s by the actions of a number of multinational companies, which pulled their operations or research facilities out of Canada[16]. These firms, indeed the industry itself, was concentrated in Quebec, making these pull-outs politically sensitive (half of the Liberal government's caucus was Quebec based). As a result, the government made domestic expansion and research and development in the pharmaceutical sector a priority policy objective. Compulsory licensing and Section 41(4) of the Patent Act came back on to the political agenda.

INDUSTRIAL AND BUREAUCRATIC DIVISIONS[18]

AGAINST COMPULSORY LICENSING	*FOR COMPULSORY LICENSING*
INDUSTRY	**INDUSTRY**
The Pharmaceutical Manufacturers Association of Canada was established in 1914, and centred in Ottawa since 1967. PMAC represented 67 pharmaceutical firms, mainly located in Quebec. These firms were the foreign-owned, patent-holding multinationals that accounted for 90 percent of the sales of prescription drugs in Canada. PMAC was an exceedingly well-organized and professional interest group, with full-time staff and institutionalized relationships with the permanent bureaucracy in Ottawa and especially with the Departments of Health and Welfare and Regional Industrial Expansion.	The Canadian Drug Manufacturers Association (CDMA) was founded in 1967. It was much smaller than PMAC (17 members), with a membership confined to Canadian-owned companies. These were all manufacturers of generic drugs, and had come into existence as a result of 41(4). These companies were mainly located in Ontario, although there were some generic companies in Quebec. While CDMA was far less powerful, professional and institutionalized than PMAC, and while it had less legitimacy and permanence in its relationship with the permanent bureaucracy, it enjoyed a relatively healthy and positive relationship with the Department of Consumer and Corporate Affairs.
BUREAUCRACY	**BUREAUCRACY**
The Department of Regional Industrial Expansion (DRIE) — particularly the Health Care Products Division of its Chemical Branch—was sympathetic to PMAC. DRIE's view was that compulsory licensing had inhibited research and development in the pharmaceutical industry.	The Department of Consumer and Corporate Affairs (C&CA) had championed compulsory licensing and section 41(4) in 1967 and had subsequently defended it. The department had been a persistent critic of the multinational pharmaceutical companies. PMAC more or less ignored C&CA, as it was a weak department politically, nowhere near the equal of DRIE. But it offered the only real government access for CDMA. C&CA constantly ridiculed the view that elimination of compulsory licensing would increase investment and research and development in the pharmaceutical sector.
	While it might have been expected that the Department of Health and Welfare would champion the consumer interest, it concentrated its attention on product safety. It enjoyed a comfortable relationship with PMAC, so took a back seat in the debate.

There was, however, a dramatic difference of opinion in both industrial and bureaucratic circles as to what direction drug patents policy should take (see Inset II).[17] In one corner was the PMAC, the organized arm of the multinationals, in February 1983 presenting an anti-compulsory licensing brief, "Proposals for Patent Reform in Relation to the Compulsory Licensing Provisions under Section 41 of the Patent Act." In the other corner was the Canadian Drug Manufacturers Association, the organized arm of the generic companies, in April 1983 countering with a brief of its own, "A Case for the Retention of Section 41(4) of the Patent Act." Complementing this split was a division in the federal bureaucracy between the Department of Regional Industrial Expansion (DRIE), which favoured the elimination of compulsory licensing, and the Department of Consumer and Corporate Affairs (C&CA), which supported its retention.

A series of tensions would shape the debate over whether drug patent law should be tilted more toward price or investment:

§ industrial tension between patent-holding and generic companies;

§ national tension between foreign and Canadian firms;

§ regional tension between Quebec interests and those of the rest of the country;

§ bureaucratic tension between DRIE and Consumer and Corporate Affairs;

§ ideological tension between equity and growth goals and about the appropriate role of the state.

These conflicts created a politically fluid situation. There was no one obvious solution that would maximize political gains or minimize political losses for the government.

Whatever the decision or viewpoint, this would be a tough political decision to make, as there was no consensus in any of the bureaucratic, regional, and interest group domains.

The situation did seem to lean in favour of the multinationals, DRIE, Quebec, and investment:

§ the pharmaceutical industry in Quebec appeared to many to be collapsing;

§ a number of provincial governments (Quebec, Nova Scotia, Alberta, Saskatchewan) were attacking 41(4);

CANADIAN POLITICS IS A SMALL WORLD

The environment in which policy is made in Canada is a small, concentrated one in which the same personnel often show up in different roles. Political, bureaucratic and interest group 'hats' are swapped amongst the same people. The following is a short, by no means inclusive, list of some of the 'players' in Bill C-22, and their various roles:

JOHN TURNER

Introduced the legislation creating compulsory licensing in 1968; in the 1970s, member of the Board of Directors of Sandoz — a multinational drug company; leader of the opposition at the time of Bill C-22.

JUDY EROLA

Minister of Consumer and Corporate Affairs who established the Eastman Commission; later, became President of the Pharmaceutical Manufacturers Asociation of Canada.

MARTIN O'CONNELL

Minister of Labour in the Trudeau government; later became a consultant to Eli Lilly, a multinational drug firm; resigned that post to become a consultant on patent law revision for the Department of Consumer and Corporate Affairs.

ALLAN MacEACHEN

Minister of Health and Welfare when compulsory licensing was introduced; Liberal leader in the Senate at the time of Bill C-22 .

IVAN FLEISCHMAN

Executive assistant to Liberal Minister John Roberts; consultant for the Canadian Drug Manufactuers Association.

SKIP WALLIS

Campaign manager for Peter Pocklington; consultant for CDMA.

GARRY OUELLET

A founder of Government Consultants Inc., a powerful Ottawa lobby firm, used by PMAC; a chum of Brian Mulroney; recruited Michel Côté, Minister of Consumer and Corporate Affairs.

GERALD DOUCET

A founder of GCI, longtime Nova Scotia MLA, and brother of Fred Doucet, Prime Minister Mulroney's chief of staff.

§   a variety of medical and scientific groups were lobbying for change, for strategic technological reasons, arguing that the pharmaceutical industry was at the leading edge of the biotechnological revolution;

§   a federal task force on biotechnology argued that the pharmaceutical industry should be considered from a national security perspective and expressed concern about 41(4);

§ the Liberal government was disappointed in the low degree of investment in this sector;

§ the Quebec caucus was a formidable political force pressing for change and its whip (André Ouellet) was the Minister of Consumer and Corporate Affairs.[19]

Ouellet assembled a committee of officials to review the need for compulsory licensing, in the process excluding some of the C&CA officials who were sympathetic to 41(4). He appointed Martin O'Connell as a consultant on the issue. O'Connell was an ex-Liberal labour minister in the previous Trudeau administration, who had gone on to work as a consultant to Eli Lilly, a major multinational pharmaceutical company. He had also helped prepare the 1983 PMAC brief against compulsory licensing. O'Connell's appointment was but one example of the fact that Canadian politics is a 'small world' (see Inset III). Many of the players in the saga of Bill C–22 wore different 'hats' in the private and public sectors at different times. Compared to the United States, Canada has fewer constraints on ex-politicians and officials working as government consultants for the private sector.

O'Connell carried out his own study (outside of the public bureaucracy), and recommended to the minister that drug firms receive eight years of patent protection (during which time compulsory licensing would not be available). In June 1983, the Department of Consumer and Corporate Affairs produced a Red Paper on the issue, whose content was nothing short of schizophrenic. The bulk of the report was written by C&CA officials, and was more or less pro-compulsory licensing. The conclusions, apparently emanating from the O'Connell study, emphasized investment considerations and questioned the usefulness of compulsory licensing.[20]

By spring 1983, then, the Liberals had decided to review and revise the Patent Act. Appearing before a House of Commons committee, Ouellet argued that changed conditions in the 1980s warranted a shift of focus away from price to investment concerns. The price of drugs had stabilized, he claimed, but investment in this sector was too low:

The degree of investment in Canada was in danger, because of Section 41(4) of the Patent Act....We have decided to change the Act ...in order to create a better climate for investment and research in Canada.

The government position was that it was willing to undo licensing if the pharmaceutical industry promised to increase the degree of research and high-tech investment in Canada.[21]

Alarm bells rang immediately in CDMA headquarters. When in doubt in the Ottawa policy game, hire a high-powered consultant — the CDMA purchased the services of Ivan Fleischman, a former executive assistant to another ex-Liberal minister, John Roberts. He gained the ear of Tom Axworthy, Trudeau's principal secretary, and managed to inject concern over the price impact of the undoing of 41(4). This temporarily neutralized the tilt toward investment.[22]

Judy Erola was named Minister of Consumer and Corporate Affairs in the August cabinet shuffle. She was at this time less convinced than Ouellet of PMAC's case for change, and was less sensitive to Quebec pressures. However, the issue had by this time been pitched up to the international level. PMAC developed and nurtured relations with the White House, and President Reagan made it clear to Canadian ambassador Allan Gotlieb that the United States considered 41(4) to be as offensive as the National Energy Program. Potential Canadian-American tension was thus added to the industrial, bureaucratic, and regional tensions mentioned earlier.

Given these conflicts, Erola made a quintessential Canadian move — she called for a Royal Commission study. When the Liberal's Quebec caucus heard about the move, it tried to block it but Prime Minister Trudeau approved Erola's manoeuvre. A Commission of Inquiry on the Pharmaceutical Industry was to be carried out by Dr Harry C. Eastman of the University of Toronto, a noted expert in the field. Its purpose was to assess the industry and to "identify proposals that might form the basis for reaching a consensus on licensing policy." The Commission was to report within a year, and, it was hoped, would lay the basis for a policy consensus that could be given legislative form by the Liberal government.

By the time the Commission issued its report in May 1985, there were some fundamental changes on the scene. The Conservative party was in government and Judy Erola had returned to the private sector — as president of PMAC.

THE ODYSSEY OF THE MULRONEY GOVERNMENT'S BILL C-22

A Progressive Conservative government would review the Patent Act to ensure that intellectual capital is protected and to allow innovating companies to profit from the investment made in research and development without causing the consumer to pay unduly higher prices for medications.

Progressive Conservative Party campaign promise, 16 July 1984

With the landslide election of the Progressive Conservative government in the fall of 1984, the political die was cast; compulsory licensing and section 41(4) were effectively doomed. The government brought with it a new political agenda, planning to regenerate private enterprise and the marketplace through a rolling back of government involvement in social and economic life. Private enterprise was to be the engine of economic growth, and the government planned to support its adoption of new technology, which the government considered to be the major spur to this growth. The elimination of compulsory licensing was one of a number of ingredients in this strategy. With an unprecedentedly large proportion of the seats in Quebec, the Quebec caucus would be a formidable regional force pressing for changes that would please its provincial pharmaceutical industry. Indeed, a Quebec M.P., Michel Côté, was named Minister of Consumer and Corporate Affairs.

Despite these propitious conditions for change, it took more than three years to pass Bill C–22 . When it wants to, a strong majority government in a parliamentary system can pass almost any legislation. But this does not mean that there will not be difficulties or a political price to pay in doing so.

Round One

In early 1985 Côté revealed that he intended to table a new pharmaceuticals policy by spring 1985 (the legislation did not appear until summer 1986). Over the winter of 1985, the minister tried to end the industrial guerrilla warfare between the multinationals and the generic companies, by attempting to engineer a 120 day moratorium to allow legislation to be created in a calmer atmosphere. The generic drug companies, through their institutional arm, CDMA, were asked to introduce no new generic drugs during this time period. The multinationals in turn, through PMAC, were asked to drop their lawsuit battles with the generic companies over old patents.[23] This attempt failed.

Each of the industrial sides hired high-powered lobbyists to ensure that their respective cases were made as effectively as possible. CDMA's main lobbyist was Skip Wallis, who had been Peter Pocklington's campaign manager when the Edmonton Oilers owner ran for the leadership of the Progressive Conservative party. The political tide, however, had turned, and CDMA and its lobbyists were unsuccessful in gaining access to those politicians and bureaucrats with authority and influence on this matter.

PMAC, on the other hand, was riding the crest of a political wave, and a considerable degree of this momentum was generated through the efforts of its lobbyist. Its sole political consultant was *Government Consultants Inc.*, perhaps the most powerful and successful lobbying organization in Canada. Its current chairman, and founder, is Frank Moores, the former premier of

THE EASTMAN REPORT

The purpose of the Eastman Commission was "to identify proposals that might form the basis for reaching a consensus on licensing policy."[25] The commission showed that:

§ the adoption of Section 41(4) had spawned the growth of (mainly Canadian) firms producing compulsorily licensed (generic) drugs;

§ compulsorily licensed drugs comprised about 20 per cent of the $1.6 billion ethical drug market in 1983, amounting to 3 per cent of the sales of all pharmaceutical products in Canada;

§ the prices of generic drugs in 1983 was 51 percent of their patented equivalents — which had saved consumers $211 million as a result. The patent-holding firms emphasis on a *promotion* strategy saw promotion costs amounting to 21 per cent of sales over the previous five years (the equivalent figure for R&D was 4.5 per cent);

§ the traditional (multinational) pharmaceutical industry had *not* shown adverse effects as a result of compulsory licensing. Profits were more stable and higher on average than in most industries, and the Canadian industry was more profitable than pharmaceutical industries in France, Japan, Switzerland, Germany, and England.[26]

Newfoundland. Its staff included a variety of ex-politicians and senior civil servants who knew the names and phone numbers needed to influence policy decisions and its two other owners were particularly close to the Mulroney government. Garry Ouellet was a Quebec City lawyer and Mulroney crony who had screened potential PC candidates in Quebec before the 1984 election, approving, amongst others, Michel Côté. The other owner was the lobbying front man for PMAC, Gerald Doucet. He had been a long-term Conservative MLA in Nova Scotia and was the brother of Fred Doucet, then senior adviser to Mulroney. Doucet took the lead in organizing PMAC's public relations campaign (he organized a PR seminar in the Bahamas) as well as in bringing PMAC and Côté together (he organized meetings between PMAC and Julien Beliveau, Côté's chief of staff).

The commission concluded that "compulsory licensing is an effective component of an appropriate patent policy for the pharmaceutical industry." Without compulsory licensing, it maintained that there would be less competition, higher prices and product differentiation.[27]

On the critical issue of research and development, the commission concluded that:

§   the industrial research programs of drug firms are established on a world-wide basis, and compulsory licensing in one country does not affect these global decisions appreciably: "in the commission's opinion, *Canada is not well placed to become a major world center for pharmaceutical research or for the production of active chemical ingredients.*"[28]

The commission proposed three policy alterations:

§   new drugs should be given *four* years of protection from generic competition;
§   after this period, generic companies would pay a royalty, whose rate would be determined by the industry's ratio of worldwide R&D expenditures to sales plus a 4 percent charge for the benefits of promotion costs (estimates varied, but it appeared that the effective royalty rate would be about 14 percent and increased royalties would raise prices by about $30 million a year);
§   these royalties would be paid into a pharmaceutical royalty fund, which would be distributed to pharmaceutical firms according to each's share of Canadian R&D and the sales of their compulsorily licensed products.[29]

PMAC's efforts were perhaps a case of lobbying overkill, as the government already intended to change the Patent Act. Minister of Health and Welfare Jake Epp's comment in the House of Commons evoked the policy mood of the time: "The government wants to have research and development in Canada. The government wants to ensure that we are a member of this high tech field, especially with regard to new drugs."[24] Compulsory licensing thus had to go. In April, the Prime Minister himself made what turned out to be a rare direct intervention into this discussion, when he declared that Canada was a scavenger in the area of intellectual property.

Unfortunately for the government, a political chicken came home to roost in the spring of 1985. On budget day that year, the Commission of Inquiry on the Pharmaceutical Industry (the Eastman Commission) issued its report. This Royal Commission had been a stopgap measure adopted by the previous Liberal government in order to buy time before having to make a tough and divisive political decision. To the Conservative government, the Commission's report was unwanted and unnecessary, not least because the Commission defended compulsory licensing and section 41(4) (See Inset IV). The Eastman Report demonstrated exhaustively that the Canadian pharmaceutical industry was in excellent shape, and that multinational firms had not been adversely affected by the advent of compulsory licensing and the generic companies. Without compulsory licensing, the Report argued, there would be less competition, leading to higher prices, leading to product differentiation and even higher prices. On the critical issue of research and development, Eastman was not optimistic. Given the global strategies of the pharmaceutical industry, no amount of incentives, no matter how generous, would bring basic research investment to Canada. Canada was simply "not well placed" to become a major player. The Report suggested some policy changes, including the establishment of four year patents for new drugs and the creation of a royalty fund that would reward firms doing research in Canada.

Predictably, PMAC was critical of the Eastman Report, declaring that the Commission's policy approach would not stimulate new investment in Canada. The proposed four year period of exclusivity was an empty gain, as the average time for a generic drug to appear on the market was about eight years. The multinationals had asked for fifteen years of exclusivity.

The Eastman Report was not good news for the government either. Consumer and Corporate Affairs Minister Côté attempted to put a positive light on matters. In a classic statement of political balance and moderation, he declared that

> ...the general recommendations of the Eastman Report are acceptable to us, to the extent that they advocate research and development in the pharmaceutical industry. However, I (do have) reservations with respect to the reaction to higher royalties on consumer prices...We will try to promote research and development in Canada, while at the same time making sure that consumers pay as little as possible for pharmaceutical products...We will give priority to finding a solution...so as to boost research and development in the provinces of Quebec and Ontario as well as in the rest of Canada.[30]

Of course, this was the trick: to balance the interests of consumers and producers, generic companies and multinationals, Quebec and the rest of Canada, price and investment, equity and growth. Neither Côté nor anyone else had pulled that particular rabbit out of the hat.

The Eastman Report slowed the building political momentum to abolish compulsory licensing. Indeed, the government made no pronouncements and issued no legislative plans in this area for over a year; the issue disappeared from public sight. The government was on the verge of introducing the legislation on a few occasions, but plans were cancelled at the last minute, apparently on the Prime Minister's orders. On 23 June 1986 a *Globe and Mail* columnist informed readers that "legislation on the subject has been ready for a long time, but will not be introduced until autumn at the earliest," because the government was concerned that the Eastman Report had undermined the credibility of the case for patent reform.[31] Four days later, on 27 June 1986, the government attempted to introduce Bill C–22. (Presumably this cost some 'informed source' the columnist's friendship.)

The government's first attempt to change the Patent Act was a fiasco, although its political strategy appeared to be sound. It waited until the last day before the summer recess to introduce Bill C–22. Over the summer recess, the government could then gauge public reaction while carrying out a political selling job on its own terms, beyond the scrutiny and hectoring of the Opposition in the House of Commons. However, the job was bungled. A few hours before the parliamentary recess was to begin, the bill was sent by private courier to Parliament Hill, where it got lost. More accurately, it sat anonymously on a security guard's desk, as he would not allow the courier to deliver it. Literally metres away, frantic government officials watched the minutes slip by. The minister had no bill to present. The Speaker asked the Opposition to allow the legislation to be tabled. Characteristically, the opposition refused, maintaining formally but perhaps nastily that it could not agree to the tabling of a bill that it had not actually seen. The minutes sped by, MPs left Ottawa for the summer, and Bill C–22 remained sitting safely on a security guard's desk.

Round Two

Harvie Andre replaced the ill-fated Michel Côté as Minister of Consumer and Corporate Affairs. (Côté went on to Supply and Services, and then was removed from the cabinet after revelations that he had not disclosed a major financial campaign contribution; he did not run for re-election in the 1988 election.) On 6 November 1986, the government finally managed to introduce Bill C–22 in the House of Commons. It was inauspiciously entitled "An Act to Amend the Patent Act and to Provide for Certain Matters in Relation Thereto," and contained four major provisions:

§   the system of compulsory licensing (41(4)) would end;

§   discoveries of new drugs would be given patent protection for *ten* years;

§   the price of drugs would be regulated by a review board;

§ $100 million would be allocated to the provinces over four years to defray the increased cost of drugs financed by provincial health plans.

The pharmaceutical industry in turn promised to carry out $1.4 billion of investment in Canada (this promise was *not* part of the legislation). The legislation also contained mechanisms allowing the government to review the situation periodically, particularly with regard to the legislation's impact on drug prices.

A *Globe and Mail* columnist described Bill C–22 as a "tremendous political gamble...It's the kind of sleeper that, treated properly by the opposition, could produce big trouble for the Conservatives."[32] This turned out to be a shrewd observation. The government soon discovered just how willing the Opposition was to politically exploit Bill C–22. In an act that foreshadowed the legislative process over the next year, the Opposition parties tied up the House of Commons for two days over the simple introduction of the bill. It is highly unusual for a bill to be challenged at this stage, but a vote had to be called as the Opposition did not offer unanimity. For the next month, Question Period was acrimoniously dominated by Bill C–22, and legislative discussion was heated and tense.

In the fortnight between first and second reading, the Opposition assaulted Bill C–22 on two issues. First, the government was accused of giving in to American pressures. This was an issue that would intensify once the Canada-United States Free Trade Agreement appeared. Opposition leader John Turner pointed to "the government's cave in to the United States on the question of drug prices." NDP leader Ed Broadbent posed this question:

> Will the Prime Minister acknowledge that at the "Shamrock Shuffle", President Reagan asked that this item be placed on the agenda, that Special Envoy Yeuter complained about Canada's dragging its feet in terms of changing our patent law, and that last spring Vice-President Bush also urged the Canadian government to change this law so that multinational American drug companies could gouge Canadian consumers the way Americans are gouged at home?[33]

This dimension was also exploited in questions about the American Pharmaceutical Manufacturers Association's involvement in the drafting of the legislation, and its president's apparent advance knowledge of its content.[34]

The Opposition also raised the populist theme of the impact of the legislation on drug prices. There was a widespread perception that Bill C–22 would lead to higher drug prices. Turner thundered that the government "has used the sick and the elderly as a pawn...in the free trade negotiations...Was it not enough to attempt to de-index pensions for our older people?" Liberal spokesperson Killens asked rhetorically, "Why does the minister not favour the sick, the weak, and the elderly?" — and contrasted this anticipated situation with the regime of 41(4) — "we have had among the lowest drug prices in the world." Turner reminded his audience that he had "had the honour of bringing in the current drug price legislation in 1968."[35]

The debate over the probable impact of C–22 on drug prices intensified as a result of an interview given by Harry Eastman on the CBC's *The Journal* on 18 November. Eastman observed that the price of *new* drugs would likely be higher as a result of Bill C–22 because there would be less generic competition to keep prices down.[36] The Opposition pounced on this interview, and railed against the government's insensitivity in raising drug prices — giving the impression that *all* drug prices would rise.[37]

Andre was a combative minister, whose style of defending Bill C–22 exacerbated the bitter mood and divisiveness surrounding the legislation. He hung tough on both the price and American issues. With respect to the Eastman interview, he made the unfortunately over-general statement that "prices will not go up by single penny as a result of Bill C–22." The logic of this reply was sound, albeit tortured. The price of *already existing* drugs would not be affected by the legislation; and it was impossible to talk about a rise in the price of drugs that did not yet exist. Discussion degenerated into semantic confusion, with the Opposition calling for Andre's resignation for misleading the House, and Andre accusing the Opposition of scaremongering. On the question of American involvement, Andre was just as blunt: "No one made representations to me either from the United States, through the Trade Office, or through the External Affairs Office or in any other way." In defending Bill C–22, he emphasized investment rather than price goals:

> In exchange for granting patent protection to inventors or creators, we will gain at least 3,000 high-tech jobs in an area from which it is unforgivable that Canada should be excluded....If there is to be research in this important area of biotechnology and drugs...there has to be patent protection provided. [38]

After these two weeks of guerrilla warfare, the real legislative battle began with the start of second reading on 20 November 1986. In a preamble to explaining and defending the legislation, Andre evoked the character of the Conservatives' political agenda, and patent law's place in it:

> Bill C–22 will create a climate favourable to new investment in research and development to reward private initiative and to adjust investment to support government efforts aimed at promoting sustained economic growth, job creation and the protection of Canadian consumers.[39]

This was an evocative depiction of the government's priorities in this and other areas: to give support to private investors to produce economic growth and jobs. He characterized the previous Liberal government's adoption of compulsory licensing in 1969 as "a regressive step for Canada." The Patent Act had been misused to control prices, and in the process had frustrated inventors and creators. André claimed that 41(4) had done as much damage to investment and economic growth as other Liberal initiatives, such as the Foreign Investment Review Agency and the National Energy Policy (this was a claim rejected by the Eastman Commission). Over the next year, Andre delivered a standard presentation of the raison d'être of Bill C–22, organized around five major themes: the principle of intellectual property rights, improved multilateral relations, the promise of high-tech economic development, regulation of drug prices, and improved health care (see Inset V).

Debate at the second reading stage took place over five days (21, 24, 25 November and 5, 8 December), and Bill C–22 continued to have pride of place during Question Period. The debate was incredibly hostile, with little humour or give-and-take. It was a classic zero-sum battle: the Opposition wanted the legislation blocked or withdrawn while the government wanted the legislation passed quickly and with no substantial changes. The Opposition devised a variety of procedural tricks to drag out the debate, hoping to exploit what it perceived to be substantial political fallout from the bill. The government became increasingly frustrated about Opposition tactics, which were seen as frustrating the parliamentary process. On 21 November, House Leader Mazankowski announced the addition of two extra days of debate and hinted at the use of closure.

A number of basic opposition themes emerged during the course of debate at this stage:

§ the Liberals declared their support of the Eastman Report, which was seen as "a proper balance between the interests of consumers and those of the drug industry"; 10 years' patent protection was seen to be too long and the prices review board too weak;

§ both the Liberals and the NDP argued that there were no guarantees in the legislation that the promised jobs and investment would be forthcoming;

§ the government continued to be accused of giving in to the pressures of the multinationals and the Reagan administration.[40]

A number of issues were also raised outside the House of Commons:

THE GOVERNMENT'S RATIONALE FOR BILL C–22

Consumer and Corporate Affairs Minister Harvie Andre explained and defended Bill C–22 on countless occasions, in the House of Commons as well as before House and Senate committees. On each occasion, he delivered more or less the same presentation, in which he elaborated the five major 'pillars' or themes of Bill C–22:

§ the government was committed to the principle of *intellectual property*; the invention of a new drug should be treated no differently than the writing of a novel or any other creation; Canada was presently getting a 'free ride';

§ Bill C–22 was necessary to improve Canada's multilateral relations: "Since 1969 (when 41(4) was adopted), every single one of our partners in the Western world has been after us to restore patent protection" — and to re-enter the world of open, free markets for inventions;

§ Canada has an opportunity to enter the high-tech world of biotechnology and related areas; this bill promises to create 3,000 new jobs and $1.4 billion in investment from 1986 to 1995 (doubling the ratio of investment to sales from 5 per cent to 10 per cent); this will create opportunities for Canada's young scientists;

§ with regard to possible price increases, the situation will be regulated by a Drug Prices Review Board, and by Parliament as a whole after 10 years; in any event, most people are covered under government health plans;

§ the accelerated discovery of new and improved drugs will lead to better health care for all Canadians and lower medical costs.

§ on 23 November, Harry Eastman admitted that it would be difficult to monitor drug prices, because of the wide variation in drug prices around the world;

§ André continued to deny that drug prices would rise, even with the decline of generic competition; his argument was that it now took 11 1/2 years for generic companies to get a drug on to market, and C–22 would not affect prices inasmuch as it afforded only 10 years of patent protection; CDMA president Calenti retorted that the minister's figures were based on 1969 data and that the average was now six to seven years, and four to five for important popular drugs;

§ the Consumers Association of Canada declared that "the bill is flawed beyond repair," that drug prices would increase, that the Bill provided no investment guarantees, and that hospitals would be seriously affected by higher drug costs;

§ Ontario Health Minister Murray Elston announced that Bill C–22 would cost the Ontario government an extra $35 million a year;

§ Joyce King, president of the lobby group, United Senior Citizens of Ontario, declared that "the legislation is immoral"; the Ontario Coalition of Senior Citizens Organizations called Bill C–22 "regressive."[41]

By 4 December, the government had had enough. Mazankowski rose in the House of Commons and stated that it was "with a great deal of regret that I rise to put this motion of closure." He defended his move on the grounds that the opposition was frustrating debate, detailing how difficult it had been for the government to even introduce the bill, and how 14 hours of House time had been consumed in votes and procedural wrangling, including votes on 13 motions that had cost 19 hours. The opposition accused the government of tyrannically gagging Parliament.[42]

Opposition leader Turner effectively closed debate at the second reading stage the next day. After reviewing the bill's alleged weaknesses and re-rehearsing Liberal criticisms, he concluded that the government had carried out a "secret deal...with the multinationals...The Minister and his government have capitulated to an American lobby. There is no doubt in anybody's mind that the only reason the government is prepared to sell out with this bill is to keep the Americans happy and the Prime Minister's personal free trade agenda on track."[43]

On 8 December 1986 Bill C–22 finally emerged from second reading and was passed on to the legislative committee assigned to examine the Bill, headed by Conservative M.P. Arnold Malone. Bill C–22 would not re-emerge from this committee for over three months. As is typical, the Bill more or less disappeared from public sight and scrutiny during this committee stage — a calm before the next storm.

During the committee stage, various interests and groups were able to have their kick at the legislative cat. This process began in earnest on 10 December, with the announcement of the formation of a coalition of interest groups against the bill — the National Coalition on Patent Act Changes. The line-up of organized interests for and against Bill C–22 was formidable and extensive (see Inset VI). This is in itself a commentary on the changed character of politics in the 1980s. Politics is interest group politics, and both established groups and ad hoc organizations rally for and against most legislation. This presents a political challenge for governments in accommodating such a division of interests, with legitimate and authoritative opinion on both sides. During the course of the Malone Committee's 20 meetings on Bill C–22, the arguments for and against were rehearsed over and again with each group or individual before the Committee essentially re-inventing the wheel. In broad terms, the medical establishment, doctors, and life science researchers favoured the bill, while consumers, health care and social workers, and churches were against it.

The provincial picture was just as muddy as the interest group scene.

INTEREST GROUPS AND
BILL C-22

Groups Supporting Bill C-22

Canadian Association of Retired Persons
Canadian Medical Association
Canadian Chamber of Commerce
Science Council of Canada
National Biotechnology Advisory Committee
Patent and Trade Mark Institute of Canada
Canadian Federation of Biological Societies
Canadian Manufacturers Association
Canadian Pharmacy Association
Canadian Society of Industrial Pharmacists
Biological Council of Canada
Kidney Foundation
Canadian Cardiovascular Society
Canadian Dermatology Foundation
Canadian Paediatric Society
Canadian Diabetes Association
La Federation de l'Age d'Or
Bureau de valorisations des applications de la
recherche
Association Canadienne Francaise pour
l'avancement des sciences
Coalition nationale pour la recherche en sciences
de la sante
L'Association des médecin de la langue francaise
Cystic Fibrosis Society

Groups Against Bill C-22

National Anti-Poverty Organization
National Action Committee on the Status of
Women
National Federation of Nurses
National Pensioners and Senior Citizens Federation
United Senior Citizens of Ontario
Coalition of Provincial Organizations of the Handicapped
Canadian Association of Social Workers
Consumers Association of Canada
Canadian Labour Council
Public Service Alliance of Canada
Federal Superannuates National Association
Canadian Autoworkers Union
Royal Canadian Legion
Canadian Council on Social Development
Canadian Health Coalition
United Church
Catholic Health Association of Canada
National Council on Welfare
Canadian Federation of University Women
Canadian Conference on Catholic Bishops

Given the clustering of multinationals in Quebec, there was considerable political support for Bill C–22 in that province. The Quebec National Assembly passed two resolutions in its favour, on 20 June and 19 December 1985. However, there was also a broad provincial interest in keeping drug prices down, as the provinces paid health insurance costs (this point should not be exaggerated: prescription drugs comprise about 5 per cent of provinces' total insurance costs). Six provinces came out against Bill C–22 over the course of its evolution into law. The PEI legislature passed a resolution against it in March 1987, as did the Manitoba legislature in April. Ontario sent the government a letter of protest against the bill. A senior deputy minister from Saskatchewan expressed opposition before the Malone Committee, but a provincial election and some grain subsidies later concentrated Saskatchewan's attention in favour of C–22. Newfoundland, New Brunswick, Alberta, and Nova Scotia expressed concern about the higher prices that seemed inevitable after C–22, but not all of these provinces came out publicly against the legislation. While there was a policy tension between the industrial interests of Quebec and the social or budgetary interests of the rest of the provinces, this was not a 'do-or-die' type of provincial tension, as it was in the CF–18 case. To anticipate, the key issue was the strength or intensity of the Quebec interest in the issue, relative to the far less intense involvement of the other provinces. Moreover, the other provinces were offered a 'sweetener' in the bill — $100 million to help defray their increased health insurance costs.

Andre appeared before the Malone Committee on 11 December and predicted that "we are on the verge of a biotechnology revolution.... I am convinced that we are going to see a spurt of investment and activity as a result of what we are doing in terms of this bill." Opposition concerns and criticisms shook neither his optimism nor his resolve to give positive encouragement to the private sector. He did move slightly on the question of the bill's impact on prices, admitting that "generic competition causes the price to come down." If the generic companies did not bring their products on to the market as quickly as a result of Bill C–22, then there would be a delay in price decreases. He termed this "potentially delayed savings," an awkward and effectively confusing euphemism for rising prices.[44]

In mid-March, the Malone Committee returned Bill C–22 to the House of Commons substantively unchanged. Legislative debate began on the Committee's report on 31 March, with the House's mood with respect to Bill C–22 unchanged as well. The Opposition continued to press the government on by now familiar themes: the impact of rising drugs prices on the sick and the elderly; the absence of investment and research and development guarantees; concern that investment would centre on low level testing of products and not on pure research; disquiet that multinational corporations were dictating policy terms to the Canadian government. During this stage of the debate, spanning 31 March, 1, 2, and 7 April, the Opposition managed to issue 47 report stage motions (there had been only 11 in committee). For the government, this was slow, tedious and frustrating. Moreover, it was politically damaging to day after day be typified as having neglected the interests of the poor and the elderly in selling out to the Americans.

On 7 April, the government for the second time used closure to end the debate. However, it was not until 1 May — the day the Meech Lake constitutional accord was announced — that debate continued (and concluded) on the Committee report. In the interim, the spotlight was taken by the Canadian Conference of Catholic Bishops, which had become exceedingly active in criticizing government economic policies. It issued a letter to Andre expressing concern that "the impetus for this legislative change has not come from the people of the country... national organizations representing...Canadians have been unanimous in calling not to proceed with the proposed legislation....[these were] determined efforts of average Canadians, especially the elderly and the poor. We urge your government to resist the pressures from the multinational drug industry and from the

United States administration."

Debate on the third reading of the bill was perfunctory and predictable. Andre accused the Liberals of having in 1969 "decided to deal Canada out of the biotechnological revolution...If we want to attract the capital funds required to be competitive on the international scene, our country must convince foreigners that it is a good place to invest." The Liberals concluded the debate, arguing that the government was trading away the interests of the old, the sick and the poor in return for increased prices and profits to the multinationals, which might or might not result in increased investment.[45]

On 6 May 1987, final reading was given to Bill C–22, which passed by a vote of 117-39. This brought to an end a torturous legislative journey. Literally dozens of motions had been introduced and debated, procedural tricks had abounded, three months had been spent in committee, the NDP and the Liberals together presented almost 2000 petitions against the bill, containing about 150,000 names, and the government had been forced to impose limits at each stage of debate. The overwhelming Conservative majority in the House of Commons finally prevailed. But the worst was yet to come.

Bill C–22 was now sent on to the Senate.

Round Three

For the next three months of summer 1987, Bill C–22 was in the Senate's hands. This was an especially lively summer in Canada, with a variety of issues competing for attention: the capital punishment debate, a national postal strike, free trade talks, the appearance of the Meech Lake constitutional accord, and various discussions about AIDS, pornography legislation, day care and tax reform. As a result, public attention was not especially focused on patent law reform.

Canadians had become accustomed to a passive and predictable Senate, given the Liberals' decades of electoral dominance and a Senate dominated by a vast majority of Liberal appointees. But the 1984 election changed all that. A vast Conservative majority in the House of Commons confronted an overwhelming Liberal majority in the Senate. While the latter had lost almost all political legitimacy over the years (as a result of its appointed nature), Canadians were soon to learn that the Senate actually holds some substantial political power.

A foreshadowing of what was to come had occurred in February 1985, when the Senate withheld authority for more than a month for a routine borrowing bill. The government was furious, and Justice Minister Crosbie introduced a constitutional amendment that would have effectively eliminated the Senate's existing power to alter or indefinitely delay a bill.[46] The bill died on the order paper in 1986. In July 1986, the Senate again delayed legislation, this time dealing with reform of the country's penal system. In April 1987, the Senate vowed to veto any legislative change that re-introduced capital punishment, and was subsequently very involved in legislative debates over immigration and copyright law.

But it was Bill C–22 that most dramatically illustrated the changed character, under the Mulroney Government, of the relationship between the House of Commons and the Senate. On an unprecedented three occasions, the House of Commons had to send the same legislation to the Senate for its approval. This was the longest parliamentary stand-off between the two chambers in 40 years. The case also illustrated the extent to which the Senate is the only real opposition to the government in certain political circumstances. Given an overwhelming government majority in the House of Commons, given party discipline that muted any non-Quebec caucus criticism, and given intense support for the bill from a major province (and only tepid reactions from the other provinces), the Senate was really the only effective political channel for opposing the legislation.

It all started on April Fool's Day 1987 when the Senate created a special committee to examine Bill C–22. The committee was chaired by Senator Lorne Bonnell, a Trudeau-appointed Liberal who had spent four decades of his life as a country doctor in Prince Edward Island. He had previously acquired hundreds of signatures for a petition against Bill C–22, so he was familiar with the legislation and particularly unsympathetic to it.

In mid-May, the Bonnell Committee was assigned a $315,000 budget to hold public hearings across Canada. In late May through mid-June, Bonnell, his Senate committee colleagues, and the committee staff travelled to all of the provincial capitals. They heard for themselves the arguments and representations for and against Bill C–22 that Arthur Malone's House of Commons committee and the Eastman Commission had heard earlier. At the same time, the Senate committee ensured that the public remained aware of the legislation, particularly its negative features. The committee heard from CDMA and PMAC, industrial spokespersons, specialists, organized interests, civil servants, and others. Harvie Andre twice appeared before it, on the latter occasion assuring the committee that Bill C–22 was not part of the Free Trade Agreement; he had raised the issue with chief negotiator Simon Reisman, who reported that the issue had never come up in bargaining with the United States. While the committee was in Quebec City, the government of Quebec accused the Senate of acting to delay patent change, which would bring $660 million in new R&D activity to Quebec. On 16 June, the Bonnell Committee presented its first (of seven) reports to the Senate, which then discussed the report and returned it to the committee. On 28 June, the committee voted to spend several more weeks studying the bill.

On the eve of Canada Day 1987, an extraordinary legislative session came to an end. 82 bills had been introduced, and half of them had actually passed. But with regard to the main, high profile government items, there had been little or no action. The government was frustrated and furious; over a year had passed since Michel Côté's tragi-comic introduction of Bill C–22, and the legislation was still not law. After 82 hours of debate in the House of Commons, 65 hours of hearings in committee (which included hearing 96 witnesses from 46 organizations), 75 hours of debate in the Senate, and a cross-country Senate committee, Bill C–22 was still not law. The government stewed while the Senate sat on the bill.

On 3 July, the government asked Speaker John Fraser to recall Parliament intending to pressure the Senate into committing itself one way or the other on the patent legislation (as well as on some transportation legislation, which was also stalled in the Senate). The plan was to have the House debate emergency immigration legislation, while the Senate concluded its work on Bill C–22 and Bills C–18 and C–19, the transportation bills. The Speaker enjoyed an especially large amount of political freedom at this time, because he had been elected in an unprecedented free secret vote. On the evening of evening of Saturday July 4, the Speaker decided to exercise his power; he declined the government's request to recall Parliament. The government was foiled again.

The issue continued to heat up over the summer. PMAC announced in early July that all new research in Canada would be held up until the Senate passed Bill C–22, and published a list of delayed projects worth $553 million. Judy Erola, ex-minister of Consumer and Corporate Affairs and current PMAC president, declared that "without the change the industry in Canada would die."[47] Deputy Prime Minister Mazankowski demanded that the Senate deal with the legislation before the end of July, or else Parliament would be recalled. "What else can I do?" he asked rhetorically.

On 7 July, the Senate Committee promised that it would finish its work by 10 August and the Senate promised to conclude its discussions by 14 August. In striking this compromise with the House, Senator Allan MacEachen stated: "The Senate established its own timetable. Presumably, the Senate was expected to crack up and collapse. It has not yielded to the unjustified pressures placed upon it by the government."[48] The tone of this statement was ominous. More ominous still was Senator Bonnell's comment that his committee would probably propose amendments to the legislation.

On July 30, the government bit the bullet and recalled Parliament, marking only the thirteenth resort to this since Confederation. The ostensible reason was to debate the issue of illegal immigration, but the government had other legislative objectives as well. On 10 and 12 August, the Bonnell Committee issued its final reports, which were debated in the Senate from 10 to 13 August. Following the Bonnell Committee Report,[49] the Senate proposed a set of ten amendments to Bill C–22. These proposals included:

§   a four year (as opposed to ten year) period of exclusivity;
§   a 14 percent royalty rate for use of the patent after the four year period of exclusivity;
§   the creation of a royalty fund, which would be distributed according

to firms' share of the Canadian drug market and their rate of spending on R&D in Canada. (This was attached as a 'recommendation,' as the Senate was concerned that this was a tax measure, an area in which it clearly had no jurisdiction).

These amendments were essentially an endorsement of the Eastman Report. The Senate scuttled the bill's proposal for a prices review board and interim financial compensation to the provinces. It also insisted that there be no retroactive feature to the bill, that the new patent regime should come into effect only when the bill was passed into law.

On 13 August 1987, Bill C–22 was returned by the Senate to the House of Commons — with its ten amendments. The House of Commons would have to debate the legislation again.

Round Four

Reaction to the Bonnell Report and the Senate's amendments was swift. Andre accused the Senate and the Liberal party of "keeping Canada in the Dark Ages" in the field of drug research. The Senate's proposals would ensure the perpetuation of Canada's "pirate reputation" in the area of intellectual property, he claimed, and would create only 10 percent of the 3,000 jobs anticipated by Bill C–22. As for the propriety of the Senate's action, he stated, "I don't know whether they just want to make their point, and they'll be satisfied with that, or whether they're going to use their legal authority to kill the bill." If the Senate decided to kill the bill, "I don't think that very many people would accept that the Liberal party still has the right to dictate their policies because what will happen is that we would be allowed to pass only those policies that the Liberal Party agrees with."[50]

John Turner quickly endorsed the Senate recommendations. The Liberal strategy had become clear: promote the Eastman proposals. For the NDP, the situation was deliciously ironical. It disliked the Senate on principle, as an illegitimate-because-unelected body, and its members had traditionally refused Senate appointments. On the other hand, the NDP was in favour of the legislative status quo with regard to Bill C–22. House Leader Nelson Riis summed up the NDP position: "We feel that the bill is bad, that it's not in the best interests of Canada or Canadians. We will do everything we can to stop it, and we'll applaud those whose acts stop it."[51] The NDP thus applauded the Senate, an institution it despised.

Bill C–22 and the Senate's amendments sat on Andre's desk for a week, as the government pondered its next move. The whole process had become politically expensive; the government was losing valuable legislative time dealing with this bill and it had other measures, such as the immigration and transport bills, that needed urgent attention. The longer the process lasted, the greater the chance of political embarrassment. For example, the famous American consumer advocate Ralph Nader wrote an open letter to Prime Minister Mulroney stating that "your government is close to making a very serious mistake by choosing corporate welfare over the Canadian public's health and welfare." He cited studies indicating that the 17 year period of market exclusivity in the United States had effectively priced drugs out of the reach of low income earners.[52]

The longer the process was extended, the more symbolic issues came to dominate the actual substantive issues of the bill. The role of the Senate, in particular, dominated public discussions at this time. The Prime Minister himself set the tone when he gave one of his off-the-cuff interviews to a scrum of reporters outside the House of Commons. He characterized the Liberals in the Senate as a cabal, whose actions were "having the effect of choking off $700 million of investment going right into the province of Quebec and 1,300 jobs in science and technology — the kind of jobs Quebec has been dying for years.... [these] non-elected Liberal senators...are...in the process of inflicting very serious and perhaps irreparable damage to the scientific well-being of Quebec." (The Prime Minister also characterized opponents of the Meech Lake constitutional accord as 'anti-Quebec' — see Chapter 5). Later, in response to a question in the House of Commons, Mulroney declared that "the Liberal party is inflicting a type of industrial catastrophe on Montreal." On 25 August the Prime Minister told a group of pro-C–22 demonstrators to go to the Senate "but you might wake them up. Some days they're either on hunger strikes or fast asleep."[53]

Discussion of the Senate continued in the House of Commons, when the Senate amendments were introduced on 21 August and debated on 21, 24, 25, 26, 28, and 31 August. The debate was no less intemperate or hyperbolic than the Prime Minister's remarks, and took some odd turns. Harvie Andre led off the discussion by asserting that "there is no way one can morally justify a non-elected body vetoing legislation." If the Senate can veto this legislation, he continued, then "we in essence have Allan MacEachen...sitting at the cabinet table. We cannot have two federal governments."[54]

On 22 August, again to reporters outside of the House of Commons, Mulroney revealed that during the Meech Lake constitutional discussions he had proposed abolishing the Senate, but that the offer was not taken up as certain premiers had wanted to think about it.[55] In response to a question in the House of Commons on 25 August, the Prime Minister indicated that, if the Liberal and NDP parties gave their approval, "we can arrange for a resolution to provide for the abolition of the Senate [and] I can guarantee...I will bring it in as quickly as I can." The suggestion was ridiculed by Opposition leader John Turner, who told the Prime Minister he couldn't be serious, as the Meech Lake constitutional accord had injected the principle of provincial unanimity into constitutional change with respect to the Senate. Turner countered with his own offer: "Would [the Prime Minister] accept my offer to bring in a resolution for an elected Senate....If he does that he will get our unanimous consent immediately." The Prime Minister was caught off guard by the proposal, and rambled a bit, noting that "this gets more and more interesting." He then asked for a show of good faith from the Liberals; Turner was asked to instruct the Liberals in the Senate to approve Bill C–22.[56]

This was all a bit silly and was more interesting as an example of the macho gamesmanship that each of the leaders was prone to play than it was as a bit of constitution-building. But nothing came of this big talk. Of course, the Liberal leader himself was on the political spot. On the one hand, Bill C–22 was divisive in itself, as the Quebec Liberal caucus, a disproportionately large group, was in favour of the legislation and its promise of benefits for Quebec. On the other hand, while the Liberals were gaining tremendous political mileage from the government's embarrassments over Bill C–22, the Liberal Senators' behaviour involved a potential political and constitutional time bomb that Turner did not want to see explode. On 26 August, then, Turner declared: "Our position is quite clear on the jurisdiction of the Upper House....As long as the Senate remains a nominated chamber...at the end of the day the elected House of Commons must prevail."[57] This was also the NDP's position. It argued that the government was raising this issue only to deflect public attention from the unacceptable substance of Bill C–22.

The other symbolic issue at this time was the American connection. The Opposition continued to portray the government caving in to American wishes and the multinational drug companies' voracious appetite for ever higher profits.[58] In a major speech on 26 August, Turner delivered his most intense attack to date on the American issue. He asserted that Parliament had not been re-called to deal with the immigration situation, but rather because of "the absolutely obscene desire of the government of Canada to bow to American pressure to amend our drug patent legislation and dramatically increase prices in order to maintain the free trade negotiations with the United States....This is the first time a legislature of a sovereign nation was ever called into emergency session just to abide by and conform to the wishes of another nation."[59]

The only substantive issue that persisted in discussions was the issue of investment guarantees. Bill C–22 was premised on a promise by the multinationals that, if compulsory licensing were eliminated and increased patent protection assigned, then $1.4 billion in additional investment would be forthcoming. This promise was not part of the legislation — it was a promise. For the Liberals, this became perhaps the key substantive issue, as they came to realize that the passage of the bill was inevitable. Turner demanded that the government provide "guarantees instead of these government promises" that Bill C–22 would lead to an explosion of high-tech pharmaceutical investment. "If we want the guarantees," said Liberal MP Jacques Guilbault, "it's because we don't have any trust whatsoever in the promises of foreign multinationals." There was a question in many Liberal minds as to whether this investment would even cost the multinationals very much, as the tax system provided up to 60 cents on the dollar in write-offs and credits. Former Minister of Consumer and Corporate Affairs André Ouellet called the legislation "toothless": "we want the investment to be clear and binding."[60]

The government remained unmoved during the debate on the Senate amendments. Minister of Science and Technology Frank Oberle summed up the government's position in stating that "this debate concerns Canadians in the 21st century. This debate is about using science and technology and research and development to carve a niche for Canada in the new age." Andre pleaded: "Do not deal Canada out of this biotechnology revolution."[61] The government adopted only one of the Senate amendments, a technical one concerning when the legislation would come into effect.

Although the government introduced a closure motion on 26 August, debate was concluded on 28 August 1987 by the government's simple call for the question to be put. This was unexpected and caught the opposition unprepared, leading to Opposition charges of 'muzzling'. On 31 August 1987, the Senate amendments were dealt with by the House of Commons, and Bill C–22 returned to the Senate.

Bill C–22 arrived back in the Senate on 2 September. That chamber, having perhaps forgotten about it, or being unsure what to do with it, delayed discussion for 24 hours. The next day, it decided that the legislation should be sent for further study to the Senate Standing Committee on Banking, Trade and Commerce (the Sinclair Committee). The government was enraged. Andre accused the Senate of "mischief for political purposes...I really don't believe there are any more facts and I don't believe the Senators believe there are any more facts to be advanced."[62] Nonetheless, the Sinclair Committee set about to do its business through September and October, issuing a report only by 21 October.

The impact of the issue on the Liberal party continued to grow. Various MPs and senators from Quebec broke political rank, feeling the pressure from their constituents and supporters. (Defectors included Senator Pierre de Bane and MP J.C. Malépart.) Outside of Quebec, Liberal MP Roland de Corneille accused the Senate of hypocrisy, contrasting its present activism with its passivity during the Trudeau years.

Public scrutiny of the role of the Senate continued to grow. If nothing else, the debate over Bill C–22 reminded the public and political scientists of a seldom-used political device called a *free conference* used to break a stalemate between the House of Commons and the Senate. Each side names an equal number of representatives to a committee, which tries to work out a deal. In this situation, the Senate has the upper hand, since if no deal is produced the legislation dies and the government has to wait until the next session to reintroduce it. This tactic has been used 10 times in this century, the last time in 1947 to resolve a stalemate over changes to the Criminal Code

(Bill C–364). The idea of a free conference began to be bandied about at this time, but the government was adamantly opposed to it. As André put it, the use of a free conference "would be inviting Allen MacEachen to sit at the cabinet table. If we have to negotiate with him on this, we will have to negotiate with him on tax reform, trade and the constitution." As for Mac-Eachen, when he was reminded of Liberal leader Turner's view that "at the end of the day" the House of Commons should prevail, he responded that he was sure Turner did not have a particular day or hour in mind.[63] In the interim, the Senate managed to approve Bill C–84 (changes to the immigration act), after extensive scrutiny and delay. Liberal Senators were able to distinguish between popular and unpopular legislation, and delays on the immigration bill would have backfired politically.

On 2 October Andre dutifully appeared before the Sinclair Committee. "I have not prepared an opening statement," the exasperated minister began. "I could not possibly find a new set of words that would not be repetitive of what I have already said about this bill." Nonetheless, he was exceedingly articulate in once again explaining the political raison d'etre of Bill C–22: "The government feels that Bill C–22 is instrumental in fulfilling the mandate the government sought and received from the people in 1984 to emphasize technology and research and development in economic areas generally." He admitted that the bill had its opponents but reiterated that it had supporters as well: "I have been pleading...for recognition that we have a diversity of interests...I think that we have to look at the benefits as well as the costs. On that basis the package balances those interests in what we consider the best way." On the question of investment guarantees, the minister concluded that public scrutiny would be a sufficient check: "I would rather have the companies meeting a judgmental test than a numerical test." [64] The multinational companies themselves were not keen on having the government scrutinize and interfere with their capital investment decisions.

The political debate shifted back to the question of the American connection when the Free Trade Agreement was tabled in the House of Commons on 5 October. What should have been a political triumph for the government instead turned into yet another misfortune (or goof). In briefing reporters shortly after the deal was signed, the Canadian Embassy in Washington released a draft of the agreement dated 3 October. This draft of the agreement was different from the one that had been tabled in the House of Commons, and included the following incriminating passage:

Canada has agreed to pass the pending amendments contained in Bill C–22 in respect of compulsory licensing of pharmaceuticals.

An enraged Opposition attacked the government for misleading the House about the relationship between Bill C–22 and the free trade negotiations. André continued to deny any link: "Bill C–22 was not part of the negotiations at the table." Later in the day, though, he was contradicted in a written statement by Pat Carney, the Minister of International Trade that declared that a commitment on Bill C–22 was agreed to by officials of both countries, but was rejected by senior Canadian negotiators at the last minute. The *Globe and Mail* on 9 October carried a report of what had happened. The original version of the Free Trade Agreement had included a commitment by Canada to pass the drug bill, and this document was initialled by negotiators for both countries on 3 October. A subsequent version, dated 4 October, did not contain this commitment and it was this version that was tabled in the House of Commons on 5 October. On 13 October Finance Minister Wilson stated that when the working parties passed the draft agreement up to their ministers, those ministers said "absolutely not, this is not part of the trade agreement." On 16 October, Canadian ambassador to the United States Allan Gotlieb revealed: "Canada never intended to make the drug bill part of the Free Trade Agreement. The matter was raised mistakenly at the table and dropped in 'four seconds'."[65]

All of this looked like a government cover-up, and was tremendously embarrassing to the government in general and Harvie Andre in particular. On countless occasions André had adamantly and abrasively denied any link between C–22 and free trade negotiations. He later admitted that he was 'surprised' when he saw the 3 October document with the Bill C–22 passage in it. Suspicions about the linkage between the legislation and the Free Trade Agreement were not allayed when Lowell Murray, government leader in the Senate and Minister of State for Federal-Provincial Relations, observed that

> If the Senate were to defeat Bill C–22, I believe that many congressmen and senators would think twice about their support for the Free Trade Agreement because, surely, they would take such action as meaning that one of the houses of the Canadian Parliament was thumbing its nose at the Free Trade Agreement. [66]

All of this hardened the Liberals' position in general, and the Senate's position in particular. MacEachen concluded that "Senator Murray's statement is a clear concession of what we have suspected all along, that the United States regards the passage of this bill as an essential part of the deal and that Canada has committed itself to that end." NDP leader Broadbent said he had been informed that US senators were told that Canada promised to pass the drug law. Turner said that he was now more convinced than ever of the link between the bill and the Free Trade Agreement.[67]

On 21 October 1987 the Sinclair Committee delivered its report to the Senate. It accepted the 'spirit' of the bill, including the idea of a 10-year period of market exclusivity; this indicated that the government had won the battle over abolishing compulsory licensing. However, the committee concluded that the bill was too 'industry-oriented.' The 'ends' were considered to be appropriate, but the 'means' had to be changed. In short, the committee suggested that there be tougher statutory guarantees on industry performance and proposed that:

§ companies 'earn' their patent protection; a royalty fund would be established and operate as in the Eastman proposal; however, specific investment targets would be written right into the legislation; if a company did not reach its target, it could lose its patent protection;

§ companies whose drug prices rose faster than the increase in the Consumer Price Index be penalized, by lifting their monopoly rights on their drugs;

§ the 10-year period of exclusivity apply only to drugs that came on to market after the bill became law (and not to those drugs that had come on to market since Bill C–22 was first introduced).[68]

The Senate accepted this report on 29 October 1987 and sent Bill C–22 back to the House of Commons. The Liberals in the House of Commons supported the Sinclair Committee report. Turner told an audience of Bill C–22 supporters in Montreal that investment guarantees should be written into the legislation. Raymond Garneau revealed that the Senate amendments had the unanimous support of the Liberal caucus in the House of Commons.

On 3 November Bill C–22 returned to the House of Commons. This was the first occasion in Canadian history in which the House of Commons had been asked to approve the same legislation three times. Andre declared wearily that "There has been more said about this bill than any other bill in the history of this Parliament."[69] Unfortunately for the government, no more would be said about the matter that day. Its bad luck continued: a French translation of the government motion to reject the Senate recommendations was not available, so the motion could not be tabled until the next day. On 4 November the opposition asked again and again for guarantees to be put into the legislation. The government toughed it out. On 5 November Bill C–22 passed for the third time and was sent back to the Senate for the final showdown.

The Senate immediately adjourned for two weeks.

As Bill C–22 neared passage, the merits of the bill were lost in discussion of the Senate's constitutional authority. For the government, the position was starkly put by Lowell Murray:

The matter has become a constitutional issue as to whether the majority in the Senate in the year 1987 intends to exercise to the full the right of vetoing legislation that comes from the elected house....it is inappropriate in 1987 for this appointed body to exercise to the full [its] constitutional rights...to defeat or amend substantially government legislation.[70]

On the other hand, the 'dean' of constitutional experts, Senator Eugene Forsey, maintained that the Senate was fully within its rights to suggest amendments to the bill.[71]

On 17 November 1987, the Senate received Bill C–22 for the third time. Senator Murray announced, "we have arrived at 'the end of the day'...Shall the Senate allow this matter to come to a final vote?...Shall the elected chamber prevail over the will of the appointed chamber?" For the Liberals, Senator Sinclair replied that "the time of day cannot be before a conference."[72]

The Senate did not formally demand a free conference. Rather, on 18 November a showdown was averted as the Senate voted to inquire whether the government would agree to face-to-face negotiations. Senator Murray reluctantly agreed to bring this proposal to Cabinet. Harvie Andre called the process "antiquated and just a little bit weird."[73] On 19 November Senator Murray reported to the Senate that "ministers are convinced that the conference would serve no useful purpose at this stage of the process unless...the purpose was to kill the bill indirectly rather than directly." [74]

When push came to shove, Liberal senators and the Liberal party had to judge what would be gained and lost in the defeat of the bill. Caucus members from Quebec insisted that the legislation should be allowed to pass. Defeat of the bill would cause a regional grievance, and damage the unity of the Liberal party. The party had already gained substantial political mileage in engineering such a protracted political debate. At a caucus meeting on 18 November, the issue was decided.

Senator Allan MacEachen rose in the Senate on 19 November and brought the issue to a close. He first noted that "the Senate has flexed its legislative muscles. It has decided to become a true legislative body and to deal with legislation in a serious way." Presumably the government could expect the Senate to continue dealing with its legislation in a serious way in the future. Then, the die was cast:

If all the senators decided today to defeat this bill...I think their decision would be widely applauded by the Canadian people. However, defeating the bill would relieve the government of its commitments...The defeat of the bill could become a victory for the government. Its energies would then be devoted to fanning the flames of regional grievances. It would blame the Senate for denying the people the alleged benefits of Bill C–22...It would be much more appropriate that the government take the responsibilities for the impact of the legislation rather than the Senate should do so....I think it is time for the Conservative government...to be saddled entirely with the results of their own mistakes and to be allowed to face this issue in the next election...

...our duty has been done.[75]

In the final vote, 27 senators voted 'yes', 3 senators voted 'no', and 27 Liberal senators abstained. Bill C–22 had concluded its odyssey.

DISCUSSION

It would be misleading to suggest that the preceding story is typical of the way that legislation is passed in Canada's parliamentary, majoritarian system. Indeed, the case more closely resembles the legislative processes of the United States, where the system of separation of powers has produced an extraordinarily complex policy system. Nonetheless, there have been a significant number of legislative initiatives in the Mulroney era that have had similar experience — immigration regulation, copyright law, the Free Trade Agreement, broadcasting policy, and the Meech Lake constitutional accord. In the many worlds of Canadian politics, different issues and different contexts produce a wide variety of legislative processes and experiences. It is important for the student of politics to recognize that there are these different processes and to understand what conditions lead to which processes.

There were three conjunctural conditions that made changes to the drug patent legislation so difficult to realize: the policy agenda was undergoing an abrupt transformation, there was a 'balance of power' surrounding Bill C–22, and the bicameral character of Canada's legislature became operative.

With the election of the Mulroney government in 1984, the Canadian policy agenda was given a new direction, with 'neo-conservative' concerns replacing the 'Keynesian/welfare state' approach that had shaped the postwar policy agenda. Not every election generates this kind of fundamental transformation in policy orientation. Indeed, one would be hard-pressed to point to an equally significant election in the postwar period. Typically, the electoral return of a Liberal government would result in a policy agenda comprising basically marginal or incremental legislative initiatives that fine-tuned the Keynesian/welfare state system. Once elected, the Conservative government pursued a very different policy agenda that reflected their very different values. In the process, they had to 'undo' a number of the policy accomplishments of the previous Keynesian/welfare state era. While the Conservatives did win an unprecedentedly large majority, they did in fact receive only about half of the votes cast. A large segment of the Canadian population perceived that the Keynesian/welfare state approach benefitted them, and their interests and values (and political energy) would not simply disappear as a result of an election. On the one hand, then, the kinds of policy that the Conservatives initiated would involve not marginal or incremental tinkering, but fundamental changes that reflected a profound change in philosophy. On the other hand, these initiatives would stimulate intense reaction from groups and interests that supported the policies of the previous regime and who espoused a different philosophy.

Bill C–22 was not 'typical' in this respect. Drug patent legislation in the previous regime was organized around compulsory licensing, which reflected a certain political philosophy and set of priorities — regulation of multinational drug companies, control of drug prices, making drugs widely accessible. It also created certain interests that benefitted from the policy, particularly consumers, generic drug companies, and most provinces. The Conservatives' neo-conservative philosophy produced a different set of priorities — 'freeing' of private enterprise (the multinationals), deregulation of prices, increasing investment and research and development in the new field of biotechnology. Bill C–22 was supported by a different set of interests: scientists and researchers, the multinational drug companies, the province of Quebec.

To an outside observer, it would be hard to imagine how the issue of drug patent legislation could produce such passionate debate and divisive controversy. Bill C–22 generated a kind of 'morality play' precisely because it was a concrete legislative manifestation of the fundamental change in policy direction brought about by the election of the Conservative government. As Bill C–22 was being debated, there was another debate going on simultaneously, a debate for and against the neo-conservative philosophy. This made Bill C–22's legislative passage especially tense and more complicated than usual.

A second complicating factor was the unusually balanced array of forces that surrounded the bill. This was, in part, related to the ideological debate just discussed. Typically, though, there is an asymmetry in the way a legislative proposal is championed, particularly within the bureaucracy and within the private domain affected by the legislation. More often than not, a legislative proposal has the twin blessing of the dominant (or dominating) interest group in a particular policy area and the bureaucratic arm of government with responsibility in that area. By the time the legislation is formally introduced into the House of Commons, the legislative battle is effectively over. The policy is perceived as legitimate, because the major interests are in favour of it. And the policy is seen to be rational, because the trained, expert and experienced bureaucracy says that this is the right policy. Critics of the legislation are outside of this closed world, a minority that is no match for the powerful bureaucratic-interest group alliance.

Bill C–22 was introduced in a very different setting. There was a fundamental difference of opinion and interest in the pharmaceutical industry, between the multinational and the generic drug companies. The latter had benefitted from (indeed, were created by) compulsory licensing and so were staunchly against the bill that undercut their foundations. The former had violently opposed compulsory licensing from day one and favoured Bill C–22 as it was designed to directly benefit their operations. For the industry, then, Bill C–22 was a zero-sum battle: what one side would gain the other side would lose. There was no possibility of consensus.

The bureaucratic scene was no different. The Department of Regional Industrial Expansion supported Bill C–22, seeing it as a way of generating the increased investment Canada needed to break into research and development in the exciting new field of biotechnology. The Department of Consumer and Corporate Affairs had responsibility for applying the policy of compulsory licensing, so it had a vested interest in perpetuating Section 41(4) and had built up a comfortable and understanding relationship with the generic companies. It saw DRIE's argument as a pipedream. While it certainly did not have the political clout, authority, or effectiveness of DRIE, its claims were essentially backed up by the Eastman Report.

This was an impossibly difficult situation: the industry was split, each side had a champion in the bureaucracy and so the government was not able to say, "we are going to do this, because the industry wants it and the experts say this is the thing to do." The absence of technocratic or interest consensus made the process surrounding Bill C–22 transparently *political* and not a matter of course. The government would have to stand up and be counted, and take the political fallout produced by literally discriminating against the losing side. This is not normal political practice, as governments typically try to make policy appear as if in the interests of all, and to minimize their political losses if not maximize their political gains. In the case of C–22, there were as many, if not more, potential losses than there were gains.

Of course, the issue of patents is a technical one, and it generated a series of in-depth statistical and policy studies (see Inset I). From the Ilsely Commission, through the reports of the Restrictive Trade Practices Commission and the Hall and Eastman Royal Commissions, to the various department and specialist reports, governments were presented with a wealth of analysis and recommendations. This is typical of the policy process in a modern, technological world, where legislation deals with scientific and complex matters only vaguely understood by the elected policy-makers. On some occasions, governments attempt to 'let the experts decide,' as this can help them escape political responsibility for what might turn out to be unpopular actions. But at bottom, these technical features really only obscure fundamental discussions about interests and values. This was made abundantly clear in the case of Bill C–22, when the government rejected the analysis and advice of the Eastman Commission, and particularly the commission's view that Canada was unlikely to play a major research role in this area. Politically, the government was committed to this policy change, and it was abundantly clear that Bill C–22 was a political decision.

The third complicating (and atypical) factor was the behaviour of the Senate. The Canadian legislature is a bicameral one, with an upper house, the Senate, and a lower house, the House of Commons. The bicameral character of the Canadian legislature weakened over time, mainly because the Senate is nonelected. The obvious contrast to make is with the United States, where an elected Senate (since the 17th Amendment in 1913) plays a full legislative role in the political give-and-take between it and the House of Representatives. The United States Senate is so effective that it appears to play a larger role than the individual states in representing regional interests at the national level. In Canada, the failure of the Senate as a legislative representative of regional interests has contributed to the strengthened role of the provinces as regional spokespersons at the national level.

Canadian governments have been incapable of resisting the patronage temptations associated with the Senate's appointive nature. Aside from the Diefenbaker interlude (1957-63) and the short-lived Clark administration (1979), Liberal governments have dominated Canadian political life and Senate appointments in the postwar era. When the Mulroney government was elected, it faced a Senate mainly composed of Liberal political appointees. This created an atypical Canadian situation of an upper house controlled by one party and a lower house controlled by another. In conjunction with the two factors just discussed, the Liberal senators decided to use their legislative authority to intensely scrutinize, criticize and delay the passage of Bill C–22. In the first place, Bill C–22 aimed to undo a piece of legislation that had been created and administered by many of the Liberal senators themselves in their earlier political lives. In effect, then, the constitutional stalemate between the two bodies was an institutional expression of the policy and ideological transformation that was taking place in Canada in the mid-1980s. Plus the Senate turned out to be the only 'effective' opposition available in the political system at that time, given the Tories' overwhelming majority and the bureaucratic and interest group balance just noted. Once the government made the political commitment to abolishing compulsory licensing, the Senate was the sole channel through which consumers, the generic companies, and other opponents of Bill C–22 could articulate their feelings.

Bill C–22 is a good illustration of how difficult it can be to pass a bill, even when the government enjoys a large majority. Indeed, a large majority can create certain tactical problems for a government. The media and the public are particularly on guard for signs of government arrogance. At the same time, given the ideological debate and interest group and bureaucratic divisions, it made good political sense for the Liberal party to engineer as many legislative delays as possible, and there are dozens of procedural tricks to employ in dragging out debate.. The Opposition does in fact have the constitutional responsibility of keeping the government on its toes. In this case, the Liberals (and the NDP) felt that there were substantial political gains to be made in keeping Bill C–22 in the public eye for as long as possible. If a frustrated government decides to use closure — as it did on three occasions in this case — there is even more political mileage to be gained in portraying the government as using its huge majority to crush opposition in an undemocratic way. The Senate's actions were a variant on this theme: the extraction of the maximum political benefits in exploiting the ideological and political opposition to the legislation.

Bill C–22 produced a legislative marathon rather than a sprint, because the policy agenda was undergoing fundamental change, there was a balance of political forces, and because the Senate decided to kick up its heels. These were relatively special conditions. But there were a variety of other issues surrounding Bill C–22 that are suggestive of more typical ingredients of the real worlds of Canadian politics. These included the regional dimension of the process, the government's difficulties in controlling the issue, and the importance of political credibility.

Similar to other studies in this volume, Bill C–22 illustrates the regional character of Canadian politics. Depending on the circumstances, this can be a political resource for the government or a constraint on its actions. In this case, there was no intrinsic reason why drug patent legislation should have raised regional issues; there is nothing in the regional experiences of Canadians that lends itself to certain regions being for or against a price or investment approach to patent legislation. One might have expected the case to divide along class lines with consumers taking a price approach and business taking an investment approach. Indeed, this was one feature of the debate, with the government accused of favouring the interests of corporations over the interests of the poor, the sick, and the elderly.

The class theme was muted, though, by the regional one. As with most features of the Canadian economic experience, pharmaceutical activity is not distributed evenly across the country. The multinationals are concentrated in Quebec and the generic companies are concentrated in Ontario, with a number of generic firms situated in Quebec as well. For all intents and purposes, the pharmaceutical industry is a Quebec industry. Within a producer province like Quebec, an investment orientation to drug patents policy was clearly predominant. As a result, Quebec was intensely against compulsory licensing and supportive of Bill C–22. For most of the rest of the provinces, a price orientation to drug patents prevailed over an investment one. But the other provinces' experience of the issue was far less intense than was Quebec's. Hence, there was a regional dimension to C–22. This turned out to be a political resource for the government in its effort to pass the legislation. The fortuitous concentration of the industry in Quebec allowed the government to portray opponents of C–22 as being 'anti-Quebec,' which effectively neutralized the class and price dimensions of the issue. At the same time, it weakened Liberal opposition to the legislation, as the Liberal party was itself divided by the regional question.

The regional dimension of the issue was handled by the government on its own terms, inasmuch as the provinces did not have much of a formal involvement in the process. On one level, patents are uncontroversially a matter of federal jurisdiction. On another level, the Conservative party had a large enough caucus from each of the regions to ensure the perception that each region's interests were being adequately represented. The government effectively maintained the party discipline that fettered criticism of the legislation by Conservative party representatives from outside of Quebec. While there was a degree of declared opposition to Bill C–22 from six provinces, this was easily deflected by the government. Provincial concerns about the budgetary impact of higher prices were alleviated by promising the provinces $100 million in 'bridging' funds. The 'Quebec card' was really the trump card in this context.

The regional dimension of the Bill C–22 saga is but one example of how the *substance* of policy can, in the course of the policy process, ultimately take a back seat to other *symbolic* events. More often than not, a government cannot control this process, as issues take on a life of their own, often far removed from their original context. Sometimes this can work for the government, as did the regional dimension in this case. Whether Bill C–22 would lead to higher or lower prices became increasingly irrelevant. Bill C–22 was good for Quebec — period. Similarly, the bill became identified with embracing the wonderful new world of high tech and biotechnology. Was Canada going to remain stuck in the technological Dark Ages or was it to leap into the technological future? Regardless of what the Eastman Report or other studies said about this possibility for Canada, the government could easily exploit this evocative and compelling ideal. The trick for governments is to direct public discourse to the 'substance' of the issue (as they define it) and/or to exploit symbolic features of the issue that reflect well on the legislation.

However, this is more easily said than done. The Conservative government at times completely lost control of the legislative process when Bill C–22 was linked to another enduring Canadian theme: Canadian-American relations. There were two related stories here. The first is the persistent albeit ambivalent apprehension about the role of multinational companies in Canada. It was abundantly clear to all Canadians that, outside of the generic sector, the drug industry was controlled by foreign (mostly American) companies. And it was no secret to anyone that the multinationals demanded an end to compulsory licensing and that the government was willing, indeed anxious, to help them out. On one level, then, the issue became a symbolic question of whether American or Canadian companies should benefit from patent legislation. This is a continuing theme in economic policy debates in

Canada. If nothing else, the Bill C–22 saga demonstrated the immense power and influence of multinational corporations in the policy process in Canada. PMAC was an immensely powerful lobby, and its monetary and specialist resources, lobbyists, and influence dwarfed those of the generic companies and consumers. The multinationals enjoyed privileged access in the policy process, while consumers and citizens were much farther removed from the reins of power. As Inset III suggested, the policy world surrounding Bill C–22 was a relatively small one.

Canadians seem resigned, though, to be observers of the policy process rather than participants in it, and the disproportionate influence of the multinationals is more or less taken for granted. The more persistent, dangerous, and compelling issue was the question of the relationship between Bill C–22 and the free trade negotiations. Despite heroic efforts, the government was simply unable to shake the idea that the passage of Bill C–22 was a *quid pro quo* for America's participation in a free trade deal. This issue had powerful symbolic value. The Liberals portrayed Bill C–22 as a selling out of Canadian sovereignty. The question of political sovereignty and nationhood is itself far removed from the issue of patent legislation, but, in the real world of Canadian politics, governments can lose control of a specific issue and see it replaced by a traditional symbolic one like nationhood.

Why did the Conservative government endure the political costs, embarrassments, and misery associated with Bill C–22? After all, when faced with a popular reaction against the de-indexing of pensions, it backed down. That was precisely one of the reasons the government had to stick it out this time. A government can get a certain amount of political mileage out of retreating from a controversial or divisive issue. It can then portray itself as responsive, open, and accommodating. But this sort of action can also be portrayed as being weak, vacillating, and indecisive, particularly if it appears to be a habit. Of course, *how* a government retreats is as important as that it retreats. However, no one would take any pronouncements or initiatives of the government seriously, if there was perpetual expectation that the mustering of serious opposition would cause the government to cave in.

Without political *credibility*, a government is lost; it must have this political resource in order to carry out its aims. Lacking it, a government will not be able to count on the political support it requires to carry out policy initiatives. Credibility is also a resource that a government must earn over the course of its term in office, precisely by doing what is expected of it and by carrying through on its promises and commitments. Once election time rolls around, who is going to vote for a government that lacks credibility?

This was an issue that hounded the Mulroney government. Despite real accomplishments, the public did not assign it much political credit. Bill C–22 was an issue that was perceived by the government as being a test of its credibility. Here was a piece of legislation that reflected in the clearest terms its ideological position and political promises. It had promised to revive the

Canadian economy by encouraging the private sector to embrace the new technology that would lift Canada into a prosperous future. It was a piece of legislation that was supported by some of its staunchest political supporters: the corporate sector, Quebec, the Americans. It was an issue that, regardless of government intentions, affected the fate of the free trade negotiations with the United States, the centrepiece of its economic renewal plan.

The Conservative government had no choice. It had to pass Bill C–22, regardless of cost. It had the legislative majority to pass the legislation, but it turned out to be politically costly. These are the hard realities of the real worlds of Canadian politics.

DISCUSSION QUESTIONS

1) Governments often commission studies by experts to examine complex issues. To what extent should governments feel bound by the results?

2) Would the process of Bill C-22 have been significantly different if there had been interest group consensus? If there had been bureaucratic consensus? Both?

3) Does this policy example strengthen or weaken the case for an elected Senate?

4) Should an appointed Senate have the right to defeat or substantially amend a piece of legislation passed by the elected House of Commons?

5) Discuss the role of political parties in this case. What did they have to win or lose from the various possible outcomes? What role did they play in the process?

6) Discuss the role of the Prime Minister in this case. How much power did he have to affect the outcome?

7) How effective was the legislature in representing regional and sectional interests?

8) All other things being equal, how difficult should it be for a majority government to pass a piece of legislation?

9) How important were ideological and political cultural factors in this case?

10) Did the government have a mandate from the Canadian people to abolish compulsory licensing? To what extent should political parties 'spell out' during elections what they plan to do if elected as the government?

11) What strengths and weaknesses does this case illustrate about Canada's political institutions?

CHRONOLOGY

1960	Ilsley Royal Commission recommends compulsory licensing.
1961	Green Book (Henry) documents high drug prices.
1963	Restrictive Trade Practices Commission Report recommends abolition of patents.
1964	Hall Royal Commission recommends compulsory licensing.
1967	Harley Special Committee on Drug Costs and Prices recommends compulsory licensing.
	Department of Consumer and Corporate Affairs created. Bill C–190 introduced by John Turner
1968	Bill C–102 introduced by Ron Basford (passed March 1969) to revise Patent Act. Section 41(4) establishes compulsory licensing.
1969ff	Multinational drug companies battle to undo 41(4).
1976	Department of Consumer and Corporate Affairs issues Working paper on Patent Law Revision. No changes recommended.

1980	Department of Industry, Trade and Commerce issues 5 background papers on health care products. Multinationals threaten to pull out of Canada.
1981	Economic Council of Canada study concludes that compulsory licensing should be retained. Federal task force on bio-technology: the pharmaceutical industry should be considered from a national security perspective.
1982	Plant closings in Quebec. Ayerest, McKenna and Harrison shift research facility to New Jersey; Hoffman La Roche follows Smith, Kline and French out of Montreal.
1983	Pharmaceutical Manufacturers Association of Canada submits *Proposals for Patent Reform* (February). Canadian Drug Manufacturers Association submits *A Case for the Retention of Section 41(4) of the Patent Act* (April). Martin O'Connell retained by Department of Consumer and Corporate Affairs (February); Minister André Ouellett requests a departmental study of compulsory licensing. Ouellett announces decision to review 41(4) to Senate Committee on Health, Welfare and Social Affairs (May). Conclusions of departmental study of 41(4) different from those of 1976 study — emphasis on high tech and investment (June). Judy Erola becomes Minister of Consumer and Corporate Affairs (August).
1984	Eastman Royal Commission established.
1984	Conservatives' election campaign includes promise to review the Patent Act. Conservative landslide election victory. Michel Côté named Minister of Consumer and Corporate Affairs.
1985	Côté promises spring legislation (February). Talks with PMAC and CDMA in search for compromise (March). Eastman Royal Commission issues report; recommends retaining compulsory licensing, with some changes (May).
1986	Côté fails in attempt to introduce Bill C–102 (27 June).
1986	Minister Harvie Andre introduces Bill C–22 amidst

procedural wrangling (6–7 November). Controversial CBC interview with Harry Eastman (18 November). Second reading of C–22 (21,24,25 November; 5, 8 December), with government use of closure (4 December) to terminate debate. Creation of National Coalition on Patent Act Changes to fight Bill C–22 (10 December). House of Commons Legislative Committee on Bill C–22 established (chaired by Arthur Malone; meets 20 times).

1987	
10 March	PEI passes unanimous motion against Bill C–22 Malone Committee reports (March). Debate begins on Committee Report (31 March, 1,2,7 April, 1 May); 47 report stage motions; closure invoked (7 April). Report stage concluded (4 May); third reading and on to Senate (5,6 May).
8 April	Senate refers Bill C–22 to Bonnell Committee. Committee tours the country in late May and early June, holding public hearings.
29 April	Manitoba passes a motion against Bill C–22.
12 June	Quebec attacks Senate for delaying.
16 June	Bonnell Committee issues first report.
25 June	Senate sends report back to committee.
1 July	Parliamentary session ends.
3 July	Government asks Speaker John Fraser to recall Parliament to deal with transportation, immigration, and patent legislation.
4 July	Fraser declines the request.
6 July	Multinational drug companies declare an investment strike.
7 July	Bonnell Committee promises to finish its work by 10 August.
30 July	House of Commons recalled to deal with illegal immigration.
11 August	House of Commons sits.
12 August	Bonnell Committee issues final report, recommending retention of compulsory licensing and Eastman changes
13 August.	Senate sends Bill C–22 back to House of Commons, with 10 amendments.
19 August	Prime Minister Mulroney makes direct intervention, attacking the Senate and playing the Quebec card.
21 August	House of Commons debates Senate amendments (21,24,25,26,28,31 August).

	Debate shifts to constitutional and free trade issues.
25 August	Quebec groups demonstrate on Parliament Hill in support of Bill C–22
26 August	Opposition leader John Turner declares that House of Commons must ultimately prevail. Government invokes closure (not actually used, as a procedural device ends debate on 28 August).
31 August	House of Commons rejects Senate amendments; Bill C–22 sent back to Senate for second time.
3 September	Senate sends Bill C–22 to Banking, Trade and Commerce Committee (chaired by Ian Sinclair).
9 October	Question Period dominated by issue of link between Bill C–22 and free trade negotiations.
21 October	Sinclair Committee reports, recommending substantial changes.
29 October	Senate accepts Sinclair Committee Report.
3-5 November	House of Commons debates Senate amendments, which are rejected; Bill C–22 sent back to Senate for the third time. Senate adjourns for two weeks.
18 November	Senate inquires whether the government would like to meet to discuss a compromise.
19 November	Government declines the offer to meet with the Senate. Senate quits battle; Bill C–22 passed.

NOTES

1. See B. Doern, in *How Ottawa Spends, 1988-89* K. Graham (Ottawa: Carleton University Press, 1988), 233-68.

2. M. Atkinson and W.D. Coleman, *State and Industry: Growth and Decline in the Canadian Economy*, chapter six, in press.

3. The 'Green Book' is Appendix 'Q' of Restrictive Trade Practices Commission, *Report Concerning the Manufacture, Distribution and Sale of Drugs* (Ottawa: 1963).

4. Restrictive Trade Practices Commission, *Report Concerning the Manufacture, Distribution and Sale of Drugs* (Ottawa: 1963).

5. Royal Commission on Patents, Copyrights and Industrial Designs, *Report* (Ottawa: 1960).

6. Royal Commission on Health Services, *Report* (Ottawa, 1964).

7. Ibid., 40, recommendations 67,68.

8. House of Commons, Special Committee on Drug Costs and Prices, *Final Report* (Ottawa: 1967).

9. House of Commons, *Debates*, 15 December 1967, 5467, and 12 February 1968, 6727.

10. Ibid., 14 February 1968, 6727.

11. See Ronald Lang, *The Politics of Drugs: A Comparative Pressure Group Study of the Canadian Pharmaceutical Manufacturers Association and the Association of the British Pharmaceutical Industry.* (Lexington: Lexington Books, 1974). See also Atkinson and Coleman, op. cit.; John Sawatsky and Harvey Cashore, "Inside Dope,", *This Magazine*, July–August 1987.

12. Commission of Inquiry on the Pharmaceutical Industry, *Summary of the Report* (Ottawa: 1985), 6 (hereafter referred to as the Eastman Report); P.K. Gorecki and I. Henderson, "Compulsory Licensing of Drugs in Canada: A Comment on the Debate," *Canadian Public Policy* 4 (Autumn 1981), 562; D.J. Fowler and M.J. Gordon, "The Effect of Public Policy Initiatives on Drug Prices in Canada," *Canadian Public Policy* 10 (March 1984), 71.

13. See Sawatsky and Cashore, op. cit.

14. Eastman Report, 5.

15. The Gorecki and Henderson article was an offshoot of this study.

16. For example Smith, Klein and French; Hoffman LaRoche; Ayerst, McKenna and Harrison.

17. Atkinson and Coleman, op. cit.

18. Ibid.

19. Sawatsky and Cashore, op. cit.

20. *Financial Post*, 5 March 1983.

21. House of Commons, Standing Committee On Health, Welfare and Social Affairs, *Proceedings*, 27 May 1983, 67–69,10,11,12.

22. Sawatsky and Cashore, op. cit.

23. See House of Commons, *Debates*, 4 and 6 March 1985, especially 3113–14, J. Epp.

24. Ibid., 8 March 1985, 3114.

25. Eastman Report, 1.

26. Ibid., 5-7.

27. Ibid., 7.

28. Ibid., 17. Emphasis added.

29. Ibid., 8. Referring to the international investment strategy of the multinational drug companies, Economic Council of Canada economists Gorecki and Henderson concluded, "it may be better for Canada to rely on the fruits of foreign innovation than to attempt to build our own R&D capacity." Gorecki and Henderson, op. cit., 565.

30. House of Commons, *Debates*, 23 May 1985, 4997–98

31. Hugh Windsor, *Globe and Mail*, 23 June 1986.

32. Jeffrey Simpson, Ibid., 18 November 1986.

33. House of Commons, *Debates*, 6 November 1986, 1137. The issue of compulsory licensing was item #3 on the agenda of the 'Shamrock Summit' between Prime Minister Mulroney and President Reagan held in Quebec City in March 1985. In April 1986 Clayton Yeuter complained publicly about how long it was taking the Canadian government to undo compulsory licensing.

34. Ibid., 19 November 1986, 1316ff.

35. House of Commons, *Debates*, 6 November 1986, 1137; 19 November 1986, 1316ff; 7 November 1986, 1178–79. On the story of the attempt to de-index pensions, see Elizabeth and Gretta Riddell-Dixon, "Seniors Advance, The Mulroney Government Retreats: Grey Power and the Reinstatement of Fully Indexed Pensions," in Robert J. Jackson (et al), *Contemporary Canadian Politics: Readings and Notes.* Scarborough: Prentice-Hall, 1987.

36. *Globe and Mail*, 19, 20 November 1986.

37. House of Commons, *Debates*, 19 November 1986, 1316.

38. Ibid., 19 November 1986, 1319, 1319-20, 1318; 7 November 1986, 1179.

39. Ibid., 20 November 1986, 1368-71.

40. Ibid., 20 November 1986, 1375, 1379; 21 November 1986, 1415-7; 2 December 1986, 1695.

41. *Globe and Mail*, 21, 24, 26, 27, 28 November 1986.

42. House of Commons, *Debates*, 4 December 1986, 1776ff.

43. Ibid., 5 December 1986, 1833,1839.

44. House of Commons, Legislative Committee on Bill C–22, *Minutes of Proceedings and Evidence*, 11 December 1986, 11-17.

45. House of Commons, *Debates*, 5 May 1987, 5743–44, 5750.

46. The Crosbie amendment proposed that any 'money bill' presented to the Senate 30 days before the end of a session, but not passed by the Senate with amendments within 30 days, would be considered passed. Any other bill forwarded to the Senate at least 45 days before the end of the session would be considered passed by the Upper Chamber unless the Commons directed otherwise; if the Senate amended a bill, and the House of Commons did not accept this within 15 days, the original bill would be considered passed.

47. *Globe and Mail*, 7 July 1987.

48. Ibid., 8 July 1987.

49. Senate, Special Committee of the Senate on Bill C–22, *Seventh Report*. 12 August 1987.

50. *Globe and Mail*, 11, 13 August 1987.

51. Ibid., 14 August 1987.

52. *Toronto Star*, 19 August 1987.

53. *Globe and Mail*, 20, 24 August 1987.

54. House of Commons, *Debates*, 21 August 1987, 8283.

55. *Globe and Mail*, 23 August 1987.

56. House of Commons, *Debates*, 25 August 1987, 8393ff.

57. Ibid., 26 August 1987, 8433ff.

58. Ibid., 21 August 1987, 1298ff.

59. Ibid., 26 August 1987, 8433, 8437.

60. *Globe and Mail*, 20, 25 August 1987.

61. House of Commons, *Debates*, 25 August 1987, 8304; 21 August 1987, 8280.

62. *Globe and Mail*, 4 September 1987.

63. Ibid., 2 September 1987.

64. Senate, Standing Committee on Banking, Trade and Commerce, *Minutes of Proceedings and Evidence*, 37-22,23,27,39.

65. House of Commons, *Debates*, 9 October 1987, 9863-70; *Globe and Mail*, 16 October 1987.

66. *Globe and Mail*, 10 October 1987.

67. *Toronto Star*, 14 October 1987.

68. Senate, *Debates*, 21 October 1987, 2009-45.

69. House of Commons, *Debates*, 3 November 1987, 10667.

70. Senate, *Debates*, 22 October 1987, 2060-1,2062.

71. *Globe and Mail*, 7 November 1987.

72. Senate, *Debates*, 17 November 1987, 2157-9.

73. *Globe and Mail*, 18 November 1987.

74. Senate, *Debates*, 19 November 1987, 2212-3.
75. Senate, *Debates*, 19 November 1987, 2223.

SEXUAL POLITICS:

PORNOGRAPHY POLICY IN CANADA

From the late 1970s on, there has appeared to be a growing public con-sensus that pornography is a 'problem' that governments should deal with. The Mulroney government twice introduced tough anti-pornog-raphy legislation, which was met by fierce opposition both within Par-liament and in society at large. On both occasions, the government decided not to use its huge majority to force the legislation into law. This continued a pattern established during previous Liberal ad-ministrations, which saw five legislative initiatives come to naught. The story of recent anti-pornography policy initiatives illustrates how difficult it is to legislate in the area of 'moral regulation.' In the con-text of a bewildering array of interests and moral and ideological claims, the government did not appear to have the authority to act. While legis-lative initiatives were not successfully pursued in Parliament, pornog-raphy policy was actually being made by the other branches of government — the judiciary through court decisions and the executive through customs regulations. The case also illustrates the political im-pact of feminism, which substantially transformed and complicated the political discourse around pornography in Canada.

In 1959 a Montreal judge declared that D. H. Lawrence's novel *Lady Chatterly's Lover* was obscene. The decision was appealed and was finally resolved in a famous Supreme Court case, *R. v. Brodie, Dansky and Rubin*. The Supreme Court ruled that the book was not obscene. Reading Lawrence's novel now, many Canadians would wonder what the fuss was all about. After all, today one can walk into most corner convenience or video stores and purchase or rent graphic depictions of scenes that Lady Chatter-ly could not have dreamed of. This is but one feature of our sexual age, in which we think, talk, practice, discuss, experiment, dissect, report, compare, represent and advertise sex in an amazingly open and energetic way. Tech-nological advances in printing have made possible mass marketing of inex-pensive books and magazines with sexual content. Even more strikingly, the video revolution has resulted in the widespread and inexpensive availability of films presenting sexually explicit activity.

Governments have, to an extent, been involved in the sexual transformation of society. In one of the most famous political aphorisms of the 1960s, former prime minister Trudeau declared that "the state has no business in the nation's bedrooms," and as justice minister he changed the Criminal Code to decriminalize previously outlawed sexual practices. By and large, though, modern governments have not been anxious to legislate moral standards and behaviour. These are divisive social issues, where deeply held personal convictions inhibit the construction of social consensus. In sexual matters in particular, society has led and governments have followed. In another famous political quip, former Conservative British Prime Minister Macmillan insisted that "if you are looking for morality go see your preacher." There are many political votes to lose telling citizens how to live their (sexual) lives. While most sectors of the economy have been regulated by governments over the postwar period, the multi-billion dollar pornography industry has gone largely unregulated.

Nonetheless there are occasions when governments conclude that the times call for legislative initiatives in these areas. In the late 1970s, increasing numbers of Canadians expressed concern about the widespread availability of 'pornography,' although the term was not used with much precision. What most people meant was naked bodies visually presented as being involved in some kind of sexual activity. A distinction emerged between soft-core and hard-core pornography, the latter generally referring to material involving explicit representation of sexual acts, violent sex and the involvement of children. It was the increasing prevalence and availability of this latter category that appears to have triggered a public reaction in the late 1970s. The outcry emanated from a variety of sources, including women's groups, and coincided with a broad 'neo-conservative' reaction against many features of modern existence, from bureaucracy and the welfare state to sexual promiscuity and the breakdown of the traditional family unit.

The Mulroney government decided to make the problem of pornography a policy priority. This decision reflected, at the time, a happy political coincidence of necessity and choice. Political momentum had been building since the late 1970s to create tougher Criminal Code sanctions against pornography. Previous Liberal governments initiated various studies and introduced three legislative measures in response to widespread demands for controls on violent and child pornography. In addition, the Conservative party was itself infused by a sense of morality and purpose and was willing to talk about right and wrong in the sexual domain. It proposed to treat most sexually explicit material as being pornographic, to impose harsh penalties on the producers and distributors of both hard- and soft-core pornography, and to stringently control public access to erotic material.

When the Conservatives faced the electorate four years later in 1988, the Criminal Code remained unchanged and pornography had fallen off the policy agenda. Two tough anti-pornography bills had been introduced — Bill C–114 by John Crosbie and Bill C–54 by Ramon Hnatyshyn. Neither bill came even remotely close to being passed. Previous Liberal initiatives in this area (Bills C–21, C–53 and C–190) met a similar fate. After a decade of legislative studies, committee reports, commissions, and policy initiatives, the Criminal Code statutes dealing with pornography remain the same as in 1959.

Why has it been so difficult to change Canada's pornography laws? This case illustrates many hard political realities of the real worlds of Canadian politics. It demonstrates how, despite the best efforts and energies of governments, very often *nothing gets done*, even in priority areas. The Mulroney government enjoyed the largest electoral majority in Canadian history; caucus support of harsh restrictions on pornography was especially strong and energetic; substantial parts of the Canadian community, including most women's groups, demanded increased restrictions on pornography; pornography had been extensively studied and widely discussed; the issue had considerable political momentum and a certain degree of legitimacy. Yet the government chose not to use its huge majority to pass its legislation in this area.

In the area of 'moral regulation,' Canadian governments face serious political constraints and appear to lack the authority required to act. There certainly was 'conservative' momentum in the late 1970s and early 1980s to deal with pornography. But the Canadian political culture is by no means homogeneous. While Canadians may be depicted as being fairly conservative on moral issues, and willing to defer to and accept leadership in these areas, there is a substantial liberal impulse in Canadian society. Canadians remain ideologically and publicly divided on this issue, and this has made it difficult for governments to proceed, even in propitious circumstances.

Despite its huge majority, the government's authority to take strong moral action was fatally weakened by the fragmented moral and political context in which it was legislating. The ideological and moral character of the issue also undermined the possibility of transforming the issue into a 'technical' one. Studies and expert advice were inconclusive and not terribly useful in telling the government what to do.

The pornography case also demonstrates just how hard it is to design a law. Governments are often frustrated by the difficulties involved in 'translating' basic commitments or views into workable and effective legislation. Words are blunt instruments, and laws are comprised of words that can be abused, misinterpreted, and misshaped. Devising appropriate wording and language in this area has turned out to be particularly challenging, and this problem alone has made changing the law on pornography all but impossible.

The pornography case also presents two increasingly important worlds. First, the chapter will show how the courts have played a substantial role in implementing government's pornography policy. Indeed the courts have ef-

IDEOLOGICAL APPROACHES TO PORNOGRAPHY

Ideologies take complex problems and issues and 'translate' them into terms simple and comprehensible enough for people to understand. Ideologies in effect offer a choice of simple options about what to think about pornography and what ought to be done about it. Most people orient themselves to the issue of pornography along *conservative*, *liberal*, or *feminist* lines.

The *conservative* view of pornography assumes that individuals are lustful, violent, and evil rather than inherently good. The purpose of the law is to generate moral rules, values and traditions that successfully repress individual lust. Conservatives thus support 'community values' that will discipline and channel our passions. Sexual desire is particularly dangerous and potentially destructive, unless it is directed to procreation within the family unit. Conservatives expect governments to ensure the strength of a community's moral values even if this entails interfering in the personal lives of individuals. On this view, pornography inflames and excites sexual passions with no other end than enjoyment, no other purpose than satisfaction, and nothing more noble than gluttony of the flesh. As individuals are incapable of resisting this temptation, governments are urged to prohibit the production and consumption of pornography. The conservative approach is thus a *moral* one and conservative policy is directed to making pornography a *criminal* matter.[1]

Liberals take the exact opposite position. For them, pornography is not a matter of morality and should not be criminalized. Liberals see the individual as a rational being capable of developing his or her talents and capacities without guidance from others. Indeed, the law, the state and traditions — the moral values of the community — are seen as potential constraints or inhibitions on the free and full development of the individual. Liberals thus demand that the state not interfere in the life of the individual, who should be given 'space' in which to grow and develop. The sexual domain is considered no different than any other aspect of life, the individual should be allowed to use and develop his or her sexuality on the basis of private decisions and experiences. Artists, writers and communicators should be allowed freedom of expression regardless of whether the subject matter is sexual. Individual citizens should not be denied the right to see, read, or consume this material. Whether this material is 'immoral' or in 'bad taste' is for the individual to decide, not the government. Pornography would not be considered by liberals to be a criminal matter or

fectively *made* pornography law and have played a more important role than Parliament. The same can be said of customs, which has regulated and controlled Canadians' access to sexually explicit material (most of which is imported into Canada). This raises the important question of who should make laws that touch on moral issues — elected politicians or appointed judges and officials. Second, the case illustrates the extent to which the women's movement has changed politics in Canada. Over and above the obvious impact of the women's movement as an interest group, feminism has changed the nature of political discourse on many aspects of Canadian political life. This chapter illustrates how the women's movement created a new conceptual terrain upon which the issue of pornography was debated.

Before analysing in detail the events surrounding the government's

something for the law to be concerned about, unless it could be shown that pornography results in some harm to individuals (anti-social behaviour, rape, violence). Unlike conservatives, though, this harm is not assumed but must be established empirically.[2]

Feminist analysis portrays society as organized around a 'sexual class system'. Men are seen to have disproportionate (if not monopoly) power in the economic and political worlds, while women retain responsibility for the private world of the family and children. This division of labour has resulted in vast asymmetries of power, status, and wealth. Feminists direct the state to increase women's opportunities in the economic and political worlds, while redressing women's position in the private world as well. Feminists see pornography as reflecting the dominance of men's sexual needs and their definition of what sexuality is. This reinforces the inferiority that women experience as a result of the sexual class system. Pornography presents women as 'different' from men, serving the limited function of satisfying men's sexual needs. The harder, more violent forms of pornography portray women as enjoying pain, degradation, and subservience. Feminists look to state prohibition of pornography as an act of social engineering or 'empowerment,' which will contribute to the breaking down of sexual stereotypes and constraints, thereby allowing women to participate fully in society.

This feminist approach is conceptually different from that of liberals and conservatives. Feminists argue that the liberal 'free speech' approach ignores the fundamental inequality experienced by women; freedom of speech with respect to pornography perpetuates sexism, subservience and degradation. For feminists, pornography is not a free speech issue but a matter of equality. There is, though, a liberal dimension to the feminist position. Like liberals, feminists argue for state prohibition of pornography that harms women, both with regard to the violence and physical harm done to women by the consumers of pornography, as well as with respect to the misogyny and trivialization of women's existence that bars equal access to society. While liberals focus on the *direct* harm that might be caused by pornography, feminists also consider the *indirect* harm that results, allowing pornography to be considered a legitimate matter for criminal concern. Thus, while allied politically with conservatives, feminists distinguish their position from conservatives' by differentiating pornography from 'erotica' — which is seen as healthy and acceptable. Feminists do not see sex as 'bad' or 'sinful in itself.[3] There is also a socialist variant of feminism that analyses pornography in terms of its relationship to capitalism. *Socialist feminists* do not favour prohibitions on pornography, as they fear that this will lead to further denials of human (particularly sexual) rights. [4]

failure to pass Bills C–114 or 54, we will establish a backdrop by reviewing the evolution of Canadian law in this area from the late 19th century to the late 1970s. A chronology of events is appended to the chapter to assist the reader in following the case.

PORNOGRAPHY AND CANADIAN LAW: 1867-1977

Pornography is about sex. Traditionally, it has been used as a pejorative or derogatory term (it is derived from the Greek, meaning to write about prostitutes). To label something as 'pornographic' is to declare that it is an objectionable depiction of sex. Like beauty, though, this is something that is very much in the eye of the beholder. In a society increasingly open and frank about sex, many view the depiction of a naked body or a sexual organ as completely natural and mundane. Others consider it to be offensive. A third category, 'erotica,' is often distinguished from pornography as an 'acceptable' item which arouses sexual desire (in Greek mythology, Eros was the god of love). Are Calvin Klein jean ads pornographic, erotic, or neither?

Most people address these questions with the aid of some very broad ideas about sexuality, ideas that reflect a spectrum of moral and cultural standards and are value-laden. Hence people disagree in their reactions to these questions, because these ideas are not compatible with each other. We can distinguish three broad orientations to pornography, each of which has influenced the evolution of Canadian pornography law (see Inset I). There are, first, many who see pornography as a 'freedom of speech' or censorship issue, and argue that there should be no legal prohibitions on sexual material unless that material can be shown to harm people. This is the liberal position. Others see it as a moral issue, with pornography to be outlawed lest it undermine community standards. This is the conservative position. A third and more recently articulated attitude is that pornography should be outlawed if it demeans and degrades people, particularly women. This is the feminist position.

Various interests have rallied around each of these ideological positions. Generally speaking, church groups, police groups, municipal organizations, and educational associations have taken a conservative approach. Civil liberties groups, gay organizations, library associations, and professional associations of artists and writers have taken a liberal approach. Women's organizations have been split, in three ways. A substantial number of women and women's organizations take a conservative approach. They are now affiliated with the wider neo-conservative reaction against liberalism and the alleged evils of modernity, such as drugs, abortion, and the decline of family values. A large number of feminists also favour prohibition of pornography, but for radically different reasons. Mainstream or liberal feminists wish to foster women's roles in society, including free development of women's sexuality. They do not wish to deny sexual expression and women's sexual development, but seek, rather unsuccessfully, to differentiate between the erotic and the pornographic. These feminists thus find themselves unhappy bedfellows with the New Right. Finally, socialist feminists disagree with the first two groups, and take a position akin to the civil libertarian one, fearing that censorship of pornography will increase state authority and lead to other forms of repression, including sexual repression.

Like many other countries, Canada's pornography laws have reflected more of a conservative orientation than a liberal one. For both liberals and conservatives, the challenge has been in translating philosophical or moral objectives into precise and operative legal terminology. Sadly, the principle *nullum crimen sine lege, nulla poena sine lege* (no judicial decision without a law, no punishment without reference to a law) has not held to any great extent in this area. The criminal law on pornography has never been very precise, with the result that Canadians have not really known in advance whether their conduct would infringe a legal rule.[5]

Until recently, policy discussions focused on the issue of 'obscenity' rather than 'pornography'. Obscenity is a broader and less sexually specific term, referring to matters that offend standards of decency (the term is derived from the Latin word meaning ill-boding or offensive). Even now, Canada does not have a pornography law *per se* but rather has an obscenity law, under which the (perhaps narrower) category of pornography is applied. For almost a century, Canada's law regarding obscenity was based on the English common law. It was not until 1959 that the Canadian Parliament defined 'obscenity.' In the interim, it was essentially the courts that determined pornography policy, with the tacit support of the political branches. Judges have had to fill the legal and policy vacuum in this area of moral regulation, and have implicitly been assigned the critical role in setting standards and determining what is pornographic.

The 'Hicklin' Test

The origins of legal action against obscenity can be traced to 1724, with a charge of obscenity laid against *Venus in the Cloister*, subtitled *The Nun in her Smock*. The English Parliament enacted legislation in 1857 — The Obscene Publications Act — that restricted sexually stimulating material. However, it was the case *R. v. Hicklin* (1868) that shaped the implementation of pornography laws for almost the whole of the next century.

The case involved a book entitled *The Confessional Unmasked*, which revealed the techniques allegedly used by priests to extract erotic confessions

---

Inset II

THE CRIMINAL CODE, 189   Section 179

Everyone is guilty of an indictable offence and liable to two years' imprisonment who knowingly, without lawful justification or excuse —
(a)publicly sells, or exposes for public sale or to public view, any obscene book, or other printed or written matter, or any picture, photograph, model or other object, tending to corrupt morals; or (b)publicly exhibits any disgusting object or any indecent show; or (c)offers to sell, advertises, publishes an advertisement of or has for sale or disposal any medicine, drug or article intended or represented as a means of preventing conception or causing abortion.
2. No one shall be convicted of any offence in this section mentioned if he proves that the public good was served by the acts alleged to have been done.
3. It shall be a question of law whether the occasion of the sale, publishing, or exhibition is such as might be for the public good, and whether there is evidence of excess beyond what the public good requires in the manner, extent or circumstances in, to or under which the sale, publishing or exhibition is made, so as to afford a justification or excuse therefor; but it shall be a question for the jury whether there is or is not such excess.
4.The motives of the seller, publisher or exhibitor shall in all cases be irrelevant.

from female penitents. In declaring the work obscene, Lord Chief Justice Cockburn enunciated the following definition:

> I think the test of obscenity is this, whether the tendency of the matter charged as obscenity is to deprave and corrupt those whose minds are open to such immoral influences and into whose hands a publication of this sort may fall....it would suggest to the minds of the young of either sex, or even to persons of more advanced years, thoughts of an impure and libidinous character.

This came to be known as the Hicklin test for obscenity, and was used in the Canadian courts through to the 1960s. The Hicklin test is based on a conservative view of the matter; the test is informed by moral standards, that are assumed to be self-evident, as is the moral harm done to society by the consumption of the obscene material. Proof of harm or social impact is not required — 'impure thoughts' (by a very narrow range of people) are considered to be sufficient moral harm to warrant criminal action.

The Hicklin case had a profound legal impact in Canada. Canada's first Criminal Code was established in 1892, and in it, Section 179 (see Inset II) prohibited the public sale, or exposure for sale, of any obscene book or printed matter. The term 'obscene' was not defined by Parliament. The result was that the courts used the Hicklin test in obscenity trials. In the House of Commons debates on the creation of the Criminal Code, discussion centred on the difficulty of creating an acceptable definition of obscenity, a problem that would plague lawmakers for the next century. There was also discussion of how technology was changing the character of obscenity; photography was shifting pornography from the printed word to the visual presentation.[6] This foreshadowed the 20th century developments of cheap printing and the video revolution. Section 179(2) of the Criminal Code established that no one would be prosecuted for obscenity if it were proved that the publication of the material served the public good. This was the origin of the 'reverse onus' test, in which a defendant would have to prove his or her innocence against an obscenity charge.

Over the next century, legal experts and civil libertarians criticized the Hicklin test for vagueness in its meaning, subjectivity in its application, focus on impact on the most vulnerable, and the absence of a requirement of actual proof of harm. It also did not allow the admission of expert testimony in defence of a work, did not allow any effective defence on the basis of literary or artistic merit, and allowed the examination of selected passages separated from the work as a whole.[7]

Despite its alleged defects, the Hicklin test survived the trials of time, perhaps because it reflected Canadians' conservative values. It certainly met the approval of successive governments. The 1949 Royal Commission on the Revision of the Criminal Code did not find Section 179 either unclear or ambiguous.[8] The 1952 Senate Select Committee on the Sale and Distribution of Salacious and Indecent Literature concluded that the Hicklin test was "enforceable if there is a will to enforce it".[9] In the mid-1950s, Justice Minister Garson repeatedly maintained that there was no better definition of obscenity than that devised by Chief Justice Cockburn.[10]

On the other hand, court decisions led to the narrowing of the grounds upon which an item could face criminal charges. In an important and influential American case dealing with James Joyce's *Ulysses* (1933), Justice Woolsey shifted the issue of impact away from the young and the abnormal to the same hypothetical 'reasonable man' as in the law of torts. *R. v. Martin Secker Warburg Ltd.* (1954) established the idea of 'contemporariness,' the idea that what 'corrupts' and 'depraves' changes from generation to generation. *R. v. American News Co. Ltd.* (1957) confirmed the principle that the entire work in question should be considered. Standards of obscenity were thus being changed by judges and not by politicians. Nonetheless, the essentially conservative approach to obscenity continued: works were to be judged by their expected impact on the morals of the community.

Court decisions had the effect of loosening the law and allowing the publication and distribution of works that would previously have been declared obscene. At the same time, changes in printing technology allowed high volume, low cost printing of books and magazines (particularly comics). The result was that 'indecent' material — which had previously been relatively expensive and available only to the elite — became cheap and widely accessible to the masses, particularly youth. In the 1950s, 'decency in writing' became a public issue.[11]

Bill C-58

It was in this context that Davie Fulton, as an opposition Conservative MP, in 1953 requested the creation of a joint committee on 'Filthy Literature'. He argued that there was

> evidence of a disturbing increase in the volume of filthy literature circulating in Canada...It comes as an eyesore to go in and browse around a newsstand and pick up some of the things...available at 5, 10 or 15 cents to the youth of the country.... Supermen and gangs of thugs, G-men and sadistic murderers carve their way through the 'funny pages' talking plain talk and giving people the works...

He cited American studies which indicated that these 'crime comics' and other magazines had "a direct influence upon the motivation of youthful offenders." Freedom of speech and literary and artistic expression had to be "reconcile[d].... with the necessity of preventing abuse, preventing a situation under which liberty becomes licence and degenerates...into lewdness or obscenity." Fulton argued that the Criminal Code was inadequate to deal with a changing situation, and that obscenity had to be defined with more clarity and precision.[12]

Fulton became Justice Minister in 1957, and in 1959 initiated Bill C–58, amendments to the Criminal Code's section 179 provisions on obscenity (renumbered to Section 150 in an earlier Criminal Code amendment). Fulton claimed that Bill C–58 responded to a "problem which is real and urgent in Canada...It is apparent from discussions I have had with law enforcement officers....that the present law is clearly not adequate to deal with this type of trash."[13] A new subsection 150(8) defined obscenity:

> For the purposes of this Act, any publication a dominant characteristic of which is the undue exploitation of sex, or of sex and any one more of the following subjects, namely, crime, horror, cruelty and violence, shall be deemed to be obscene.

This section was designed to complement the Hicklin test by providing an objective test of obscenity to supplement the more subjective one. This would allow the law to catch certain (trashy) publications that could escape under the Hicklin test. According to Fulton, the tests would be:

> does the publication deal with sex, or sex and one or more of the other subjects named? If so, is this a dominant characteristic? Again, if so, does it exploit these subjects in an undue manner?

Fulton admitted that two terms remained relatively subjective: 'dominant' and 'undue.' With regard to the former, the amendment was aimed at 'muck' and 'trash' that had no literary or artistic merit, but was exclusively 'filthy.' The idea here was that the term 'dominant' would force the courts to look at the whole publication, and not just parts of it. Other types of publications would continue to be judged by the Hicklin test. With respect to 'undue exploitation,' Fulton explained:

> The word 'undue' is one with which the courts are familiar as meaning generally something going beyond what men of good will and common sense would normally tolerate.

Implicit in this argument was the position that scientific books or works of literary or artistic merit would not be in jeopardy.[14]

This change to the Criminal Code exists to this day as the legal basis upon which charges of pornography are laid. Bill C–58's obscenity provision perpetuated a rather conservative orientation to pornography. It made it easier for publications to be charged, and created new categories under which publications could be charged. The law remained infused with the moral purpose of protecting society from this sort of material, whose potential for harm remained assumed and self-evident. As opposition MPs pointed out at the time, the new law was not as 'clear, precise and practical' as had been promised. The application of the new definition of obscenity would still require subjective judicial interpretation and reaction. Judges would determine precisely who men of 'good will' might be in determining whether a matter was 'undue' in its exploitation of sex. Judges would determine what 'common sense tolerates.' Fulton acknowledged the Opposition's points: "I am not maintaining...that the definition we have is perfect. It is the best definition we could achieve...."[15]

The Criminal Code amendment had relatively smooth sailing in Parliament. There was some concern expressed (by the CCF) about freedom of expression. But Liberal opposition leader Pearson supported the bill, as did most MPs. Indeed, a substantial number wanted tougher legislation.[16]

Despite its conservative underpinnings, the passage of Bill C–58 was followed by an explosion of activity in the industries producing sexually explicit material. By the late 1970s, pornography was a multi-billion dollar enterprise. *Penthouse* regularly outsells *Time* and *Newsweek* combined, and 'adult videos' are enormously profitable. The pornography industry outgrosses the combined total of conventional movie and recording businesses in North America. Like ships passing each other in the night, consumers purchased more and more sexually explicit material while public authorities in Canada continued to apply the conservative values enunciated by Fulton and others. For example, the provinces had boards that censored movies. The scrutiny of books was left to the courts and especially to Customs (on the role of Customs, see p. 132 below). Some provinces took 'preemptive' action in response to Bill C–58. For example, the Ontario government set up an advisory panel on obscene publications, consisting of a sociologist, a librarian, a lawyer, and a specialist in literature. If a citizen discovered a book for public sale that he or she considered obscene, the title could be sent to the Attorney General or to this panel, which would review the publication. If the panel considered the publication to be acceptable, it communicated the decision to the citizen with reasons for this evaluation. If the publication was assessed as obscene, it would be pulled from the stores. This was a procedure agreed to by wholesale distributors, who saw in this process a way of defending themselves from criminal charges. This informal system of 'self-censorship' was used in many ways through the next decades. Even such a traditionally staunch champion of freedom of speech as *Saturday Night* agreed with this procedure:

Any close observers of the bookstalls today would agree that it is reasonable to set one [of these procedures] up. There are so many lurid and detailed accounts of sexual aberrations, particularly of sadism and lesbianism, that even the most liberal-minded person is disturbed.[17]

In the late 1950s and early 1960s a number of critical judicial decisions further liberalized the implementation of pornography regulations (see Inset III, p. 121). These decisions effectively eliminated the Hicklin test for obscenity and operationalized the 'meaning' of Bill C–58's attempt to define obscenity. The phrase 'dominant characteristic' had turned out to be relatively uncontroversial in application; over time, no one tried to challenge a court claim that sex was a dominant characteristic of a publication under scrutiny. The phrase 'undue exploitation' caused far more problems, but the courts determined this to involve a 'community standards' test. A work would not be considered obscene as long as it was considered acceptable by the standards of the community, which the courts saw as changing over time and as reflecting the views of the average person. The idea of relative degrees of tolerance was validated by the courts, and was to be related to the purpose of the work (scientific, artistic, literary, etc.). This required that the whole work be assessed, not simply the incriminating passage or picture.

While the 'black hole' quality of the Hicklin test was eliminated, these changes did not really amount to the advent of an objective or 'scientific' test. Indeed, the criteria laid out above remained difficult to apply with any degree of consistency or predictability, and the courts' obscenity judgments continued to be varied and uneven. As one observer commented on the conduct of obscenity trials, the question was,

> Does the publication shock the judge? If it does, it will be interpreted as being in conflict with community standards, unredeemed by purpose or merit, and the causal link between the publication and the social dangers will be assumed.[20]

Moreover, the defence based on literary or artistic merit and the contribution to the public good turned out to be a non-starter, and does not really exist in Canada. Over and above the problem of the lack of clarity in the idea of the public good, defendants have had difficulty establishing that an otherwise obscene work was in the public interest. Further, defendants have had to prove that the impact of the book did not extend beyond its contribution to the public good — an impossible claim to prove. In practice, this defence has proven to be impracticable.

Nonetheless, the decade that followed the introduction of Bill C–58 saw an effective narrowing of the conditions under which a material could be charged with obscenity. It was in this period that previously banned classics, like *Ulysses* and *Lady Chatterly's Lover*, were legalized. In 1964, the Ontario County Court of Appeal ruled that *Fanny Hill* was not obscene. These changes were the result not of political decisions, but of the manner in which the courts applied the law. Moreover, 'expert opinion' created further momentum for the liberalization of attitudes toward pornography. The United States Commission on Obscenity and Pornography study concluded that no direct relationship could be established between the consumption of pornography, and anti-social behaviour like crime, delinquency, and degeneracy. This was the first round in a series of studies that attempted, inconclusively, to establish whether pornography caused any 'harm.' The Law Reform Commission of Canada concluded that, while it was reasonable to proscribe what it termed 'public obscenity,' 'private obscenity' like softcore pornography privately purchased and consumed ought not to be considered a criminal offence.[21] This in turn was the first round in a series of proposals that sought to decriminalize large areas that would previously have been deemed to be obscene.

REACTION AGAINST PORNOGRAPHY — ROUND ONE: THE LIBERALS

Changes in legal interpretation made sexually explicit material more widely available, and Canadians appeared to have a taste for it. This raised some concern. In 1969, *Maclean's* observed:

The proliferation of pornography in the past decade can only be described as an explosion....the freshet of pictorial and verbal pornography has become a torrent....Book titles run into the thousands and range through every possible heterosexual activity to masochism, fetishism and bestiality. In film scenes the nude scene is almost mandatory. Lesbianism, homosexuality and autoerotism are explicitly portrayed.

The article presented pornography as a "burgeoning social problem" that the government was ignoring, and it predicted that the ultimate result would be "mindless permissiveness or ugly reaction."[22] It was not until the late 1970s, though, that pornography became a matter of policy concern. This coincided with two broad and conflicting developments. The organized women's movement took on increasing political force, and prohibition of pornography was on its agenda. In addition, the late 1970s saw an ideological swing to the right in the Western world, a swing against the welfare state, bureaucracy, 'permissiveness,' and modernity in general.[23] In the process, there developed a call for the diminution of the welfare state and the role of the government in the economy, and the reassertion of traditional values and personal morality. Ironically, this neo-conservative shift called for government deregulation of the economy at the same time as it called for increased state moral regulation.

There was evidence of increased public concern about pornography. In 1975 Canada's first anti-pornography squad was formed in Toronto. Project P consisted of two Toronto policemen and two Ontario Provincial Police officers. It attained a remarkable success rate in laying obscenity charges, and trained other police forces in this area. Grass roots organizations were set up in suburban neighbourhoods to force merchants to keep sex magazines out of the reach of children.[24] In 1977, an informal committee of five Progressive Conservative and three Liberal MPs was established to pressure the government into introducing harsher anti-pornography measures. This was the parliamentary wing of a Joint Church-Parliamentary Committee on Pornography and Obscenity that had launched a national campaign to stamp out pornography.[25]

Political momentum on the pornography issue built up in the fall of 1977. Ten private members' bills to amend the Criminal Code prohibitions on pornography were introduced. These bills set the tone for the political discourse on pornography, and foreshadowed the types of legislative initiatives that would be forthcoming over the next decade. Typical of these bills was Progressive Conservative John McGrath's Bill C–207, which proposed to broaden the legal definition of obscenity to include "any explicit representation or detailed description of a sexual act and any pictorial representation tending to solicit partners for a sexual act". 'Sexual act' would include masturbation, and anal, oral or vaginal intercourse with or upon any person, animal, dead body, or inanimate object, including an attempted or simulated sex act. McGrath's bill would have criminalized almost all printed and pictorial material that dealt with sex.[26]

The efforts of the joint church-parliamentary group were successful, as the Liberal government agreed to send the private members' bills for study to the Standing Committee on Justice and Legal Affairs. This effectively placed the issue of pornography on the political agenda. Chaired by Liberal MP Mark MacGuigan, the committee issued a report in 1978 that legitimized the position of those who were arguing that pornography should be made a priority issue: "The Committee was impressed by the urgency of the problem of sexually explicit material...The situation has seriously degenerated...." The report was very much informed by the feminist analysis of pornography, pointing to the increase in violent or hard-core pornography that portrayed women as "passive victims who derive limitless pleasure from inflicted pain...sexual objects whose only redeeming features are their genital and erotic zones." In the committee's view, pornography abused the principle of equality by "reinforc[ing] male-female stereotypes to the detriment of both sexes."[27] It proposed to redefine obscenity as existing where "a dominant characteristic of the matter or thing is the undue exploitation of sex, crime, horror, cruelty, or violence, or the undue degradation of the human per-

LADY CHATTERLY'S LOVER

In 1959, a Montreal judge declared that D.H. Lawrence's novel *Lady Chatterly's Lover* was obscene. This set the wheels in motion for a famous Supreme Court case, *R. v. Brodie, Dansky and Rubin* (the Brodie case). This was the first obscenity case heard by the Supreme Court after Bill C–58. The court ruled that the book was *not* obscene, by a 5-4 decision; the fundamental split in the court was reflected in the fact that seven different judgments were issued. The court's problem was whether to consider Parliament's new definition of obscenity to be exhaustive; four judges held that the Hicklin test was excluded under the new section, two held that the Hicklin test *might* still apply, and three reserved judgment. The court also struggled over the interpretation of the phrase 'undue exploitation' and Fulton's depiction of 'tolerable' standards; what emerged from this case was the idea of a *'community standard of acceptance,'* as enunciated by Justice Judson:

> Surely the choice of the courts is clear cut. Either the judge instructs himself or the jury that undueness is to be measured by his or their personal opinion and even that must be subject to some influence from contemporary standards — or the instruction must be that the tribunal of fact should consciously attempt to apply these standards. Of the two, I think that the second is the better choice.[18]

Operative meaning was given to the idea of a community standards test in a 1963-64 case (*R. v. Dominion News and Gift Ltd.*):

> The standards are not those set by those of lowest taste or interest. Nor are they set by those of rigid, austere, conservative or puritan taste or habit of mind. Something approaching a general average of thinking and feeling has to be discerned.[19]

son,"[28] and proposed separate criminal sanctions against child pornography. The committee also recommended the *requirement* of trial by jury in pornography cases, to ensure the application of local community standards, and to make inadmissible the use of 'expert' testimony to establish these community standards.[29]

Speaking to the report in the House of Commons, MacGuigan noted that the recommendations were "particularly aimed at bringing the woman's point of view into our law in this area for the first time...that was our purpose in introducing the concept of the degradation of the human person."[30] This new and feminist approach to the definition of pornography was one that would continue to inform judicial decisions in this area (viz., the Towne Cinema (1974), Rankine (1984), Ramsingh (1984) and Wagner (1985) cases).

Justice Minister Basford appeared before the committee, and expressed reservations about the approaches to pornography taken in the private members' bills. In particular, he argued that

> It is...our duty...neither to fetter freedom of speech nor to impose the taste of one segment of the community upon another segment...if you are going to write a code that tries to define in explicit language every sort of act that would corrupt, or morally corrupt, you would first have a very long list and you would undoubtedly exclude conduct that should be included.

In general, he agreed that child pornography was a matter that needed legislative attention but, for the rest, stricter enforcement of the present Criminal Code provisions would suffice.[31] Later, speaking to the report in the House of Commons, he expressed concern about a number of recommendations, including the necessity of trial by jury and the inadmissibility of expert evidence.[32]

In November 1978, Basford introduced legislation to alter Canada's obscenity laws. Bill C–21 was the first of five legislative proposals that would be introduced on pornography over the next decade, and was an omnibus bill dealing with rape, prostitution, child abuse, and loansharking as well as with pornography. The bill followed the MacGuigan committee's report in three ways:

§   it introduced harsh prohibitions against child pornography;
§   it recast the definition of pornography to include 'undue degradation of the human person';
§   it 'uncoupled' sex from violence in the definition of obscenity.

Bill C–21 did not receive wide media or public attention, although it did generate a certain amount of controversy. Alan Borovoy, general counsel for the Canadian Civil Liberties Association, maintained that the bill was repressive:

> The key problem is that it goes far beyond the sexual component of obscenity. They talk about undue exploitation, but that gives rise to the question of what is due degradation of the human person.

The bill was also criticized for its vague language and its failure to specify what would be considered to be criminal. As well, there was concern that the bill created a potential for encouraging overzealous prosecutions of sexually explicit material.[33] Some feminists agreed with the overall philosophy of the bill, but criticized its definition of obscenity for being far too broad as it did not distinguish between pornography and erotica.[34]

The merits and demerits of Bill C–21 were not given parliamentary scrutiny, as the legislation was never debated in the House of Commons or sent to committee for study. Legislative time was running out for the Liberal government, which anticipated an election in 1979. It had critical legislation that it wanted to pass before then, particularly revisions to the Bank Act. In this context, pornography remained low on the government's list of priorities. Over the next decade this would become a familiar pattern: legislation would be introduced but neither debated nor passed into law.

In December 1977, the Toronto newspaper *Body Politic* was charged under the obscenity laws for publishing an article entitled "Men Loving Boys Loving Men." For the next six years the issue was fought out in court, as the Ontario government waged a campaign against the gay newspaper. In the first of its three acquittals, Justice J. Sydney Harris argued in February 1979 that "Parliament has failed to provide the court with sufficiently precise guidelines to enable the court to come to any conclusion as to what would be guilty conduct." The courts, he concluded, should not be placed in the position of having to determine what is moral or immoral.[35] For many, this case abundantly illustrated why the Criminal Code provisions on obscenity needed amending and tightening.

In December 1980, the Liberals were returned to power after the short Conservative interregnum in 1979. The government announced plans to study one aspect of the issue. The Committee on Sexual Offences Against Children and Youth was commissioned by the ministers of Justice and Health and Welfare. Chaired by a University of Toronto sociologist, Robin Badgley, the committee included representatives of social, health, and youth services, women's groups, psychiatry, and the law. It was directed to investigate the extent of sexual exploitation and abuse of children (including child pornography) and to examine the adequacy of laws in this area. The Badgley Committee took almost four years to complete its work and to issue a report.

Long before this, the Liberal government proposed changes to the Criminal Code to deal with child pornography. Responding to mounting public pressures, Justice Minister Jean Chrétien in January 1981 introduced Bill C–53 which, like Bill C–21 before it, was an omnibus bill that dealt with an extensive array of Criminal Code matters of which the child pornography section was only a small ingredient. The bill proposed to change the existing Criminal Code to specify child pornography as a criminal offence. The minister argued that "children are innocent victims of vicious people. They cannot protect themselves and we have to protect them." He also maintained that child pornography resulted in child abuse. The prohibitions on child pornography were quite harsh, and were designed to send a clear message to the public and to the courts.[36]

The bill did not receive second reading for a year, and in December was sent on to the House of Commons Committee on Justice and Legal Affairs. The committee heard from the usual array of expert and interest group witnesses, from women's groups to police and legal associations, from periodical distributors to federal and provincial bureaucrats. The proposal generated a considerable amount of criticism. The vagueness of the bill's language was criticized, particularly the phrase 'sexually explicit conduct.' Judicial difficulties were predicted in dealing with material involving actors and models who *appeared* to be less than 16 years of age but were older. It was anticipated that artistic and socially acceptable material like Franco Zefferelli's film version of *Romeo and Juliet* could be censored. Some critics maintained that child pornography legislation was being used as a 'Trojan horse' to pass tougher obscenity laws. Others pointed to the fact that child pornography was not extensive in Canada and could be dealt with under the existing Criminal Code provisions.[37]

The issue came to a head in the committee hearings on 15 July. Chrétien accused Committee members of not really wanting to deal with child pornography. Concern over 'legal interpretation' of vague language was brushed aside by the minister with the comment that "I know child pornography when I see it." "If you want to have child pornography in every goddam store," he said, "it is your business. I want to take it out. You vote for it. I will vote against it". With that, he stormed out of the committee room. [38] The committee never completed consideration of the amendments or issued a report, as, once Chrétien left the committee meeting, the bill was dead. The government ultimately withdrew the bill.

Despite these continuing legislative failures, two fairly dramatic events kept pornography in the spotlight. In early 1981, a chain of 13 adult video stores was established in British Columbia with the evocative name *Red Hot Video*. This set the stage for a heated battle in the province over what kinds of sexually explicit films should be available for public sale and consumption. The battle turned nasty in the fall of 1982, when two of the video outlets became red hot indeed — they were burned down. Responsibility was claimed by a group called the *Wimmin's Fire Brigade*, which issued the following manifesto:

> Red Hot Videos sells tapes that show wimmin [sic] and children being tortured, raped and humiliated. We are not the property of men to be used and abused. Red Hot Video is part of a multi-billion dollar pornography industry that teaches men to equate sexuality with violence. Although the tapes violate the Criminal Code of Canada and the British Columbia guidelines on pornography, all legal attempts to shut down Red Hot Videos have failed because the justice system was created and controlled by rich men to protect their profits and property.
>
> As a result, we are left no viable alternatives but to change the situation ourselves through illegal means. This is an act of self-defence against hate propaganda.[39]

In early January 1983 a coalition of 45 women's groups made a formal complaint to the British Columbia ombudsman over the failure of the BC government to take action against violent pornography.[40]

The other widely publicized event that kept pornography on the political agenda was the First Choice/Playboy incident in 1983. First Choice had been issued a licence by the Canadian Radio-Television and Telecommunications Commission (CRTC) to establish a pay-TV channel. In January 1983 it announced that it had contracted with Playboy productions to produce 'soft-core' pornographic films for its subscribers. This feature of First Choice's programming had not been presented during the CRTC licence hearings. There was immediate and intense negative reaction to this announcement, led principally by women's groups. Demonstrations were organized in ten cities, protests were lodged with Communications Minister Francis Fox, and women were encouraged to boycott Eaton's (which was involved in Baton Broadcasting which in turn had an interest in First Choice). Communications Minister Fox initially lambasted First Choice for its decision, then softened his position, warning critics that a distinction had to be made between 'adult programming' and pornography. Fox wrote the cable companies, warning them to police themselves or else face the possibility of stiffer government regulation. He admitted that the government had no means of preventing the telecast of erotic films that did not transgress the obscenity laws. The CRTC insisted that the industry develop a 'voluntary code of ethics,' to ensure that cable stations would not transmit films containing gratuitous violence against women. First Choice and other companies defended themselves by articulating the principles of freedom of speech while suggesting that no one would be forced to watch these films. But it agreed to develop a code of ethics. A year later, these voluntary guidelines were yet to be set. Indeed, by early 1984 the CRTC announced that it would not impose any new anti-pornography regulations, for fear of toppling the fledgling and apparently struggling pay-TV industry. Women's groups were outraged. On 18 January the Canadian Coalition Against Media Pornography staged nation-wide noon-hour demonstrations on this issue.[41]

While the Red Hot Video and First Choice incidents generated increased support for tougher anti-pornography laws, other events had countervailing effects. In 1981, the National Film Board released a film entitled *Not a Love Story: A Film About Pornography*. The NFB had established a separate division (Studio D) in 1974 to make documentaries from a feminist point of view. *Not a Love Story* was one of the results. Directed by Bonnie Sherr Klein and produced by Dorothy Todd Henaut, the film explored pornography explicitly and graphically from a feminist perspective. It ran into difficulties with the Ontario Censor Board (OCB), which had become increasingly assertive and interventionist in this period. The OCB's actions were challenged by the Ontario Film and Video Appreciation Society (OFAVAS), a group with anti-censorship and feminist positions. In 1982, the OCB refused to allow screening of a number of films at an OFAVAS event, which led the latter to take the Censor Board to court. OFAVAS won its battle all the way up to the provincial Supreme Court, on the grounds that the OCB's powers were unconstitutional. This led the Ontario government to write a far more precise censorship law and to rename the OCB as the Ontario Film and Video Review Board (OFVRB). More recently, in August 1988, the Ontario government amended its Theatres Act to exempt film festivals and institutions like art galleries from having films cleared by the OFVRB.

Throughout 1983, it was widely anticipated that the government would introduce anti-pornography legislation. In the Throne Speech debate, Justice Minister MacGuigan commented that

> We do not have the weapons in our current sexually oriented concept of obscenity to deal with forms of expression that are fundamentally degrading to the individuality, the integrity, and indeed the personality of victims.

He announced plans to change the Criminal Code to deal with "degrading expressions which are fundamentally opposed to the values of our society," noting that the "heart of the problem is the definition of obscenity itself." Perhaps controversially, he concluded that "I don't think it's possible to have a satisfactory definition of obscenity which departs from community standards — because what else are you going to use?"[42] In October 1983 there was all-party agreement to study the problem of radio and television pornography. Stimulated by Lynn McDonald's introduction of a private member's bill to amend the Broadcasting Act, the House of Commons Communications and Culture Committee called witnesses and studied the issue. [43]

In May 1983, MacGuigan announced that he planned to create a committee to examine the issues of pornography and prostitution. On 23 June 1983, the Special Committee on Pornography and Prostitution was established, chaired by Paul Fraser, the respected former head of the Canadian Bar Association. Its seven members included experts on the law, family, prisons, and women. With respect to pornography, its mandate was "to consider the problems of access to pornography, its effects, and what is considered to be pornographic in Canada...to ascertain public views on ways and means to deal with [pornography]...to consider alternatives, report findings, and recommend solutions...."[44] The committee released a discussion paper in December and carried out extensive public hearings throughout Canada in the first half of 1984. Fraser admitted at the outset that "there may not be a legal solution to these problems...There is a widespread divergence of opinion as to solutions."[45] The Fraser Committee did not issue its report until February 1985, after the Liberals had lost power to the Conservatives.

Private groups continued to call for stricter anti-pornography measures. For example, a statement was read from the pulpits of all Anglican churches in November 1983, calling on the government to pass tougher restrictions and suggesting that church members boycott stores that sold pornographic material. Bishop Lackey, chairman of the church's continuing education committee, noted that pornography was rampant in Germany before the rise of Hitler.[46]

On 7 February 1984 — a year before the Fraser Committee issued its report — Justice Minister MacGuigan introduced Bill C–19, which included his long-awaited changes to the Criminal Code sections on pornography. As with Bills C–21 and C–53, the Criminal Law Reform Act was an omnibus bill. It was 300 pages long, and included sections on drunk driving, drug trafficking, fraud, and prostitution as well as pornography. With respect to pornography, Bill C–19 contained a new definition of obscenity:

> For the purposes of this Act, any matter or thing is obscene where a dominant characteristic of the matter or thing is the undue exploitation of any one or more of the following subjects, namely, sex, violence, crime, horror or cruelty, through degrading representations of a male or female person or in any other manner.

This definition tracked what appeared to be an emerging consensus that pornography should be considered as something that dehumanized or degraded human beings. The definition also disentangled sex and violence so that something could be considered pornographic even though it had no sexual content. Both features of the definition generated a certain degree of criticism. The terms 'degradation' and 'dehumanization' were seen to be so vague that too many materials would be open to prosecution. Moreover, some critics noted that most 'horror' movies presented violent scenes with no sexual content, and they wondered if these would be prosecuted under the proposed Criminal Code provisions. There was also criticism that the introduction of Bill C–19 preempted the work of the Fraser Committee.[47]

Once again, the merits and demerits of MacGuigan's proposals were not rehearsed in Parliament or scrutinized in committee. On 9 July 1984 Prime Minister Turner announced that a federal election would be held in September. Bill C–19 never proceeded to second reading.

Over the decade 1975–1984, the issue of pornography was scrutinized and debated. Despite a distinct shift in ideological mood, despite increasing social concerns about degrading and child pornography, despite the Liberal government's apparent commitment to toughen anti-pornography measures, the Criminal Code provisions on obscenity in 1984 remained the same as they had been 25 years earlier when Davie Fulton proposed Bill C–58.

REACTION AGAINST PORNOGRAPHY —
ROUND TWO: THE MULRONEY GOVERNMENT

In a feature story in October 1984, *Maclean's* predicted that the debate over pornography would heat up under the Conservatives. Polls showed public support for curbs on pornography, but Canadians were purchasing and viewing pornographic material at an increasing rate. All the while, pornography was becoming an increasingly divisive issue. Conservatives and Liberals were divided on the question of free speech and the state's responsibility in moral matters. Women were divided between those who saw pornography as debasing women and those who saw its control as potentially increasing the powers of the state in a dangerous way.[48]

It was widely anticipated that the Conservative government would quickly introduce tough or even harsh anti-pornography measures. The Conservatives had endorsed, in broad measure, the neo-conservative strategy pursued by the Reagan and Thatcher governments in the United States and the United Kingdom. This strategy included reviving traditional values, from the work ethic to family life, in the effort to generate increased economic initiative and growth. Whatever its economic or industrial merits, pornography was seen by the Conservatives as an offence to the moral standards of the community and a challenge to the traditional family unit.

As Opposition leader, Brian Mulroney had enquired of the Liberal government, "what about immediate action to tighten anti-pornography laws?"[49] Once elected, the Conservative government declared that it gave "high priority to support and strengthen the Canadian family, which is the cornerstone of our society" and planed to introduce measures "to control pornography and sexually abusive broadcasting."[50] Prime Minister Mulroney promised to take "whatever legislative steps are necessary to define and control pornography...swiftly and decisively,"[51] a commitment which Justice Minister Crosbie later stated "will certainly be carried out."[52] A year later, the Throne Speech reiterated this commitment, and the Prime Minister himself articulated the relationship between pornography and the family:

> Our Canadian family is the cornerstone of all decent social initiatives. The Canadian family will be defended in this Parliament by this government, at all times and in all circumstances....With more threats to the fabric of our family life, it is the government's duty to act in response. That is why we will be moving in this session against pornography, child abuse and drug abuse.[53]

Before proceeding to introduce legislation, the government inherited two reports from the previous Liberal administration. As is so often the case, one government commissioned a study or report, and a different government received it, because the study or commission process can take so long (which might actually have been the purpose in commissioning the study in the first place). Depending on its content, the report can bring either good or bad news for the government that did not commission it. While the Badgley Report was useful to the government, the Fraser Report was troublesome.

The Badgley Committee on Sexual Offences Against Children and Youths issued its report[54] in August 1984 during the election campaign, and the timing lessened its potential impact. It recommended that there should be a specific Criminal Code prohibition against child pornography, defending this position as follows:

> The justification for the stringent legal regulation of child pornography is the state's transcendent interest in protecting and fostering the well-being of its children and in punishing and deterring criminal conduct which is inimical to their well-being.

Child pornography was seen to have a special character, "the circumstances of its production, namely the sexual exploitation of young persons," and this required a separate proscription. Its recommendations followed along the lines of the MacGuigan Report and Chrétien's Bill C–19, including tightening of federal regulations (customs, broadcasting) and increasing the capacity of law enforcement agencies. The committee's approach was tough and was very much in tune with the Conservative government's ideological orientation. The area of 'criminalization' was quite widely established; even simple possession of certain material could be considered as an offence. Certain terms remained vague and morally informed, such as the use of the word 'lewd.' In general, though, the committee took the approach of 'spelling things out' — an accounting was given of what 'sexual activity' comprised. The committee also recommended that strict restrictions be placed on young people's accessibility to pornography. Specifically, it recommended that the Criminal Code be amended to prohibit accessibility and sale of pornographic materials to those under 16 years of age. These materials would include magazines, videos and sex aids. Vendors of visually explicit material would have to cover and seal materials or else be charged.

While the recommendations of the Badgley Committee were useful for the Conservatives, the report of the Fraser Committee offered good news and bad news. The committee performed a thorough job of producing a substantial report (see Inset IV. p. 130). Its recommendations combined liberal, feminist and conservative concerns, although no one ideological group would be happy with the total package. The recommendations reflected public

THE FRASER COMMITTEE

The Special Committee on Pornography and Prostitution examined the *availability and use* of sexually explicit materials, and discovered that one of nine Canadians over 18 years of age had purchased an 'adult entertainment magazine' in the past year; a further three of ten had looked at one; one out of eight adult Canadians had purchased or rented an adult-only video in the past year; half of the population had seen television with nudity or sex in the previous year; Penthouse and Playboy magazines have monthly sales of 500,000 and 300,00 respectively.[55] With respect to pornography's *impact* it wrote:

> ...we have to conclude, very reluctantly, that the available research is of very limited use in addressing these questions...The Committee is not prepared to state, solely on the basis of the evidence and research it has seen, that pornography is a significant causal factor in the commission of some forms of violent crime, in the sexual abuse of children, or in the disintegration of communities and society.[56]

Its hearings had demonstrated the *absence of social consensus* on the question of pornography, with a variety of women's organizations, churches and church groups, community organizations, education associations, and police and municipal officials in favour of stricter regulations, while other women's groups, civil liberties associations, professional representatives of the film and video business, distributors, and gay rights organizations were against censorship.[57]

Its recommendations were informed by a well-considered *philosophical discussion*, which attempted to balance liberal 'freedom of expression' concerns with feminist 'equality' goals. On the one hand,

> We see the zone of no regulation (of pornography) as that where...conduct does not coerce others;[58]

On the other hand, pornography law

> must be founded upon the rights of women and men to legal, social and economic equality...We agree with the argument that the phenomena of pornography...[is] at least [a] reflection of perceptions that women are inferior, and that men can expect women to be available to service their sexual needs.... We believe that Canada should be ready, collectively, to reject the view of women that is involved in much contemporary pornography.59

It adopted a *conceptually different approach* to pornography as the basis for Criminal Code amendments:

> [Our] emphasis on equality will...require a shift from the traditional focus on immorality as a basis of criminal prohibitions...[to] a theory that views pornography as an assault on human rights...Our recommendations are..to create offences not on concepts of sexual immorality but rather on the offences to equality, dignity, and physical integrity which we believe are involved in pornography.[60]
>
> In the same way that freedom of expression may not extend to statements wilfully promoting hatred, or be outbalanced by the need to protect the equality

rights of others, so the same conclusions can be reached in the case of certain forms of pornographic representation. We believe this to be so in particular in those cases in which the pornographic representation depicts a particular group, typically women, as less than human, and their mistreatment as a legitimate subject of sexual stimulation, typically male.... In our opinion the most hateful forms of pornography are subversive of policies and values favouring equality.[62]

Its recommendations embraced a two-pronged strategy, which reflected a diminished concern about 'moral corruption' and an increased concern with 'degradation and denial of human dignity'; the committee proposed to increase criminal sanctions against the latter (violent and degrading pornography) while decreasing criminal sanctions and decriminalizing the former (other, non-violent depictions of sexual activity); it distinguished 'three tiers' of pornography, with varying criminal sanctions:[62]

Tier One

§ visual representations of children under 18 participating in sexual activity, and material which advocates, encourages, condones, or presents as normal the sexual abuse of children;

§ visual pornographic material that was produced in such a way that actual physical harm is caused to the participants;

§ no defences based on artistic merit, educational or scientific merit;

§ penalties of up to five years for producers and distributors of pornography causing physical harm; up to two years for its rental or sale;

§ penalties of ten years for producers and distributors of child pornography and five years for its sale or rental.

Tier Two

§ matter that depicts or describes sexually violent behaviour, bestiality, incest, or necrophilia. Sexually violent behaviour includes sexual assault, and physical harm depicted for the apparent purpose of causing sexual gratification or stimulation to the viewer, including murder, assault, or bondage of another, or self-infliction of physical harm;

§ availability of defences of artistic merit and artistic or scientific purpose;

§ penalties of five years for producers and distributors of sexually violent and degrading material; penalties of up to two years for its rental or sale or display without notice;

Tier Three

§ a criminal sanction would only apply to these materials when displayed to the public without a warning as to their nature or made accessible to people under age 18;

§ material includes visual pornographic materials in which are depicted vaginal, oral, or anal intercourse, masturbation, lewd touching of the breasts or the genital parts of the body or the lewd exhibition of the genitals, but no portrayal of a person under 18 or sexually violent pornography is included.

§ less onerous criminal sanctions.

The Committee also recommended that civil rights protection should be enacted that would consider pornography to be a form of 'hatred' and to include 'sex' as an identifiable group in the Criminal Code prohibitions on hate literature. [63]

anxiety about the increasingly violent quality of pornography. At the same time, they reflected liberal values that insisted that the state should not interfere in individual choices that appeared to cause no harm to others. (The committee had concluded that no link had been established between pornography and anti-social behaviour.) In stark terms, only degrading and violent (hard-core) pornography was to be subject to (increased) criminal sanction. The rest (soft-core pornography and erotica) was to be decriminalized, unless it was displayed improperly or without warning. This was to be accomplished by creating three tiers of materials, with criminal sanctions changing from tier to tier. While the Conservative government could and would accept the first half of the Fraser formula, it could not and would not accept the second half.

It is interesting to note the extent to which the Fraser committee was alive to feminist discourse on pornography, particularly that associated with the writings and activities of Jillian Riddington, Helen Longino, Catharine MacKinnon, and Andrea Dworkin.[64] The Committee more or less approved of Longino's definition of pornography as

> verbal or pictorial material which represents or describes sexual behaviour that is degrading or abusive to one or more of the participants in such a way as to endorse the degradation.[65]

The committee stopped well short of recommending that *all* degrading or dehumanizing representations of women be criminalized. While it was sympathetic to the feminist claim that vast quantities of everyday media and advertising presented false depictions of women, it concluded that criminalization of this material would simply overwhelm the law (bringing it into disrepute) while potentially leading to the curtailing of freedom of speech. The Fraser Committee concluded that the law should criminalize in a precise way those areas of pornography that could be effectively prohibited by the law. As for the rest, other forms of social control would have to be devised.[66]

The Courts and the Curious Case of Canada Customs

The Fraser Committee report neutralized the momentum for tightening anti-pornography law; its conclusions and recommendations did not mesh well with a government committed to tough anti-pornography measures. Through 1985 and early 1986, the government continued to consider the issue and study the Fraser Committee report. While no legislative initiatives were forthcoming, a law did exist even though it was seen by many to be inadequate. And that law continued to be applied by police, customs, and the courts.

The Supreme Court case *Towne Cinema v. R.* (1985) illustrated one of the fundamental problems in applying Section 159(8) of the Criminal Code. An Alberta movie house was charged and convicted of obscenity for showing the movie *Dracula Sucks*. The Alberta Court of Appeal upheld the conviction but, after an appeal to the Supreme Court, a new trial was ordered. The court was split on the question of the now-crucial 'community standards.' Chief Justice Dickson's view prevailed:

> The task is to determine in an objective way what is tolerable in accordance with the contemporary standards of the community as a whole and not merely to project one's own personal ideas of what is tolerable...Here, the trial judge had wrongly applied a standard of taste in holding that the majority of the community would feel the same revulsion for this film as he did.

Dickson maintained that the court ought to consider which audience would be viewing the film. Justice Bertha Wilson disagreed with this orientation, and agreed with the previous opinion of an Ontario County Court judge:

> In my opinion, contemporary community standards would tolerate the distribution of films which consist substantially of scenes of people engaged in sexual intercourse. Contemporary community standards would also tolerate the distribution of films which consist of scenes of lesbian sex, group sex, fellatio, cunnilingus and anal sex. However, films which consist substantially of or partially of scenes which portray violence and cruelty in conjunction with sex, particularly where the performance of indignities degrades and dehumanizes the people upon whom they are performed, exceed the level of community tolerance.[67]

The courts struggled to make concrete the slippery and elusive notion of community standards. All the while, they pushed back the frontiers of acceptability of sexually explicit material. But they were not alone in determining and changing the law as they implemented it. Another agency of the state created law as it implemented the Criminal Code statutes on obscenity — Canada Customs.

For example, in December 1983, customs officials seized the entire shipment of that month's edition of *Penthouse* as it was entering Canada. In response to a question in the House of Commons about the matter, Minister of National Revenue Perrin Beatty stated:

> The government will do everything possible to ensure that violent

pornography is not imported into Canada. What I found distressing in this instance was the suggestion that it was appropriate to have naked women bound in ropes hanging from trees, and that it was considered art work. It is not art work, and there is no place whatsoever for this sort of material in Canada.[68]

This case highlighted two phenomena. First, almost all of the hard-core pornographic material purchased in Canada is imported, about 85 percent from the United States. Only about 3 percent is domestically produced. Second, historically the most effective way of prohibiting pornography has been to prevent it from being imported into Canada. Canada Customs has played as critical a role as the courts, and a more important role than Parliament, in establishing the effectivness of Canada's pornography laws (see Inset V). Customs has the capacity to examine only 7 percent of persons and 5 percent of goods crossing the border. Nonetheless, from 1978 to 1982, there were 7,700 seizures or detentions of material considered to be 'indecent' or 'immoral'. In the first half of 1984, there were 223 cases involving 1,083 items. The moderate number of cases recently reflects the impact of a system of voluntary restrictions. Regular importers of sexually explicit material often voluntarily present to the Prohibited Importation Unit advance copies of material about to be imported. The unit then offers a judgment in advance. If the judgment is positive, this allows the importer to send the material across the border with confidence. If the judgment is negative, or if the unit points out a specific but limited number of 'problems,' then the importer can react accordingly; the material might not be imported, or material can be 'adjusted' (pages torn out, certain material blacked out, or whatever). This is more or less regular procedure for mass market publications such as Playboy and Penthouse, and the process saves them considerable bother and expense. Local field officials carry out investigation of material and enforcement of the guidelines at points of entry like border crossings and airports. When there is uncertainty about the status of certain material, it is sent off to the Prohibited Importation Unit in Ottawa. An importer who wants to appeal a decision made at the field level can have a 'commodity specialist' at the regional level review the case and make a decision. If the original decision is upheld, an appeal can then be made to the deputy minister and, finally, to the courts. These last steps are, of course, prohibitively expensive.[69]

This process is not especially satisfactory from the perspectives of the principles of objectivity and consistency: its results are subjective and uneven (see Inset VI). In the late 1950s, Minister of National Revenue George Nowlan commented on this process:

I really think that we are much better qualified to deal with increasing the seasonal tariff on cabbages and cucumbers than to pass moral judgment on literature coming into this country.

I do not think that the tariff board is necessarily the best judge of impurity in books and literature. Perhaps I could say that the courts are not either, but someone has to take the responsibility.[73]

It was Customs that effectively prevented James Joyce's *Ulysses* and other classics from being available in Canada for decades.

This process was substantially weakened as a result of a judicial decision. In 1985, Tom Luscher tried to import a 40 page copy of *Flying High — Gourmet Edition*. The item was seized by customs, and Luscher appealed the ruling at the regional level, then to the deputy minister, and finally to the Federal Court of Appeal. The court overturned the ruling, maintaining that the customs regulations of the Tariff Act were too vague and subjective to qualify as 'reasonable limits' on press freedom under the Charter of Rights (Section 2b). As a result of this judicial decision, for a short time there were no prohibitions on the importing of any pornographic material. The government moved quickly to remedy this situation. Bill C–38 was introduced to restore to customs officials the authority to stop pornography at the border. Tariff Item 99201-1 of Schedule C to the Customs Tariff was eliminated and replaced by more precise and specific reference to existing Criminal Code provisions on obscenity, particularly Section 159(8). In anticipation of new anti-pornography legislation, a 'sunset' clause was placed on the bill, whose provisions would expire on 30 June 1986. The bill required only two hours of debate and moved from first reading to Royal Assent in three days. Subsequent results have varied, but the fact remains that Customs has the continuing authority to ban books from entering Canada.

Crosbie' Bill C–114: The Conservative's First Try

A Gallup poll released in July 1985 showed that Canadians were divided on the issue. The legalized sale of 'explicit pornography' was favoured by 57 per cent of Canadians, with 36 per cent against. The issue also divided Canadians along lines of sex: 67 per cent of men were in favour of the sale of pornographic material, but women were split half and half.[74] Regardless of what was happening in the judicial, legislative and executive areas, decisions about pornography were being made in society. On the one hand, Canadians were voting with their wallets, as the pornography industry thrived. On the other hand, 'self-regulatory' devices began to appear. For example, in April 1986 the 7-Eleven chain of convenience stores in Canada announced that it was discontinuing the sale of Playboy and Penthouse magazines. This followed Moral Majority leader Jerry Falwell's 'deterrence strategy': "Our goal is to make it [the case] that to buy one of Hugh Hefner's magazines, you're going to have to go to Sleazetown."[75]

In September 1985, Justice Minister Crosbie promised that legislation

CUSTOMS AND PORNOGRAPHY

The Customs and Excise Branch of Revenue Canada is given authority by Section 14 of the Customs Act to prohibit the importation of various materials listed in Schedule C number 99201-1, as follows: "books, printed paper, drawings, paintings, prints, photographs, or representations of any kind of treasonable or seditious, or of an immoral or indecent character."

This part of the Act is implemented by the Prohibited Importation Unit of the Department of National Revenue.[70] The Unit compiles an index of prohibited material, which is updated monthly. In 1980, there were 35,000 items in this index. The Unit is guided by Section 159(8) of the Criminal Code in determining what is to be prohibited as works of "an indecent or immoral character." More specific guidelines are set and periodically updated by the ministry to help the Unit in its work, but these guidelines have no legal status. In the early postwar period the infamous 'G' list gave a long and detailed account of what was to be prohibited from entry, and also offered 'rules of thumb' to assist customs officials. For example, paragraph 6 of G-2 suggested that "examination of calendar pictures...should be made with the realization that they are likely to be on display for a full year and a higher standard would be required."[71]

The following were the guidelines used in the 1970s and 1980s:[72]

The following material will be dealt with at field level for initial classification and will be prohibited:

§   i)Illustrated material containing hard-core pornographic pictures which lewdly and explicitly display the male and female sexual organs, sexual intercourse, sexual perversions and such acts, including bestiality;

§   ii)Reading material, containing explicit hard-core fictional text dedicated entirely to sexual exploitation and containing no redeeming features. The primary source of material of this character is the paperback...

The following material will be referred to headquarters for initial classification:

§   iii)...the so-called 'grey areas,' with illustrations depicting similar subjects to those described in 2 (i) but in a less explicit fashion with emphasis,

would be introduced before Christmas; in March 1986, he promised to introduce legislation in April; in the interim periods, he promised tough — much tougher — legislation against pornography because "I do not believe that the expanded commercial exploitation of sex reflects contemporary attitudes and values in Canada."[76]

Crosbie's legislation was finally introduced on 10 June 1986. Bill C–114, An Act to amend the Criminal Code and the Customs Tariff, was different from the Liberal government's legislative attempts to deal with pornography.

§ however, mainly on sexual activities and apparently designed to appeal in the same way as hard-core type pornography. In this category are the pseudo or so-called "nudist" and "film" magazines which make pretensions to being bona fide but which include lewd or other pornographic displays.

§ iv)Any publication which despite its format or alleged scientific, medical or artistic purposes appears to be in essence an indecent or immoral publication in disguise.

Generally speaking, items which do not fall within the foregoing categories may be allowed to be imported including the so-called 'naughty' or 'spicy' girlie type magazines where the models are partially clad so that the genitals are not exposed and perversions are not depicted. Cultural and educational publications and bona fide nudist magazines, although illustrated with nude males or females but not including indecent poses or over-emphasis of the sexual organs, are also considered admissible...

Inset VI
THE UNPREDICTABILITY OF CUSTOMS

In early 1986 customs banned Charles Silverstein's *The Joy of Gay Sex*, because the book depicted acts of 'sodomy,' which were prohibited under its guidelines. The Glad Day Bookshop appealed this decision and won. In December, customs officials examined a shipment of 811 books destined for Little Sisters, a gay bookstore in Vancouver, detaining 379 of them, including *Hot Studs: Homo Encounters*; *Meat: How Men Look, Act, Talk, Walk, Dress*; *The Joy of Gay Sex*; and the 19th century homoerotic novel *Teleny*. It also seized Jean Genet's *Querelle*; Allen Ginsberg's *Straight Hearts Delight*; Richard Plant's study of Nazi treatment of gays in World War II, *The Pink Triangle*; and *Erotic Poems from the Greek Anthology*. Little Sisters appealed to the regional office of Revenue Canada, which released only one title, *Best Guide Amsterdam*. Another appeal was launched, this time to the deputy minister, and 27 more titles were released including *The Joy of Gay Sex*, *Teleny*, and *The Gay Touch*. *Fag Rag*, *Surfer Sex*, *Leather Blues*, and *Hard: True Gay Encounters* (volume 2) remained banned. The different results at each stage of the appeal process indicated that the customs process remained unpredictable and subjective. The gay community in particular felt targeted.

The Liberals had presented omnibus bills containing a series of amendments to the Criminal Code in a wide variety of areas. Bill C–114 dealt exclusively with pornography, and other bills would deal with other Criminal Code amendments. The bill moved away from an approach that provided a broad definition of pornography to be applied by the judicial and executive branches, providing a set of quite specific definitions of different categories of pornography. Implementation of the law would involve material being assessed as falling within a particular category (see Inset VII).

This 'categorization' approach bore some resemblance to the Fraser Committee recommendations, as did some of the language of the bill. But the resemblance ended there. Bill C–114 comprised some of the toughest anti-pornography measures in the western world. The Fraser Committee had recommended that only a narrow range of pornography be considered a matter for criminal prohibition; if material was not child-related or violent and degrading, it would be considered perfectly legal, with some restrictions on its display and sale. Crosbie's legislation proposed to make all types of pornography subject to criminal prohibition, and restricted the display of any sort of erotica.

Bill C–114 provided a detailed and exhaustive definition of pornography that implied that anything leading to sexual arousal would be considered pornographic. A puzzling category of 'other sexual activity' seemed designed to ensure that every type of sexual activity known or yet to be discovered would be caught in Bill C–114's net. This detailed approach resulted in a certain degree of bluntness in the categorization of sexual activity. No distinction was made between what might be called 'odd' or 'bizarre' sexual practices and 'mainstream' ones. All types of sexual intercourse, bestiality, and necrophilia were lumped together with lactation and menstruation. No distinction was made between rape and sex between consenting adults. Defence based on artistic and literary merits was allowed in certain categories, but only on a 'reverse onus' footing; defendants would have to establish their innocence in court.

Crosbie had promised tough measures, and he certainly delivered what had been expected of him. His defence of Bill C–114 was as intense as the legislation itself:

> I am not a zealot. I'm not opposed to the erotic, believe me.
> I am, I think, tolerant in this area. [But] this flood of material in the last 15 years has just gone too far. I think public opinion supports far less permissiveness in response to pornography. The pin-up has now become depictions of sodomy, incest, bestiality, sadism, masochism and degrading sexual conduct, and society must act to prevent this going any further. In fact we want to drive back this kind of material from where it now exists.[77]

He brushed aside both 'narrow,' legal concerns about the difficulty of defining pornography and 'liberal' claims that pornography caused no harm:

> A work of artistic merit might be a 60 to 90 minute movie with a story which eventually leads to a bedroom scene. But if it's just a movie of 20 minutes, with two, four, six, ten adults cavorting having intercourse in every conceivable manner without any story, then it's obviously just porn.

People have intercourse with one another in all manners of ways...that's pornography and unfortunately...the greatest customers for this material are those who are more likely to have their attitudes warped by it and this is teenagers between the ages of 13 and 18.[78]

The child pornography measures of Bill C–114 were widely applauded by Canadians and were given all-party support in the House of Commons. Had they been introduced separately, they might very well have been accepted by Parliament. There was, however, little consensus on the other measures in Bill C–114. The police lobby, customs officials, and church and certain women's groups were enthusiastic about the legislation. "We think Crosbie has been very bold and courageous and we intend to support him," declared Brian Still, executive director of the Evangelical Fellowship of Canada. "Maybe some erotica will be caught in the net. But so be it."[79] Conservative pollsters had indicated to Crosbie that there was a 'moral majority' on the pornography issue, and the government's political sense was that the civil libertarians were poorly organized. The Inter-church Committee on Pornography (a subcommittee of the Evangelical Fellowship of Canada) placed effective pressure on the government. It had initiated a massive letter-writing campaign and had gained the support of Tory backbenchers, including the caucus justice committee. Crosbie claimed to have received thousands of letters criticizing the Fraser Committee's decriminalization approach, as well as hundreds of letters supporting Bill C–114. The message from the Conservatives' electoral constituency had been made clear, as it had at an earlier party convention where Crosbie had been politically assaulted for the government's decision to end discrimination against homosexuals in the armed forces.[79]

On the other hand, there was substantially widespread and thorough criticism of the bill, both within Parliament and in the community as a whole. Opposition spokespersons Nunziata (Liberals) and Deans (NDP) attacked the bill for being too broad and for not distinguishing between obscenity and erotica. Civil libertarians called the bill dangerous. Human rights activist Jack London described the bill as the product of "right-wing, fundamentalist, puritanical thought" that "would give a sense of orgasmic ecstasy to Jerry Falwell". Alan Borovoy, general counsel of the Canadian Civil Liberties Association, worried that the legislation would establish the police as arbiters of public taste: "the danger is that its language is broad enough to include actions like kissing, touching and holding." Even women's groups that had supported tougher anti-pornography legislation, like the YWCA and the National Action Committee on the Status of Women (NACSW), spoke out against Bill C–114. "We wanted laws that outlaw the degradation of women," said Reva Dexter of the Vancouver Coalition Against Media Pornography, "We didn't want laws that were going to be Victorian and outlaw healthy human sexuality." Louise Dulude (NACSW) argued that "it seems that they

BILL C–114

The act defined four categories of pornography and a separate category of child pornography:

Pornography that Shows Physical Harm
§ "means any pornography that shows a person in the act of causing or attempting to cause actual or simulated permanent or extended impairment of the body of any person or of its functions";

Degrading Pornography
§ "means any pornography that shows defecation, urination, ejaculation or expectoration by one person onto another, lactation, menstruation, penetration of a bodily orifice with an object, one person treating himself or another as an animal or object, an act of bondage or any act in which one person attempts to degrade himself or another";
§ defence of artistic, scientific, medical grounds allowed, in conjunction with an appropriate warning being displayed to the public;

Violent Pornography
§ "includes sexual assault and any behaviour shown for the apparent purpose of causing sexual gratification to or stimulation of the viewer, in which physical pain is inflicted or apparently inflicted on a person by another person or by the person himself";

Pornography
§ "means any visual matter showing vaginal, anal or oral intercourse, ejacula-

have listened too closely to the religious and fundamentalist groups that are against pornography because they think sex is dirty. They are reaching much too far in the hope of making political capital out of this very issue." "This government has never understood the difference between hate and sex," suggested Maude Barlow, former adviser to Pierre Trudeau on women's issues. Many critics joked nervously about what "other sexual activity" might include, and worried that kissing and hand-holding might become illegal. [80]

Bill C–114 was an ambitious piece of legislation in an area where there was no social consensus. As a general rule, this sort of legislation is not introduced in Canada, where piecemeal, incremental changes are the normal approach to policy. Moreover, governments usually try to avoid entering areas where there is intense social disunion. To pass this type of legislation, particularly in the absence of consensus, is simply too politically divisive and costly to the government, unless it enjoys such an incredibly high degree of authority that it can deflect criticism and controversy. It may have been true that the government was indeed ambitious and threw caution to the wind, underestimating the inevitable negative reaction to the bill. Whatever the case, the divisiveness generated by this legislation overwhelmed whatever authority the government might have had to deal with the issue.

tion, sexually violent behaviour, bestiality, incest, necrophilia, masturbation or other sexual activity.

Different penalties were assigned for each of the categories.

Child Offences

pornographic material is defined as meaning

§   "i (a) any material the dominant contents of which are a description of masturbation or vaginal, anal or oral intercourse; or (b) any matter showing masturbation or vaginal, anal or oral intercourse; or (c)any matter showing or describingi)ejaculation, sexually violent behaviour, bestiality, incest or necrophilia, or

§   (ii) any act referred to in the definition of 'degrading pornography' or of 'pornography that shows physical harm'..."

§   selling or renting such material to a person under the age of 18 is an offence, with a due care and diligence defence allowed, as well as defence on scientific, artistic, or medical grounds;

§   those convicted of involving persons less than 18 in pornographic material, or of importing, distributing or producing material with persons under 18, face sentences up to ten years; conviction for rental or sale of such material involves sentences up to five years;

§   possession of visual material involving persons less than 18 years old engaged in sexual activity is a criminal offence, where sexual activity means "an actual or simulated act of vaginal, oral or anal intercourse, bestiality, masturbation, sexually violent behaviour, exhibition of the breasts or the genitals for a sexual purpose or any act referred to in the definition of "degrading pornography" or of "pornography that shows physical harm";

§   similar penalties for producing or distributing material that shows child sexual abuse.

There were some observers who suggested that the government's action was a public relations gesture. Maude Barlow concluded that the bill had no chance of passing, and stated that "some people might be cynical enough to say they [the government] don't even want it to go through."[81] This view was given some credibility by the introduction of Bill C–111. The purpose of this legislation was to extend the period of effect of Bill C–38, which had been passed the previous year to reassert customs authority over the import of pornography (see p. 135 above). Bill C–111 would extend this temporary coverage until December 1987. This suggested to the NDP in particular that the government was not going to act in haste, if at all, on Bill C–114.[82]

An unusual silence then fell over the issue of pornography in the second half of 1986, as if the intensity of the response to Bill C–114 had consumed all of the passion surrounding the issue. In fact, it turned out to be the silence of a wake for the bill. As the session ended, Bill C–114 died on the order paper, along with 20 other pieces of legislation. Like Jean Chrétien, Mark MacGuigan, Ron Basford and Otto Lang before him, John Crosbie would leave the Justice Department with Criminal Code Section 159(8) intact. On 30 June 1986, Crosbie was transferred to the Department of Transport and replaced by Ramon Hnatyshyn. Just before the shuffle, Crosbie took one last kick at the critics of Bill C–114. In response to an opposition member's assessment that in light of the vehement criticism of the bill it should be withdrawn, Crosbie replied:

> For the first time in 20 years this country has a government not afraid to deal with the question of pornography. We have not appointed some commission or committee on which we may slough off our responsibility. ...I have received hundreds of letters indicating support for our legislation...The Honorable member can be impressed by those who write for the media. We all know their tendencies, in any event...I am prepared to listen to the ordinary people of Canada.[83]

Bill C–54: The Conservatives' Second Try

Over the next year, conditions appeared to be ripe for the reform of Canada's pornography laws. A US commission on pornography issued a two-volume report in July 1986, which failed to prove that pornography was harmful to the public, but nine of the eleven commissioners agreed that "substantial exposure" to pornography "is a cause of sexual violence, sexual coercion and unwanted sexual acts." The commission called for mandatory 20 year terms for second convictions of selling obscene material, prosecution of pornographic film-makers, and state authority to seize the assets of obscenity-related businesses. [84]

In early October, a Gallup poll indicated that two of three Canadians felt Bill C–114 was acceptable or should be stronger; three of five felt that pornography leads to violence against women; half felt that government should censor books, and three of five felt that government should censor films.[85] These results suggested that Canadians were willing to introduce strict regulations in the area of pornography.

Customs officials continued to defend Canada against the introduction of immoral and indecent material. The seizure of books being shipped to Little Sisters Bookstore has already been noted (see Inset VI). In November 1986, Playboy magazine contained a pictorial feature of the punk rock singer Wendy O. Williams jumping from a parachute with her body entangled in the cords. 25,000 copies of the magazine made it across the border before Customs seized the remaining 75,000 copies and turned them back, on the grounds that this was an unacceptable representation of bondage. These copies eventually found their way back to Canada, with the appropriate pages ripped out.

Throughout the winter and spring of 1986-87, there were mixed reports as to the government's legislative intentions. 'Overwhelming numbers of letters of support' for Bill C–114 were apparently received by the government.[86] The Interchurch Committee on Pornography was reported as having

been successful in getting the legislation back on the agenda (the most effective lobby they had ever seen, said some Western MPs), and as having
faith in Justice Minister Hnatyshyn as a 'strong family man'.[87] Against all this,
the Anglican Church announced its view that Bill C–114 was too restrictive.[88]
There were reports that Ottawa was dropping its controversial legislation as
a result of criticisms from civil libertarians, arts associations and women's
groups.[89] And supporters of the legislation expressed concern about the
'fuzzy promises' in the Throne Speech, which suggested a sell-out to civil
libertarians, women's and arts groups, and the central Canadian media.[90]

In October 1986, the Liberal party issued a six-page position paper on
pornography. It attacked the government's legislation for failing to recognize sexuality as a part of life." The paper cautioned against giving too much
discretionary power to limit freedom of expression:

> Any law which gives wide discretion to the police to decide what to
> condone and what to prosecute tends to a police state. The law
> should be ascertainable by reading it and not by consulting police
> about their attitude toward prosecutions.

The Liberal party proposed that policy reflect the recommendations of the
Fraser Committee.[91]

Throughout this period, the government claimed that it would re-intro-
duce anti-pornography legislation. "It is a priority," claimed Justice Minister Hnatyshyn, "I want to go at an early time to my colleagues in cabinet to
see what changes [to Bill C–114] they think might be appropriate. There is
political will to proceed."[92] In the October Throne Speech, the government
reaffirmed its commitment to the family and its intention to take action
against violent pornography; a few days later, Hnatyshyn reiterated that "the
Speech from the Throne underlined the priority which these initiatives take
in the view of the government. I propose to come forward with legislation
at an early date," an assurance made again in January 1987.[93]

In the event, Hnatyshyn's legislation was not introduced until 4 May
1987. Bill C–54, An Act to amend the Criminal Code and other Acts in consequence thereof, was similar to Crosbie's Bill C–114. It presented a similar
set of categories of pornography, with penalties geared to the particular
category. These categories included child pornography, pornography showing physical harm, violent pornography, degrading pornography, 'unnatural'
pornography (bestiality, incest, and necrophilia), and simple pornography
(masturbation, ejaculation, all forms of intercourse). In this, the legislation
was more or less the same as C–114. The 'reverse onus' defence on scientific, medical, or artistic grounds remained. The universally ridiculed
category 'other sexual activity' was dropped. Bill C–54 also included an
amendment to the hate laws, which made sex an 'identifiable group,' as
recommended by the Fraser Committee.

The biggest difference from the earlier bill was the attempt to distinguish between erotica and pornography. Bill C–54 defined erotica as meaning

> any visual matter a dominant characteristic of which is the depiction, in a sexual context or for the purpose of the sexual stimulation of the viewer, of a human sexual organ, a female breast or the human anal region.

This appeared to equate erotica with nudity. The production, distribution or sale of erotic material was not in itself to be considered a criminal offence. Rather,

> Every person who displays any erotica in a way that is visible to a member of the public in a public place, unless the public must, in order to see the erotica, pass a prominent warning notice advising of the nature of the display therein or unless the erotica is hidden by a barrier or is covered by an opaque wrapper, is guilty of an offence punishable on summary conviction.

The display or sale of erotica to a person less than 18 would be considered a criminal offence.

Bill C–54 was only marginally different from Bill C–114. Some of the latter's more obvious defects were eliminated and a touch more subtlety was injected into the categorization of sexually explicit material. Overall, though, Bill C–54 comprised very harsh anti-pornography measures. It rejected the Fraser Committee's recommendation to decriminalize all but violent and child pornography, and continued to treat as criminal all material that generated sexual arousal. After first reading, Hnatyshyn explained to reporters that the government was by no means backing off the attack, and wished to deal 'head on' with pornography:

> What this has to do with is the dissemination of pornography across the country....The legislation is an attempt to bring a balanced approach to this issue, to find out if we want to have this material in the confectioneries and corner stores around the country. This particular legislation tries to...bring precision, clarity, and guidelines...It will mean law-enforcement agencies and crown prosecutors have some basis upon which to understand what is unacceptable material in our society, rather than taking a totally subjective view of what is obscene.[94]

In question period, he defended the bill against criticisms that it was too harsh and all-encompassing:

I do not believe that there is anyone in the House who thinks it is an easy question to define these matters...The Bill is light years ahead of the present law...It is in accordance with the values and traditions which the overwhelming majority of Canadians hold respecting acceptable material.[96]

The immediate reaction to Bill C–54 was similar to that which followed the introduction of Bill C–114. Predictably, right-wing and church groups supported the bill. Lynne Scime, head of REAL women, praised the bill: "Now that Hnatyshyn has said what we wanted him to say, it's up to us to get co-ordinated and urge him to hold firm." The Interchurch lobby group, rural Tory MPs, and most of the federal caucus were elated. There was moderate support for the bill in some quarters, including the women's movement. Louise Dulude, President of the National Advisory Council on the Status of Women, gave qualified praise, particularly for the child pornography measures as well as for the bill's largely overlooked proposal to amend the hate laws to include women as an identifiable group. "We've been asking for this change for years," Dulude stated. [97]

Others were less sanguine about the bill. NDP spokesperson Svend Robinson — who would later declare his homosexuality before the nation — described the bill as a "combination of Jimmy Swaggart and Queen Victoria." Liberal critic Kaplan urged the government to "get away from this idea that all sexuality is pornography," and asked that the child pornography sections, which were widely supported, be separated from the rest of the bill. Critics and even some Conservative MPs worried that the definition of pornography was overly broad. Some claimed that the measures directed at youth were too harsh, as it would be a criminal offence to show a female breast in the presence of a person under 18 years of age. Various arts groups expressed concern that Bill C–54 would seriously endanger the vitality of the arts; these groups included the Playwrights Union of Canada, the Writers Union of Canada, the Association of non-profit Artists Centres, the Alliance of Canadian Theatre and Radio Performers, the Ontario Association of Art Galleries, the Canadian Museums Association, and the Canadian Conference on the Arts. [98]

Canadian historian and author Pierre Berton was one of the bill's harshest critics, launching a personal crusade against the bill. "The rednecks are using a cannon to kill a gnat," he wrote in the *Toronto Star*.[99] Hnatyshyn replied that the bill represented the broad consensus and that the "anything goes philosophy" conflicted with Canada's legal and social traditions (see Inset VIII).[100] Librarians feared that the legislation criminalized as child pornography books that explained sex to teens, 'true to life' books for adolescents that dealt with sexuality (such as Judy Bloom's), books that explained AIDS, and more obvious candidates like Marian Engel's *Bear*, Ayn Rand's *The Fountainhead*, Margaret Atwood's *The Handmaid's Tale*, Margaret

PIERRE BERTON ON BILL C-54

The yahoos and rednecks who run our lives have managed to turn the clock back and inform us that sex is naughty and we must be protected from it...I can see films, photographs and TV crime shows in which men and women shoot each other, knife each other, blow each other up and burn each other alive — as long as they don't do it in a sexual context. But I am forbidden by a new law to watch a man and a woman lying in each other's arms making passionate and explicit love...

Old fashioned censorship is with us again. If the Charlottetown Festival revives *Johnny Belinda*, it will have to plead artistic merit in order to get the rape scene okayed...If you show any sexual activity on the screen or on the stage that involves anybody who looks as if he or she is under 18...it's pornography by definition and the maximum sentence is 10 years. This means that Zefferelli's great film *Romeo and Juliet* will be outlawed as pornographic in Canada. *Blue Velvet* is now by definition pornographic...we adults have been told that we cannot see the...breakthrough film of the year...because the plot hinges on a teenager watching a sexual act.... What librarian will dare to stock *Show Me*, the pictorial sex education book for children? Or *The Joy of Sex*, the pictorial education book for adults?

The new amendments have a darker purpose. They are especially hard on homosexuals. By banning any depiction of masturbation, oral or anal intercourse, they deny the gay community all forms of visual stimulation; and it's a community that is especially vulnerable.

We are all in the hands of...the same people who are now baying for blood in a futile debate over capital punishment.... What they...want to do is return us to the Victorian Age when sex was safely in the closet, to be sniggered at but never to be met honestly...With that moral certitude that places them above the common herd, they operate under...the firm conviction that the depiction of physical love is depraved and...fear that it will stimulate the consumer into passionate acts of wild abandon that most of us would categorize as good, clean fun.

Pierre Berton

Laurence's *The Diviners*, William Golding's *The Lord of the Flies*, and Plato's *Phaedo*. Librarians anticipated that they might either have to create 'adult only' sections in order to protect themselves from prosecution or begin to impose 'self-censorship'.[101]

Hnatyshyn retorted by stating if the law were read closely "they'd find there is absolutely no basis in this concern...If there is an artistic, medical, or scientific purpose to the books, they are completely outside of the pornography law." Richard Mosley, senior general counsel in the criminal and family law policy directorate of the Department of Justice, argued that it was highly unlikely that police would consider charging librarians. "It is a worst case scenario, which is extremely unlikely to happen because the police take direction from the provincial Attorneys General and ultimately the courts."[102] This was small solace to the critics. "Anybody who has lived in the real world for longer than an hour," said Alan Borovoy of the Canadian Civil Liberties Association, "knows that judgments about things like artistic merit are completely subjective." It would be unwise to simply say "trust the

RAY HNATYSHYN'S RESPONSE

Bill C–54....represents the broad consensus in the Canadian public that there is no place for portrayals of child pornography, sexual violence, or degradation in a sexual context...this bill contains provisions which safeguard artistic expression...Mainstream films are not the target of this bill...

This 'anything goes' philosophy is in direct conflict with our legal and democratic tradition which always seeks to preserve a balance between freedom of expression and the protection of human dignity...

The current law has been criticized as being vague, subjective and incapable of equal application across the country. The Fraser committee... found that the present law and penalties...were inadequate.... One of the principles of criminal law...is that [it] should with clarity and precision set forth the conduct declared criminal and the rights and defences available to accused persons....The bill also strikes an appropriate balance between the need to circumscribe the dissemination of vile and exploitative material on the one hand and freedom of expression on the other...

It is important to remember that the police, deciding whether to lay a charge, and the Crown, in deciding when to proceed with a prosecution, would be unlikely to proceed where there is artistic merit....

Another positive feature of Bill C–54 is that it provides a definition of 'erotica'...Some commentators have equated the government's definition of erotica with nudity. This is, quite simply, wrong...Those who claim that statues of nudes will need to be clothed, and that cherubs will need to be painted over, clearly do not understand the bill...

The government has four objectives...: to ensure the dignity of the individual, to strengthen and clarify the law dealing with pornography, to protect our children from gratuitous violence, emotional or physical, to protect people from sexual exploitation.
Justice Minister Ray Hnatyshyn

authorities and assume that the police won't do it." If a 'zealot' pressed charges, it was maintained, a library's defence could only be on reverse onus grounds. The cost of proving innocence on artistic grounds could scare libraries into self-censorship.[103]

A period of six months separated the introduction of the bill from second reading, which did not begin until 26 November and continued on 30 November, 2, 4, and 7 December. When Hnatyshyn spoke during second reading, it was the first parliamentary statement on pornography by a government in almost thirty years. Since Davie Fulton's Bill C–58, debates on pornography policy had essentially taken place outside of the House of Commons as various legislative initiatives failed to progress past first reading.

Hnatyshyn's presentation was predictable but not particularly spirited or thorough. "We are showing leadership on a question of national interest whose solution is not easy to come by," he began, and claimed that "the Canadian public expects a strengthening of the present law, not greater licence to trade in the exploitation of private acts." The minister maintained that the government was following the Fraser Committee report, in treating pornography as a form of hate propaganda and in aiming at "ensuring the dignity of the individual." The strength of Bill C–54 was that it "defines pornography as precisely as possible" and distinguishes it from erotica. The government had responded to the concerns of the artistic community by having the law provide for a defence based on literary or artistic merit. The minister denied that the bill made nudity illegal, and assured art galleries that the cherubs in their paintings need not be painted over. Freedom of speech was defended by Hnatyshyn, so long as it did not cause injury or damage, or exploit or degrade.[104]

The Opposition response was simultaneously generous and critical. The bill's purpose was lauded. "Its aims are honorable and its intents justified," declared Lucie Pépin. Svend Robinson approved the bill's attack on violent, degrading, and child pornography. The NDP's Lynn McDonald stated that "Bill C–54 is an attempt to go in the right direction. At least I give the government credit for wanting to bring in tough and careful legislation."[105]

The government was, however, chastised for fumbling the opportunity. While its aims are acceptable, said Pépin, "its methods are repressive." "Unfortunately, it makes a lot of mistakes," claimed McDonald. The result was that the government had created a "repressive law which takes us back to the Victorian era," declared Pépin. Robinson described the legislation as "a right-wing obscenity...[that] will make Canada the most puritanical country in the Western world." The Opposition criticized the bill's denial of the presumption of innocence; maintained that it created an opportunity for police interference with artistic freedom; insisted that the government was rejecting the Fraser Committee approach ("we can stamp out pornography without getting rid of erotica and sexuality"); pointed to the fact that artistic, women's, and civil liberties groups were against it; and accused the government of paternalism: "It is quite curious that a government which applauds the free market as the best way to allocate the economic pie seems to be deathly afraid of the free market of ideas and expression," observed Liberal Lloyd Axworthy.[106]

The NDP assured the government that "we will support the bill at third reading if we see a good bill because...we really want to get moving on this." The Liberals reacted similarly: "we are willing to cooperate 100 per cent with the government, and make some changes in order to have more effective legislation against pornography."[107]

The government suggested that the Opposition's criticisms could be dealt with in committee, if only the bill were to be given second reading. The Opposition declined to give second reading and go to committee, declaring that it did not trust the government's intentions. It feared that the government would use its huge majority to push Bill C–54 through committee without amendments, as it had done earlier in the hotly contested immigration bill.[108]

Throughout the Opposition's attack on Bill C–54, there were no major government spokespersons or cabinet ministers who came to its defence.

After five days of debate, second reading simply fizzled out. The government chose not to use its majority to push Bill C–54 through second reading to the committee stage. Indeed, C–54 was not been debated in the House after 7 December 1987.

Since then, various groups have continued to protest the legislation. The National Film Board reported that under Bill C–54, *The Decline of the American Empire* or *Not a Love Story* could not have been made or shown.[109] The Art Gallery of Ontario protested the bill by displaying posters beside 38 art works in its collection that it claimed would be affected by Bill C–54.[110] The Book and Periodical Development Council used the "Freedom to Read Week" to spotlight the 'defects' of Bill C–54, and libraries across Canada protested the bill in various walk-outs and demonstrations.[111]

After the Christmas recess, the House of Commons re-adjourned and confronted a dense legislative agenda, which included the refugee bill, indexing of civil servants' pensions, the Atlantic Canada Opportunities Agency, day care, tax reform, tobacco advertising, amendments to the Electoral Act, conflict of interest legislation, official languages legislation, free trade, constitutional changes, and pornography. Backbench Tory MPs continued to press the government to proceed with Bill C–54; 12 petitions were made by Tory MPs between January and May.

In late winter, however, Bill C–54 looked to be in serious jeopardy. With the Supreme Court decision on abortion (see p. 200ff.), a second and apparently more pressing moral issue was jettisoned into the policy agenda. Suddenly pornography was not a top priority. Pornography's move to a back burner reflected emerging divisions in the Tory caucus, particularly between rural and urban MPs. "Nobody is really pushing it," revealed a government source. Hnatyshyn "has done his bit for that element of the party that wants it. At least we can say we introduced it."[112] In response to a loaded question in the House of Commons in May, Hnatyshyn asserted that pornography legislation was still a government priority. [113] However, when the Prime Minister began to talk about the House of Commons sitting all summer, a long list of legislative matters was presented — and the anti-pornography legislation was noticeable by its absence.

In the autumn of 1988, the government finally admitted that it was not going to proceed with Bill C–54. Deputy House leader Douglas Lewis stated: "I think it is fair to say in terms of priorities, proceeding with the porn bill as it is now is not possible because of the controversy surrounding certain parts of the bill." A senior government adviser concluded that "it is a bad piece of legislation. No one wants to know about it." Rev. Hudson Hillesden, chairman of the Interchurch Committee on Pornography, observed that "the government has backed away from the bill because of media attacks. I think it is going to be asked a lot of questions about this. One of these days it is going to have to stand up and bite the bullet."[114]

Bill C–54 was dead. Crippled by criticism and ridicule, it ultimately died of neglect, as the government decided not to use its huge majority to pass the legislation and other matters squeezed it off the policy agenda. Section 159(8) of the Criminal Code had survived its fifth attack.

DISCUSSION

In the real worlds of Canadian politics, many bills fail to pass. Indeed, through the course of a government's four or five years in office, dozens of bills may die on the order paper. The adage 'many are called and few are chosen' is as apt for laws as it is for people. The hard reality is that a government has only a certain amount of legislative time in which to get things done. That is why priorities are set. Important, even pressing, matters may be discussed and studied, and legislation designed. But there is no guarantee that the government will pursue the matter with the time, energy and political resources — or the luck — required to ensure the passing of legislation.

Bills C–114 and C–54 did not command the government's commitment. On one level, this appeared to be surprising. After all, the Conservative government had been elected on a platform that had included the commitment to reinvigorate family and moral values. There was widespread caucus and extra-parliamentary party support for aggressive measures to be taken on the pornography front. And the government made a strong public commitment to 'do something' about the pornography problem. On another level, though, it was hardly surprising that Criminal Code Section 159(8) was not amended. Canadian governments have passed legislation in this area on precisely two occasions: when the Criminal Code was established in 1892 and when obscenity was finally defined by the Conservative government in 1959. The historical record suggests that governments have not been anxious or able to legislate in moral areas in general and with respect to sex and pornography in particular. And they have had a lot of bad luck.

More often than not, issues press themselves onto the political agenda, regardless of government intentions. What governments do is *process* issues, and *how* they deal with an issue is as important as the issues themselves. Pornography became an issue in the mid-to-late 1970s. The proliferation of sexually explicit material was the result of a combination of changing social tastes and court decisions. This was not the government's doing. Indeed, governments were criticized in the 1960s and 1970s for not doing something about it. Pornography as an issue was forced on to the political agenda in the late 1970s as a result of lobbying efforts by church groups in alliance with backbench Conservative MPs.

The Liberal government at the time did not consider pornography to be a pressing issue or to rate priority status. Moreover, it continued to see the issue in terms of 'freedom of speech' as least much as in 'moral' terms. But the government *had to be seen* to be doing something. Over the next seven years the government appeared to be very active in this area: private members bills' were sent to committee, the committee issued a report on pornography, three bills were introduced, and two commissions were established. This was all quite admirable, but the ultimate result of all this was...nothing. The Liberals proceeded cautiously with a low cost strategy. Their legislative strategy reflected this: pornography amendments were buried deep in huge omnibus bills.

The Conservative government, though, reacted to the pornography issue in a different way. Politically and ideologically, it was predisposed to actually do something. It saw the issue in moral and social terms, with freedom of speech a secondary consideration. It did not commission any more studies or send the matter to committee or bury its proposals in omnibus bills. It stormed ahead and designed specific and tough anti-pornography legislation, which it presented proudly and aggressively. And the result of this was....nothing. The Conservative government's failure to translate its position on pornography into Criminal Code changes demonstrates how difficult it is to pass laws in general and to legislate in the realm of morality in particular. Despite strong caucus, party, and public support for anti-pornography measures, it chose to pass neither Bill C–114 or Bill C–54.

The hard reality was that Canadians were, and are, fundamentally divided on this issue. Moral and sexual issues divide people on ideological, religious and cultural grounds. The Conservative government proposed to deal with pornography in a way that coherently reflected a particular moral approach. The existing legal regime with regard to pornography was perhaps sloppy, unpredictable, uncertain, and incoherent. In a sense, this reflected the fundamental divisions in Canadian society. In its attempt to impose order on the Criminal Code, the Conservative government gave concrete expression to these social and ideological divisions and opened itself up to widespread criticism and ridicule. On the one side stood those who believed that the state should impose moral standards; on the other side were those who argued that morality is a personal not a public matter. For some, the matter was a question of free speech and censorship; for others this translated as personal irresponsibility and protecting the defenseless. To liberals, the issue was individual rights, to feminists the issues were equality and group rights. These principles were articulated equally effectively by well-organized and active interest groups: civil libertarians, librarians, artists, gays, and socialist feminists on the one side and church groups, police and customs officials, and radical feminists on the other. Most governments simply lack the authority to act in a situation like this, or are unwilling to pay the political costs that would inevitably result from pursuing one position over another. Only a matter of the highest political priority will be pursued under these daunting conditions.

Of course, governments can attempt to build up a consensus on a policy issue. They can 'horse-trade,' giving opposing sides 'a victory' in different areas so that each gets a benefit as well as a wound. But this tactic is not easily employed in the realm of morality. The Conservative government could not trade, say, abortion rights or capital punishment to one side in return for pornography legislation on the other. Moral issues don't allow these inconsistent but useful policy approaches. Similarly, a government can introduce a small or incremental change that is not divisive and make it appear that it is listening to both sides. (Indeed, a more moderate bill may have been less divisive and so might have passed). But, this is difficult to do in the moral area. Even if the government had decided to simply tinker with Section 159(8), policy debates would have remained on the high moral plane and dealt with freedom of expression, censorship, and other explosive themes.

Another consensus-building tactic is to use expert studies to make the case for one side or the other, which can then be presented as a technical necessity rather than a political choice. What the government desperately needed was a study that proved that pornography harms people or society. If it could be established beyond reasonable doubt that the consumption of pornographic materials results in, say, rape or violence, then a government could make the case that its legislation had nothing to do with morality *per se* but was rather designed to protect society. However, studies on the impact of pornography have not produced conclusive results. The Fraser Committee concluded ("reluctantly") that studies had not established that pornography caused harm. Two US Commissions on Pornography drew opposite conclusions on the matter.[115]

Governments in Canada initiated various studies and commissions, each of which presented them with recommendations on how to proceed. But their recommendations were not scientific or based on established truths. These reports were certainly not able to translate a moral issue into a technical one. For example, the Fraser Committee devoted pages to elaborating various philosophical and moral options, and presented one such particular option as the basis upon which its recommendations were made. The government did not like the report's recommendation to decriminalize most sexually explicit material. This signalled the normative character of the Fraser Committee's recommendations and the political nature of the decisions being made by the government in the area of pornography policy. The lack of expert consensus made it harder to build up a public consensus, and the Fraser Committee recommendations weakened the acceptability of the Conservative government's approach.

As time passed, the government found itself with an unwieldy and divisive issue on its hands. There was no chance of building up a consensus on pornography policy, without the government's appearing to 'sell out' its principles to the 'enemy.' What did it have to gain? If the pornography legislation were not passed, who would the Conservatives' right-wing supporters vote for in the next election — the NDP? the Liberals? The Conservative caucus had been very effective in acting as a liaison between grass roots anti-pornography groups and the government. But this was not the only pro-family, anti-permissiveness issue on the agenda. There was abortion to deal with, and the capital punishment debate had taken place as promised. Moreover, the caucus appeared to be assuaged by language legislation. If the government persisted with Bill C–54, it would lay itself open to charges of ridicule (the 'prudish' party) as well as to the charge of being manipulated by the extreme right-wing of the party. There were more middle of the road votes to be gained by dropping the legislation than there were right-wing votes to gain by pursuing it. Once abortion was forced on to the agenda (see p. 200ff.), the government decided to cut its losses. By early 1988, pornography was no longer a matter of government priority. The government had moved from a position of actually doing something to a position of appearing to do something about pornography.

For many, this was yet another frustrating example of watching a government *say* that it wants to do something while not being *able* to do it. In various cases, governments face countervailing pressures or don't have adequate resources, or they don't really want to act. The pornography case was one in which the government really wanted to act, but somehow ended with nothing. On one level, this was because the government was politically inept and greedy. Regardless of one's political orientation, it is clear that Bills C–114 and C–54 were incredibly ambitious; they tried to do far too much. In this way, the government overshot its authority and its public support. There was a quality of vengeance to the legislation, as if Conservatives were attempting to undo 40 years of permissiveness in one bill. This ensured that there was no room for compromise or for moderate discussion. The Conservatives created an all-or-nothing situation. And they got nothing.

On another level, though, the case indicates how hard it is to actually *make* a law. Laws comprise words, and words in a legal context can be very imprecise instruments. Canadians have been trying to define obscenity and pornography for a century, and the right words have not yet been found. Take, for example, the attempt to distinguish pornography from erotica. Most people would report that they have a gut feel for the difference between the two. But to translate this gut feeling into precise *legal* words is quite another matter. Alan Borovoy may be correct in asserting that "there simply are no words in the English language significantly precise to make the distinction between pornography and legitimate art." Two legal strategies have been pursued in this regard. Earlier governments decided to formulate very loose legal definitions of obscenity. Section 159(8) casts a very wide net, and that has been its intention. The courts are then in turn asked to operationalize the loose definition. Liberals argue that this is dangerous, inasmuch as artistic and literary work can get caught by this loose definition. Conservatives worry about the exact opposite, that the loose wording is slippery and allows pornographers to wriggle free. Nobody seems happy!

Alternatively, one can attempt to make the Criminal Code prohibitions on pornography very precise and specific. This was the approach taken by the Conservatives in Bills C–114 and C–54. Various definitions of pornography contained specific documentation of meaning and detailed accounting of almost every possible infraction. This approach was criticized as well, for effectively legalizing anything that is not on that list — unless a catch-all category is included like the infamous 'other sexual activity.' As well, the more words and definitions that are used and the more detailed the accounting, the more there is to criticize as being inappropriate — and the approach can get 'nit-picked' to death. The legislation can also be criticized for creating the opportunity of making too many things illegal. This can bring the law into disrepute.

Whenever a committee, commission, or government introduced a definition of obscenity, its words and language were dissected and criticized. The response would usually then be "It's not perfect but...." or "It's better than the present law...." Unlike suggested definitions or legislative proposals, the existing law has one crucial feature in its favour: it already exists.

A historical survey of pornography policy also illustrates in a dramatic way one of the more critical of the real worlds of Canadian politics: the separation of powers. Parliament, the legislative branch, passed pornography legislation in 1892 and in 1959. In 1892, the law was so loosely constructed that it did not contain a definition of obscenity. Almost 70 years later, obscenity was finally defined by Parliament, but in a very imprecise way. Who *actually* devised pornography policy in the face of what was in effect a vacuum? Pornography legislation is not unusual in this way. Laws have to be formulated with a certain amount of laxness, to cover all the varied situations in which they have to be applied, as well as to remain flexible enough to adapt to changing conditions. Indeed, much contemporary legislation delegates authority to officials in the executive branch to flesh out the skeletal legislation in its application.

For the last century, pornography law has effectively been made by the executive and judicial branches. At the provincial level, the police and the offices of the Attorneys General take the loosely worded legislation and apply it in particular cases. As has been seen, this is a very subjective and unpredictable process. More important, probably, has been the role of customs. Here again, customs officials take the loosely worded legislation and translate it into more detailed and specific guidelines. These latter have no legal status, but they are effectively the law. Customs and the police have had far more impact than Parliament in determining what pornography is and what is legal or illegal. The lines of responsibility between these two groups and the legislators in Parliament are very slender.

Most police and customs decisions are accepted, but some cases are appealed and may end up in the courts. Indeed, judicial decisions have guided the executive branch's activities in this area to a far greater extent than has

Parliament. Overall, judicial decisions loom largest in the determination of Canada's laws on pornography. Up to 1959, Parliament had not defined obscenity, and directed the courts to rely on the Hicklin test. This was an extremely subjective process whereby judges effectively applied their own moral standards. Even after Parliament defined obscenity in 1959, the courts were asked to sort out the relationship between the new definition and the Hicklin test as well as to figure out what the new definition actually meant. Ironically, the courts effectively liberalized the pornography scene even though it was anticipated that Section 159(8) would tighten the net. This two-track process has continued to the present: while political momentum has shifted to the right and to a tougher view on pornography, the courts continue to push back the frontiers of what it considers acceptable. Finally, with the adoption of the Charter of Rights and Freedoms, the courts are being asked whether the Charter's Section 2b (freedom of expression) is contravened by obscenity law; whether the vagueness of the law offends the 'prescribed by law' phrase of Section 1 of the Charter; and what the relationship is between individual rights (like free expression) and group rights (like women's equality guarantees).

This raises the traditional question of whether these sorts of matters should be determined by elected members in Parliament or by non-elected judges and bureaucrats. Whatever one's views, the fact remains that Parliament has effectively delegated responsibility for regulating pornography to the courts, customs and the police. This was a situation that Bills C–114 and C–54 proposed to remedy.

The pornography case illustrates as well the continuing and growing impact of the women's movement on the real worlds of Canadian politics. Pornography is but one of many issues that can be used to demonstrate how feminist issues have been catapulted onto the political agenda and how a new political discourse changes the way we talk about politics. Women's groups have been effective in widening the political agenda to deal with 'private' matters. Traditionally, liberal democratic politics has dealt with 'public' matters of the state and the economy. Private matters, like the family and relationships between the sexes, were not the concern of government. As women became organized, and demanded and received access to the public world, it became clear to them that full and satisfactory access to that world required a transformation of the private world as well. Hence day care, family support, wife battering and incest — and pornography — became feminist issues of concern, and have gradually been placed on the agenda. The underpinning view is that women cannot possibly be afforded equality in the realms of political and economic power if vast numbers of men continue to harbour misogynous attitudes and to treat women as no more than sex objects. A prohibition on pornography is thus seen as a necessary precondition to women's effective access to the public world.

The political discourse on obscenity has changed completely over the last decade as a result of the women's movement. To a considerable extent, arguments on pornography now rest less on principles of morality and far more on the notion that pornography degrades human beings. This is not to suggest that victories are automatic for women's groups (see the discussion of Meech Lake, p. 270). Nor is it meant to suggest that the women's movement is a homogeneous force. Indeed, the pornography case illustrates that various divisions exist within the women's movement on different issues. Pornography has actually divided the women's movement: radical and mainstream feminists support state regulation of child and violent pornography; socialist feminists see pornography as part of the capitalist economic system and fear that government regulation of pornography will increase state control of sex and sexuality. The tension between individual rights and group rights divides women's groups as it does society as a whole.

When the first Criminal Code was introduced and debated in the House of Commons in 1892, three issues dominated discussion of obscenity. First, it was noted that technological change (viz., photography) was enlarging the possibilities for the creation of obscene material. Second, there was broad agreement that it was impossible to come up with a perfect definition of obscenity. Third, it was acknowledged that the prohibition of obscene material should not interfere with freedom of expression. These issues continued to predominate over the next century. Seven decades later, changes in printing technology created the possibility of cheap mass market paperback books and magazines. And a century after the first debate, video technology has created new frontiers of presenting sexually explicit material. While creating these new possibilities and challenges, technology has not improved the capacity to define the problem nor to devise solutions that do not threaten freedom of expression. Thirty years after the last Criminal Code changes, the all-but-universally criticized Section 159(8) endures, and customs and the courts do Parliament's work. The mix of politics and morality creates odd results in the real worlds of Canadian politics.

DISCUSSION QUESTIONS

1) To what extent can expert studies help governments legislate in moral areas? Should governments feel bound to follow their recommendations?

2) What role did Parliament play since 1977 in the development of por-

nography policy? How effective were individual MPs in affecting the course of events? What role did political parties play?

3) Prime Minister Mulroney did not play an important role in this case. Why didn't he play a more active role?

4) To what extent does the concept of political culture help in understanding this case? Do the different ideologies have anything in common in the way in which they characterize pornography and pornography policy?

5) How important has the judicial branch been in affecting the prohibitions on pornography? What impact will the Charter of Rights and Freedoms have on the development of policy on pornography?

6) Canadians buy substantial amounts of sexually explicit material while supporting the principle of state regulation of pornography. How do you explain this?

7) To what extent should ordinary people be allowed to decide what sort of sexually explicit material they have access to?

8) Is the Canadian political system well designed to deal with moral issues?

CHRONOLOGY

1868	R. v. Hicklin — obscenity test
1892	Bill 7 — Criminal Code S.179 — statutory prohibition on obscenity
1933	US v. One Book Entitled 'Ulysses' (rejects Hicklin test)
1944	Conway v. The King (Canada follows Ulysses decision)
1949-52	Royal Commission on the Revision of the Criminal Code
1952	Senate Special Committee on the Sale and Distribution of Salacious and Indecent Literature
1954	R. v. Martin Secker Warburg Ltd. and others (community standards principle, contemporaneity, whole

	work)
1954	Bill C-7 amendments to the Criminal Code; content same as 1892, only numbers change (s.150-4)
1957	R. v. American News Co. Ltd. (Hicklin too vague and subjective)
1958	Ontario Attorney General: Committee on Obscene and Indecent Literature
1958	*Peyton Place* admitted to Canada
1958	Bill C-58 — defines obscenity
1960	R. v. Munster (159[8]) and Hicklin can coexist
1962	R. v. Brodie, Dansky and Rublin (*Lady Chatterly's Lover* not obscene)
1963-4	Dominion News and Gifts Ltd v. R. (community standards test, national criteria and changing over time)
1964	Ontario Court of Appeal rules that *Fanny Hill* is not obscene
1970	US Commission on Obscenity and Pornography
1973	Miller v. California (establishes what is outside First Amendment protection)
1975	Law Reform Commission of Canada proposes decriminalization of 'private obscenity'
1975	Project P established in Toronto: Canada's first anti-pornography squad
1977	Committee of MPs formed to pressure government; 10 private members bills sent to House Justice Committee; *Body Politic* case begins ("Men Loving Boys Loving Men")
1978	MacGuigan Committee reports; introduces notion of 'undue degradation'; Bill C-21 — Criminal Law Amendment Bill (omnibus bill, with section on child porn); first reading only
1979	*Body Politic* acquitted (also June 1982, September 1983)
1980	Badgley Committee established (on Sexual Offences Against Children and Youth)
1981	Bill C-53 — Criminal Code Amendments, including section on sexual exploitation of children, stuck in committee; Red Hot Videos Inc. established in British Columbia; National Film Board's *Not a Love Story*
1982	Ontario Censor Board Case; two Red Hot Video Stores set on fire
1983	First Choice announces contract with Playboy

	productions Fraser Commission established (on Pornography and Prostitution); Customs seizes December issue of Penthouse
1984	Bill C-19 — Criminal Law Reform Act, includes new definition of obscenity; dies on order paper; Badgley Committee reports
1985	Fraser Commission issues report, recommending decriminalization of soft porn, harsher penalties for hard porn; Luscher/Flying High case with Customs; Customs' power declared unconstitutional; Bill C-38 — tightens up Customs Act
1986	Glad Day Bookshop wins case (The Joy of Sex Case); 7-Eleven Stores remove Playboy and Penthouse; Bill C-114 — Crosbie's tough anti-porn bill; never gets passed first reading; US Attorney General's Report on Pornography; reports link between pornography and anti-social behaviour; Customs turns back November Playboy Customs seizure of gay material at Vancouver airport
1987	Bill C-54 — Hnatyshyn's anti-porn bill; minor changes to C-114; goes to second reading
1988	12 petitions from MPs in January-May to proceed with C-54; government decides to proceed with abortion legislation, but not with pornography; talk of all-summer sitting — pornography not included

NOTES

1 Special Committee on Pornography and Prostitution, *Report* (Ottawa: 1985), 17-8. Hereafter referred to as the Fraser Committee report.

2 Ibid., 15-6.

3 Ibid., 18-22.

4 For an articulation of this position see D. Lacombe, *Ideology and Public Policy: The Case Against Pornography* (Toronto: Garamond Press, 1988).

5 Richard G. Fox, "Obscenity,", *Alberta Law Review*, XII, (1974), 173.

6 House of Commons, *Debates*, 8 March 1892, 106, 133, 1312, 1319, 2457, 2958.

7 See Fox, 173ff; Fraser Committee report, 111ff.

8 Royal Commission on the Revision of the Criminal Code, *Report* (Ottawa: 1954).

9 Senate Committee on Salacious and Indecent Literature, *Proceedings* (Ottawa: 1952). 246.

10 House of Commons, *Debates*, 1953, 1198, 1200-2

11 H. Alexander, "Obscenity and the Law," *Queen's Quarterly*, 60 (2).

12 House of Commons, *Debates*, 1953, 1193-7.

13 Ibid., 1959, 5518.

14 Ibid., 5517-8.

15 Ibid., 5319

16 Ibid., 5309-10, 5318, 5520, 5524, 5530.

17 *Saturday Night*, 11 June 1960, 8.

18 Cited in Fox, 208.

19 ibid

20 Ibid., 209.

21 "Limits of Criminal Law: Obscenity: A Test Case" (Ottawa: Law Reform Commission: 1975).

22 *Maclean's*, September 1969, 8.

23 See Lacombe, 10-5, 39ff.

24 *Toronto Star*, 31 March 1977.

25 *Globe and Mail*, 2 February 1977.

26 Other bills included C–206 (Epp), C–209 (Whiteway), C–241(Dinsdale), C–318 (Epp), C–325 (Appolloni), C–348 (Friesen),C–399 (Appolloni), C–400 (Reid), and C–401 (Mc-Grath).

27 House of Commons, Standing Committee on Justice and Legal Affairs, *Report on Pornography* (Ottawa: 22 March, 1978). 18:3-4. Hereafter referred to as the MacGuigan report.

28 Ibid., 18:6-8.

29 Ibid., 18:5-6, 8-9, 10.

30 House of Commons, *Debates*, 19 April 1978, 4658.

31 House of Commons, Standing Committee on Justice and Legal Affairs, *Minutes of Proceedings and Evidence*, 7 February 1978, 5:9, 35.

32 House of Commons, *Debates*, 19 April 1978, 4656.

33 *Financial Post*, 24 February 1979.

34 E. Wachtel, "Our Newest Battleground: Pornography", *Branching Out*, v. 13, 1979, 33-7.

35 *Globe and Mail*, 15 February 1979.

36 House of Commons, Standing Committee on Justice and Legal Affairs, *Minutes of Proceedings and Evidence*, issue 103, (1982), 9ff. See also the Speech from the Throne, 22 April 1982.

37 *Globe and Mail*, 29 June 1982; 14 July 1982,A9; 16 July 1982; *Toronto Star*, 22 April 1982. *Maclean's*, 7 June 1982, 50.

38 House of Commons, Standing Committee on Justice and Legal Affairs, op. cit., 15-7, 104-32. *Globe and Mail*, 16 July 1982.

39 *Globe and Mail*, 23 November 1982. The use of the word 'wimmin' as opposed to 'woman' was used to create distance from the word 'man.'

40 Ibid., 4 January 1983.

41 *Maclean's*, 31 January 1983, 11.

42 *Globe and Mail*, 20 April 1983; *Toronto Star*, 23 April 1983.

43 *Globe and Mail*, 6 October 1983.

44 Fraser Committee report, 5-6.

45 *Toronto Star*, 9 January 1984.

46 Ibid., 12 November 1983.

47 *Globe and Mail*, 3 March 1984, 9 February 1984.

48 Maclean's 29 October 1984, 54.

49 House of Commons, *Debates*, 7 February 1984, 42

50 Ibid., 5 November 1984, 7.

51 *Maclean's*, 29 October 1984, 54.

52 House of Commons, *Debates*, 13 November 1984, 178.

53 Ibid., 1 October 1986, 13; 3 October, 49

54 Committee on Sexual Offences Against Children and Youths, *Report* (Ottawa: 1984). Hereafter referred to as the Badgley report.

55 Fraser Committee report, 87-92.

56 Ibid., 49

57 Ibid., 76-82.

58 Ibid., 26.

59 Ibid., 24.

60 Ibid., 22

61 Ibid., 267

62 Ibid., 254-72, 276-8, 691.

63 Ibid., 317-24.

64 Helen E. Longino, "Pornography, Oppression and Freedom: A Closer Look", in, *Take Back the Night: Women on Pornography* Ed. Laura Lederer (Toronto: Bantam Books,

1984). Catharine A. MacKinnon, *Feminism Unmodified: Discourses on Life and Law* (Cambridge: Harvard University Press, 1987). Andre Dworkin, *Pornography: Men Possessing Women* (New York: Perigree Books, 1979). Jillian Riddington, *Freedom from Harm or Freedom of Speech*. Discussion paper, (Ottawa: National Association of Women and the Law, 1983).

65 Longino, 60.

66 Fraser Committee report, 52, 263-64.

67 "Would you believe the issue of 1984 is free speech?" in *This Magazine*, November 1984, 22-26.

68 House of Commons, *Debates*, 14 November 1984.

69 Fraser Committee report, Chapter 9, 147-62; *Saturday Night*, May 1964, 12-14; *Saturday Night*, December 1980, 9-10; *Globe and Mail*, 15 August.

70 Fraser Committee report, Chapter 9, 147-62

71 *Saturday Night*, May 1964, 12.

72 The guidelines were presented to the MacGuigan committee.

73 House of Commons, *Debates*, 27 August 1958, 4177.

74 *Toronto Star*, 22 July 1985.

75 *Globe and Mail*, 12 April 1986.

76 House of Commons, *Debates*, 1 September 1985, 6 March 1986. *Toronto Star*, 7 February 1986.

77 *Toronto Star*, 12 June 1986.

78 *Alberta Report*, 23 June 1986, 13; CTV interview, reported in *Globe and Mail*, 16 June 1986.

79 *Montreal Gazette*, 17 June 1986; *Globe and Mail*, 14 June 1986; *Alberta Report*, 29 June 1986, p.52 and 7 July 1986, pp. 34-5; *Toronto Star*, 11 June 1986.

80 *Toronto Star*, 11,12 June 1986; *Globe and Mail*, 13 June 1986.

81 *Globe and Mail* 13 June 1986.

82 House of Commons, *Debates*, 12 June 1986.

83 Ibid., 25 June 1986, 14, 217.

84 *Globe and Mail*, 10 July.

85 *Toronto Star*, 3 October 1986.

86 Ibid., 19 September, 1986, A10; 3 October 1986.

87 *Alberta Report*, 22 September 1986, 34-5.

88 *Toronto Star*, 19 September 1986.

89 Ibid., 3 October 1986.

90 *Alberta Report*, 20 October 1986, 10-1.

91 *Toronto Star*, 4 October 1986.

92 Ibid., 19 September 1986.

93 House of Commons, *Debates*, 6 October 1986, 102; 27 January 1987, 2744.

94 *Toronto Star*, 6 May 1987.

95 House of Commons, *Debates*, 11 May 1987, 5952.

96 *Maclean's*, 18 May 1987, 44.

97 *Toronto Star*, 13 May 1987.

98 *Globe and Mail*, 5 May,1987; 16 May 1987; *Toronto Star*, 16 May 1987; 27 May 1987; House of Commons, *Debates*, 7 May 1987, 5898, 11 May 1987, 5952.

99 *Toronto Star*, 16 May 1987.

100 Ibid., 23 May 1987.

101 Ibid., 16 May 1987; *Globe and Mail*, 14 August 1987.

102 *Toronto Star*, 17 November 1987.

103 *Globe and Mail*, 20 November 1987; 21 November 1987.

104 House of Commons, *Debates*, 26 November 1987, 11,226-9.

105 Ibid., 11,230, 232; 30 November 1987, 11,426.

106 Ibid., 11,230, 11,426, 11,232.

107 Ibid., 11,298-9(McDonald), 11,438(Kaplan).

108 Ibid., 11,425 (Axworthy), 11,532 (Hovdebo).

109 *Globe and Mail*, 1 December 1987.

110 Ibid., 17 December 1987.

111 *Globe and Mail*, 21 November 1987.

112 *Toronto Star*, 14 March 1988.

113 *Maclean's*, 5 September 1988, 10,1.

114 House of Commons, *Debates*, 2 May 1988, 15,015.

115 See Fox, 187-9; Fraser Committee report, 95-102; *Globe and Mail*, 7 April 1986.

COURTS, POLITICS, AND MORALITY: CANADA'S ABORTION SAGA

It took the Supreme Court of Canada fifteen months to reach a decision on the Morgentaler case. In what was certainly the most dramatic and delicate decision to date regarding the Charter of Rights and Freedoms, the court in January 1988 upheld the Morgentaler appeal and declared Canada's abortion law unconstitutional. A law that had been passed in 1969, that had been criticized by both pro- and anti-abortionists, and that had defied political efforts at compromise, was struck down with a single judicial decision. The story of Canada's abortion law throws several things into stark relief. It exposes the difficulty of trying to make public policy for extremely sensitive moral issues, and may be compared to the problems of legislating in the area of pornography. It shows the increasing importance of feminism as a political force. It reveals the growing prominence of a "rights-based" mentality in Canadian political discourse, especially since the Charter. It uncovers the pivotal role and special dynamics of courts in the policy process: Canadian pro-abortionists, realizing that politicians were unwilling to tackle reforms in the 1970s, decided to aim at judicial victory instead. Finally, the abortion issue challenges our ability to reconcile rights with obligations, technology with humanity, and public laws with personal morality. The Supreme Court's 1988 abortion decision did not resolve these or any other issues. Abortion politics promise to be even more divisive and agonizing in the 1990s than they were in the previous two decades.

Rarely are an issue and an institution so starkly contrasted as are abortion and the Supreme Court. No matter what one feels about abortion, it is clearly an issue defined by feelings: feelings about life, motherhood, and the rights of women. No one who has thought seriously about abortion can resist its tremendous emotional undertow. Abortion forces a consideration of the archetypal human experiences: birth, life, and death. In contrast, the Supreme Court, which in January 1988 declared Canada's abortion law unconstitutional, is deliberately designed to suppress passion and extinguish feeling. Issues are addressed and resolved in the cold, clean language of legal reasoning.

Nine judges (seven in the abortion case) sit surrounded by dark oak and frozen marble, betraying passion only when their reason has been offended. And so the abortion issue as it is seen on the streets — with all of its confusion and depth of feeling — is rendered calm and precise in the serenity of the judicial chamber.

Most Canadians, of course, have only a dim sense of the Supreme Court as an institution. The role of this court and of others in the Canadian judicial system has increased substantially with the adoption in 1982 of the Charter of Rights and Freedoms. Yet most Canadians know the courts only by their judicial decisions, and these are usually filtered by the media. Since the Charter guarantees constitutional rights, and since only the courts (and ultimately the Supreme Court) can determine precisely what the Charter means, these decisions will assume increasing significance, both for elaborating what the Charter says and for guiding legislatures as to what is legally permissible. In this new game, interest groups and other policy actors will increasingly see the courts as a means whereby they can win their political battles through constitutional interpretation. This is what happened in Canada's abortion saga. Supported by the pro-choice movement, Henry Morgentaler deliberately broke the law in the hopes of forcing the issue into the courts. Joe Borowski, Canada's best known anti-abortion crusader, went before the Supreme Court in October 1988 to press his case that the fetus is a person and thus protected by law.[1]

Canada's abortion saga has passed through several stages. The first was the period of agitation for reform in the 1960s, which eventually led to amendments in the Criminal Code in 1969. Before those amendments, abortion was illegal, and anyone convicted of "procuring a miscarriage" was liable to life imprisonment. From the perspective of the 1980s this agitation assumed a curious form: it was *not* led by women or feminists convinced of the right to abortion, but by physicians and lawyers who wanted to minimize criminal liability for performing abortions. The second period comprises the first of Henry Morgentaler's judicial assaults on the law. Only a year after the new abortion law was passed, Morgentaler was arrested in Montreal for performing abortions at a clinic he had established exclusively for that purpose. Between 1970 and 1976, Morgentaler faced two separate arrests, three jury trials, and an 18-month jail sentence (he served ten months). In 1976 he retreated from the field.

The third stage begins with Morgentaler's re-entry to the fray. Convinced that abortions were becoming harder to get because of agitation by anti-abortion forces, and incensed that Joe Borowski was preparing a court case to argue that the fetus is a person under Canadian law, Morgentaler decided in 1982 to open abortion clinics in Winnipeg and Toronto. Both opened in 1983 amid demonstrations of support and protest, and a few incidents of violence. Morgentaler was once again arrested, and his Toronto case eventually made its way to the Supreme Court in October 1986. On 28 January 1988 the Court upheld Morgentaler's appeal and struck down the law that he had been fighting against for almost 20 years.

While this complex story highlights the role of the courts and the Charter in modern Canada, it also illustrates several other aspects of the real worlds of politics. It demonstrates, as do all the chapters in this book (particularly the one on pornography), the importance of political symbols and language in struggles over public policy. Real politics in a pluralistic, democratic state is about argument and debate, about winning hearts and minds. It is not simply a matter of raw numbers or brute force. This was clear in the abortion saga, which pitted one man, Henry Morgentaler, and a minority political movement "pro-choice") against a law that elected politicians would have preferred to leave alone. They made their case in the courts by *argument*, and they took that argument and others into the public square. This chapter will provide glimpses of how those arguments were shaped, what assumptions they took for granted, and the ways that they evolved in light of new circumstances. The vital core of the arguments on both sides, however, was symbolic. It was not so much (though this was also important) a matter of rational claims for or against abortion, but the question *what did abortion mean*? Did it *mean* the decline of the family and a de-valuation of life, or did it *mean* the new dawn of women's rights and the primary basis of their liberation from a patriarchal power structure? This dimension of meaning was deliberately tapped on both sides to evoke responses from people, responses that would dispose them towards the competing rational arguments. In the early 1970s, the Abortion Caravan dragged a coffin, filled with knives and coat hangers, from one end of the country to the other. Years later, Joe Borowski would paint the outside wall of his health food store with the picture of a graveyard and a sign reading "Pro-Choicers Have a Place for Unwanted Babies."

This chapter will also throw some light on the difficulties governments sometimes face in making and passing laws. In some areas, such as free trade and Meech Lake, governments seem prepared and able to move quickly. Both free trade and the Meech Lake Accord are enormously controversial, and both are singularly important to the future of the country, but in both cases governments seemed to take the bit in their teeth and forge ahead despite opposition. In cases like pornography and abortion, governments seem paralyzed. Nothing is done, agreement seems impossible, legislation languishes, and people agitate fruitlessly for decades. So, as these contrasting issues show, governments are not by any means always incapacitated, vacillating, or undetermined. The question then, is why the resolve and backbone in some cases but not others? The abortion and pornography issues provide clues to some of the types of policies that are particularly difficult to address. They both deal with the body and sexuality, though in different ways. They are both entwined with what has perhaps been the most fundamental challenge to traditional post-war politics in Western states:

feminism. They both touch on issues of religious belief. Finally, both invite debates about rights — in the case of abortion, reproductive rights; in the case of pornography, rights to free speech and freedom from censorship. Opposition to free trade or the Meech Lake Accord is not organized as a sexual protest, a gender protest, or a religious protest. These forces have, of course, made themselves evident to some degree in these issues (for example in the objections of some churches to free trade and the opposition of some feminist organizations to the Meech Lake Accord), but these are not the principal axes of debate. Abortion, like pornography, is burdened with so many of society's most volatile convictions, that it is enormously difficult to find a middle ground.

Finally, the abortion case illuminates the practical politics of Canadian feminism since the 1960s. The complex tapestry of Canada's abortion saga reveals how a movement, an issue and a man came to be interwoven. They remained distinct, as patterns on a tapestry must always be, but they needed each other to have full effect. This chapter will show how Canadian feminism, with its early roots in the radical student movement of the late 1960s, was casting about for an issue, a focus, and a platform that would broaden its appeal to Canadian women and men. Abortion rights, or "free abortion on demand" as the early slogan put it, became that focus. The "pro-choice" slogan emerged in the mid-1970s, and continued to dominate the feminist agenda, even as other issues like Charter rights and equity employment were added to the list. Early on, the movement decided on a strategy of court challenges, but it needed to find a doctor who would be prepared to break the law, face life imprisonment and the loss of his or her medical licence and reputation, and bear some of the enormous legal costs involved in going to the courts. Henry Morgentaler entered the picture, not because he was a feminist (indeed, his old world male mannerisms irritated some in the women's movement), but because of a personal agenda to prove to himself the power of his will. And so they helped each other: Morgentaler by steadfastly refusing to obey the law and being prepared to risk everything in his court challenges; feminist pro-abortion networks by providing volunteers to staff clinics and raising funds to pay the lawyers. After the 1988 Supreme Court decision that struck down the abortion law, Morgentaler went quietly back to his Toronto clinic. The battles over local abortion clinics, a new permissive law (or no law at all), and ultimately the broader question of reproductive rights, now fall to the movement, and promise to continue to absorb much of its energies for years to come.

Canada's first abortion law[2] simply copied an 1803 British law that first made abortion a statutory offence. Before 1803, Britain relied on the common law understanding that abortion was an offence after "quickening" — the sensation a woman has of fetal movement sometime between the 13th and 16th week after conception. The 1803 legislation made abortion a punishable offence both before and after quickening, and those provisions were included in Britain's 1861 Offences Against the Person Act.[3] Women who tried to self-induce as well as those who tried to procure an abortion were liable to imprisonment for life. The relevant passage from the Offences Against the Person Act was in Section 47:

> Every one who, with intent to procure the miscarriage of any woman, whether she is or is not with child, unlawfully administers to her or causes to be taken by her any poison or other noxious thing, or unlawfully uses any instrument or other means whatsoever with the like intent, — Is guilty of felony, and liable to imprisonment for life.[4]

Canada's first Criminal Code was consolidated in 1892, and the relevant parts of the Offences Against the Person Act were incorporated as sections 271-274[5] with two changes. The first was to reduce the maximum penalty for self-induced abortions from life imprisonment to seven years (by 1969 it had been further reduced to two years). The second was the addition of an explicit "saving" provision, which absolved those who in good faith did something considered necessary for the preservation of the mother's life, and as a consequence killed the fetus. This latter provision was introduced to protect physicians in cases where, in trying to save the mother's life, they inadvertently caused an abortion. These provisions, with some small changes in numbering and wording, remained as Canada's abortion law until 1969.

Interestingly, another section of the Criminal Code lumped abortion and contraception together, making it an indictable offence to "offer to sell, advertise, publish an advertisement of or have for sale or disposal any medicine, drug or article intended or represented as a means of preventing conception or causing abortion."[6] Today, when condoms are an acceptable subject for dinner conversation and stand-up comedians, it takes some effort to recollect the formal sexual mores of the early 20th century, along with its implications for intercourse, contraception and abortion. While pre-marital and adulterous liaisons of course did occur, the prevailing standards called for sexual intimacy only within the confines of marriage. Natural means of contraception such as *coitus interruptus* (withdrawal), *coitus reservatus* (refraining from ejaculation), and rhythm (avoiding intercourse during the woman's fertile period) were recommended by physicians for married partners, but mechanical contraceptive techniques such as the condom or the diaphragm were associated with prostitution.[7] Up to the 1930s, the most prevalent means of contraception in Canada was *coitus interruptus*, which has a comparatively high failure rate. Consequently, self-induced abortion was an important back-up method of family restriction.[8] The medical profession at this time had not yet clearly established its pre-eminence over other types of healers, and so turn-of-the-century newspapers were filled with advertisements for abortifacients (thinly disguised as remedies for female ailments, *not* to be taken if pregnant).[9]

Despite its legal coupling to contraception, abortion was not a significant political issue until the late 1950s. Up to that time, the most vigorous pressure on the reproductive front focused on liberalizing the birth control laws. The birth control movement gathered force through the 1920s and 1930s, and had reached a degree of respectability by World War II. In Canada the provision of birth control information was illegal, and so the issue finally came to court in the 1936 *Palmer* case. In its 1937 ruling, the court found in favour of Dorothy Palmer (a nurse at a birth control clinic), and accepted the saving provisions of the Criminal Code that she had acted in the public good. Thus, while the sale or promotion of information or means of contraception remained technically illegal until 1969, administration of the law was relaxed.[10]

The absence of agitation for liberalized abortion in the 1950s did not mean that no abortions were being performed. Abortions were done in practically every major Canadian city. The Abortion Squad of the Metropolitan Toronto Police Force estimated that before the 1969 legislation, thousands of criminal abortions were procured annually in that area alone.[11] At that time, there were several ways, most of which were expensive or dangerous, for a woman to get an abortion. She could try to self-induce, she could go to a back-street abortionist, or she could approach a physician. Since the only exception allowed under the law was an abortion done to save the mother, most physicians were reluctant to perform a procedure that could land them in jail for life.[12] There are no reliable figures on the incidence of abortion, and estimates of the number of alleged illegal abortions vary predictably according to whether the pro-abortion or anti-abortion side is making the argument. Most pro-abortionists argue that the number of illegal abortions was very high (and that the law was therefore both ineffective and unjust); anti-abortionists aver that the number was low (and that the law was consequently appropriate). Anecdotal evidence suggests that illegal abortions were a fact of Canadian life in back streets, motel rooms, and even hospitals, where records would be discreetly fudged (e.g., abortions entered as "routine D & C's" [dilatation and curettage] for menstrual complications). Women with money or access to a sympathetic physician were the most likely to get safe abortions.

The first credible call for a change in Canada's abortion law came not from an organized movement or political party, but surfaced as a short article by Joan Finnigan in a 1959 issue of *Chatelaine*.[13] The article deserves attention for of its faithful rendering of the pro-abortion arguments, or discourse, that came to prevail in the 1960s. The first stage of the argument was a *mise en scène*, describing the agony of a 14-year old girl made pregnant by a brutal gang rape. Her compassionate physician, clearly believing that termination of pregnancy was warranted in this case, risked criminal prosecution under Canada's abortion law.

Claiming that while in other countries (Sweden, Denmark, Iceland, China, Russia, Japan, India, and some unspecified Roman Catholic states in South America) the girl could have been legally aborted on humanitarian grounds, Finnigan concluded that Canada had the "stiffest abortion law in the world."[14] Its "unyielding harshness" contrasted with the suggestions of some observers (again, largely unspecified) that the permissible grounds for abortion be broadened to include rape, eugenic considerations, or threat of serious mental or physical breakdown. The next step was to argue that illegal abortions were widespread in Canada — Finnigan's estimate was 33,000 per year (her method was to take an estimate of illegal American abortions, and multiply it by 1/10, the ratio of Canadian to American population).

Finnigan closed with a philosophical reflection. Foreshadowing what was to become a key slogan of the pro-abortion movement a decade later ("Every child a wanted child"), she said that

> the unwanted pregnancy — not always, but often — results in the unwanted child. Surely one fact stands as unquestionably true: the child needs to be wanted in order to develop into a stable productive individual. Every year our society sanctions hundreds of "forced" marriages. Some of them work, but many don't. What of the child's needs then?[15]

Finally, she alluded to religious forces that might try to forestall legislative reform. No religion had the right to impose its views on a democratic, pluralist society; organized religion had to give way to individual moral choice; women of all faiths, whatever their beliefs, in practice get abortions; religious objections had to confront the hard choice of mother against fetus in life-threatening circumstances, as well as the fact that the fetus is "an unknown quantity and the mother is a grown experienced member of human society."[16]

Finnigan's 1959 article is important both for what it said and for what it did not say. The piece, short as it was, contained the core pro-abortion arguments of the next decade: (1) the focus on "hard" cases such as raped teenagers, incest, fetuses with potentially severe deformities, the burdens of additional children, (2) the stress on the allegedly large number of illegal abortions, (3) the claim that competently performed abortions were safe and untraumatic (later to develop into the idea that pregnancy was riskier than abortion and moreover that abortion actually had beneficial psychological effects such as mild euphoria and a sense of release), (4) the assertion that unwanted children would grow up to be sociopaths, (5) the argument that abortion was a matter of individual choice and that religious organizations (by clear implication, the Roman Catholic Church) had no right to speak on the issue or force their views on others, and (6) the bold declaration that some lives are worth more than others, that the fetus is less than human, and that quality of life ultimately matters more than the simple fact of living.

Surprisingly, however, Finnigan was silent on other claims that after 1970 were to become vital rhetorical weapons for pro-abortionists. The most obvious omission was the concept of abortion as a "women's issue." Naturally, Finnigan wrote passionately about the plight of women, but she never directly identified abortion as a women's issue in the sense that the absence of legalized abortion services reflected societal oppression of women. Moreover, the only passage in which Finnigan invoked the concept of "rights" was when she compared the opposing "right to life" of the mother and fetus. (By the 1970s and certainly after the adoption of the Charter, it was inconceivable that any pro-abortionist would neglect to claim abortion as every woman's right.) Finally, Finnigan overlooked the notion of equity among different categories of women — poor v. rich, rural v. urban, educated v. uneducated. A major pro-abortion theme after the 1969 changes was that the law worked inequitably, and hence unjustly, with regard to women in different parts of the country or in different social classes. In short, Finnigan's silence on these issues simply confirms that there was no feminist (in the modern sense of the term) pro-abortion lobby until the early 1970s.[17]

If there was no organized feminist pressure to liberalize the abortion law, where was the impetus for change? According to one careful study of the origins of the 1969 law that finally legalized abortion in some cases, Canadian abortion agitation went through two distinct phases before entering the political arena.[18] The first was a preparatory phase in which the issue was championed almost solely in the press. After *Chatelaine*'s 1959 article, the abortion question was ignored for two years until the *Globe and Mail* carried a series of editorials, op-ed pieces, and letters to the editor between 1961 and 1963.[19] The *Globe*'s key argument was that "thousands of illegal abortions are performed in Canada every year, generally by unqualified persons, and they leave behind them a wake of death and physical and mental wreckage." A law so widely disobeyed "brings all law into contempt."[20] The *Globe and Mail* and other media were not indulging in an empty crusade, since the public's perception of abortion was powerfully affected by the thalidomide tragedy during these years. The famous Sherri Finkbine case threw a sharp light on that tragedy and on the abortion issue. Mrs. Finkbine had access to thalidomide (a drug to treat nausea due to pregnancy) during her pregnancy. After stories of thalidomide-related birth deformities surfaced in Europe, Mrs. Finkbine tried to get an abortion in Arizona in 1962. She was refused and flew to Sweden for one. The fetus was deformed. Her story made world headlines, no doubt in part because of the sad irony of her profession: she was a local host of Romper Room, a children's show.[21]

The second phase of agitation over abortion began in 1963 and consisted of a review of the abortion question by several professional associations, principally the Canadian Bar Association (CBA) and the Canadian Medical Association (CMA). Both had an interest in the issue because of its criminal law and medical aspects. The CBA wrestled unsuccessfully with a liberalizing resolution from 1963 to 1965. In 1966 the tide turned; despite a vocal minority the association voted in favour of legalized abortion on grounds of danger to the mother's life or health, unwanted pregnancy due to rape, or danger of a defective child. [22] The CMA took its lead from a proposal developed by the Ontario Medical Association between 1963 and 1965. The resolution called for legalized abortion in cases requiring the preservation of the "life or physical or mental health" of the mother.[23] Added to the considerable prestige and pressure of the CBA and CMA were the yearly calls between 1963 and 1966 by the National Council of Women of Canada for a review of the abortion law.

These pressures for review of abortion might have been fruitless had the federal government not already been in the midst of a review of other issues regarding the family and sexuality — the legalization of contraceptives and widening the grounds for divorce.[24] These legislative initiatives reflected the sexual revolution of the 1960s. The long battle to make contraceptive techniques and information widely available laid the foundation for the debate about abortion (indeed, the 1960s review of the abortion law was often coupled with debate over contraception). The advent of the birth control pill in the early 1960s had severed the link between copulation and procreation — whereas before the pill, pregnancy was always a plausible outcome of intercourse, after the pill, as Henry Morgentaler would put it to a legislative committee, pregnancy could be considered an "accident." While there had always been "accidents," the pill made birth control seem so completely foolproof that it radically redefined our cultural concepts of sex, pregnancy, and abortion. The status of sex went from procreational to recreational; a contracepting woman with an unwanted pregnancy was an almost entirely innocent third party, and abortion was a way to rectify the error. Added to this were the tragic thalidomide cases, which focused world attention on the issue of "quality of life," for both newborns and their parents. In combination, these broad changes defined the new social landscape upon which abortion would be situated in the 1960s.

Another important factor behind the political success of the pro-abortion lobby in the 1960s was the absence of any articulate and organized opposition to a liberalized law. It was not until April 1967 that the Roman

COMPARISON OF THREE PRIVATE MEMBERS' BILLS ON ABORTION, 1967

Sponsor	Grounds	Decision
Grace MacInnis (Bill C-122)	1. "serious risk to the life or grave injury to the health, either physical or mental, of the pregnant woman" 2. "substantial risk of a defective child being born" 3. "pregnancy is a result of rape or incest"	2 doctors
Ian Wahn (Bill C-123)	1. where pregnant woman is "in danger of losing her life" 2. where pregnant woman "will suffer in health as a result of pregnancy"	TAC or 2 doctors
H.W. Herridge (Bill C-136)	1. "that the continuance of the pregnancy would involve risk to the life or of injury to the physical or mental health of the pregnant woman or the future well-being of herself and or the child or her other children" 2. "in determining whether or not there is such risk of injury to health or well-being account may be taken of the patient's total environment actual or reasonably forseeable" 3. "that there is a substantial risk that if the child were born it would suffer from such physical or mental abnormalities as to be seriously handicapped"	2 doctors

Catholic bishops of Canada announced that they would review the abortion question.[25] The appointment of Pierre Trudeau as justice minister in April 1967 brightened the outlook for liberalized abortion (as well as birth control, divorce, and homosexuality), since Trudeau was a known supporter of relaxed legislation. Abortion finally reached the parliamentary arena in October 1967.

On 3 October 1967 the House of Commons Standing Committee on Health and Welfare began hearings on three private member's bills regarding abortion (Inset I). The three members were Grace MacInnis (NDP, Vancouver-Kingsway), Ian Wahn (Lib, St. Paul's), and H. W. Herridge (NDP, Kootenay West). The Conservatives and Créditistes (a party at that time based largely in Quebec) were strongly opposed to liberalizing the abortion law. Wahn's bill merely tried to tidy up the Criminal Code's hazy provisions, where Section 237 absolutely forbade abortions, Section 209(2) exempted such action if it were done to preserve the life of the mother, and Section 45 protected from liability in surgical operations as long as the operation was done competently and of necessity. By 1967, many Canadian hospitals already had therapeutic abortion committees (TACs — usually consisting of a small number of physicians who reviewed applications to perform abortions in their hospitals), and so Wahn's bill simply recognized prevailing practice. Herridge's bill, modeled after the 1967 British abortion law, would have provided for abortion on demand because its grounds (e.g., the mother's "well-being") were so broad. MacInnis's bill fell between these extremes.

The committee heard from several organizations in its October-December meetings.[26] Henry Morgentaler, as past president of the Humanist Fellowship of Montreal, was asked to present its brief on 19 October 1967. He recommended that "any woman should have the right to have termination of pregnancy on request up to three months of pregnancy."[27] He was to suggest a standard of viability: when the fetus is capable of living, with assistance, outside the mother (roughly at six months after conception) it becomes a "baby" and should not be aborted. Committee exchanges with Morgentaler and other witnesses were often sharp, emotional, and sometimes sarcastic. The MPs were as divided in their opinions as their witnesses were.

The committee interim report of 19 December 1967 came as a surprise. With a bare quorum of 13 members, it voted 11-2 in favour of a relaxed abortion law. Noting that "opinion on abortion varies widely throughout Canada," the committee proposed that therapeutic abortions be permitted where "pregnancy will seriously endanger the life or the health of the mother."[28] Something was up; two days later, in a move that caught almost everyone by surprise, the government tabled an omnibus bill to amend various sections of the Criminal Code, including abortion. The bill was clearly a masterstroke designed to minimize controversy over its morality: on the same day that it was introduced, it was read for the first time and Parliament immediately adjourned for the Christmas holiday. Abortion was to be legal if a woman's continued pregnancy "would or would be likely to endanger her life or health."

Events proceeded quickly in the new year. On 13 March 1968 the Standing Committee on Health and Welfare, after hearing presentations and witnesses since January, tabled its final report. It found the government's abortion proposal too vague, and preferred tighter wording that would permit abortion only in cases where continued pregnancy "will endanger the life or *seriously* and *directly* impair the health of the mother."[29] Between March and June, Lester Pearson resigned as Liberal party leader and was succeeded by Pierre Trudeau who went on to win a federal election and become prime minister. John Turner, as the new Minister of Justice, assumed the job of re-introducing the omnibus bill (with the original phrasing for the abortion section, referring to a pregnancy that "would or would be likely to endanger her life or health") for first reading on 19 December 1968. Full debate began on 23 January 1969 and extended for four acrimonious months, with much of the acrimony arising from a Ralliement créditiste filibuster against the bill's abortion clause. The closest that the House of Commons came to a specific vote on abortion was on 9 May 1969, when the government allowed a motion to delete the abortion clause from the omnibus bill. Of 264 MPs, 143 were present (54 per cent); interestingly, 107 of them voted against deletion (i.e., in favour of the abortion clause), and 36 voted for.[30] There was a clear split on this question between the Conservatives and Créditistes, and the Liberals and the NDP. The former raised all the questions characteristic of what would soon be calling itself the "right to life" movement; the latter made its case for relaxed abortion laws in much the same terms as Finnigan had a decade earlier. The omnibus bill, including all revisions to the Criminal Code, was passed by the Commons on 14 May 1969, and became law on 27 June. With its passage, Canada had a new abortion law in the form of section 251 of the Criminal Code (see Inset II).

Section 251 can be broken down conceptually into two key parts. The first part (subsections 1 and 2) states that anyone who attempts to perform an abortion on a pregnant woman is liable to life imprisonment (self-induced abortions were liable to two years imprisonment). The second part (subsection 4) provided exceptions to the first part. Abortion was legal only if (1) it was performed by a qualified physician in (2) an accredited or approved hospital whose (3) TAC had a certified majority opinion that the "continuation of the pregnancy of such a female person would or would be likely to endanger her life or health." The TAC had to have at least three members, each of whom was a qualified physician at that hospital.[31] In terms of its legal language, the new abortion section of the Criminal Code was at best only a modest liberalization of pre-1969 practice, which absolved doctors of criminal liability if they performed an abortion to save the mother's life. The problem with the "saving provision" had been that it was somewhat narrow (action taken to save the *life* of the mother); that was why hospitals had set up TACs in the first place, to ensure that abortions were within the law.

As we will note shortly, Section 251 had several awkward features. From a feminist perspective, it still left the real control over abortions in the hands of doctors, not women. Moreover, that control was exercised through a bureaucratic process involving TACs and certificates. The justificatory language was so vague ("would be *likely to* endanger her life or *health*") that it could conceivably include anything from the simple mental stress of childbearing to a real physical threat to life. Paradoxically, the same legislation could be read as either too slack or too narrow.

Laws are rules designed and enforced by government, and applicable to all citizens. The measure of obedience a law enjoys depends on three primary factors: its textual precision, the incentives to obey (and this would include the law's legitimacy), and the government's capacity to monitor and punish infractions. A law may be considered "bad" in the technical sense if it is weak with respect to these three factors. Section 251 was a bad law in this sense. It was badly drafted, and open to widely different interpretations. The incentives to disobey were very strong, particularly when, within a few years, feminism focused attention on reproductive rights, and argued that the right to choose abortion was a human right and that restrictions on this right were illegitimate. Finally, it was difficult to enforce the law — police officers could scarcely patrol every hospital and back alley. Added to this stew, of course, were the strong moral feelings—both pro and con—that abortion engendered.

The first long phase of abortion reform in Canada was not the work of charismatic individuals or broad coalitions. It was the result of uncoordinated actions, coincidental events, and no doubt to some degree the new sexual consciousness of the 1960s. There were other considerations, of course. There was then no organized feminist movement, but women's voices were heard at key points in the debate. What Finnigan's 1959 article and the representatives of the National Council of Women shared was a horror at the consequences of back-street illegal abortions. As noted earlier, there was no call for abortion as a woman's right; the arguments were entirely pragmatic. A 19th-century law was forcing women to seek the services of quacks and butchers, and since no law would ever stop women from needing abortions, the legislation had to be relaxed in order to eradicate the back-alley carnage and exploitation that, at the height of the debate in 1967, was sometimes estimated to annually involve 100,00 Canadian women.

If women's organizations were relatively weak in lobbying for abortion reform, who led the fight in the 1960s and why was it successful? The leaders were the CBA and the CMA, supported by stinging editorials in the press, principally in the *Globe and Mail*.[32] Since 1892 Canadian physicians had had the option of performing an abortion if that were the only way to save the mother's life. By the 1960s, however, most of the purely physical risks of pregnancy had disappeared, and thus the purely medical grounds for abortions were practically non-existent. All legal therapeutic abortions were performed in hospitals, which were legally responsible for every surgical procedure undertaken by medical staff. The TACs that had been informally established by Canadian hospitals were protective devices to shield both doctors and hospitals from legal liability. The CMA and CBA lobbies in the 1960s wanted the law clarified not in order to allow more abortions, but in order to clarify the legal status of physicians who performed them.

The lobbies were helped by the fact that the Liberal government was already in the middle of a review of contraception and divorce, and thus receptive to the CBA and CMA arguments that the Criminal Code provisions on abortion also needed revisions. A second factor was the disorganized nature of the anti-abortion forces. While most key anti-abortion activists were Catholic, the Canadian Catholic Church — which might have been expected

CRIMINAL CODE, 1970: CHAPTER C-34, SECT. 251

251. (1) Everyone who, with intent to procure the miscarriage of a female person, whether or not she is pregnant, uses any means for the purpose of carrying out his intention is guilty of an indictable offence and is liable to imprisonment for life.

(2) Every female person who, being pregnant, with intent to procure her own miscarriage, uses any means or permits any means to be used for the purpose of carrying out her intention s guilty of an indictable offence and is liable to imprisonment for two years.

(3) in this section "means" includes (a) the administration of a drug or other noxious thing, (b) the use of an instrument, and (c) manipulation of any kind.

(4) Subsections (1) and (2) do not apply to (a) a qualified medical practitioner, other than a member of a therapeutic abortion committee for any hospital, who in good faith uses in an accredited or approved hospital any means described in paragraph (a) for the purpose of carrying out her intention to procure her own miscarriage, if, before the use of those means, the therapeutic abortion committee for that hospital...(c) has by certificate in writing stated that in its opinion the continuation of the pregnancy of such female person would be likely to endanger her life or health, and (d) has caused a copy of such certificate to be given to the qualified medical practitioner.

to lead the resistance — "did not play a leading role in the formation of the right-to-life movement in Canada."[33] The second Vatican Council (1962–65) absorbed so much of Canadian bishops' energy, and generated so much turmoil on the issue of contraception, that the Canadian Catholic hierarchy did not react to the abortion controversy until 1967.[34] At that point the Church's arguments against liberalized abortion were overwhelmed by pragmatic arguments in favour of change coming from the CBA, the CMA, and other scattered associations. As well, other Christian denominations such as the United and Anglican churches either vacillated on the issue or cautiously endorsed a relaxed law. The fractured Christian consensus on abortion made the Catholic Church seem isolated as well as backward.[35]

It should not be surprising, in light of all of these factors, that the 1969 abortion law generated little but dissatisfaction among committed pro-and anti-abortionists. From the pro-abortion perspective, the law simply recapitulated the prevailing practice and tidied up the legal language. Abortion in Canada would be mired in red tape and humiliating bureaucratic

(5) The Minister of Health of a province may by order (a) require a therapeutic abortion committee for any hospital in that province, or any member thereof, to furnish him a copy of any certificate described in paragraph (4c) issued by that committee, together with such other information relating to the circumstances surrounding the issue of that certificate as he may require, or (b) require a medical practitioner who, in that province, has procured the miscarriage of any female person named in a certificate described in paragraph (4c), to furnish him a copy of that certificate, together with such information relating to the procurement of the miscarriage as he may require.

(6) For the purposes of subsections (4) and (5) and this subsection "accredited hospital" means a hospital in a province approved for the purposes of this section by the Minister of Health of that province; "board" means the board of governors...of an accredited or approved hospital..."qualified medical practitioner" means a person entitled to engage in the practice of medicine under the laws of the province in which the hospital referred to in subsection (4) is situated; "therapeutic abortion committee" for any hospital means a committee, comprised of not less than three members, each of whom is a qualified medical practitioner, appointed by the board of that hospital for the purpose of considering and determining questions relating to termination of pregnancy within that hospital.

(7) Nothing in subsection (4) shall be construed as making unnecessary the obtaining of any authorization or consent that is or may be required, otherwise than under this Act, before any means are used for the purpose of carrying out an intention to procure the miscarriage of a female person.

delays, and women would continue to suffer. The anti-abortionists saw disaster of another sort: the law's ambiguous phrasing on endangerment would encourage routine abortion for almost any reason. Both sides felt that the government had outwitted and outmanoeuvred them. Both were determined to win the next time.

FEMINISM, HENRY MORGENTALER, AND THE QUEBEC TRIALS, 1969–76

For two weeks they carried the coffin across Canada, down the streets of Kamloops, Edmonton, Regina, Winnipeg, the Lakehead, Sudbury, and Toronto. In every place they stopped, they gathered petitions for abortion reform. The trek had started in Vancouver on 27 April 1970, and culminated in a two-day demonstration in Ottawa. On 9 May about 500 women rallied on Parliament Hill and then made their way to 24 Sussex Drive, brandishing coat hangers, lilies, and the coffin for the women who had died at abortionists' hands. Two days later, a small group disguised as "respectable women" chained themselves to the Commons Visitor's Gallery and shouted "Free abortion on demand" and "Every child a wanted child" to the gaping MPs below. This was the Abortion Caravan, Canada's first organized fusion of feminism and abortion.[36]

Though there were Canadian feminists in the late 1960s, there was no recognizable feminist movement in Canada. Feminism was submerged in the New Left politics of the mid- and late 1960s, a politics that hinged on student radicalism and anti-war protests. A key group in this early phase of Canadian feminism was the Student Union for Peace Action (SUPA), formed in Regina in 1964 to coordinate political action aimed at abolishing war, racism, poverty, and other social evils.[37] SUPA, for all its rhetoric of liberation, was organized along classic sexist lines: the "girls" made sandwiches and placards while the "guys" made speeches and revolution. When SUPA dissolved in 1967, many female radicals had begun to re-conceptualize their experience in feminist terms. This casual migration of activists from the New Left to feminism showed up in the Abortion Caravan, which was conceived by the Vancouver Women's Caucus, many of whose members had been SUPA activists at Simon Fraser University.[38] As one sympathetic observer put it at the time: "Abortion law reform is one of many concerns of women's liberation, but it has served as no other issue to link university and working women, the economically comfortable and the poor, young and middle-aged in an urgent personal struggle to achieve a definable goal."[39] The Abortion Caravan was the "glue that stuck the first feminist network in Canada together."[40] Not all feminists were convinced that "free abortion on demand" should be the movement's highest priority, but the left-wing of the movement (especially the Young Socialists, a Trotskyist group) kept up the pro-abortion momentum in the early years.[41]

Whereas in the 1960s the critique of the abortion law had been based on almost purely pragmatic considerations, the new feminist movement began to introduce the idea of rights into the debate. The Report of the Royal Commission on the Status of Women reflected the shift by making both arguments simultaneously, in favour of a liberalization of the law. The commission pointed out that the 1969 law would have no effect on the number of illegal abortions and consequent maternal deaths and injuries, and, moreover, that it discriminated against poor women who could not afford an abortion outside Canada. These pragmatic arguments were aptly summed up in the phrase "A law that has more bad effects than good ones is a bad law." But the commission then shifted ground to the rights argument: "We have come to the conclusion that each woman should have the right to decide if she will terminate pregnancy."[42] The commission recommended abortion on demand for women pregnant for 12 weeks or less; women over 12 weeks pregnant would have to be endangered physically or mentally by the pregnancy or face a "substantial risk" that the child would be greatly handicapped if born.[43]

The Abortion Caravan and the Royal Commission report were symptomatic of a deep dissatisfaction with the new abortion law. Scarcely a year after the law was passed, Eleanor Pelrine, a prominent pro-abortion activist, listed what were to become the movement's staple criticisms.[44] First, even with the modest liberalization in 1969, hospitals were turning away women. Canadian women continued to have illegal abortions or abortions outside Canada. Second, the legislation did not compel hospitals to establish TACs, but no therapeutic abortion was legal in Canada unless it was approved by a TAC. One estimate held that in 1976 only 20.1 percent of civilian hospitals in Canada had a TAC. This was in part because only 41 percent of Canadian hospitals had the obstetrical and gynecological staff and facilities needed to perform abortions and hence qualify as eligible to establish a TAC. Of the *eligible* hospitals, only 48 percent had TACs.[45] Hospitals failed to establish TACs for two reasons, religious and professional/ethical. Fully one-quarter of eligible hospitals without TACs were owned by or affiliated with religious denominations.[46] The professional/ethical reason was simply that the medical community tended to "look upon the abortion procedure with distaste."[47]

Pelrine's third criticism was that the vagueness of the term "health" in the legislation would make the TACs both judge and jury over hapless women. She preferred the definition of health promoted by the World Health Organization: "a state of complete physical, mental, and social well-being, and not merely the absence of infirmity or disease."[48] This terminological vagueness, added to hospital's discretion over whether to establish a TAC at all, led to a fourth problem: widely different levels of access to abortion services province by province, city by city.

Pelrine's final criticisms attacked the medical bureaucracy and red tape created by the law. The demand that TACs meet and assess every application could mean dangerous delays for women in the latter part of the first trimester — any delays past the 12th week greatly increased the threat to health posed by the abortion. Finally, even if a patient got approval, the demand that the abortion be performed in an approved or accredited hospital could create further delays while the woman waited for a bed.

As a physician in general family practice and as someone who was a known supporter of liberalized abortion, Henry Morgentaler experienced the law's limitations directly in the supplications of the desperate women who visited his Montreal office. Morgentaler's 1967 presentation of the Humanist Fellowship brief on abortion to the Standing Committee on Health and Welfare, and the subsequent publicity, attracted numerous calls from women seeking abortions. For a year Morgentaler refused to do abortions, referring the women to doctors who would. The personal risks were just too great — a possible life sentence, the ruination of his career, and the financial collapse of his family. But Morgentaler knew that he was living a lie: how could he attack the abortion law as unjust and yet refuse to help women victimized by that injustice? In 1968 he made a decision that changed the course of Canada's abortion politics, a decision that almost 20 years later would grow into one of the country's most important constitutional decisions under the new Charter of Rights and Freedoms. He decided to do abortions, without fanfare at first, but openly and even proudly. While other doctors would continue to perform abortions in the law's twilight zone, Morgentaler came out into the sunshine, dared his antagonists to arrest and prosecute him, and then fought his case implacably in the courts. Henry Morgentaler was different, even extraordinary, not because of his convictions, since these were shared by many, but because of his complete refusal to surrender. No sanction, no fine, no jail term, no law would stop him. What events shaped this man and placed him on Canada's historical stage?

Henry Morgentaler was born and grew up in the Polish textile city of Lodz. His parents were Jews who had rejected their religion in favour of socialism, and the young Morgentaler felt triply ostracized and unwanted: as a Jew, as a socialist, and by his own mother, who he was convinced did not love him.[49] Morgentaler's anti-Catholicism was first nurtured by the Polish Catholic churches, which were notoriously anti-semitic.[50] He and his family spent 1939–44 in the Lodz ghetto under German occupation. His father, sister, and girlfriend were taken away, and disappeared; in 1944 Morgentaler, his younger brother, and his mother were transported to Auschwitz. His mother was removed and he never saw her again. Morgentaler was also separated from his brother for a time, but the two were re-united after the war. The ghetto, Auschwitz, and the horror he witnessed there left Henry Morgentaler without a shred of religious conviction. Even if God existed, He must be evil to allow such suffering.[51]

Re-united with his childhood sweetheart after the war, Morgentaler pursued medical studies in Germany, and then the two of them sailed to Canada in 1950. It took Morgentaler five years to get his medical diploma, his citizenship, and finally a licence to practice medicine, but he soon established himself as a general practitioner in an east-end working class district of Montreal. In 1961, despite financial and professional success, a family, and a home, Morgentaler was unhappy. He underwent psychoanalysis to deal with his discontent and the feeling that "something deep down was unfulfilled."[52] His marriage dissolved and he began to look outside himself for a larger public role. In 1964 he became the president of the Montreal Humanist Fellowship, and gradually began to feel that being active "as a sort of mover of history" was important. His psychoanalysis had shown him that his Holocaust experiences had left him with a sense of impotence. He realized, as he put it,

that I could do something — not merely survive, but use my personality, my talents, and my abilities in a very active way. Later, I came to the conclusion that, under some circumstances, it is imperative to defy authority — necessary for my self-esteem, to prove my manhood in direct conflict.[53]

In 1968 Morgentaler decided to mesh his political convictions with his medical work, and concentrated on family practice (i.e., vasectomies, fitting IUDs, prescribing oral contraceptives, and performing abortions). At that time there were two principal abortion techniques. The one most commonly used by illegal abortionists was the insertion of some long, sharp object to puncture the amniotic sac and induce miscarriage. As well as being unsafe because of the risk of introducing infection, the operation left the woman alone to cope with the miscarriage and its aftermath. Morgentaler tried this technique with a catheter, but found it to be unsatisfactory. The other main technique was dilatation and curettage, a somewhat tricky surgical procedure that required full anaesthetic.[54] It was the safest technique available, but required a skilled surgeon as well as the full array of hospital services to deal with the anaesthetic and recovery. Morgentaler's research led him to a technique developed in 1958 in China and just beginning to be used in Europe, though still unknown in Canada — vacuum aspiration or vacuum suction. He ordered a vacuum aspirator from England, managed to get it past dozing Customs officials, and began to train himself in the technique. As its name implies, vacuum aspiration basically involves anaesthetizing the cervix, expanding the vagina with dilators, and inserting a hollow plastic rod called a cannula, which is connected to the vacuum aspirator with clear plastic tubing, into the uterus. The abortionist runs the cannula around the uterus, and the machine sucks out the fetus. The only anaesthetic required is the para-cervical block to allow dilatation; the patient is awake for the entire procedure. The transparent tubing allows the abortionist to gauge whether the fetal matter has been completely extracted, though Morgentaler added a modified supplementary curettage to ensure that nothing would remain in the uterus to cause bleeding or infection. The entire procedure lasts from about five to fifteen minutes from cervical injection to vacuum aspiration, and is virtually painless except for some uterine cramps that can be soothed with an analgesic.[55] Morgentaler charged from $250 to $300 per abortion, though he claimed to reduce his fees for indigent women.

By introducing vacuum aspiration techniques to Canada, Morgentaler dramatically changed the assumptions that both legislators and physicians had applied to abortion. A Morgentaler abortion did not require a hospital, an anaesthetist, or even a particularly skilled physician; no complicated medical histories were needed, and patients were ready to leave in thirty minutes; the investment in medical equipment was miniscule (about $5,000 in 1970), and not much more than a general practice office was needed, with only a few staff.[56] Abortion clinics no longer had to be housed in major hospitals; they could now be established in local neighbourhoods. That is precisely what

Morgentaler set out to do.

Morgentaler's first abortion clinic, established in 1969, was an unassuming Montreal bungalow at 2990 Rue Honoré-Beaugrand. He kept a low profile, taking referrals that rapidly increased as women from Montreal, Toronto, and the Maritimes heard about him. Visiting Morgentaler was usually less expensive and certainly less threatening than going to New York. Morgentaler did not openly publicize his activities or directly challenge the government, but it was only a matter of time before the authorities came after him. (In Canada, criminal law is enforced by provincial authorities.) He was clearly breaking the law, since his clinic was neither an approved nor an accredited hospital, he did not have a TAC, and he did abortions on demand without inquiring as to any threat to the mother's life. On 1 June 1970 his clinic was raided by Montreal police, and three days later Morgentaler was charged with conspiracy to commit abortion and procuring abortion.

Morgentaler had clearly violated section 251 of the Criminal Code. Police, in conducting their rather heavy-handed raid, had accumulated sufficient evidence to show (indeed, Morgentaler never denied it) that he had performed abortions outside the law. The issue was not that clear, however, because the justice system assumes that charges must be proved, and gives the accused an opportunity to defend himself. Morgentaler's Montreal lawyer was the flamboyant and shrewd Claude Armand-Sheppard, who knew that, with a jury trial, his client's only chance was to have public opinion behind him. Armand-Sheppard recognized, as did Morgentaler's subsequent lawyers in the Winnipeg and Toronto cases, that the trials were in fact political manoeuvres in the guise of courtroom tactics. The court cases were condensations of vast forces swirling around a single issue — the whole weight of the pro- and anti-abortion arguments, the entire edifice of Canada's abortion laws, rested on the thin shoulders of a Montreal doctor who could be perceived either as a saintly guardian of women's rights or as a criminal making money from human misery. Morgentaler's physical appearance — his is the epitome of the stereotypical Jewish visage — made him an easy target for the latent anti-semitism that still disfigured Quebec's predominantly Catholic population in the early 1970s. Armand-Sheppard decided that Quebec public opinion was not yet ready to support Henry Morgentaler, and he released a battery of writs, motions, and appeals that threw the charges into legal limbo for over two years. Morgentaler was out on bail during this time, and regularly attracted attention by criticizing the abortion law as well as what he considered the stupid and hypocritical legal system that upheld it. This was a new phase for Morgentaler; in his 1967 Commons committee appearance he had been restrained and civil in his criticisms. After 1970, and once again in the Winnipeg and Toronto trials, he never bothered to hide his contempt for politicians. He considered them vindictive in their enforcement of a bad law and blind to the real needs of Canadian women. Morgentaler kept up his attacks through letters to ministers and MPs, through press conferences and appearances at rallies.

Morgentaler was emboldened to take stronger action when, on 22 January 1973, the United States Supreme Court handed down its decision in *Roe v. Wade* and legalized abortion throughout America.[58] The pro-abortion movement was encouraged by the decision, and decided that it could push harder for legislative change in Canada.[59] On 16 March 1973, Morgentaler announced to a Toronto rally that he had personally aborted over 5,000 women: the meeting erupted in applause and cheers, and the crowd of feminists and civil libertarians went wild, giving Morgentaler a standing ovation.[60] Morgentaler made the same announcement several times in the next week, but while his clinic remained under surveillance, there were no raids and no new charges. His challenge to the federal and provincial authorities was stunning: from the perspective of the Criminal Code and the criminal justice system, it is as though he had publicly admitted committing 5,000 murders or 5,000 rapes. Still nothing happened. The last straw was a CTV broadcast of a *W-5* documentary showing Morgentaler performing an abortion at his clinic. The show aired on 13 May 1973 — Mother's Day.

The system finally lashed back at Henry Morgentaler on 15 August 1973. Seventeen policemen stormed into his clinic while he was doing an abortion. They arrested Morgentaler, eleven patients, three nurses and a receptionist. On 29 August Quebec Attorney General Jérôme Choquette took the unusual step of preferring indictments regarding Morgentaler's twelve charges of performing illegal abortions (the last time this had happened was with the FLQ trial after the 1970 October Crisis). This meant that the case would go directly to trial, without a preliminary hearing. Armand-Sheppard tried to have the Quebec Court of Appeal quash the indictments on various grounds, all of which failed, and Morgentaler went before a jury of eleven men and one woman on 18 October 1973, three years after the first charges against him had been laid. Armand-Sheppard's defence was based on Section 45 of the Criminal Code, which absolved anyone of criminal liability in performing a surgical procedure as long as the procedure was done with reasonable care and it was reasonable to do the operation. This was supplemented and eventually overshadowed by the "defence of necessity" granted in common law.[61] The defence of necessity, like all common law principles, is general and must be applied case by case, but implied an immunity from criminal liability for performing an abortion if the abortion was necessary to save the life of the mother.

The trial took a month. In the end, the jury deliberated for almost 10 hours, reappearing periodically for advice on the meaning of Section 45, and finally acquitted Morgentaler on 13 November 1973. The Crown immediately appealed to the Quebec Court of Appeal, but in the meantime the Quebec Revenue department came after Morgentaler for $354,799 it claimed he owed in back taxes on revenues from his self-confessed 5,000 to 7,000 abortions.[62] Provincial tax assessors seized Morgentaler's professional and private documents, diaries and tapes, and closed his bank account. At this point it became clear that the law and the government intended to make an example of this Montreal abortionist who had goaded and insulted them into action. That impression must have been confirmed for Morgentaler on 25 April 1974, when the Quebec Court of Appeal upheld the Crown's appeal of Morgentaler's jury acquittal. It ruled that the necessity defence could not properly be invoked in this case, since abortion was legally available — there had, in short, been choices and opportunities, not "necessity."[63] More astonishing than this, however, was that the Court of Appeal then proceeded to *overturn the jury acquittal and substitute a conviction*. It instructed the judge who had presided over the jury trial to sentence Morgentaler, but since Morgentaler had immediately appealed to the Supreme Court, the trial judge declined. On 14 May the Court of Appeal directly ordered sentencing, and Morgentaler was placed in the Parthenais maximum security prison to await the decision. On 25 July 1974, he was sentenced to eighteen months in prison and three years probation. His only hope was that the Supreme Court would strike down the Court of Appeal's power to substitute a conviction for a jury acquittal. His hopes were dashed when eight months later, on 26 March 1975, the Supreme Court rejected his appeal.[64] The next day Morgentaler was taken to the Bordeaux jail. Without his clinic, his bank account, or his freedom, he seemed finished.

The Quebec trials and their implications were far from over, however. The Supreme Court decision to uphold the power of a Court of Appeal to substitute conviction for jury acquittal seemed such a gross affront to the role of juries in a democratic system that the federal government in mid 1975 introduced the "Morgentaler amendment" to the Criminal Code, allowing Courts of Appeal to set aside jury acquittals and order new trials, but not to reverse those acquittals. Other developments were not as benign. On 5 May 1975, when Morgentaler had been in jail for only about a month, Jérôme Choquette once again signed preferred indictments against him on new abortion charges. It seems that Quebec officials hoped to get Morgentaler to plead guilty in exchange for being allowed to serve concurrent sentences.[65]

Morgentaler refused to plead guilty to anything, went before another jury (seven men and five women), used the defence of necessity (which the judge explicitly told the jury it could not consider), and on 9 June 1975 was acquitted. Predictably, the Crown appealed, but on 20 January 1976 the Quebec Court of Appeal upheld the acquittal. The Crown appealed this too. In a somewhat bizarre gesture of redress, Ron Basford, the new federal Minister of Justice, set aside Morgentaler's conviction on the *first* trial and ordered a re-trial before a jury. (There had been some pressure in cabinet to pardon Morgentaler, but this was as far as Basford was prepared to go.) On 18 September 1976, a jury acquitted Morgentaler on the first set of charges, on which he had been tried twice before, once before a jury and once before the Quebec Court of Appeal. That same day, the Crown announced that it would press fresh charges against Morgentaler in early November. Morgentaler's salvation came from a fitting enough source: public opinion turned against the ruling Liberal government, and on 15 November 1976 the people of Quebec elected a Parti québécois government. The new justice minister, Marc André-Bedard, announced that there would be no further attempts to prosecute Morgentaler or any other doctor performing abortions in Quebec. The federal abortion law was clearly unenforceable.

By deliberately breaking the law and provoking the authorities, Morgentaler turned himself into a martyr, and like all martyrs he suffered. He had to close his abortion clinic, his medical licence was revoked, and the revenue department pursued him for a settlement on back taxes. He had a heart attack while in prison. The woman he had lived with for years left him; his first wife demanded a divorce. It took him several years to re-establish himself. But, also like most martyrs, he had some victories. Even though his attack on the federal law had failed, he could get some satisfaction from the fact that abortions for almost one-third of the Canadian population — all of Quebec — were available and would eventually be supported by public funds. His trials had forced the Morgentaler amendment, undeniably an important buttress for civil liberties in Canada. And in September 1975, Ottawa appointed a Committee on the Operation of the Abortion Law (the Badgley committee), and while its 1977 report eschewed any recommendations, it provided credible evidence of the law's shortcomings.

Morgentaler's travails had little discernible effect, however, on public opinion. In 1976, at the height of his notoriety, a national survey commissioned by the Badgley committee showed that "there was no strong mandate either to 'tighten' or to 'reform' the existing legislation....most persons implicitly endorsed the status quo."[66] In a situation reminiscent of the glacial pace of legislative change on pornography, there was no broad, national demand for a new law. In the long run, Morgentaler's most important victory was not in changing opinions but in becoming a symbol.

Paradoxically, this *man* came to represent one of the most critical issues of *women's* rights. The balance between Morgentaler and feminism in the abortion battles of the mid-1970s was an interesting illustration of the concatenation of individual struggles and broad political movements. Feminism as a movement nurtured most of the pro-abortion thinking after 1970, but movements do not go to court; individuals do. As well, a renegade physician like Morgentaler was needed because of the medical nature of the abortion procedure. Morgentaler was not a feminist, but his personal agenda coincided nicely with that of the women's movement during the period. Nor could he pursue his crusade on his own. Later, in the Winnipeg and Toronto battles, his potent symbolic force and adamancy was wedded much more intimately to a feminist support network, which staffed the clinics and helped raise funds for his legal bills. Until then, however, Morgentaler nursed his wounds and steeled his will for the next, and final, confrontation.

Throughout the 1970s, Henry Morgentaler and his supporters claimed that
they were only exercising the right and responsibility of civil disobedience.
From the anti-abortion perspective, of course, they were simply breaking the
law. Morgentaler's deliberate disobedience incensed his opponents almost
as much as the idea that he was, in their view, a cold-blooded baby killer. One
man who had watched Morgentaler from afar became convinced that two
could play the courtroom game. Joe Borowski, a former trade unionist, a
former Manitoba NDP Cabinet minister, and an oddball character with a
strange mix of unflinching integrity and single-minded determination, became in the early 1970s a leading and outspoken opponent of abortion. His
reasons were an amalgam of legal principles (respect for the rule of law) and
religious conviction (he is Catholic).[67] He resigned his cabinet post in 1971
and left the NDP to fight abortion, and in particular to fight Henry Morgentaler.

Morgentaler's 1975 Supreme Court appeal had been the first attempt to
claim a "right to abortion" under the Canadian Bill of Rights (the 1961
predecessor of the Charter of Rights and Freedoms). While the court had
dismissed the argument, Borowski realized that it might cut both ways and
that if medical evidence could be adduced to show that the fetus was a human
life from the moment of conception, then it might gain the status of a "person" under law and receive all the protections available thereby. Borowski
engaged Morris Shumiatcher, one of Canada's most distinguished jurists and
a former president of the Canadian Civil Liberties Association, to argue the
case. The case was launched in 1977, in Shumiatcher's hometown of Regina
rather than in Winnipeg to cut travel costs. Federal lawyers immediately challenged Borowski on two points; whether he had any right whatsoever to bring
such a case to trial (whether he had standing), and whether the case should
be heard in provincial or federal court. It took four years simply to resolve
these procedural issues. They went all the way to the Supreme Court, which
in December 1981 decided, on the first question, that Borowski did have
standing and that he could challenge the 1969 abortion law on behalf of the
unborn. It took another nine months for the Court to decide that the challenge should be launched in provincial court. In August 1982, Joe Borowski
and Morris Shumiatcher began preparations for their case before the Saskatchewan Court of Queen's Bench in Regina.

Morgentaler was enraged when he heard the news in 1981 that Borowski
had been granted standing.[68] Morgentaler had lain low since 1976, rebuild-
ing his life, relatively happy with the abortion situation in Quebec. He was
less happy with developments outside Quebec. The pro-abortion movement
had become institutionalized in various committees and coalitions for the es-

tablishment of abortion clinics, and feminists had succeeded at the ground level, creating "women's health centres" that gave reproductive counselling and abortion referrals. In a brilliant strategic move, the mainstream of the movement had redesignated itself as "pro-choice." The slogan of "free abortion on demand" had little appeal for the broad Canadian public. "Choice," on the other hand, had the cachet of individual liberty and acceptance of different lifestyles. Who could oppose "choice"? But while the number of abortions had increased steadily from 1970 (in 1980 there were 65,855 abortions as opposed to 368,030 live births, for a ratio of 17.8 abortions for every 100 births), there were troubling signs that the anti-abortion forces were beginning to rally and themselves become well-institutionalized opponents of wider abortion. Morgentaler claimed that one-third of the 2,000 abortions his Quebec clinic performed annually were for out-of-province women.[69] Throughout the country, anti-abortion groups had succeeded in closing several hospital TACs; in Newfoundland, for example, there was only one hospital that performed abortions left in 1982.

These reasons led Morgentaler to once again enter the fray. On 4 April 1982, he sent federal justice minister Jean Chrétien a telegram demanding reform to the abortion law. Morgentaler also said that he was considering establishing private abortion clinics in other provinces because "no jury in any major city in Canada would find me guilty for such a humanitarian action."[70] Within a week the League for Life of Manitoba sent telegrams to Chrétien and Roland Penner, the NDP attorney general for Manitoba, vowing to fight Morgentaler if he tried to establish a Winnipeg clinic.[71] The Manitoba College of Physicians and Surgeons followed some months later by stating that it would not license a Morgentaler abortion clinic, and Roland Penner said that he would not stay prosecution if Morgentaler broke the law.[72] By this time Morgentaler had made it clear that his key targets were Winnipeg and Toronto, the former because its NDP provincial government was on record as supporting liberalized abortion, and the latter in large part because he had been invited by a coalition of feminist pro-abortion groups.[73] The strategy in both cases was the same: to deliberately break the law, force the authorities to prosecute, and then get a jury acquittal, exposing the abortion law as insupportable and unenforceable. Morgentaler was playing the Quebec card. He made this clear in a Winnipeg press conference on 30 November 1982. Roland Penner, in a meeting with Morgentaler that day, had reiterated his position that, while he was personally "pro-choice", as the provincial attorney general he was bound to uphold the law. Morgentaler said that he would go ahead and establish a clinic anyway, and as in Quebec, would use the defence of necessity if he went to trial.[74] A week later, Roy McMurtry, the attorney general for Ontario, also warned that he would have no choice but to prosecute if Morgentaler performed illegal abortions.[75]

The following year was exceedingly busy and confusing. It saw three separate court actions, the establishment of two clinics (one each in Winnipeg and Toronto), several raids and arrests, and many marches and demonstrations. Morgentaler himself was threatened by a Toronto man brandishing clipping shears, and someone else tried to burn down his Toronto clinic.

Borowski's trial was colourful but the case remained under appeal by year's end. Several groups saw the significance of Borowski's legal gambit, and sought standing in the case. On 23 January 1983, Mr. Justice Matheson of the Saskatchewan Court of Queen's Bench denied such standing to the Canadian Abortion Rights Action League, the Canadian Civil Liberties Association, and Campaign Life. He scheduled the case for 9 May. In the meanwhile, however, the Canadian Charter of Rights and Freedoms had been adopted as part of Canada's constitution, and so when the case opened in Regina, Shumiatcher changed his argument (from the old Canadian Bill of Rights) to claim that the abortion law was unconstitutional because it violated the unborn child's "right to life" under Section 7 of the Charter. Shumiatcher set out over the next weeks to show that TACs were merely a rubber-stamp for abortions and that leading international medical experts believed life begins at or around conception. Federal lawyers simply rejected the relevance of these arguments; they set out to show that the abortion law was a valid law, however it might be interpreted by TACs, and that the fetus, whether alive or not, was not a legal person until born.[76] In an astounding move, federal lawyers called no witnesses (Shumiatcher had called eight experts and several non-experts).[77] The case ended on 27 May 1983, and Justice Matheson reserved his decision until 13 October. He decided against Borowski, ruling that Section 251 of the Criminal Code was a valid law and that the fetus was not a legal person. The case had cost Borowski $350,000 (most of it raised through donations), but he freely admitted that this was only the "first round in a three-round bout," the next steps being the Saskatchewan Court of Appeal and finally the Supreme Court of Canada.[78] A month later, Borowski filed a formal notice of appeal.[79] The Saskatchewan Court of Appeal hearing did not begin until 15 December 1985.

Opponents rallied the moment that Morgentaler announced he would open a Winnipeg abortion clinic in March 1983.[80] Their first line of attack, a novel one, was to have Morgentaler's municipal permits for the property at 883 Corydon Avenue revoked.[81] An anti-abortion petition with the names of 1,800 Corydon residents was presented to the city, but Morgentaler already had a development permit to renovate the building. On 25 March, a city committee upheld Morgentaler's building permit on the grounds that he had met the relevant municipal conditions; the fact that he openly proposed to break the law on the premises was ruled irrelevant.[82] Four days later the *Winnipeg Free Press* carried a paid, 18-page list of over 35,000 names opposing Morgentaler's clinic.[83] Renovations took longer than expected (they were not helped by vandalism that defaced the clinic's exterior with swastikas and slogans such as "Jewish Revenge"), and opponents kept trying to block

Morgentaler's occupancy permit by claiming zoning violations.[84] The clinic finally received its permit and opened on 7 May, one day later than anticipated. Joe Borowski was there on 6 May with a trailer, free coffee, and about 100 supporters, ready to capture media attention at the grand opening. The protest fizzled as the doors remained closed for another 24 hours.[85]

Before opening on 7 May, Morgentaler had written to the provincial health minister asking to have his clinic declared an "approved hospital" and therefore a legal abortion facility under Section 251. The application was denied; Morgentaler opened anyway.[86] Since he was openly flouting the law, it was once again merely a matter of time before charges were laid. Police raided the clinic on the morning of 3 June 1983, arriving in six squad cars and striding through the ranks of surprised anti-abortion pickets. Borowski rushed to the clinic minutes after the raid began to express his jubilation that the clinic was closed. Eleven people were taken away, but Morgentaler was not among them. He was in Montreal.[87] He had enlisted the services of Dr. Robert Scott, an Ontario physician, to do abortions at the Winnipeg clinic. On 10 June, police laid charges of conspiracy to procure abortions against Morgentaler, Scott, and six staff. Morgentaler was far from chastened by the raid and the charges. He re-opened the Winnipeg clinic on 6 June, and two days later at a press conference in Toronto, he announced that he would open a Toronto clinic on Harbord Street in one week, despite promises by Roy McMurtry to lay charges if he did.[89] The clinic would be staffed by Dr. Leslie Smoling, and Morgentaler and his supporters showed that they were preparing for a long and expensive legal battle — they announced a Pro-Choice Defence Fund with a target of $500,000. At this point, Morgentaler began to fight a two-front war. On 14 June he appeared in Winnipeg to face conspiracy charges, and the following day he was in Toronto to open his new clinic. The Harbord clinic opening was a macabre circus: pro- and anti-abortion pickets marched before the clinic, and within an hour of opening a man attacked Morgentaler with garden shears.[90]

On 25 June police raided the Winnipeg clinic for the second time, once again arresting Scott and the clinic staff, and laying more abortion charges. They also seized the abortion equipment and files as evidence. Predictably, Morgentaler vowed to re-open.[91] On 5 July, Toronto police raided the Harbord clinic, seized equipment and files, arrested Smoling, and issued a warrant for Morgentaler's arrest. Minutes later, clinic staff defiantly re-opened the clinic. Morgentaler surrendered himself on 7 July.[92]

In 1982 a prominent Canadian feminist could write that abortion was "the forgotten issue of the women's movement in Canada."[93] Henry Morgentaler and Joe Borowski changed all that. The clinics and the court cases were merely the manifestations of a much wider struggle. The political circumstances behind the two clinics were quite different, but led to the same fusion of Morgentaler the symbol, abortion the act, and feminism the movement. In Winnipeg, Morgentaler's arrival was treated with some ambivalence in pro-abortion circles. There, the Coalition for Reproductive Choice (established in 1982 with four member groups: the Canadian Abortion Rights Action League, Manitoba Women and the Law, the Manitoba Action Committee on the Status of Women, and the Women's Health Clinic) was worried that too close an association with Morgentaler would jeopardize public funding of its birth-control services.[94] Morgentaler wanted to run the show, set up the clinic and be the "front," and his autocratic ways annoyed some of his supporters. But once the battle was joined, they had no choice but to fall in behind him. In Toronto, on the other hand, Morgentaler was invited to participate in the clinic by the Committee for the Establishment of Abortion Clinics, which itself had been formed only a year earlier. The same group, once it got Morgentaler's advice to hire Smoling, selected the clinic site and helped establish the Ontario Coalition for Abortion Clinics, an organization that would develop contacts with about sixty women's groups.[95] Morgentaler was a powerful symbol and a brilliant publicist, but even some members of the Ontario groups feared a backlash against the women's *health* movement through too close an association to abortion.[96]

We should pause at this point to reflect on how resilient the political process had been since Morgentaler's first conviction. Politicians obviously had no taste to tackle what was and is possibly Canada's most divisive public issue. They could find support for inaction from polls that showed that the broad centre of the population could live with Section 251. Pro- and anti-abortion forces, of course, could not live with the law, and had ultimately decided to pursue the judicial route. But before the Charter this had not been notably successful either; without a constitutional standard of rights (which is what the Charter provides) against which to measure laws, the courts cannot "strike down" legislation.

The judicial route had to be supplemented with a strategy to win over public opinion, however. Thus the struggle moved inevitably to the streets. Indeed, the street demonstrations were meant to send signals to politicians and conceivably even judges. "Pro-choice" rallies occurred through the summer in both Winnipeg and Toronto, and small knots of anti-abortion picketers kept vigils at the clinics. The war of street numbers eventually culminated in the 1 October National Day of Action for Choice. While pro- and anti-abortion groups turned out in small numbers across Canada, Toronto saw about 20,000 anti-abortion protesters march silently by Morgentaler's clinic (some estimates were as high as 40,000).[97] Simultaneously, a small group of 1,000 to 2,000 pro-abortion supporters rallied at Toronto City Hall. (The contrasts could not have been sharper: in the first group, families, the elderly, Roman Catholic youth groups, priests, and nuns; in the second, labour unionists, Young Socialists, and even a few "Dykes for Choice."[98]) The low turnout was a severe setback to the prestige of the pro-abortion movement, and suggested that the political momentum may have shifted against it.[99] But, in a fundamental sense, street politics mattered less now than did legal manoeuvres. The courts and the lawyers had seized the issue, and they would relentlessly pursue it to the finish.

Morgentaler faced two sets of charges and two court appearances in Winnipeg and Toronto. The Winnipeg case went forward first, with a preliminary hearing on 5 October 1983 to determine whether there was enough evidence to go to trial. The hearing ended on 20 October, and the judge decided that Morgentaler should go to jury trial sometime in January or February 1984. The Toronto trial of Morgentaler, Scott, and Smoling began on 21 November (the Ontario attorney general had decided to skip the preliminary hearing and go directly to trial) before Mr. Justice W.D. Parker of the Supreme Court of Ontario. Morris Manning, Morgentaler's lawyer, immediately launched a challenge to the abortion law's constitutionality based on its violation of several rights listed in the Charter of Rights and Freedoms.[100] Thus before the court could proceed to the charges against the three doctors, it had to decide whether the law upon which the charges were based was constitutionally valid. With the beginning of the Ontario trial, the Winnipeg case fell into limbo and was never revived. The Manitoba government and the courts agreed to postpone the Winnipeg trial until the Toronto one was completed, but the Toronto case eventually led to the Supreme Court. This was not the end of other battles with Manitoban authorities, however. Morgentaler re-opened the Winnipeg clinic on 23 March 1985. It was raided the same day and new charges were laid. Six days later the Manitoba College of Physicians and Surgeons suspended his medical licence for his "apparent wilful and deliberate resort" to breaking the law. Morgentaler vowed both to re-open the clinic and to continue to perform abortions, even without a licence. Police raided the clinic again on 30 March, and Morgentaler entered a court battle to regain his medical licence that involved appeals up to the Manitoba Court of Appeal in 1986. But these were mere skirmishes. The real action had shifted to Toronto.

The 250-seat Toronto courtroom was crammed with pro- and anti-abortion supporters as Morris Manning began his assault on the abortion law's constitutionality. Mr. Justice Parker heard Manning argue that the abortion law violated rights to life, liberty, and security of the person; the right to freedom of thought, belief, opinion, and expression; and the right not to be subjugated to cruel and unusual treatment. For good measure, Manning added that the federal abortion law, since it dealt with hospital procedures, violated provincial jurisdiction over health.[101] In support of these arguments, Manning called witnesses and tried to adduce evidence that current abortion procedures actually threatened the mental and physical health of women, were ensnarled in bureaucratic red tape, and were accessible only to middle-class women who could afford to travel. Manning went on for four weeks, but when the moment came for federal and Ontario government lawyers Arthur Pennington and Alan Cooper to rebut, they refused, simply asserting that it was not Judge Parker's job to decide how laws are to be applied. They argued that the law was valid in the strict legal sense, and that its administration was not a constitutional matter for courts to decide.[102]

Manning summed up his arguments on 19 and 20 January 1984. Pennington and Cooper summed up in March, making three arguments. The first was that the fetus is a human life, and that aborting it is not akin to removing a wart. No one has to decide — indeed, no one can — whether the fetus is a person, but it has value, and the law's purpose is not simply to regard the rights of the mother, but balance those rights against the rights of the fetus. The second argument was less impassioned but equally important: the simple fact that not all Canadians had equal access to abortion facilities did not invalidate the law, since many federal programmes were "marred" in this way. Finally, they warned Judge Parker against usurping the role of Parliament and "Americanizing" the Canadian Charter of Rights and Freedoms by imposing the views of an unelected judge on the people. Parliamentary transcripts of the constitutional debates clearly showed that neither government nor opposition had wanted Section 7 of the Charter to apply to abortion.[103] And so was raised a new and puzzling question: are the courts to judge disputes in law, or are they, armed now with the Charter, to make laws? The Charter, as part of the Constitution, is the standard against which all Canadian laws must be judged. That judgment, of course, comes from the courts. But how far can the courts go in using the Charter to strike down laws, however imperfect, that have been made by a democratically elected legislature? In this case, the evidence was clear that the politicians had thought they were *preventing* the application of Section 7 of the Charter to abortion. Henry Morgentaler had no doubts that he and his supporters, in seeking legislative change, "may succeed in the judicial sphere where we have not succeeded in the political sphere."[104]

Judge Parker took months to make up his mind, no doubt aware that the stakes were high enough that almost any ruling he made would ultimately be appealed to the Supreme Court of Canada. On 20 July 1984, he decided against Morgentaler and Manning. He rejected all of Manning's arguments on the grounds that the Charter only protects freedoms so deeply rooted in the country's traditions that they may be deemed fundamental. "No unfettered legal right to an abortion can be found in our law, nor can it be said that a right to an abortion is deeply rooted in the traditions or conscience of this country."[105] Manning was disappointed that the court had not seized this opportunity to "develop the law" through the Charter, while Morgentaler mused that he might re-open his Toronto abortion clinic, closed since the raid a year earlier.[106] As could be expected, Manning appealed Parker's decision to the Ontario Court of Appeal, but the appeal was denied. Morgentaler, Smoling, and Scott were then scheduled to a jury trial on 15 October.

A jury had to be selected before the trial could begin. Jury selection usually goes quickly, with both prosecution and defence asking short questions of prospective jurors to ensure their neutrality. This time the case was too big and the stakes too high. After much haggling among the lawyers, they agreed on three questions: Do you have beliefs on abortion that might cause you to convict or acquit regardless of the evidence? Have you formed opinions as to the guilt or innocence of the accused? and Would you be able to set aside these beliefs to reach a verdict based on the evidence and the law?[107] Manning broke the agreement, with Parker's assent, and asked prospective jurors about their work and family backgrounds. At his side in the courtroom were Marjorie Fargo and Catherine Marks, two professional jury consultants flown in from Washington, D.C.[108] In the end, it took a review of 132 people before 12 could be selected for the jury: six men and six women, six married with children and six single. Alan Cooper remarked that the selection "was probably the most important thing we will do here." The trial arguments began on 19 October.

The prosecution's case was straightforward: it had only to show that Morgentaler, Smoling, and Scott conspired to perform abortions outside of Section 251. It could show that Morgentaler had anticipated arrest and trial and had taken the precaution of circulating a "guidebook" to clinic staff so that the proper evidence of a defence of necessity would be available, and moreover that he had a contract with the clinic ensuring that he would handle all "public relations."[109] Manning's defence was essentially the defence of necessity, since he could no longer argue the constitutional validity of the law. Witness after witness, question after question, Manning strove to show that clinical abortions were safe, that access to abortion was miserably inadequate, and that women were forced to go to the United States or elsewhere to get abortions. In his formal summation to the jury, Manning urged it not simply to apply the law, but to decide whether the law was good or bad and to "send a message to the government." Judge Parker admonished him for suggesting that the jury was not bound by the law, and also pointed out that the defence of necessity applied only when imminent peril would result from obedience to the law, when there was no reasonable alternative, or when the good results of disobedience outweighed the bad.[110] On 8 November 1984, after six hours of deliberation, the jury unanimously acquitted the three doctors. It was an extraordinary verdict, since the accused had admitted to breaking the law and the judge had in essence disallowed their defence. In the technical, legal sense, the defence of necessity should not have been accepted, and yet the jury trained its attention on the inadequacies of the law.[111] Pro-abortionists sprang into jubilant action to raise donations to cover legal fees,[112] while anti-abortionists attacked the jury members as "unionists and transients" and wondered openly if now they might not also break laws to further their cause.[113] The day after his acquittal, Morgentaler promised to re-open the Harbord Street clinic and demanded that the authorities leave him alone.[114]

The weary cycle started again. On 4 December 1984, Roy McMurtry announced that the Crown would appeal the jury acquittal, Manning promised a cross-appeal against the Attorney General, and Morgentaler defiantly said that he would open his clinic. The clinic opened quietly on 10 December, and Morgentaler ignored McMurtry's plea to keep it closed until the legal issues were resolved. On 19 December the police arrested Scott outside the clinic, and Morgentaler surrendered himself the next day. The charges were never pursued because of the outstanding appeals, and on 7 January Morgentaler opened the Harbord clinic again. For good measure, he performed some abortions there himself. By now the abortion issue had become a parody of itself: protesters from both sides marched through the winter, Morgentaler announced plans to open clinics in Calgary, Nova Scotia, and New Brunswick, and the Winnipeg raids continued. Anti-abortionists were clearly frustrated by events and by Morgentaler's apparent ability to flout the law, and began to intensify their protests. Toronto Catholics were urged by Emmett Cardinal Carter to picket Morgentaler's clinic.[115] Large anti-abortion demonstrations continued through February 1985, and pro-abortion activists began to feel a shift in public mood against Morgentaler.[116]

In April several anti-abortion groups (the Catholic Women's League of Canada, the Hamilton Right To Life Association, the Alliance for Life, and the Coalition for the Protection of Human Life) sought to intervene in the Crown's appeal of Morgentaler's latest jury acquittal. They were denied and the appeal began on 19 April 1985. The Crown's main arguments to the Ontario Court of Appeal were that the defence of necessity was inapplicable and that Manning should not have enjoined the jury to ignore the law.[117] Manning had a rough ride before the Court. His counter-arguments to the appeal went back to the constitutional invalidity of the abortion law, but the judges were decidedly unsympathetic, grilling him with interjections and eventually declining to take seriously his key constitutional claims.[118] The Court's scepticism flowered into a decision on 1 October 1985 to overturn the jury acquittal because of fundamental errors in law regarding the defence of necessity and the jury's role in upholding the law.[119] Morgentaler immediately announced his intention to appeal to the Supreme Court of Canada. Another dreary year went by as pro- and anti-abortionists continued to slug and slash at each other, like numbed and bloodied boxers in the final desperate rounds of a fight. There were sit-ins at the Toronto clinic and legal skirmishing in Winnipeg over Morgentaler's medical licence; Robert Scott opened a second abortion clinic in Toronto in May 1986 and was arrested and charged in late September; anti-abortionists talked about forming their own political party, and managed to capture TACs in Newfoundland and PEI and thereby halt all abortions in those two provinces.

Finally, on 7 October 1986, the case came before the Supreme Court of Canada. This was the apex of Henry Morgentaler's long history of legal and political challenges to Canada's abortion law. Twenty years after deciding that he needed to "prove his manhood" by defying authority, he faced the highest court in the country. Winner take all. In addition to the formidable talents of his lawyer, Morris Manning, he had a weapon he could never have imagined twenty years earlier: a constitutionally entrenched Charter of Rights and Freedoms that invited appointed judges to weigh laws against rights. It was a momentous event in Canadian legal and political history, but curiously flattened by the Court's own dry and sombre procedures. Henry Morgentaler's 20-year challenge, all the raids and arrests and jail terms, came down to four days of lawyerly discourse in a room that muffles both passion and pain, placing them between the precise calipers of the law. When it was over, the issue dropped into the dark cold sea of judicial rumination, and a decision did not surface until 28 January 1988 — two years later. The only event of note in the intervening year was Joe Borowski's defeat in the Saskatchewan Court of Appeal on 30 April 1987. Unruffled, Borowski did what he always expected he would have to do: he appealed to the Supreme Court. Ironically, Borowski was claiming rights for the fetus under the same section of the Charter that Morgentaler had used to argue the constitutional invalidity of Section 251 of the Criminal Code.

R. v MORGENTALER: THE DECISION

Seven judges heard the case. Five ruled that the law was invalid, two ruled that it was not. But judicial *conclusions* can be arrived at by different forms of *judicial reasoning*, so that even though five judges struck down the law, they did so by different means. Inset III (p. 204) summarizes the opinions of the seven judges on five key questions. Manning originally proposed 13 separate grounds of appeal, but the primary focus of the oral presentations was Section 7 of the Charter.[120] Chief Justice Brian Dickson wrote on behalf of himself and Justice Lamer that Section 7 "does impose upon courts the duty to review the substance of legislation once it has been determined that the legislation infringes an individual's right to 'life, liberty, and security of the person.'"[121] Dickson went on to say that "state interference with bodily integrity and serious state-imposed psychological stress" constituted a breach of the security of the person. Commenting on Section 251, he said:

At the most basic, physical and emotional level, every pregnant woman is told by the section that she cannot submit to a generally safe medical procedure that might be of clear benefit to her unless she meets criteria entirely unrelated to her own priorities and aspirations. Not only does the removal of decision making power threaten women in a physical sense; the indecision of knowing whether an abortion will be granted inflicts emotional stress. Section 251 clearly interferes with a woman's bodily integrity in both a physical and emotional sense. Forcing a woman, by threat of criminal sanction, to carry a foetus to term unless she meets certain criteria unrelated to her own priorities and aspirations, is a profound interference with a woman's body and thus a violation of security of the person.[122]

Section 251 created delays and induced psychological stress and thus violated Section 7 of the Charter, but the next question was whether these infringements were in accordance with Section 7's "principles of fundamental justice." Dickson interpreted these principles in procedural and practical terms, and cited all the problems with Section 251 noted almost immediately after the law was passed in 1969. Dickson found that these problems made the abortion law fundamentally unfair. While he recognized that state protection of fetal interests "may well be deserving of constitutional recognition" under Section 1 of the Charter, he concluded that the abortion law did this in an unfair and arbitrary fashion.

Justice Beetz, writing for himself and for Justice Estey, also concluded that the abortion law was unconstitutional in terms of Section 7, and that its violation of the security of the person was not saved by Section 1 of the Charter.[123] He arrived at this conclusion by a different process of reasoning, however. In his view, Section 251 had indicated an overriding interest in protecting the health and life of the mother when they were endangered by the continuation of pregnancy. This standard was entrenched as a minimum when Section 7 of the Charter was adopted. Thus security of the person under Section 7 must include "a right of access to medical treatment for a condition representing a danger to life or health without fear of criminal sanction."[124] The procedural complexity of Section 251, by unnecessarily delaying access to medical help, threatened pregnant women's health in arbitrary and unfair ways. Beetz disagreed with Dickson over the intent of Section 251; where Dickson read an attempt therein to "balance" the rights of the fetus and the mother, Beetz saw a provision to protect the fetus, with only an exculpatory subsection to deal with the problem of the mother's threatened health. While Beetz viewed this intent as justified by the Charter, he did not view the means chosen to achieve it as reasonable or fair.[125]

Dickson had reasoned that the abortion law violated "security of the person," and that this violation did not accord with the principles of fundamental justice. Beetz had reasoned that Section 7 did not create a new right, but a right to "security of the person" in the sense of access to medical services to save one's life, and that the procedures under the abortion law prevented that. Justice Bertha Wilson, while also striking down the abortion law, reasoned that the law's procedures were irrelevant to the primary question of whether a woman could be forced to carry a fetus against her will. If she could not, even the best procedures in the world could not save the law. Wilson argued that Section 7 of the Charter must be read as guaranteeing "life, liberty, and security of the person," not just physical and emotional security as Dickson had presumed. The concept of liberty in particular was critical: "Thus, the rights guaranteed in the *Charter* erect around each individual, metaphorically speaking, an invisible fence over which the state will not be allowed to trespass. The role of the courts is to map out, piece by piece, the parameters of the fence."[126]

Liberty is inextricably entwined with dignity, or the ability to choose one's life and way of living. The Charter, according to Wilson, assures that "the state will respect choices made by individuals and, to the greatest extent possible, will avoid subordinating these choices to any one conception of the good life."[127] Since the Charter guarantees a degree of personal autonomy over important decisions, the question was whether the decision to abort falls into that category. Wilson felt that it clearly did, and moreover that it fell into the category of reproductive rights, which are an integral part of the recent struggle for women's rights.[128] The abortion law had clearly violated this right, and so contravened Section 7 with respect to liberty. It also affected security of the person.

Wilson's final considerations were about whether the abortion law had deprived women of their rights in accordance with "principles of fundamental justice." Her approach was different from Dickson's and Beetz's; she did not identify "fundamental justice" with fair procedures, but with the freedom of conscience and religion cited in the Charter. Once again, the abortion law failed. Section 1 of the Charter did not save the abortion law either, because although the objective of protecting the fetus was valid, the law had taken inappropriate means to do so. Wilson then echoed the *Roe v. Wade* idea of "compelling interest," and basically suggested a permissive approach to abortion for the early stages of pregnancy and a restrictive approach in the later stages.

Justice McIntyre wrote the dissent on behalf of himself and Justice La Forest. He made it immediately clear that the core of his dissent concerned the role of courts in the policy process: "But the courts must not, in the guise of interpretation, postulate rights and freedoms which do not have a firm and a reasonably identifiable base in the Charter."[129] The courts had to refrain from "imposing or creating other values."

> It follows, then, in my view, that the task of the ourt in this case is not to solve nor seek to solve what might be called the abortion issue, but simply to measure the content of s. 251 against the *Charter*. While this may appear to be self-evident, the distinction is of vital importance. If a particular interpretation enjoys no support, express or reasonably implied, from the *Charter*, then the Court is without power to clothe such an interpretation with constitutional status. It is not for the Court to substitute its own views on the merits of a given question for those of Parliament.[130]

McIntyre's approach was somewhat more prosaic than Dickson's and certainly more so than Wilson's. He noted that nowhere did the Charter guarantee a "right to abortion." To conclude that Canadian women had such a right required reading it into Section 7. McIntyre asked what the legislators had in mind when they drafted Section 7, and showed that they deliberately worded that section to *preclude court review of abortion law*.[131] A wider historical review of Canadian abortion legislation showed that abortion at will has never been generally accepted. McIntyre closed by arguing that the evidence for the procedural unfairness of the abortion law was questionable and sometimes weak, since tens of thousands of abortions were performed each year in Toronto and there was no testimony from any woman who had ever been denied an abortion.

This review of the Supreme Court "decision" shows that it was in fact, as most court decisions are, an amalgam of sometimes wildly different arguments, some with similar conclusions and others not. The 1969 abortion law was unconstitutional, that much was certain. But did Canadian women now have a "right to abortion"? Only Justice Wilson went that far. Did it mean that the government could still regulate first trimester abortions if it found more procedurally fair mechanisms? Yes, since both Dickson and Beetz had focused on the *procedural* unfairness of Section 251, hinting that cleaner rules might escape judicial sanction. Could there be an abortion law that controlled access in the later stages of pregnancy? Absolutely, since all five in the majority acknowledged the state's interest in protecting the fetus.

The court's decision, in short, did not decide very much. It struck down the old law, but ambiguously, and gave no guidance whatsoever for what might replace it. In the first days of its release, the decision was predictably hailed and reviled, but just as predictably, for all the wrong reasons. Feminist pro-abortionists claimed a "great victory for women's rights" while anti-abortionists lamented the "disaster." Only for Henry Morgentaler, standing outside on the court steps in the cold Ottawa wind, was the result an unequivocal victory: "I still cannot believe it is possible after waiting for 20 years....It is beyond my wildest dreams."[132]

DISCUSSION

For Morgentaler it was a dream; for most Canadians, and certainly the federal and provincial governments, the politics of abortion have been a nightmare. A few days after the decision, the Conservative government in Ottawa promised to "provide leadership and act quickly" to develop a new abortion policy.[133] The issue split the party caucus so severely, however, that nothing happened for four months. In May the prime minister announced that the abortion question would be put to a free vote in the Commons.[134] No guidance was given to provincial governments on how to deal with the abortion question, and so some jurisdictions, like British Columbia, Alberta, and Saskatchewan, took steps to either limit the availability of abortion services or ensure that abortions would not be paid for through provincial medicare schemes. Henry Morgentaler quietly worked at his Toronto clinic and re-opened the Winnipeg one on 27 June.

The Tory government, in the face of its severely split caucus, spent the spring and summer trying to come up with the least divisive policy options. It had to show leadership, but also allow a free vote. Finally, the government scheduled a vote in mid-July on a three-part "resolution" that set out different general approaches to drafting abortion legislation. MPs would be free to vote by conscience, and the government hoped to get some sense of Parliament's sentiments on the issue by the distribution of votes for the three options. The Opposition parties put up several pointed objections to this stratagem. It was, they said, a ploy to relieve the government of its responsibility to submit legislation on the abortion question, and moreover, coalitions of minorities of MPs could end up defeating *each* of the options. It was also procedurally peculiar, since the government wished to prohibit any amendments to the motion, thus constraining a fundamental right of parliamentarians.

After protracted negotiations, the government withdrew its original motion and re-submitted a revised version on 26 July 1988, and allowed MPs to make amendments. Rather than three options, the resolution offered a single set of principles for the drafting of future abortion legislation. MPs were to vote in favour of or against the resolution or amendments made to it. The resolution said that any abortion legislation presented to Parliament should "prohibit the performance of an abortion" except

> When, during the earlier stages of pregnancy: a qualified medical practitioner is of the opinion that the continuation of the pregnancy of a woman would, or would be likely to, threaten her physical or mental well-being; when the woman in consultation with a qualified medical practitioner decides to terminate her pregnancy; and when the termination is performed by a qualified medical practitioner; and
>
> When, during the subsequent stages of pregnancy: the termination of the pregnancy satisfies further conditions, including a condition that after a certain point in time, the termination would only be permitted where, in the opinion of two qualified medical practitioners, the continuation of the pregnancy would, or would be likely to, endanger the woman's life or seriously endanger her health.

With MPs released from the normal shackles of party discipline, amendments came from every corner of the House, some trying to reduce the conditions contained in the resolution, others trying to narrow them. The core support for restrictions came from the Tory benches, while NDP members consistently provided the pro-choice perspective. Friday, 28 July 1988 was a lesson in both Parliamentary chaos and the *immobilisme* of contemporary abortion politics. Every proposal was defeated. The government's main resolution was defeated 147 votes to 76. An amendment that would have left the choice of abortion to the woman in the early stages and demanded only one doctor's opinion in the later stages was defeated 191 to 29. An amendment that would have left the decision entirely up to a woman and her doctor was defeated 198 to 20. An amendment that would have restricted abortions to the first 12 weeks of pregnancy was defeated 202 to 17. The one amendment that came closest to victory, by virtue of having been defeated by the least number of votes, would have prohibited abortions except on the evidence of two doctors that the continuation of the pregnancy would endanger the woman's life.[135] The votes broke down almost perfectly along gender lines, with female MPs from all parties voting for the more permissive amendments. A group of about 70 male Conservatives formed the core of the anti-abortion votes, but in themselves would never have been able to defeat the government's resolution or anything else. The Parliamentary outcome showed how pro- and anti-abortion forces are entwined in an unwilling and crippling embrace. The government's resolution, its hope for policy guidance, was defeated because *both* the core of anti-abortionists and pro-abortionists, disliking it for different reasons, voted it down. Abortion did not fall completely off the agenda, however. It surfaced in several ways, for example, in the federal election campaign. At least 74 anti-abortion candidates were elected on 21 November 1988. These 74 had either voted in favour of protecting the fetus from the moment of conception or had promised in writing to do so. Also, several nomination races were fought out between pro- and anti-abortion candidates, and anti-abortion activists targeted 30 ridings in which to mount direct mail campaigns.[136] Early in the campaign a Liberal strategist admitted that his party was considering the surprise announcement — during the leaders' debates — of a policy allowing abortions on demand up to 22 weeks. The accidental admission ruined the surprise and the Liberals did not raise the abortion issue again.[137]

This indecision, drift, and the growing disparity of "abortion regimes" across the country is a harbinger of a new stage in the abortion debate in Canada. Many people thought that the Supreme Court decision would be the end of the matter. As the preceding section demonstrated, the decision is vague and quite muddled in places. The simple fact that the Charter now gives the court wide latitude in reviewing legislation does not necessarily make the judges sitting on the court either infallible or any better equipped to solve public policy problems than elected politicians or ordinary citizens. Indeed, in some ways, they are *less well equipped* to deal with knotty problems such as abortion. They are unelected, largely unaccountable, and quite removed from the daily context of politics. Moreover, they reason about policy problems through the application of legal principles. Much of the time this is useful and fruitful, but it sometimes ignores the more prosaic considerations that must be the foundation of good public policy. To give only one example from the Morgentaler decision, consider the question of access. Most people choose where to live, and where they live makes a difference in the level of public services they enjoy. While all citizens, as citizens, are and should be equal before the law, it offends common sense to suggest that public resources should be expended to put, say, a hospital and university in every community, no matter how small or large, how remote or central. Rural residents (and as a practical matter this includes most people outside of the major centres) have "unequal" access to medical services, including abortion, and will continue to have "unequal" access. The establishment of abortion clinics that do not require TACs may change this to some extent, but it remains true that most physicians and nurses look upon abortion, as the Badgley Committee noted, with distaste. In short, the unequal access to abortion services under the old law in part reflected the realities of administering and delivering public services.

The court's decision was narrowly legal, and left so much about abortion open that the political process must move forward to deal with the issue. But it is unlikely that this process will be simply an administrative matter of tidying up the legislation. The history of abortion politics in the United States since *Roe v. Wade* shows that the debate and the struggle *intensified* after the Supreme Court there apparently announced a constitutional right to abortion. The same thing happened in Britain after the liberalization of its law in 1967.[138] Anti-abortionists see the Canadian Supreme Court decision as unacceptable, and they will have considerable opportunities to affect provincial health legislation and hospital policies.[139] The moral outrage they feel over abortion is heightened by their anger over how Henry Morgentaler, from their viewpoint, used and abused the legal system to escape the consequences of blatantly breaking the law.

Abortion is obviously contentious, but it holds a special place in the new politics of morality that have swept the Western democracies in the last ten years. These new politics are partly a reflection of the new political agendas of neo-conservative governments in Britain and the United States. Ronald Reagan and Margaret Thatcher, and to some extent Brian Mulroney and Bill Vander Zalm, have pursued policies that call for the maximum of freedom in the economic sphere (hence, deregulation, privatization, tax reform, and free trade) and a heightened restraint in the moral sphere. This restraint has led to a reassertion of family values, and attacks on pornography, prostitution, drugs, and homosexuality. The anti-abortion movement, while it antedates these new politics, has been affected by them. Leading members of Campaign Life, for example, are also affiliated with REAL Women (Realistic, Equal, Active for Life), a right-wing, anti-feminist women's organization.[140] Abortion holds a special place in this galaxy of issues because it

R. v. MORGENTALER (1988): JUDICIAL OPINIONS

Issue	Dickson / Lamer	Beetz /Estey	Wilson	McIntyre / La Forest
1. Does section 7 of the Charter allow Court review of substance of legislation?	yes	no comment	yes	no comment
2. Did section 251 affect security of the person?	yes	yes	yes	no
3. Are the section 251 procedures fair?	no	no	no	not unfair
4. Is there a "right to abortion" for women?	no	no	yes	no
5. Does the state have an interest in protecting the fetus?	yes	yes	yes	no comment

condenses all of them within itself. Abortion is about women's rights, and hence about family, sexuality, promiscuity, and reproduction. It is also about the nature of human life, when it occurs, and how it should be respected.

The anti-abortion movement thus is part of a broader agenda that has seen some successes in the last few years. This may give it additional momentum, but there are several other reasons why it will probably gain visibility and strength over the next few years. The first is simply the dynamics of action and reaction that were evident in the Morgentaler saga: the more abortion clinics around, the greater the affront and the more likely people are to picket and demonstrate. The second reason is that it would seem that while Morgentaler was winning in the courts, the anti-abortion forces were winning in the streets. Their demonstrations and rallies were larger and represented a broader cross-section of Canadian society than anything pro-abortionists could muster since 1980. This may be in part because the anti-abortion movement can rely on a pre-existing network of religious and community organizations, whereas the pro-abortion movement has been largely confined to feminist groups that have only sprung up in the last decade. This is not to say, however, that pro-abortion forces could not rally and organize very quickly if Parliament passed a restrictive abortion law. The lobbying efforts around the government's abortion resolution in the summer of 1988 demonstrated the organizational capacities on both sides. The third reason is that anti-abortion groups are getting smarter by appropriating the rhetoric of their enemies. Alliance for Life, for example, now circulates an anti-abortion pamphlet entitled "Personhood and Discrimination" that draws analogies between the struggle for women's rights and the struggle for fetal rights. The whole conceptual apparatus of "rights" is increasingly being used to argue *against* abortion. Doubtless the movement will also appropriate the concept of "choice" when it comes to arguing that medicare should not pay for abortions. Surely, the anti-abortionists will argue, if someone's conscience and beliefs lead them to reject abortion as fundamentally wrong, they should not be forced to contribute taxes for that purpose. This would violate their liberty and their freedom of conscience, the very things that Justice Wilson claimed were offended by the abortion law.

Anti-abortionists may get help from an unexpected and unwilling source: modern feminism. We saw that the right to an abortion became the focus for the Canadian feminist movement in the early 1970s. While Canadian feminism certainly expanded beyond abortion by the 1980s to include economic demands such as equity employment, abortion was always near the heart of the movement. Not all feminists, of course, supported abortion, but these so-called "maternal feminists" were a minority. More recently, some feminists in the mainstream of the women's movement have begun to have second thoughts about abortion. Feminism itself had attacked the idea that pregnancy was some sort of illness that required technological medicine administered by (usually) male doctors. Pregnancy was entirely normal, and to regard it otherwise was to perpetuate sexist stereotypes of the "delicacy" of women.[141] But this completely undermined the notion of pregnancy as a "threat to the mother's health", outside of a few rare occurrences. Feminism's view of pregnancy inevitably led to the conclusion that abortion was a right, not a health necessity as had been argued up to the 1960s. But if abortion is a right, then it is hard to consider limits to that right, and any reason for aborting has to be accepted as the expression of that right.

Advances in medical technology have forced a reconsideration of the choices people make. Most feminist pro-abortionists have accepted deformity of the fetus as valid grounds for abortion, but medical technology now makes it possible to discern very small "abnormalities" and to determine such things as the fetus's gender very early. If a woman has a "right" to abort, can she abort because she wants a boy instead of a girl, or because she does not want a child genetically prone to asthma? The new technology has also provided new knowledge about the fetus and its development in the first trimester, knowledge that makes it increasingly difficult to treat the fetus as mere "tissue."[142] Some feminists are also beginning to re-evaluate women's experiences of abortion as being much less benign than previously assumed. A particularly heretical thought is that easy abortion may in fact be more in men's interest than in women's: by providing an easy way out of "accidents" it makes women more sexually available.[143]

Modern feminist discourse no longer focuses on abortion, in part no doubt because it seems as though that issue has now been won. Instead, recent thinking has turned to the broader question of reproductive rights, of which abortion is only a part. The issue of reproductive rights stems from recently available medical technologies that can (1) operate on the fetus while *in utero*, and thus treat it in practice as a person with rights separate from the mother's, (2) determine the fetus's genetic make-up, and thus provide information that might be used to abort for what most people would see as spurious or eugenic reasons, (3) allow a woman to either "rent" her uterus for surrogate motherhood, or become a producer of fetal matter for medical research by repeatedly conceiving and aborting. Some feminists also worry that these new technologies are male in spirit — since the are invasive and controlling — as well as in practice, since they are usually dominated by male physicians and researchers. These considerations are leading some radical feminists to think about "lay abortions," since the techniques are relatively simple, and women aborting women would express their power and control over their own bodies.[144] For other feminists, it raises urgent and troubling questions about an easy embrace of "abortion rights."

The politics of abortion in Canada will thus move into a new phase. Far from being resolved, the issue will continue to inflame passions and rouse bitter debates. The new politics of abortion will probably become entwined with the politics of the New Right, and in particular with a broader backlash against feminism. Anti-abortionists will develop further a discourse that stresses rights and choice, but these will be fetal rights and taxpayers' choice. They are likely to work hard to influence judicial appointments, as will the other side once its sees that it may have gained only a Pyrrhic victory. The reproductive rights issue will bedevil Canadian feminism, threatening a split between those who see medical technology as a new liberation and those who see it as a new enslavement.

These are some of the broad canvases against which Canadian abortion politics will be played out in the next few years. The immediate struggle will be over legislation. It is conceivable that governments might try to do nothing. This, after all, was the way they dealt with abortion in the past. The 1969 law was buried in omnibus legislation that made it difficult to vote against. In all the court trials and travails, with all of the opportunities to address the law, successive federal governments consistently attempted to ignore the problem. In most large political issues, it is foolish to say that one person turned the tide, but in the abortion case Henry Morgentaler, by going to the courts, clearly forced elected politicians to face the issue. It is unlikely, however, that any government will be allowed to ignore the issue. The circumstances just discussed suggest that the pressure from anti-abortionists for some kind of legislation will not abate. The normal parliamentary process of committee hearings at which the public may appear will be enormously complicated, in comparison to what transpired in the mid-1960s, by the issues of medical technology, our experience with the 1969 law, and the constraints of the Charter.

All of these, of course, are mere possibilities. The only certainty is that the Supreme Court and the Charter will continue to reshape our politics, both in terms of what we think is the proper balance of individual rights and the public good, and in terms of which institutions we look to for policy change. It is certain, for example, that if Parliament did pass new abortion legislation that was disliked by one or the other side, that legislation would somehow find its way into the courts for review and judgment. We cannot predict what the court will decide, because the circumstances of the case before it cannot be predicted, and because it may have at least three new opinions from judges who did not sit on the Morgentaler case. The very existence of the Charter encourages groups to think of their policy concerns in terms of rights. The fact that both of the extreme sides of the debate represent minority opinions tempts them to focus their political resources in an arena that explicitly rejects majoritarianism as the sole criterion of justice. Henry Morgentaler was shrewd enough to know that while he needed public opinion on his side, it would be almost impossible to get the abortion law changed by appealing through the traditional political channels (votes, parties). His was a personal challenge that eventually carried the standard for the rights of women in Canadian society. The reaction to his claims of Joe Borowski — to go in turn to the courts — illustrates a new feature on the Canadian political landscape, a new focus for political energies and aspirations, and ultimately, new questions about the way political institutions shape and reflect and reconcile competing visions. The courts, in short, are a new world, a barely explored continent, in the way that we govern ourselves.

DISCUSSION QUESTIONS

1) How does the Charter affect the role of the courts in Canadian democracy? Discuss in relation to the different court decisions regarding abortion.

2) Both pro- and anti-abortion groups are intensely devoted to their respective causes. Anti-abortion groups in particular are likely to organize all their politics around this single issue, voting, for example, only on that criterion. What might the effects of a "single issue" politics be on the political system?

3) How are "moral" policy issues different, if at all, from economic policy issues such as the CF–18 maintenance contract? How are they debated and what are their dynamics?

4) Canadian federal politicians were often criticized for their inaction on the abortion question, though this inaction might also be seen as a measure of prudence in trying not to incite further divisions over an already divisive issue. Discuss.

5) Discuss the issue of "reproductive rights." In what ways does this issue affect the question of abortion?

6) Prostaglandins (drugs that induce miscarriage) are available in Canada in forms such as the "morning after pill." Do these drugs make the whole attempt to regulate abortion pointless?

7) From an interest group perspective, what are the advantages and disadvantages of using the courts to effect policy change?

8) Discuss the nature of judicial Charter interpretation. How do courts go about reasoning in respect of "rights" enumerated in the Charter, and what are the advantages and disadvantages of such reasoning for public policy making?

9) One of the most telling critiques of the abortion law was that its application varied across the country. Since it was a federal law with national application, this seemed objectionable. But other policy fields (e.g., health and education) are within the provincial field and variations are expected. Discuss the notion of uniformity and national standards with respect both to national policies and to ones under provincial jurisdiction.

10) Set aside your personal views on abortion, and assume that you are a prime ministerial advisor. The government has decided to try to reintroduce an abortion law as close as possible to the 1969 design, but taking into account the Supreme Court's criticisms. In what ways might the 1969 law be changed to avoid the procedural criticisms raised by Justices Dickson and Beetz?

CHRONOLOGY

1967

3 October

House of Commons Standing Committee on Health and Welfare begins hearings on three private member's abortion bills.

19 December

House of Commons Standing Committee on Health and Welfare tables interim report on abortion law.

21 December

Government tables omnibus bill to amend the Criminal Code, including abortion sections.

1968

13 March

House of Commons Standing Committee on Health and Welfare tables final report on abortion law.

19 December

Omnibus bill to amend Criminal Code re-introduced into Commons.

1969

27 June

New Section 251 of the Criminal Code becomes law.

1970

4 June

Morgentaler arrested for operating Montreal clinic. Charged with conspiracy to commit abortion and procuring abortion. Arraigned and released on bail two days later.

12 June

Preliminary inquiry begins before Justice Fauteux. Defence request for postponement denied.

16 June

Defence application to Quebec Court of Queen's Bench for writs of prohibition against Justice Fauteux.

20 July

Justice Desaulniers orders Justice Fauteux to suspend further proceedings.

25 September	Application made by Morgentaler before the Quebec Court of Queen's Bench that all further proceedings against him be stopped.
30 October	Quebec Court of Queen's Bench dismisses application to prohibit charges, but finds procedural unfairness in the way that Morgentaler's clinic was raided and the preliminary inquiry handled.

1971

25 October	Quebec government appeal to Quebec Court of Appeal against dismissal and discharge dismissed.
25 November	Papers filed with Supreme Court of Canada for leave to appeal decision by Quebec Court of Appeal.

1972

25 January	Supreme Court of Canada refuses leave to appeal.

1973

22 January	United States Supreme Court hands down decision in *Roe v. Wade.*
16 March	Morgentaler makes public announcement in Toronto that he has personally aborted over 5,000 women.
13 May	*W-5* documentary on abortion broadcast on Mother's Day, with segment showing Morgentaler aborting a woman at his clinic.
15 August	Police raid Morgentaler's Montreal clinic, make arrests, and seize equipment. Morgentaler arraigned the next day and returned to jail pending bail hearing.
29 August	Quebec Attorney General Jerome Choquette takes unusual step of preferring indictment regarding Morgentaler's 12 charges of performing illegal abortions. Morgentaler's defence counsel applies to Quebec Court of Appeal to quash the indictment; application rejected 21 September.

18 October	Jury trial begins. Jury consists of eleven men and one woman.
13 November	After almost ten hours of deliberation, jury acquits Morgentaler. Crown files notice of appeal.
1974	
13 February	Quebec Superior Court upholds order that Morgentaler pay the provincial government $354,799 in back taxes for 1969–72. Provincial tax inspectors seize Morgentaler's papers, diaries and tapes, and close his bank account.
25 April	Quebec Court of Appeal upholds Crown appeal of jury acquittal, and directs trial judge to pass sentence. Morgentaler appeals to the Supreme Court of Canada.
2 May	Trial judge (Justice Hugessen) refuses to pass sentence as directed because of Morgentaler's appeal to the Supreme Court of Canada.
14 May	Quebec Court of Appeal once again orders the trial judge to pass sentence, and directs that Morgentaler be put in jail. Morgentaler seeks to appeal this ruling as well to the Supreme Court of Canada. Appeal denied; Morgentaler put in Parthenais prison two days later.
3 June	Supreme Court of Canada rejects Morgentaler's second appeal and orders him to return to trial judge for sentencing.
25 July	Morgentaler sentenced to eighteen months imprisonment and three years probation following release precluding him from performing abortions except in an accredited hospital.
1975	
26 March	Supreme Court of Canada, in 6–3 decision, dismisses Morgentaler's appeal of the 25 April 1974 ruling of the Quebec Court of Appeal, overturning the jury acquittal.

27 March	Morgentaler taken to Bordeaux Jail. Six weeks later is moved, at his request, to the Waterloo Rehabilitation Centre.
5 May	Choquette signs order for preferred indictment against Morgentaler for new abortion charges.
29 May	Morgentaler arraigned before Quebec Court of Queen's Bench on charge that he performed an illegal abortion on 15 August 1973. Jury consists of seven men and five women.
9 June	Jury acquits Morgentaler after 55 minutes' deliberation, despite instruction by presiding judge (Justice Bisson) that the defence of necessity is not available to the accused. Crown appeals to Quebec Court of Appeal, and lays 10 more charges against Morgentaler.
17 July	Otto Lang, federal Minister of Justice, introduces Bill C–71, which includes the "Morgentaler amendment," preventing a Court of Appeal from reversing jury acquittals. Bill C-71 passes in early 1976.
29 September	Badgley Committee (The Committee on the Operation of the Abortion Law) appointed.
1976	
20 January	Quebec Court of Appeal dismisses Crown appeal and upholds jury acquittal.
22 January	Ronald Basford, federal Minister of Justice, sets aside the conviction on the original indictment, and orders a re-trial.
9 February	Crown announces that it will appeal to Supreme Court of Canada against Quebec Court of Appeal upholding of jury acquittal. Leave to appeal is denied by Supreme Court on 15 March 1976.
18 September	Jury acquits Morgentaler on re-trial of original indictment. On the same day, Morgentaler ordered to appear in court in November on eight new charges of

performing illegal abortions.

1982

4 April	Morgentaler sends telegram to Jean Chrétien (Minister of Justice) urging amendment of abortion law. Says he is considering establishment of clinics in other provinces.
15 April	League for Life (Manitoba group) sends telegram to Roland Penner (Attorney General, Manitoba) saying it will fight Morgentaler's attempt to establish a clinic in Manitoba. Telegram to Chrétien as well.
24 April	In address to the Canadian Abortion Rights Action League (CARAL), Morgentaler announces that he is ready to establish clinics across the country, especially in Toronto.
9 August	Supreme Court rules that Borowski should go before the Saskatchewan Court of Queen's Bench to argue case that Bill of Rights protects fetus.
23 November	Manitoba College of Physicians and Surgeons says it will not license a Morgentaler abortion clinic. Roland Penner says that he will not stay prosecution should Morgentaler try to establish one.
30 November	Penner and Morgentaler hold joint press conference in Winnipeg. Penner says he has no choice but to prosecute; Morgentaler vows to open Winnipeg clinic.
9 December	Roy McMurtry (Attorney General, Ontario) says he too will have no choice but to prosecute should Morgentaler try to establish a clinic in Ontario.

1983

5 January	CARAL announces that it will seek standing in Borowski's Regina court case.
28 January	Mr. Justice Matheson schedules Borowski case for 9 May 1983. Denies standing to CARAL, Canadian

Civil Liberties Association, and Campaign Life.

9 February	Community group starts fight to revoke Morgentaler's occupancy permit for Winnipeg clinic. While Morgentaler has development permit, his occupancy permit will be delayed.
2 March	Morgentaler receives licence from Manitoba College of Physicians and Surgeons, empowering him to perform legal therapeutic abortions. Penner warns Morgentaler that he must use a Therapeutic Abortion Committee.
29 March	Morgentaler announces delayed opening of clinic to April 18. Winnipeg Catholic diocese denounces clinic and *Winnipeg Free Press* publishes petition with over 35,000 names against abortion.
2 May	Morgentaler's request to have Winnipeg clinic declared a hospital denied by province.
7 May	After several delays and attempts by anti-abortion groups to quash occupancy permit, Morgentaler's Winnipeg abortion clinic opens. Borowski sets up pickets for May 6 opening.
9 May	Borowski case begins in Regina.
28 May	Regina case finishes; Mr. Justice Matheson reserves decision. Borowski returns to Winnipeg for a sit-in at Penner's office.
3 June	Winnipeg clinic raided by police.
14 June	Morgentaler in Winnipeg to face charges. First time he has been in court since Quebec trials in 1970s.
15 June	Morgentaler opens Toronto clinic amid demonstrations.
20 June	Morris Manning (Morgentaler's Toronto lawyer) asks Supreme Court of Ontario for an injunction against police interference with clinic since abortion law is unconstitutional.

25 June	Police raid Winnipeg clinic for second time; Morgentaler vows to stay open.
5 July	Police raid Morgentaler's Toronto clinic. Supreme Court of Ontario dismisses application for injunction on the same day.
5 October	Preliminary hearings begin before Provincial Court Judge Kris Stefanson on Winnipeg charges.
13 October	Mr. Justice Matheson of Saskatchewan Court of Queen's Bench decides against Borowksi in Regina case.
20 October	Preliminary hearings end in Winnipeg. Judge Stefanson decides that Morgentaler should go forward to trial in January or February 1984.
14 November	Borowski files appeal of Regina decision with the Saskatchewan Court of Appeal.
21 November	Toronto trial opens in the Supreme Court of Ontario before Associate Chief Justice William Parker. Before the charges themselves can be addressed, Manning launches a challenge to the constitutionality of the abortion law. This issue must be resolved first before the substance of the charges themselves may be addressed.
8 December	Penner drops conspiracy charges against Morgentaler and staff; replaces them with charges against Morgentaler, Scott, and nurse Lynn Crocker of performing illegal abortions.
1984	
25 January	Mr. Justice Peter Morse of Manitoba Court of Queen's Bench agrees to three month-delay in Winnipeg trial so that Ontario trial may proceed first.
20 July	After several months of argument, delay and judicial reflection, Mr. Justice Parker decides against Morgentaler and rejects Manning's constitutional challenge of the abortion law. Parker sets September 17

as date for criminal trial.

10 August	Morgentaler and Manning launch appeal of Parker's decision to Ontario Court of Appeal.
15 October	Appeal denied and trial begins before Mr. Justice Parker with selection of jury.
19 October	Jury selected and Toronto trial against Morgentaler, Smoling, and Scott begins.
8 November	Jury acquits the defendants in Toronto trial. Next day Morgentaler promises to re-open Toronto clinic and demands that McMurtry not interfere.
10 November	Greg Brodsky (Morgentaler's Winnipeg lawyer) announces that the Winnipeg clinic will remain closed until appeals from Toronto trial are completed. Winnipeg trial postponed indefinitely, until the Ontario case is resolved.
4 December	McMurtry announces that Crown will appeal jury verdict to Ontario Court of Appeal. Morgentaler says he will open clinic anyway and Manning launches cross-appeal against McMurtry.
11 December	McMurtry asks Morgentaler to stop performing abortions at Toronto clinic until Crown appeal is resolved; Morgentaler refuses.
19 December	Toronto police issue warrant for Morgentaler's arrest; Scott arrested outside clinic that evening. Morgentaler surrenders himself the next day.

1985

4 January	Morgentaler and Scott appear before Ontario Provincial Court Judge Walter Hryciuk on whether a trial should proceed on new charges, or be delayed until the resolution of Crown appeal.
8 March	Manitoba College of Physicians and Surgeons renews Morgentaler's medical licence. The president of the College resigns in protest three days later.

23 March	Police raid Winnipeg clinic as it re-opens and arrest Morgentaler. New charges laid.
29 March	Manitoba College of Physicians and Surgeons suspends Morgentaler's medical licence for seven days for his "apparent wilful and deliberate resort" to performing abortions in an unapproved facility. Morgentaler promises to do abortions anyway.
30 March	Police raid Winnipeg clinic again on Saturday for the second time in eight days, and arrest Morgentaler. He vows to re-open on Monday.
4 April	Manitoba College of Physicians and Surgeons wins interim injunction from Chief Justice Archibald Dewar of the Manitoba Court of Queen's Bench prohibiting Morgentaler from practicing medicine in province until licence suspension can come to trail. Morgentaler agrees to abide by the injunction because of severe penalties attached. On the same day, Morgentaler is charged with three more abortion offences as result of March 30 raid on clinic.
9 April	Brodsky files a motion with the Manitoba Court of Queen's Bench to quash Morgentaler's licence suspension.
15 April	Crown and defence lawyers agree to delay any further court action regarding Winnipeg abortion charges until Ontario trial is resolved.
19 April	Crown appeal of Ontario Supreme Court jury acquittal begins before the Ontario Court of Appeal.
7 May	Appeal hearing ends; Ontario Court of Appeal reserves judgment.
9 September	Mr. Justice James Wilson of Manitoba Court of Queen's Bench upholds temporary injunction by Manitoba College of Physicians and Surgeons against Morgentaler until College's civil suit seeking permanent injunction comes to trial. Morgentaler appeals.

October	Ontario Court of Appeal overturns Morgentaler's 1984 jury acquittal and orders new trial. Morgentaler appeals.
21 October	Manitoba College of Physicians and Surgeons refuses to license Morgentaler's Winnipeg clinic for abortions.
15 December	Saskatchewan Court of Appeal begins hearings of Borowski's appeal of 1983 Regina decision. Hearings last three days; court reserves judgment.

1986

15 May	Manitoba College of Physicians and Surgeons refuses for a second time to licence Morgentaler's Winnipeg clinic for abortions.
27 May	Robert Scott opens Toronto's second free-standing illegal abortion clinic.
12 June	Manitoba Court of Appeal upholds College of Physicians and Surgeons' injunction against Morgentaler.
24 September	Morgentaler, Scott, and Nikki Colodny arrested and charged, but charges stayed at Crown's request. The trio are released without bail and are back at their clinics the same day.
7 October	Supreme Court of Canada begins hearing Morgentaler appeal of Ontario Court of Appeal's overturning of 1983 jury acquittal. Manning focuses on Charter of Rights and Freedoms and the unconstitutionality of the abortion law. Hearings end on October 10; court reserves judgment.

1987

30 April	Saskatchewan Court of Appeal rules against Borowski's claim that the Charter of Rights and Freedoms protects the fetus. Borowski appeals to Supreme Court.

29 July	Supreme Court of Canada gives Borowski leave to appeal.
23 September	Ontario drops 1986 charges against Morgentaler, Scott, and Colodny pending judgment by Supreme Court of Canada on Morgentaler appeal. Manitoba government decides not to drop its charges.

1988

28 January	Supreme Court of Canada issues its 5–2 decision striking down the abortion law. Next day the federal government pledges speedy action on new law.
12 May	Prime Minister Mulroney announces that there will be a free vote on abortion in Commons.
June	Supreme Court of Canada postpones Borowski hearings to October.
28 July	Commons free vote defeats government's abortion resolution as well as five amendments allowed by the Speaker. Both pro- and anti-abortion forces declare a victory.
3-4 October	Borowski appears before Supreme Court

NOTES

1   Almost everyone who writes about abortion policy must address the question of language. The sides of the debate are so clearly drawn and unalterably opposed that they concede nothing in terminology. "Pro-choice" is ideologically loaded, and moreover inaccurate, since most people in that camp want taxpayers to be forced to pay for abortions, even if they disapprove of them. "Pro-life" is also loaded, in that it implies that the other side is not, and since surveys show that many who consider themselves "pro-life" also tend to favour capital punishment. Thus "abortion clinics" become "abortuaries" (a clever play on abbatoir and mortuary), and the "fetus" or "fetal matter" becomes "the baby". Choices are unavoidable, and we have tried to make ours as dispassionate as possible. We will use the terms "pro-abortion" and "anti-abortion" because they seem better to capture the real agendas of people in the respective camps. This may seem unfair to the pro-choice side, but it must be recalled that this tag was invented in the mid-1970s to enlist broader support from the Canadian public than had the previous call for "abortion on demand." As well, it is simply incoherent to say that one is pro-choice and anti-abortion: the pro-choice posture in fact leads to a political practice that accepts more abortions. We will use the

term "clinic" for facilities such as Morgentaler's, in part because "abortuary" is so tendentious and "facility" so unspecific. Finally, we choose "fetus" over "baby," since the latter clearly carries anthropomorphic overtones inappropriate to the medical reality of pregnancy. Technically, the conceptus is called an embryo until after the eighth week after conception, and a fetus thereafter. We will use the terms as needed.

2   Canada's statutory provisions regarding abortion have, since 1892, been part of the Criminal Code, but for ease of reference we shall refer to the "abortion law."

3   Lord Ellenborough's Act, 43 Geo. 3, c. 58, s. 3. The 1861 Offences Against the Person Act attached a maximum penalty of life imprisonment for performing abortions. In practice, women attempting self-induced abortions were rarely prosecuted: the law was aimed at the back-street abortionist. See Daniel Callahan, *Abortion: Law, Choice and Morality* (London: Macmillan, 1970), 142.

4   Offences Against the Person Act, 32–33 Vict., c. 162, s. 47.

5   Diana Dimmer and Loreta Zubas, *Update on the Abortion Law in Canada* (Ottawa: National Association of Women and the Law, 1985), 2.

6   Criminal Code of Canada, 1892, s. 179(c).

7   Unfortunately, in the case of the rhythm method, the nature of the female cycle was improperly understood until the 1920s. Before then, physicians advised patients that intercourse was "safe" during the middle of the cycle, when the opposite is usually true. See Angus McLaren and Arlene Tigar McLaren, *The Bedroom and the State: The Changing Practices and Politics of Contraception and Abortion in Canada, 1880–1980* (Toronto: McClelland and Stewart, 1986), 20.

8   Ibid., 18.

9   Ibid., 32–34.

10 Ibid., 119. For a review of the American birth control movement, see James Reed, *The Birth Control Movement and American Society: From Private Vice to Public Virtue* (Princeton, N.J.: Princeton University Press, 1984).

11 Committee on the Operation of the Abortion Law, *Report* (Ottawa: Minister of Supply and Services, 1977), 67–68. Hereafter referred to as Badgley committee, *Report*.

12 Arrest and conviction remained rare, however: between 1900 and 1972, a total of 1,793 individuals were charged with procuring or attempting to procure an abortion; 64 percent of these (1,155) were convicted. See Badgley committee, *Report*, 68.

13 Joan Finnigan, "Should Canada Change its Abortion Law?" *Chatelaine 32* (17), 103–105.

14 Ibid., 103.

15 Ibid., 104.

16 Ibid., 105.

17 Anne Collins, *The Big Evasion: Abortion, The Issue That Won't Go Away* (Toronto: Lester and Orpen Dennys, 1985), 16.

18 Alphonse de Valk, *Morality and Law in Canadian Politics: The Abortion Controversy* (Montreal: Palm Publishers, 1974).

19 *Globe and Mail*, 1 September 1961; op-ed articles appeared in *Globe and Mail*, 2–10 October 1961; 2 January 1963.

20 *Globe and Mail*, 2 January 1963.

21 Raymond Tatalovitch and Byron W. Daynes, *The Politics of Abortion: A Study of Community Conflict in Public Policy Making* (New York: Praeger, 1981), 44–46.

22 De Valk, *Morality and Law in Canadian Politics*, 14–16; 23–26.

23 Ibid., 18. In June, 1967, the CMA accepted deformity and sexual offences as legal grounds as well.

24 Ibid., 27.

25 *Globe and Mail*, 11 April 1967.

26 Canadian Bar Association, Humanist Fellowship of Montreal, Inc., Canadian Medical Association, Association for the Modernization of Canadian Abortion Laws, Emergency Organization for the Defence of Unborn Children, Catholic Physicians Guild of Manitoba, Presbyterian Church of Canada, National Council of Women, Canadian Abortion Law Reform Association, Women's Liberation Group, Anglican Church of Canada.

27 House of Commons, Standing Committee on Health and Welfare, *Minutes of Proceedings and Evidence*, no. 3, 19 October 1967, 66.

28 House of Commons, Standing Committee on Health and Welfare, *First Report*, 19 December 1967.

29 House of Commons, Standing Committee of Health and Welfare, *Second Report*, 13 March 1968; emphasis added.

30 House of Commons, *Journals of the House of Commons of Canada*, vol. 115, 9 May 1969, 1016–1017.

31 Section 251 was the "abortion law," but several other Criminal Code provisions, still in effect after the 1988 Morgentaler decision, govern aspects of abortion. Section 159(2)(c) prohibits the sale or advertising of things that will cause abortion; Section 221(1) makes it unlawful to kill the fetus during the birth process; Section 252 prohibits the procurement of things that will cause abortion. Sections 159(2)(c) and 252 are weakened by their respective reliance on the terms "without lawful justification" and "unlawfully."

32 Collins, *The Big Evasion*, 17.

33 Collins, *The Big Evasion*, 41.

34 De Valk, *Morality and Law in Canadian Politics*, chap. 8.

35 There have been so many *canards* about the Catholic position on abortion that any informed analysis demands clarification. While the Church has been a convenient target for pro-abortionists seeking an adversary (see, for example, the description of the quite deliberate selection of the Catholic Church as the "enemy" for political purposes, in Bernard Nathanson, *Aborting America* (New York: Doubleday and Co., 1979), 50–51), both the American and Canadian experiences show that the Church as an institution has been almost pathetically ineffective on the abortion question. In fairness, several other common errors need to be exposed. The first is that, prior to 1869, the Church allowed abortions up to the time of quickening, and only in 1869 made abortion at any time punishable by excommunication. Thus it would appear that the Church's prohibition against abortion is both recent and hypocritical. In fact, the Church has always held abortion to be morally reprehensible. The pre-1869 distinction was with regard to penitential practice in that *punishment* for aborting the "unformed" fetus was less severe. By 1869 the distinction between "formed" and "unformed" fetuses was rendered moot by medical science, and so the punishment of excommunication was extended to all abortions in the Apostolicae Sedis of Pius IX. The second error is the claim that the Church opposes abortion because it believes that the soul is enfused at birth. The Roman Catholic Church has never officially taken a position on ensoulment; its opposition to abortion is based rather on the more general principles that God, not man, creates life, and the prohibition of harm to innocents. The third error is the claim that the Church seeks to impose its religious views on society. In Canada at least, the Church has always held that it opposes abortion because of its detrimental effects on the common good. This is a practical, not a theological argument. See John Connory, S.J., *Abortion: The Development of the Roman Catholic Perspective* (Chicago: Loyola University Press, 1977) and John Noonan, J.R., *Contraception* (Cambridge: Harvard University Press, 1965). A cogent critique of the Catholic position must proceed on other grounds, for example like those in Callahan, *Abortion: Law, Choice and Morality*, (New York: Macmillan, 1970), chap.12.

36 Myrna Kostash, *Long Way from Home: The Story of the Sixties Generation in Canada*

(Toronto: James Lorimer, 1980), 176–178.

37 Krista Maeots, "Abortion Caravan," *The Canadian Forum* 50 (July–August 1970): 157.

38 Kostash, *Long Way from Home*, 176.

39 Maeots, "Abortion Caravan," 157. Also see Eleanor Wright Pelrine, *Abortion in Canada* (Toronto: New Press, 1971), 14: "And the right to 'abortion on demand' has become the rallying cry of the women's liberation movement....their slogan 'This uterus is not government property' symbolizes the feelings of many Canadian women."

40 Collins, *The Big Evasion*, 25.

41 Kostash, *Long Way from Home*, 178.

42 Royal Commission on the Status of Women, *Report* (Ottawa: Information Canada, 1970), 286.

43 Royal Commission on the Status of Women, *Report*, 286–287.

44 Following taken from Pelrine, *Abortion in Canada*, 36–43.

45 Badgley committee, *Report*, 27–28.

46 Badgley committee, *Report*, 30–31.

47 Badgley committee, *Report*, 21. In part this reflects ethical concerns, but many obstetrician/gynecologists view the abortion procedure (especially vacuum aspiration) as so simple that it requires virtually no surgical skill.

48 Pelrine, *Abortion in Canada*, 50.

49 Eleanor Wright Pelrine, *Morgentaler: The Doctor Who Couldn't Turn Away* (Toronto: James Lorimer, 1983), 5–6.

50 Pelrine, *Morgentaler*, 6.

51 Pelrine, *Morgentaler*, 15.

52 Pelrine, *Morgentaler*, 22.

53 Pelrine, *Morgentaler*, 25.

54 Another popular technique, developed in 1960 and perfected in Sweden, was saline injection, or "insillation." This was devised to deal with aborting pregnancies after the fourteenth week. A small amount of amniotic fluid is removed and replaced with either a salt of a glucose solution that usually kills the fetus and induces labour within 36 hours. Other, less widely used techniques are hysterotomy (a mini-caesarean section — 14 to 18 weeks) and D & E (dilatation and evacuation that combines vacuum aspiration with the use of forceps to remove the larger bits of fetal matter — 13 to 22 weeks). See Henry Morgentaler, *Abortion and Contraception* (Don Mills: General Publishing Co., 1982), chap. 4.

55 Pelrine, *Morgentaler*, 35–45. These pages reproduce an article Morgentaler published on the technique in the *Canadian Medical Journal*.

56 A side issue, though one of some importance in light of the legal bills Morgentaler faced later, was whether he made any money. Even at a conservative estimate, Morgentaler likely grossed between $600,000 and $800,000 a year in 1970 dollars. He admitted that he had made lots of money; see Pelrine, *Morgentaler*, 48–49.

57 Pelrine, *Morgentaler*, 75–76; also see Bernard M. Dickens, "The Morgentaler Case: Criminal Process and Abortion Law," *Osgoode Hall Law Journal* 14 (October 1976): 230–232.

58 *Roe et al. v. Wade, District Attorney of Dallas County*, 410 U.S. 113 (1973). The majority opinion in the 7-2 decision was written by Mr. Justice Blackmun. An unmarried pregnant woman (Jane Roe) brought action against the constitutionality of several articles of the Penal Code of the State of Texas that prohibited abortions except to save the life of the mother. Roe had argued that women have a right to terminate pregnancy, and this right is grounded in the right to personal liberty and privacy. Blackmun noted that while the American Constitution did not "explicitly mention any right of privacy," the Supreme Court

itself, in a long series of decisions, had recognized such a right or "zones of privacy" as residing in the Constitution, and that that right was broad enough to encompass a woman's decision to abort. The right was absolute, however, only in the first trimester before the fetus became viable; after that point the state had an interest in protecting fetal life and could regulate abortion even to the point of proscribing it, except where the mother's life or health had to be preserved.

59 Morgentaler, *Abortion and Contraception*, x; Pelrine, *Morgentaler*, 82.

60 Pelrine, *Morgentaler*, 83.

61 Common law defences against criminal acts are supported by Section 7(3) of the Criminal Code.

62 Collins, *The Big Evasion*, 141.

63 Dickens, "The Morgentaler Case," 235.

64 For this appeal, Armand-Sheppard had for the first time prepared several Canadian Bill of Rights arguments to claim that women had the right to abortion; see Dickens, "The Morgentaler Case," 237.

65 Pelrine, *Morgentaler*, 190.

66 Badgley committee, *Report*, 135.

67 Collins, *The Big Evasion*, 1–13. Borowski quit the cabinet of NDP Premier Ed Schreyer in 1971 after he discovered that provincial medicare was paying for abortions performed on Manitoba women outside of Canada. He considered this illegal.

68 Collins, *The Big Evasion*, 34–35.

69 *Globe and Mail*, 20 November 1982.

70 *Winnipeg Free Press*, 5 April 1982.

71 *Winnipeg Free Press*, 15 April 1982.

72 *Winnipeg Free Press*, 23 November 1982.

73 Collins, *The Big Evasion*, 73.

74 *Winnipeg Free Press*, 1 December 1982.

75 *Globe and Mail*, 10 December 1982.

76 *Globe and Mail*, 10 May 1983.

77 *Winnipeg Free Press*, 21 May 1983.

78 *Winnipeg Free Press*, 14 October 1983.

79 *Globe and Mail*, 15 November 1983.

80 He made the announcement on 27 January at a University of Manitoba debate with Borowski; *Winnipeg Free Press*, 28 January 1983.

81 *Winnipeg Free Press*, 9 February 1983.

82 *Winnipeg Free Press*, 26 March 1983.

83 *Winnipeg Free Press*, 30 March 1983.

84 *Winnipeg Free Press*, 27 April 1983.

85 *Globe and Mail*, 6 May 1983.

86 *Winnipeg Free Press*, 3 May 1983. Morgentaler had tried this ploy during the Quebec trials, and while on the surface it appeared a reasonable way out of the impasse, it was in fact unworkable. Section 251 referred to "accredited" or "approved" hospitals. Accreditation is done by the Canadian Council on Hospital Accreditation, and its minimum standards for the range of diagnostic, surgical, and obstetrical services far exceeded those available in Morgentaler's clinic. While standards for provincial approval vary widely, most demand a minimum physician/bed ration. As it happened, Manitoba did not have such a ratio re-

quirement, but it was simply absurd to label his little operation a hospital — it was analogous to a dentist demanding that his or her office be declared a "hospital." For a fuller discussion see Badgley committee, *Report*, chap.5.

87 *Globe and Mail*, 4 June 1983.

88 *Winnipeg Free Pres*, 11 June 1983.

89 *Globe and Mail*, 8 June 1983.

90 *Globe and Mail*, 16 June 1983.

91 *Winnipeg Free Press*, 27 June 1983.

92 *Globe and Mail*, 6 July 1983. Morris Manning, Morgentaler's Toronto lawyer, had earlier tried to get an injunction against police interference with the clinic, and the court's denial of injunction was delivered virtually in the midst of the raid; see Kirk Makin, "Clinic's Bid Rejected But Right of Courts Affirmed by Judge," *Globe and Mail*, 6 July 1983.

93 Kathleen McDonnell, "Claim No Easy Victories: The Fight for Reproductive Rights," in *Still Ain't Satisfied: Canadian Feminism Today*, ed. Maureen Fitzgerald, Connie Guberman, and Margie Wolfe (Toronto: The Women's Press, 1982), 33.

94 Collins, *The Big Evasion*, 65–66.

95 *Globe and Mail*, 22 June 1983.

96 Collins, *The Big Evasion*, 86.

97 *Globe and Mail*, 30 October 1983.

98 Collins, *The Big Evasion*, 87.

99 A little over a year later, Morgentaler's clinic staff and other supporters worried openly about this shift; see *Globe and Mail*, 21 February 1985.

100 *Globe and Mail*, 22 November 1983.

101 *Globe and Mail*, 22 November 1983.

102 *Globe and Mail*, 17 December 1983. Pennington and Cooper cross-examined Manning's witnesses in an effort to undermine the claims of capricious administration of the abortion law by TACs. They also developed an initial defence that the fetus was human and therefore had rights too.

103 *Globe and Mail*, 21 March 1984; *Winnipeg Free Press*, 22 March 1984; *Globe and Mail*, 6 April 1984. Pennington, the federal lawyer, made the arguments about the fetus and the law's application, while Cooper, the Ontario government lawyer, made the Charter argument.

104 *Globe and Mail*, 7 May 1984.

105 *Globe and Mail*, 21 July 1984.

106 *Globe and Mail*, 21 July 1984.

107 *Globe and Mail*, 16 October 1984.

108 *Toronto Star*, 17 October 1984; *Globe and Mail*, 19 October 1984.

109 *Globe and Mail*, 24 October 1984; *Globe and Mail*, 25 October 1984.

110 *Winnipeg Free Press*, 6 November 1984.

111 Jury deliberations are secret, but it is plausible that this jury took a common sense approach to assessing the doctors' guilt. Abortions were performed in hospitals everyday for largely non-medical reasons, and these three physicians were doing exactly the same thing but without bureaucratic permission. Alternatively, though this is speculative, the jury may have been swayed by Bora Laskin's dissent on the defence of necessity decision by the Supreme Court in 1975. Laskin had allowed for a greater degree of jury latitude than had his brothers on the court. The jury, in the midst of its deliberations, asked to see the text of this earlier decision.

112 *Globe and Mail*, 9 November 1984.

113 *Globe and Mail*, 9 November 1984.

114 *Globe and Mail*, 10 November 1984.

115 *Globe and Mail*, 12 February 1985.

116 *Globe and Mail*, 21 February 1985; 22 February 1985.

117 *Globe and Mail*, 30 April 1985.

118 *Globe and Mail*, 1 May 1985; 4 May 1985.

119 *Globe and Mail*, 2 October 1985.

120 Section 7 reads: "Everyone has the right to life, liberty and security of the person and the right not to be deprived thereof except in accordance with the principles of fundamental justice."

121 *R. v. Morgentaler,* Reasons for Judgment by the Rt. Hon. Brian Dickson, 11.

122 *R. v. Morgentaler*, Reasons...Dickson, 16.

123 Section 1 reads: "The Canadian Charter of Rights and Freedoms guarantees the rights and freedoms set out in it subject only to such reasonable limits prescribed by law as can be demonstrably justified in a free and democratic society."

124 *R. v. Morgentaler*, Reasons...Beetz, 3.

125 *R. v. Morgentaler,* Reasons...Beetz, 57. Beetz also addressed some ancillary questions regarding the constitutionality of appeal procedures.

126 *R.v Morgentaler,* Reasons...Wilson, 5.

127 *R. v. Morgentaler,* Reasons...Wilson, 7.

128 *R. v. Morgentaler*, Reasons...Wilson, 14–15.

129 *R. v. Morgentaler*, Reasons...McIntyre, 6.

130 *R. v. Morgentaler*, Reasons...McIntyre, 7.

131 *R. v. Morgentaler,* Reasons...McIntyre, 12–13.

132 *Globe and Mail*, 29 January 1988.

133 *Globe and Mail*, 30 January 1988.

134 *Globe and Mail*, 13 May 1988.

135 *Globe and Mail*, 29 July 1988.

136 *Globe and Mail*, 23 November 1988.

137 *Globe and Mail*, 21 October 1988.

138 Gilber Y. Steiner, ed., *The Abortion Dispute and the American System* (Washington D.C.: The Brookings Institution, 1983) and David Marsh and Joanna Chambers, *Abortion Politics* (London: Junction Books, 1981).

139 Another natural target is the Supreme Court itself. Now that the Charter gives the Court greater latitude to review and strike down government legislation, we can expect to see more American-style politicking over court appointments. Campaign Life, the largest anti-abortion group in Canada, moved quickly to try to influence the selection of a new Supreme Court judge to replace Justice Estey upon his retirement; see Kirk Makin, "Reduced Role for Politicians Urged in Naming of Judges," *Globe and Mail*, 16 May 1988. Its efforts did not seem successful, however, since the eventual appointee, John Sopinka, was not noted for his views on abortion.

140 Karen Dubinsky, *Lament for a "Patriarchy Lost"?: Anti-Feminism, Anti-Abortion and R.E.A.L. Women in Canada* (Ottawa: Canadian Research Institute for the Advancement of Women, 1985).

141 Several passages from *Our Bodies, Ourselves*, a feminist health guide, demonstrate these

points: "Pregnancy, labor, and birth are normal bodily processes, uncomplicated most of the time when healthy, self-confident women receive skilled and caring support for the entire childbearing year." In fact, feminism came to argue that pregnancy is potency, since it is the quintessential female experience. For example, consider this description of positive symptoms during the first trimester: "You may feel an increased sensuality, a kind of sexual opening out toward the world, heightened perceptions, a feeling of being in love. A lot of new energy. A feeling of being really special, fertile, potent, creative. Expectation. Great excitement. Impatience. Harmony. Peace." See The Boston Women's Health Book Collective, *The New Our Bodies, Ourselves* (New York: Simon and Schuster, 1984), passages at 327 and 344, respectively.

142 One of the ironies of Canada's abortion saga is that Henry Morgentaler constantly argued that his position was "rational" and "scientific," when in fact medical science was steadily undermining the validity of his view that the fetus is just a lump of tissue. Dr. Bernard Nathanson, who was the Henry Morgentaler of the United States, was persuaded by this medical evidence, not by moral or religious conviction, to change his views. See Nathanson, *Aborting America*, 160–161.

143 Kathleen McDonnell, *Not An Easy Choice: A Feminist Re-Examines Abortion* (Toronto: The Women's Press, 1984). McDonnell points out that one of the leading American funders of abortion reform has been the Playboy Foundation. In any case, this thought may not be as heretical as it first appears, since it echoes the feminist re-evaluation of the social effects of the birth control pill. Before the pill, fear of pregnancy was a useful defence against sexual advances. The pill removed that defence, and fear of pregnancy was replaced by fear of prudishness. The pill thus had come under feminist attacks both for its worrisome physical effects and for its false promise of sexual liberation. For example, see Germaine Greer, *Sex and Destiny: The Politics of Human Fertility* (Toronto: Stoddart, 1984), esp. chaps. 6 and 8.

144 McDonnell, *Not An Easy Choice*, 128–129.

ELEVEN MEN AND A CONSTITUTION:

THE MEECH LAKE ACCORD

In the spring of 1987 the federal and provincial governments struck a constitutional accord, which changed the face of Canadian federalism. After five years in the constitutional wilderness, the Quebec government agreed to sign a revised Canadian constitution whose major innovation was the increased power and authority assigned to the provincial governments. The success of the 1987 constitutional process was unanticipated, as was its breathtaking pace. In contrast to previous protracted constitutional experiences, the 1987 agreement was first broached and then agreed to by the 11 first ministers within a five week period.

The Mulroney government engineered a controlled and secret constitutional process, which saw the accord poised for ratification in late 1988. This closed, elitist process has generated as much comment and reaction as has the substance of the constitutional change itself. The eventual ratification of the agreement was put in serious doubt, as a result of political reaction to Premier Bourassa's use of the 'notwithstanding' clause over the issue of language rights. Constitutional change has had a permanent place on the policy agenda for decades, and is a political 'world' unto itself, which best illustrates the real character of Canadian politics and the roles of its major players. [1]

At 5:30 on the morning of 3 June 1987, Prime Minister Mulroney and the 10 premiers emerged from the fourth floor boardroom of the Langevin Building across from Parliament Hill. Their suits were rumpled and they looked tired and drawn. For the previous 20 hours, these 11 men had been locked up together in one of the biggest card games in Canadian history. It was an invitation-only affair: no press, bureaucrats, citizens, cabinet ministers, or MPs were there. Only heads of government had been invited to play. The stakes were high: power, money, and status. It was a game of constitution-making. The 11 men emerged to face an equally dishevelled media throng awaiting news of the winner. The extraordinary announcement was that all players had won — there were no losers. Canada had a "new" constitution.

This all-night session in the Langevin building formalized the 'accord' that the eleven men had struck in a nine hour meeting at Meech Lake a month earlier. The centrepiece of the deal was Quebec's agreement to sign the Constitution, after five years of refusing to sign. The key issue was a constitutional recognition of Quebec as a 'distinct society.' The 10 other governments agreed to this clause in return for a series of *quid pro quo's*.

How these deals were made tells us much about one of the key worlds of Canadian politics: federal-provincial relations; and one of its key activities: amending the Constitution. Indeed, federalism is probably the dominant 'world' of Canadian politics, and the idiosyncracies of Canadian federalism make Canada politically unique. One of the foremost activities in this world has been the attempt to amend the Constitution, mainly because it has been so difficult to do. An extraordinary amount of time, energy, and creativity have been expended, first, in attempting to patriate the Constitution, second, in ensuring that constitutional arrangements and practice reflect changing social and economic realities and, third, in accommodating the specific needs and assurances of the provinces, particularly Quebec. This has resulted in a variety of federal-provincial institutional mechanisms and processes whose importance rivals the parliamentary process itself. It has also created one of the most decentralized federal systems in the world, in which the premiers command a substantial amount of political authority.

In themselves, then, those intense days of 30 April and 2-3 June 1987 illustrate the closed, relatively secret processes of federal-provincial relations and of amending the constitution. These events also demonstrate the political dominance of the executive branch of government and the immense political power of the Prime Minister and the provincial premiers. Prime Minister Mulroney played an absolutely crucial role in reactivating the constitutional process as a political priority and in engineering the arrangements reached among the governments. Similarly, Quebec's Premier Bourassa demonstrated political will and skill in realizing his own promise to make Quebec a party to the Constitution on acceptable terms. The 1987 constitutional deal-making was a classic example of what has aptly been called the system of 'executive federalism' in Canada.

Ironically, while the 11 first ministers themselves accomplished so much in two or three days, they created a ratification process that could extend as long as three *years*. The constitutional agreement has to be passed by the Parliament of Canada and each of the ten provinces — by June 1990. This far more 'leisurely' and relatively 'open' ratification process has been in stark contrast to the hectic, indeed frenetic, pace set at the closed meetings at Meech Lake and the Langevin Building and the secret negotiations leading up to these meetings. This has allowed the 'other' worlds of Canadian politics to deal themselves into the constitution-making game. Since June 1987, the ratification process has been directly affected by elections, interest groups, the territories, the courts, political parties, and legislatures, and has demonstrated the uneasy relationship between the federal-provincial 'world' (a world of government-to-government relations) and the other 'worlds' (of government-to-people relations). The former seemed to have neutralized the latter, but this dominance ended a few months after the Langevin meeting, as the result of a series of key political events (including the elections in New Brunswick and Manitoba, which produced new governments not party to the arrangements struck in June 1987). Over time, non-governmental 'interests' against the arrangements took shape (women, the territories, native groups, minority language groups, labour, human rights groups), and doubts were articulated about the arrangements whenever 'open' public hearings were allowed (House of Commons, Senate, some provinces).

As this book goes to press in early 1989, the fate of the Meech Lake arrangements remains unclear. Regardless of the outcome, the story has to this point been both fascinating and instructive, and has had many twists and turns that can be followed in a chronology appended to this chapter.

AMENDING A CONSTITUTION:
DEMOCRATIC OR ELITE PROCESS?

The amendment process in a constitution must balance the requirement of stability with the need for change. Constitutions comprise political system's basic rules of the game: they establish who has political power, how is it to be used and what the rights of citizens are. These are not the sorts of issues that should be constantly tinkered with, as predictability is an important criterion of the functioning of political regimes. One wants the constitution to be altered only with difficulty, precisely to ensure that power is not easily seized, say, by one level of government at the expense of another, or by the government to the detriment of citizens. On the other hand, times change and constitutions must reflect these changes where necessary. The framers of constitutions cannot anticipate all possible national conditions or needs, and an overly rigid constitution may very well constrain effective governance.

There are two 'ideal types' of constitutions, flexible and rigid ones. Most countries, including Canada, have a rigid constitution (see Inset I). Canada is a federal political system, with constitutional mechanisms designed to inhibit the central government from usurping the power of the provinces. One distinguishing feature of federal systems is that they allow the sub-national governments to be involved in the process of constitutional change, with the provision of some sort of 'minority veto.' Hence, amending the constitution

AMENDING THE CONSTITUTION : A SURVEY

There are two 'ideal types' of constitutions. A *flexible* constitution is one that is relatively easy to change. Perhaps the best example is New Zealand, whose constitution declares (in the first article), "It shall be lawful for the Parliament of New Zealand by any Act or Acts of that Parliament to alter at any time all or any provisions of the New Zealand Constitution Act of 1852." That is, all that is required to change the New Zealand constitution is a simple act of Parliament. By contrast, a *rigid* constitution is one that is difficult to change. In order to amen. the constitution of the United States, an amendment must be passed by 2/3 majorities in both the Senate and the House of Representatives and by majorities in 3/4 of the state legislatures.

In Arend Lipjhart's scheme of the 21 continuously existing democracies since World War II[2], only 5 countries are presented as having flexible constitutions: New Zealand, Britain, Israel, Sweden, and Iceland. The vast majority of democratic countries have rigid constitutions. The amending process of these countries allows intentionally for 'minority vetoes', at either the local level or in both houses of the legislature. For example, the United States' amending formula offers a veto to 1/4 of the states – the smallest of which comprise less than 5% of the population. In Switzerland, both a national majority and majorities in a majority of cantons is required in a referendum for a constitutional amendment to be accepted. Exceptional majorities are often required in both upper and lower houses. For example, a 2/3 majority is required in both houses in Belgium and Germany, where one of the houses directly represents regional or linguistic interests. Both approaches are based on the principle of double or 'concurrent' majorities – a national one as well as a sectoral or regional one. This is designed to ensure that constitutional changes have strong support throughout the country. Whether a nation's constitution is flexible or rigid is no predictor of how often a nation amends its constitution. There has been little constitutional change in New Zealand, whereas in the first eight German Bundestags (parliaments) 70 of the constitution's articles have been changed by 34 amendments[3]

Federal systems normally also have a process of 'judicial review' to resolve constitutional squabbles between the two levels of government. There are only three countries comparable to Canada, as federal, with judicial review and a minority veto: Australia, Germany, and the United States. As previously noted, the FRG amendment process requires that an amendment be passed by a 2/3 majority in both houses. The Bundesrat is the German Federal Council, and is composed of 3-5 appointed representatives of each of the Laender (provincial governments). These representatives are actually members of the Laender. So, the German 'provinces' are directly involved and there is a minority veto available. The United States process comprises a system of 'double majorities' in which the state governments can trigger a minority veto. Australia is the only system with a minority veto and judicial review that offers a degree of direct, popular involvement in the process of amending the constitution. A proposed constitutional amendment must be passed by an absolute majority of both houses, or – after an interval of 3 months – twice by either house with an absolute majority (the Australian upper house is elected). Then, a constitutional referendum is held, and a further double majority is required: an overall majority of electors and a majority of electors in 4 of the 6 states.

FLEXIBLE CONSTITUTIONS

New Zealand, UK, Israel:	simple legislative change
Sweden, Iceland:	legislative change by two successive majority governments

RIGID CONSTITUTIONS

West Germany, Belgium:	concurrent majorities — 'special' (greater than (1/2) majorities in both upper and lower houses)
US, Canada:	concurrent majorities — majorities in both the national legislatures and in a 'special' majority of the sub-national governments

REFERENDUM

Italy:	after amendment passed by 2/3 majority in both houses, a referendum can be triggered by *one* of 500,00 voters, or 1/5 the members in either chamber, or 5 regional councils
Austria:	optional
Japan:	mandatory
Switzerland:	mandatory referendum, requiring majority of voters nationally, and a majority of voters in a majority of cantons
Belgium, Holland, Denmark, Sweden	'disguised' referendum; amendment must be passed by majorities in two successive governments

COUNTRIES MOST COMPARABLE WITH CANADA

Switzerland:	federal, with minority veto, but no judicial review and direct referendum
Austria:	federal with minority veto, but amendment can be passed by a 2/3 majority in the representative chamber, thereby by-passing the sub-national government representatives in the upper chamber
Japan, Norway:	judicial review, with minority veto, but unitary systems
Australia:	federal, with minority veto and judicial review, but also requires a referendum

is a complicated and often cumbersome business. On the other hand, the process is simplified by the absence of popular involvement. Canada has little to no tradition of using the referendum mechanism. (There have been federal referenda on prohibition and conscription; Newfoundland entered Confederation on a referendum; Quebec canvassed popular attitudes to independence via a referendum in 1980.) It has been the *governments* of Canada that have changed the Constitution, and the public has been involved only indirectly via electing those governments.

Up to 1982, Canada's Constitution was the British North America Act, 1867. A statute of the Parliament of the United Kingdom was required to change the Constitution. In 1931, the United Kingdom transferred all legislative powers to the Dominion parliaments via the Statute of Westminster. Canada was asked by the UK to devise an amending formula so that constitutional/legislative ties with the UK would be severed completely. Canada's politicians could not devise a formula, with the result that Canada's Constitution could not be amended except via an act of the British parliament.

Various conventions and practices emerged out of this arrangement. The British parliament would not amend the Canadian Constitution unless asked; it would pursue any request for constitutional change made by a joint address of the Canadian parliament; it never changed the Constitution if the provinces alone requested a change; it never rejected a federal request for a change even if the federal government had not consulted the provinces.

The federal government managed to carry out some constitutional changes in this arrangement, both with and without provincial compliance. Provincial compliance was obtained when the federal government acquired jurisdiction over unemployment insurance in 1940, gained shared jurisdiction over old-age pensions in 1960, and changed the retirement age of judges in 1960. No provincial compliance was sought in 1946, 1952, and 1974, when representation was changed in the House of Commons. Most important, though, was the 1949 amendment (S91(1)) in which the federal government, without consulting the provinces, specified that it could change the Constitution in areas of exclusive federal jurisdiction. This had the unintended effect of limiting the federal government's amending authority to a severely restricted area, and this was subsequently used only five times, in insubstantial areas. The constitution had become exceedingly rigid: a federal initiative to amend the constitution could be effected only with provincial unanimity.

The 1960s and 1970s saw an extended but unsuccessful public debate on developing a 'home grown' amending formula (see Inset II). This extended constitutional debate developed increased momentum as a result of the election of the Parti québécois and the holding of a Quebec referendum on independence in 1980. During the course of the referendum, Prime Minister Trudeau promised a 'new deal' for Quebec if the province rejected independence. This set the stage for the patriation of the constitution in 1982, and the adoption of a indigenous amending formula. In October 1980,

PROPOSALS FOR AN AMENDING FORMULA

In the 1960s and 1970s the policy agenda was dominated for periods of tome by extensive, exhaustive efforts to develop a workable, Canadian amending formula. The two most widely-known and discussed formulae centred on a *governmental* process.

The Fulton-Favreau formula (1964) comprised two parts; if a proposed amendment would change the division of powers between the two levels of government, then unanimity of the federal government and all of the provinces was required; in areas of mutual concern, the approval of 2/3 of the provinces and the federal government was required.

The Victoria Charter (1971) rejected the unanimity approach of the Fulton-Favreau formula in favour of a 'national consensus' approach. A proposed constitutional amendment would have to be approved by all provinces that had (presently or at some time in the past) 25% or more of the population, at least 2 Atlantic provinces, and at least 2 of the western provinces (with at least 50% of the population).

The Pépin-Robarts Commission (1976) (The Task Force on Canadian Unity) proposed an amending formula similar to that of Australia: a majority in both the House of Commons and an *elected* Senate as well as a majority of voters in each of the four regions in a national referendum. Approval of the provincial governments was not part of its proposal.

In 1978, Prime Minister Trudeau made a constitutional initiative in which he offered four options: the Fulton-Favreau formula, the Victoria Charter approach, a variant of the Victoria Charter approach (including various referendum mechanisms), or a national referendum. These proposals were not pursued with any significant degree of political energy or enthusiasm.

Trudeau announced his plan to unilaterally patriate the Constitution. The government was taken to court over its unilateral action; the Supreme Court ruled that this approach was, strictly speaking, 'legal,' but "offended the federal principle" and its conventions. Under Opposition pressure, a special joint committee on the Constitution was established. A political compromise was reached in November 1981, and the Constitution Act 1982 was passed in April 1982.

The constitutional process of the early 1980s was complicated and eventful; four points can be highlighted in this context. First and most dramatic was the fact that the Province of Quebec did not agree with the constitutional settlement, and never signed the new Constitution. Indeed, it was not part of the informal process that led to the constitutional consensus (which was cobbled together in a famous late night 'kitchen meeting' that was not attended by any representatives of the Quebec government). The Quebec government felt betrayed by the other provinces which, in its eyes, had ganged up and acted behind its back in coming to a consensus without Quebec's involvement. The substance of the constitutional settlement did not address the fundamental question of Quebec's role or place in Confederation. It did not acknowledge Quebec's 'collective' or 'distinct' identity, nor it assign Quebec powers to protect this identity. It did not address the issue of guarantees for the French language in Quebec, particularly given the advent of the Charter of Rights and Freedoms. And Quebec appeared to have lost its constitutional veto. It felt that Trudeau had betrayed it by not delivering on his promise of a 'renewed federalism.' Hence, the constitutional accomplishment of 1981-2 was seriously flawed, and was considered by most Quebecers to have been illegitimately imposed on it. While Quebec did not sign the new constitution, it did remain legally bound to it.

Second, a new amending formula was set (in Section 38(1)). There were four features to the formula:

§   the basic formula was to be parliamentary approval plus approval by two-thirds of the provinces (comprising more than 50 percent of the population);
§   if the issue or area being altered was not a national matter, then a dissenting province could chose to 'opt out' and not be party to the new arrangement;
§   unanimity would be required in certain 'national' areas, like the creation of new provinces or the altering of national institutions;
§   unilateral action could be taken by federal or provincial governments in areas of exclusive jurisdiction.

The creation of a new amending formula was a hollow accomplishment, given Quebec's attitude to the new constitution. Unanimity was required for constitutional alterations of a national sort (e.g. Senate reform), and it was hardly likely that the Quebec government would be willing to take part in these sorts of discussions until its own 'grievances' had been dealt with. After 1982, Quebec participated in constitutional conferences in only a limited way.

Third, the constitutional experience of 1981-82 had a 'popular' or citizen dimension to it that was unanticipated and unusual. This was the result of two factors. While participation in the formal constitutional process was restricted to governments, confrontation between the federal and the provincial governments sent each side looking for popular support to back up and legitimate its position. And the constitutional package's including a Charter of Rights and Freedoms only encouraged popular involvement. Various groups and interests rallied around this so-called 'people's package,' particularly through the joint committee process. As a result, there was an unusually high degree of public participation in this constitutional process, particularly by women's, native and multicultural groups. This led many Canadians to genuinely feel that the new Constitution, or at least parts of it, was 'theirs,' and created expectations about public involvement in future constitutional exercises.[4] The 1982 amending formula itself, though, reproduced the principle of government, as opposed to popular, control of amending the Constitution.

Fourth, the effective domain of the Charter of Rights and Freedoms was limited by Section 33, the so-called 'notwithstanding' or *non obstante* clause. This entitled parliament or provincial legislatures to assert that a particular law could operate without being subject to the rights guaranteed by the Charter. This feature of the Charter balanced the authority of the legislature with that of the judiciary. Future events would demonstrate that this was an unstable balance. The provinces requested the inclusion of this clause; only Ontario and New Brunswick would likely have agreed to the Charter without it. In the period before Meech Lake, the province of Quebec used the notwithstanding clause to limit the Charter's impact on its existing and newly passed statutes.

THE ROAD TO MEECH LAKE, 1984-1987

In a rain-soaked ceremony on 17 April 1982, the Queen participated in a constitution-signing that marked the final stage in the saga of patriating the Canadian constitution. After the defeat of the 'Oui' forces in the May 1980 referendum in Quebec, a degree of political momentum built up and culminated in the 5 November 1981 constitutional agreement between the federal government and nine of the provincial governments. The Quebec government refused to sign the new constitution, and this lacuna was a blemish on the constitutional accomplishment.

Five years later, on 30 April 1987, the federal government and all ten provinces reached a new constitutional agreement at Meech Lake. For many, this was a surprising development, as constitutional concerns had fallen off the policy agenda as a priority matter since 1982. After two decades of constitutional squabbling, Canadians appeared to have had enough of constitutional discussions, and looked to other areas for government action. Moreover, an ongoing constitutional stalemate appeared to be inevitable, given the rigidity of the new amending formula and given that all attempts to bring Quebec into the constitution would look like 'favouritism.' As Ron Graham put it, "any deal with Quebec would have to pass through that [mending] process, which was guaranteed to reject giving any powers and advantages to Quebec without granting equivalent powers and advantages to everyone else."[5] This turned out to be a shrewd insight.

Two elections changed this constitutional situation. On 4 September 1984, the Progressive Conservatives won a landslide victory in the national election. This included an historical electoral breakthrough in Quebec, where it won 58 of 75 seats. And in the Quebec provincial election of 2 December 1985 the Liberals defeated the Parti québécois in a solid victory. Instead of a federal Liberal party confronting a Parti québécois government, a federal Conservative government faced a provincial Liberal party. Gone were the towering, indeed mythic, figures of Pierre Trudeau and René Lévesque, each antagonistic to the other and committed to diametrically opposed visions of Canada and Quebec's role in it. They were replaced by the less imposing but pragmatic figures of Brian Mulroney and Robert Bourassa — who also happened to be close friends.

Mulroney and the Federal Tories

Like Pierre Trudeau, Prime Minister Mulroney was a Quebecer, fluently bilingual and well-versed in the nuances of Quebec politics. In contrast to Trudeau, though, Mulroney was a 'process' person, not an 'ideas' person. His political skills were honed in the backrooms of politics, and he developed superb negotiating skills in his managerial capacity in the private sector. While Trudeau's 'intellectual vision' of Canada had acted as a constraint on constitutional negotiations, Mulroney's lack of a 'formal' or fully developed vision of Canada would allow him to be more flexible in negotiations. Indeed, for Mulroney a constitutional deal itself would be a more important consideration than the substance of the deal. During his leadership campaign in the spring of 1983, he promised to bring Quebec into the Constitution, but he provided neither strategic details nor guiding principles.[6]

During the 1984 election campaign, Mulroney pledged to bring Quebec into the Canadian constitutional family. At his nomination meeting at Sept-Iles on 6 August 1984, he told his Manicouagan constituents that he would "breathe a new spirit into federalism." He promised to respect provincial jurisdictions "scrupulously" and to end the federal government's centralizing invasions, "the Liberals' favourite sport." With regard to Quebec's participation in the constitution, he said:

> I know that, in the province of Quebec, there are wounds to be healed, worries to be calmed and bonds of trust to be established. The men and women of this province have undergone a collective trauma. They were faced with the impossible choice between Canada and Quebec, a situation no more possible than that of a child having to choose between its father and mother. There is room in Canada for all identities to be affirmed, for all aspirations to be respected, and for all ideals to be pursued. I know many young men and women will not be satisfied with mere words. We will have to make commitments and take concrete steps to reach the objective that I have set for myself and that I repeat here: to convince the Quebec National Assembly to give its consent to the new Canadian Constitution with honour and enthusiasm. But, knowing the importance and the complexities of federal-provincial issues, I will not undertake a constitutional path with ambiguity and improvisation. To proceed otherwise would risk making things much worse rather than better.[7]

However, he did not offer any specifics on the amending formula or a Quebec veto, declaring that this issue would not be a top priority for his government. More urgent, he argued, was the task of placing his 'new federalism' at the service of economic recovery, and creating a mood for constitutional renewal on the basis of open dialogue and good examples. He did propose the creation of a federal-provincial advisory and coordinating body to end the "to-and-fro-ing at the two levels of government." But his overall strategy appeared to centre on creating ongoing improved relations with the province of Quebec, with constitutional negotiations to take place "at the opportune moment...pursued in the framework of Canadian federalism, with the authorities legitimately elected by Quebec."[8]

This approach to constitutional change continued once the Conservatives became the government. Its first Speech from the Throne stated that

> This is the inauguration of a new Parliament. Let it also be the beginning of a new era of reconciliation, economic renewal and social justice...a priority of my government will be to breathe a new spirit into federalism and restore the faith and trust of all Canadians in the effectiveness of our system of government...it is obvious that the constitutional agreement is incomplete so long as Quebec is not part of an accord. *While their principal obligations are to achieve economic renewal*, my ministers will work to create the conditions that will make possible the achievement of this essential accord.[9]

In response to a question in the House of Commons, Mulroney stated that "it has always been my intention to try and create a climate that will make it possible for Quebec to sign the constitutional agreement with enthusiasm and with honour."[10] He also declared, though, that economic recovery was the first order of government business. Other than his 'meteorological' approach, Mulroney offered no details or plans for constitutional negotiations. He was biding his time waiting for the results of the Quebec election.

Bourassa and the Quebec Liberals

Robert Bourassa had previously served as premier of Quebec in the early 1970s. A committed federalist, he was a technocrat by training and temperament, and an extremely experienced and able one. For Bourassa, the first objective of any constitutional deal with Canada would be the "goal of strengthening the position of Quebec."[11] Unlike the federal Conservatives, the Quebec Liberals were quite open and specific in setting out what were the 'conditions' of Quebec's signing the constitution. In early February 1985, the party released the policy paper *Maitriser l'avenir* ("Mastering Our Future"), which was prepared for the impending provincial election. This document reflected the party's main constitutional policy concerns of the late 1970s and early 1980s, and became the basis for the constitutional process that led up to Meech Lake. The five conditions were:

§ explicit recognition of Quebec as a 'distinct society' in the preamble of the Constitution;

§ extension of Quebec's right in the recruitment and selection of immigrants into Quebec, in order to protect its cultural security;

§ granting to Quebec the key role in the appointment of the three Supreme Court justices with expertise in civil law;

§ limitation of the federal government's spending power in areas of provincial jurisdiction;

§ granting to Quebec a full veto on all constitutional questions, with the veto entrenched in the amending formula.[12]

Compared to previous lists of considerations presented by Quebec governments, this was not an especially ambitious list. This reflected Quebec's relatively weak bargaining position in the post-referendum, post-patriation period.[13] There was little public reaction to the issuing of this document.

During the run-up to the December 1985 election, Bourassa sent a variety of encouraging political signals to Ottawa and the rest of Canada. In August, he declared that a Quebec government would accept the 'priority' of the Canadian Charter over the Quebec Charter: "The Canadian Charter has its place in the Constitution, because there are values common to all Canadians and this does not aggravate in any way the rights of Quebecers to accentuate these values."[14] In an October interview with *Le Devoir*, Bourassa stated that "I am confident, I am optimistic that a Liberal government will be capable of signing the constitutional accord...I know that the climate could allow us to sign much more easily than in past years." To the question, "Is this negotiation a priority?" he replied, "Certainly otherwise we risk compromising the constitutional negotiations if we do not succeed with the present federal government which has shown its interest in having Quebec accept the constitutional accord." He also declared that any agreement reached would not be submitted to a referendum: "I have no intention of submitting Quebecers to another political debate."[15]

In late October 1985, it was announced that Gil Rémillard, a professor of constitutional law, would run as a Liberal candidate in the provincial election. The ties between the federal Conservatives and the Quebec Liberals appeared set: Rémillard had been, up to this time, a special adviser to Brian Mulroney.

The foundation for the constitutional deal was laid in the 16 months preceding the Meech Lake meeting. This preliminary process was characterized by two features. On the one hand, the lead players in the process, Quebec and Ottawa, took extraordinary care at each stage to assuage the doubts and concerns of the various regions of Canada. On the other hand, this process was so closed (indeed underground) that few in Canada, including the media, knew what was taking place. The process was tightly controlled and engineered for the purpose of increasing the likelihood of success. Only the 11 governments were involved.

The Liberal government made a quick political overture after the December 1985 election. In early March 1986, Intergovernmental Affairs Minister Gil Rémillard announced that Quebec was willing to recognize the preeminence of the federal Charter of Rights over Quebec's Charter, and hoped that constitutional talks could start as early as October 1986. The suddenness of this overture appeared to catch Ottawa by surprise.[16] In a CBC (French language) television interview in April, Premier Bourassa stated that he hoped to reach a constitutional settlement during the Mulroney government's term in office: "We would like to sign an agreement before the next federal election, otherwise it will be constantly put off."[17]

On 9 May 1986, at a conference in Mont-Gabriel ("Quebec and its partners in Confederation"), Rémillard presented the Quebec government's five conditions for signing the Constitution. This was the formal government declaration of the five principles that had been articulated in *Maitriser l'avenir*. Rémillard hoped that this would "start the ball rolling." He warned, though, that "it is not only up to Quebec to act....Our federal partners must not sit back idly; we expect concrete action on their part, action that is likely to steer the talks in the right direction. The ball is not only in Quebec's court, but also in the court of Ottawa and the other provinces."[18] There continued to be little to no public reaction to these Quebec initiatives.

Ottawa's reaction was not especially encouraging. Secretary of State Benoit Bouchard warned governments to "be careful about the haste in wanting to finish so quickly that we sacrifice almost everything....Nothing would hurt this country more than a constitutional bidding war, which would plunge us into endless negotiations and delay indefinitely the repatriation of Quebec."[19] Rémillard concluded that Ottawa did not appear to be in any hurry to start the constitutional process.[20] In response to a question in the House of Commons on Rémillard's proposals, the Prime Minister was noncommittal; he was playing his political cards very close to his chest.[21]

While the Prime Minister initially appeared to be reticent, Opposition leader John Turner responded with alacrity and enthusiasm. In an interview with *Le Devoir* on 13 June 1986, Turner by and large endorsed Rémillard's position:

I have no difficulty in inserting in the preamble of the Constitution a recognition of the unique and distinct society in our Confederation... I am also ready to recognize that the Constitution has to be amended to allow Quebec, jointly with Canada, to control immigration to preserve the cultural balance of Quebec... I am ready...to support a right to veto for Quebec...If there were to be transfers of competence or powers, from the province to the federal government, one can consider full monetary compensation... I am ready to consider the summoning of a federal-provincial conference to discuss [the] spending power... I am ready in any way to consult the provinces [on Supreme Court appointments]. I am ready to commit myself to persuade the [Liberal] party to adopt this position.[22]

Turner's position involved a substantial break from Liberal party traditions in this area, as articulated by Pierre Trudeau and Jean Chrétien over the last two decades. Bourassa responded positively to Turner's statement, and Rémillard announced on 16 June that Quebec would be sending senior officials on a tour of provincial capitals over the next weeks to explain its constitutional position. The Quebec wing of the Liberal party voted at a meeting in St.-Hyacinthe to support Quebec's 'distinct society' requirement.[23]

On 4 July 1986, after a meeting of the Priorities and Planning committee (a kind of 'inner cabinet' of top ministers), Prime Minister Mulroney announced that "I think it's timely" to renew the constitutional process.[24] All through July, Bourassa's 'advance team' toured the provincial capitals selling Quebec's five conditions.[25] Provinces were somewhat wary, particularly with regard to the veto, which was seen as a stumbling block. Ontario Premier Peterson stated that the 'distinct society' clause would not cause problems, but that the veto and opting out were complicated issues.[26] Nova Scotia Premier Buchanan declared that "no province should have an individual veto. We've got to have equality within the Constitution of Canada."[27] Constitutional experts noted that the chance of a breakthrough was 'poor to fair.'[28]

The premiers met in Edmonton on 10-12 August 1986 for the 27th Annual Premiers' Conference. Bourassa wanted the premiers to place Quebec's status in Confederation on the agenda, but Premiers Getty, Pawley, and Devine wanted the meeting to centre on the economy and agricultural issues. While Getty in particular seemed to have poured cold water on the Quebec initiative, Bourassa played a trump card. He predicted that "if we cannot reach agreement in the next few days or weeks or months, the whole thing will be put off until the next decade because there will be a federal election and a provincial election, and it would be hard to settle anything before the end of the 1980s." Quebec held some political leverage since, even though it had not signed the constitution, major constitutional changes still required its involvement and approval to satisfy the principle of provincial unanimity. In private discussions, Quebec stated that it would not participate in any constitutional discussions that did not first address its grievances. This was unsettling to premiers who wanted to pursue constitutional change, such as in the area of Senate reform.[29]

Before the Edmonton meeting, Prime Minister Mulroney wrote each of the nine premiers, asking that they put aside their own constitutional demands and concentrate on adapting the Constitution to get Quebec to sign. On 12 August 1986, the premiers released "The Edmonton Declaration," which proposed a two-stage constitutional process:

> The premiers unanimously agreed that their top constitutional priority is to embark immediately upon a federal-provincial process, using Quebec's five proposals as a basis for discussion, to bring about Quebec's full and active participation in the Canadian federation.
>
> There was a consensus among the premiers that then they will pursue further constitutional discussions on matters raised by some provinces which will include, amongst other items, Senate reform, fisheries, property rights, etc.[30]

No timetable for negotiations was set and nothing specific was said as to what might be included in a new agreement. During an informal lunch session, Bourassa submitted an 'improved formula for amendment' (seven provinces with a minimum of 75percent of the population, effectively allowing a regional veto). This formula was "more Canadian," Bourassa maintained, because "Canada is first of all a country of regions."[31] After the release of the declaration, Bourassa declared that "it's a great day for Canadian unity, for Canada."[32] The federal government was supportive of the declaration, but predicted that formal negotiations would not begin before 1987. Senator Lowell Murray, recently named Minister of State for federal-provincial relations, stated that the process should not be rushed, and ruled out the possibility of talks at the November First Ministers' Conference: "We cannot as a country afford to fail a third time....We should have good indications that Quebec, the federal government, and the other provinces will be able to come to an agreement before we begin formal negotiations." Ontario Premier Peterson commented that "Everyone was really trying hard to find accommodation today....In my opinion there's a sense that the time is right. The mood is right. There's a sense of urgency."[33]

Over the next few weeks, Rémillard went on a follow-up tour of all the provinces.[34] Senator Lowell Murray and Norman Spector (secretary to the cabinet for federal-provincial relations) did the same for the federal government. Within Quebec, the opposition Parti québécois assailed Bourassa's approach. Opposition leader Pierre-Marc Johnson declared that Bourassa "wants a deal so much, he's ready to go against Quebec's interests." He complained that the proposed amending formula would reduce Quebec to 'just another region': "Quebec would have a veto not because it's a distinct society but because, for the time being, it's got the numbers."[35]

By late September, Prime Minister Mulroney had yet to respond formally to Quebec's five demands.[36] After a meeting with his Quebec counterpart Rémillard, Senator Murray announced that none of the five demands was unacceptable, or else the Prime Minister would not have encouraged the premiers to discuss them.[37] In the Speech from the Throne on 1 October 1986, the government reiterated that:

> The Canadian Charter of Rights and Freedoms and the Constitution remain incomplete without the assent of Quebec. My ministers have begun consultations with the provinces on this important subject. Should there appear reasonable prospects for settlement, formal negotiations will proceed in the expectation that Quebec will take its rightful place as a full partner in the Canadian Constitution.[38]

In the debate on the Speech from the Throne, Mulroney repeated this position:

> ...we have begun preparation for a new round of discussion which could bring Quebec finally to sign our Constitution....We are not going...to re-open everything, and the Quebec Premier is in complete agreement on this point...Unless we feel there is a reasonable chance for all parties to carry out the negotiations to a successful conclusion, we will not reopen the constitutional debate.[39]

In early November, the federal Liberals in Quebec held a convention at which the resolutions of the St.-Hyacinthe general council meeting were adopted. This convention marked a sound defeat for the 'traditional' Liberal position associated with Pierre Trudeau and Jean Chrétien. The latter did not attend the meeting, and the party rallied around John Turner and his support for Quebec's five demands.[40] In early January 1987, the NDP in Quebec took a far more nationalist position, which included the assertion of Quebec's right to self-determination and the entry of Quebec into the Canadian constitution as a sovereign state.[41] At its national congress in March, the NDP accepted the idea of including the 'distinct society' clause in the preamble to the Constitution and recognized that Quebec should have the right to veto or opt out with financial compensation, but refused to consider giving Quebec the exclusive right to legislate in linguistic matters.[42]

On 12 March 1987, Premier Bourassa announced that he would not attend the First Ministers' Conference on native self-government later that month. Quebec's refusal to participate indicated the extent to which constitutional discussions on a host of matters could not proceed until Quebec was a party to the Canadian Constitution. It boycotted the conference in retaliation for what it saw as the lethargic pace and lack of results of the informal discussion of Quebec's five demands that took place during the winter.[43]

Five days after Quebec declared its boycott, the federal government announced that a First Ministers' Conference would be held at Meech Lake on 30 April to discuss the Constitution and Quebec. The Prime Minster stated:

> With the cooperation of the government of Quebec, we have started a series of consultations that have led to increasingly valid and important definitions.. I think the time is ripe for the premiers of the provinces and the Prime Minister of Canada to give this matter further consideration.

Asked for details of his government's position entering the conference, Mulroney replied:

> I have no intention of tabling specific proposals today. It would be up to me and the provincial premiers to discuss them, as agreed within the process ratified by my provincial colleagues in Edmonton....If you want to know more about our basic philosophy, read my Sept-Iles speech and you will see there is a possibility of agreement between Quebec and Canada.[44]

Premier Bourassa was optimistic about the possibilities for a settlement in April, but Premier Getty announced that he would not go along with any plan that would give Quebec 'special status': "It is our fundamental position that Canada must be made up of ten provinces with equal status in all respects."[45] A week later, Bourassa announced that Quebec would boycott all future constitutional conferences until Quebec's constitutional demands were met: "There is no question of the premier of Quebec participating in constitutional conferences before Quebec adheres to the Canadian Constitution on the basis of our five conditions...[This is] a reminder that Quebec's situation in the Canadian federation is not normal and we don't accept it."[46]

In anticipation of the meeting at Meech Lake, Prime Minister Mulroney had Senator Murray write to each of the provincial governments, outlining Ottawa's response to Quebec's five conditions.[47] In the ten days before the Meech Lake meeting, the Prime Minister telephoned each of the premiers.[48] In the House of Commons on 27 April 1987, Liberal Raymond Garneau referred to the letters and demanded that Mulroney table the correspondence. When the Prime Minister declined, Garneau accused him of having no position.[49] Manitoba, Alberta, British Columbia, and Nova Scotia all appeared opposed to one or two of the demands, particularly opting out and the veto. On 24 April, four national aboriginal leaders wrote the Prime Minister, demanding a role at Meech Lake: "It is incredible that Brian Mulroney and the premiers can contemplate such major amendments to Canada's Constitution without us, especially when most of the agenda items affect us."[50]

As the Prime Minister and the premiers arrived at Meech Lake, it could hardly be anticipated that Canada was on the verge of a constitutional breakthrough. Media coverage on the eve of the event was insubstantial; the media was essentially caught napping. Governments had portrayed the event in low key terms, as a 'tentative' or 'preliminary' meeting in which views and feelings would be canvassed. Only Quebec and Alberta had declared their constitutional positions. The federal government, in particular, had refused to make public its negotiating or constitutional position — if indeed it had one. The mood going into the meeting was by no means buoyantly optimistic, although both Mulroney and Bourassa were absolutely keen on making a deal: they had both made formal electoral commitments to do so. As Newfoundland Premier Peckford put it, "Going in, I thought our chances for a deal were limited."[51]

Within Quebec, nationalist critics were attacking Bourassa. Opposition leader Johnson accused Bourassa of having only a vague position that had not been debated by the Quebec people. 'Hard- line' separatists like Camille Laurin wrote Bourassa, to insist that he demand the Constitution recognize Quebecers as comprising a 'people' and as having a right to self-determination. In an advertisement in *Le Devoir*, the Mouvement national des québécois and the Société Saint-Jean Baptiste de Montréal assailed Bourassa for not adequately consulting the people:

> While he is speaking in their name, the citizens of Quebec have never been consulted on the content of the Quebec claims...under this condition, any conclusive agreement will be considered as illegitimate...we insist on reminding you that this constitution is not ours and that it will never be ours.[52]

FROM MEECH LAKE TO LANGEVIN

The Prime Minister and the premiers met at Meech Lake in a second storey meeting room in Wilson House, a building frequently used for cabinet meetings. The closed door session lasted for more than nine hours. Each leader had a small 'team.' For example, the Ottawa team comprised Senator Lowell Murray (Minister of State for federal-provincial relations), Mulroney's personal secretary, Bernard Roy; federal-provincial relations secretary Norman Spector; Quebec Senator Arthur Tremblay (a constitutional expert); and Frank Iacobucci, deputy minister of justice. Other than the Prime Minister, no one on the federal team had been elected.

The meeting started at lunch time and was organized around discussion of Quebec's five conditions. The least controversial items were discussed first, in order to create momentum. Early (and apparently easy) agreement was reached on three of the five Quebec conditions. The immigration and judicial appointments issues were predictably easy to settle. The shared cost programmes discussion was settled before supper as well which was surprising, as many provinces were committed in principle to a federal presence or predominance in this area. The 'distinct society' issue was divisive, since many provinces were not keen on assigning special status to Quebec. Discussion then shifted to Senate reform. Once that was settled, the final compromise was made on the 'distinct society' issue. By 9:45 PM, it was all done: agreement had been reached.[53]

The 'agreement in principle' contained six ingredients, which reflected the strategy enunciated in the Edmonton Declaration (see Inset III for the text of the accord). The first five dealt with Quebec's proposals, while the sixth dealt with the next round of constitutional discussions. The 'principles' were stated rather informally, and each government's officials would have the task of 'translating' these principles into 'constitutional' language for discussion at a later constitutional conference.

The first ministers agreed with Quebec's proposal that its existence as a *distinct society* should be explicitly acknowledged in the Constitution. This was the key proposal, which generated the most discussion and controversy. The Meech Lake communiqué stated that the Constitution should recognize the existence of both French and English-speaking Canada, the former centred but not limited to Quebec and the latter centred outside but existing also in Quebec. All governments would have the responsibility of preserving this 'fundamental characteristic,' and the Quebec government would have the further responsibility of preserving and promoting Quebec's distinct identity.

The first ministers also agreed to Quebec's proposal in the area of *immigration*. In February 1978, federal Immigration Minister Bud Cullen and his Quebec counterpart Jacques Couture reached a voluntary agreement to establish an intergovernmental committee to regulate immigration levels and select immigrants in accordance with the province's needs. Quebec wanted this approach to be extended and entrenched in the Constitution. The first ministers dealt with this issue rather easily. Each province would be given the right to negotiate an immigration agreement with the federal government "appropriate to [its] needs and conditions." This agreement could then be entrenched, if the province desired. Any such agreement would have to meet with continuing federal standards and objectives, such as the overall national level of immigration and the determining of the inadmissibility of potential immigrants. At Meech Lake, the federal government reached such an agreement with Quebec. This agreement incorporated the principles of the Cullen-Couture agreement, and established certain guarantees for Quebec

THE MEECH LAKE ACCORD

(First Ministers' Meeting on the Constitution: Draft Statement of Principles)

At their meeting today at Meech Lake, the Prime Minister and the ten Premiers agreed to ask officials to transform into a constitutional text the agreement in principle found in the attached document.

First Ministers also agreed to hold a constitutional conference within weeks to approve a formal text intended to allow Quebec to resume its place as a full participant in Canada's constitutional development.

QUEBEC'S DISTINCT SOCIETY

(1) The Constitution of Canada shall be interpreted in a manner consistent with

a) the recognition that the existence of French–speaking Canada, centred in but not limited to Quebec, and English–speaking Canada, concentrated outside Quebec but also present in Quebec, constitutes a fundamental characteristic of Canada; and

b) the recognition that Quebec constitutes within Canada a distinct society.

(2) Parliament and the provincial legislatures, in the exercise of their respective powers, are committed to preserving the fundamental characteristic of Canada referred to in paragraph (1)(a).

(3) The role of the legislature and Government of Quebec to preserve and promote the distinct identity of Quebec referred to in paragraph (1)(b) is affirmed.

IMMIGRATION

– Provide under the Constitution that the Government of Canada shall negotiate an immigration agreement appropriate to the needs and circumstances of a province that so requests and that, once concluded, the agreement may be entrenched at the request of the province;

- such agreements must recognize the federal government's power to set national standards and objectives relating to immigration, such as the ability to determine general categories of immigrants, to establish overall levels of immigration and prescribe categories of inadmissible persons;
- under the foregoing provisions, conclude in the first instance an agreement with Quebec that would:

  - incorporate the principles of the Cullen–Couture agreement on the selection abroad and in Canada of independent immigrants, visitors for medical treatment, students and temporary workers, and on the selection of refugees abroad and economic criteria for family reunification and assisted relatives;

  - guarantee that Quebec will receive a number of immigrants, including refugees, within the annual total established by the federal government for all of Canada proportionate to its share of the population of Canada, with the right to exceed that figure by 5% for demographic reasons; and

  - provide an undertaking by Canada to withdraw services (except citizenship services) for the reception and integration (including linguistic and cultural) of all foreing nationals wishing to settle in Quebec where services are to be provided by Quebec, with such withdrawal to be accompanied by reasonable compensation;

- nothing in the foregoing should be construed as preventing the negotiation of similar agreements with other provinces.

SUPREME COURT OF CANADA

- Entrench the Supreme Court and the requirement that at least three of the nine justices appointed be from the civil bar;

- provide that, where there is a vacancy on the Supreme Court, the federal government shall appoint a person from a list of candidates proposed by the provinces and who is acceptable to the federal government.

SPENDING POWER

- Stipulate that Canada must provide reasonable compensation to any province that does not participate in a future national shared–

cost program in an area of exclusive provincial jurisdiction if that province undertakes its own initiative or programs compatible with national objectives.

AMENDING FORMULA

- Maintain the current general amending formula set out in section 38, which requires the consent of Parliament and at least two–thirds of the provinces representing at least fifty percent of the population;

- guarantee reasonable compensation in all cases where a province opts out of an amendment transferring provincial jurisdiction to Parliament;

- because opting out of constitutional amendments to matters set out in section 42 of the *Constitution Act, 1982* is not possible, require the consent of Parliament and all the provinces for such amendments.

SECOND ROUND

- Require that a First Ministers' Conference on the Constitution be held not less than once per year and that the first be held within twelve months of proclamation of this amendment but not later than the end of 1988;

- entrench in the Constitution the following items on the agenda:
  1) Senate reform including:
     - the functions and role of the Senate;
     - the powers of the Senate;
     - the method of selection of Senators;
     - the distribution of Senate seats;
  2) fisheries roles and responsibilities; and
  3) other agreed upon matters;

- entrench in the Constitution the annual First Ministers' Conference on the Economy now held under the terms of the February 1985 Memorandum of Agreement;

- until constitutional amendments regarding the Senate are accomplished the federal government shall appoint persons from lists of candidates provided by provinces where vacancies occur and who are acceptable to the federal government.

to ensure her cultural security. Quebec would be guaranteed a level of Canada's total immigration proportional to Quebec's share of the Canadian population. For example, if Quebec's share of the population was, say, 27 percent, then it would be guaranteed a minimum of 27 percent of immigrants into Canada in that year. Moreover, for demographic reasons, Quebec was given the right to exceed that figure by 5 percent in a given year. Quebec would also be given financial compensation for undertaking certain immigration services previously carried out by the federal government. All provinces were given the right to negotiate similar agreements.

Quebec's proposals with regard to the *Supreme Court* caused no great difficulty. Quebec had asked for the key role in the appointment of the three Supreme Court justices with expertise in civil law. The first ministers agreed in the first instance to entrench both the Supreme Court and this provision that three of the nine justices be from the civil bar. Moreover, it was determined that appointments to the Supreme Court would be made by the federal government from lists of candidates proposed by the provinces.

It was widely anticipated that Quebec's proposal in the area of *shared-cost programmes* would be a major stumbling block. Quebec had proposed that the federal government's spending power be limited in areas of provincial jurisdiction. This proposal turned out to be a surprisingly easy matter to deal with. All provinces were given the right to opt out of any future national shared-cost programme in an area of provincial jurisdiction. Moreover, a province would be given 'reasonable' compensation if it opted out, as long as it developed a similar programme compatible with 'national objectives.' Two critical provincial concessions should be noted here: this principle would apply only to future programmes, and would not affect existing programmes such as medicare. Second, any province opting out of a national plan would receive compensation on two conditions: that it establish a programme of its own and that this programme meet *national* objectives.

The last of the Quebec proposals dealt with the *amending formula*. Quebec had requested a full veto on constitutional matters, to be entrenched in the amending formula. The first ministers agreed to maintain the existing formula laid out in Section 38 of the Constitution (i.e. Parliament plus two-thirds of the provinces containing at least 50 percent of the population). They also agreed to continue to allow opting out of amendments that involved the transfer of provincial jurisdiction to the federal level (with reasonable compensation to be granted). The critical issue, though, was the agreement to establish the unanimity principle for constitutional amendments relating to Section 42 of the Constitution, where opting out is obviously not possible. In other words, each province was to be given a veto with respect to any proposed constitutional amendment dealing with alterations in national institutions, such as the powers of the Senate and the Supreme Court, the method of selection of members of the Senate and the Supreme Court, the creation of new provinces, and so on.

The political logic of these five ingredients was relatively clear. Quebec proposed that it be given increased powers in the area of immigration, selection of Supreme Court justices, shared-cost programmes and the constitutional amending process. It received all that it requested (indeed, more than it requested), but at the same time all the other provinces received exactly what Quebec received. Quebec 'won' the 'distinct society' clause — which was the necessary condition for any deal — but the rest of Canada established the principle of the right of governments to preserve the 'fundamental characteristic of Canada.' In short, a consensus was formed around assigning to all the provinces that which Quebec presented as conditions for its signing the Constitution.

The last ingredient of the agreement reached at Meech Lake was titled the "Second Round," and reflected the second half of the Edmonton Declaration. Basically, the accord proposed the institutionalization of constitutional conferences — a uniquely Canadian idea. The first ministers agreed that a conference on the Constitution be held before the end of 1988, and every year thereafter. As well, the annual First Ministers' Conference on the Economy would be entrenched in the Constitution. The agenda for future constitutional conferences was also entrenched, and would include Senate reform and fisheries. These last items reflected the particular political priorities of Alberta and Newfoundland. As Senate reform would not be pursued until a later date, the first ministers agreed that until new arrangements were made, the federal government would appoint senators from lists of candidates provided by provincial governments.

Upon completion of the agreement (see Inset IV), Prime Minister Mulroney declared to the other First Ministers, "Now, gentlemen, we can go out there and tell Canadians their federation works." Premier Bourassa enthused that Quebec was "on the verge of becoming a full partner in Confederation." Newfoundland Premier Peckford exclaimed that "It is, no question, an historic breakthrough. A new kind of tone and tenor, constitutionally and otherwise, has been set in the way Canada is going to go in the future." Ontario Premier Peterson stated that "It means there's a new spirit. It means that Quebec's in. And that's extremely important." Saskatchewan Premier Devine interpreted the agreement as involving "an historic maturing of Canada. It means we're all going to be together."[55]

The next morning, 1 May 1987, Prime Minister Mulroney reported in the House of Commons that a constitutional agreement had been reached the previous evening "which will allow Quebec to rejoin the Canadian constitutional family." He declared that the "Meech Lake agreement is good for Canada, and good for Canadians. It will unblock the constitutional reform process....It reflects a new spirit of partnership — and not one of endless power struggles."[56] Opposition leader Turner rose to "congratulate the Prime Minister of Canada, as well as Quebec Premier Robert Bourassa and the other provincial premiers for their constructive work and the result achieved yesterday. It is a happy day for Canada and for Quebec...Bringing Quebec into our constitutional fabric, fully into the Canadian family, was an objective worth [Prime Minister Mulroney's] time and worth the time of the first ministers. We are very encouraged by the result."[57] NDP leader Broadbent stated that "all Canadians...were pleased to hear that an agreement in principle was reached...The coming together of the Canadian family is desired by us all..."[57] Both Opposition leaders expressed certain 'reservations' which they did not pursue, awaiting both a chance to read the text as well as a more appropriate moment. Foreshadowing the debate over the agreement, Turner made a crucial self-congratulatory comment:

> We refrained from politicizing this question in the House of Commons. I as much as the Members of the Official Opposition and the New Democrats purposely avoided embarrassing the government about this issue. We knew that...it was desirable that the interest of

the country take precedence over partisan considerations."[59]

Outside the closed circle of first ministers and federal political leaders, immediate reaction to the Meech Lake deal was not exclusively positive. While there was genuine and general enthusiasm for the prospect of Quebec signing the Constitution, particular concerns about the agreement began to spring up around the country. Acadian groups, for example, expressed concern that the agreement would result in francophone minorities outside of Quebec being sacrificed to the English majorities. The government leader of the Yukon, Anthony Penikett, concluded that "this is a good day for Canada but it is a bad day for the Yukon", as any one province had been given the right to veto a move to make the territory a province.[60] Senator Eugene Forsey, the dean of constitutional experts in Canada, predicted that reform of the Senate had become as likely as his becoming "the Archbishop of Canterbury, the Pope or the Dalai Lama."[61] By and large, though, reaction to the events of 30 April 1987 was relatively quiet — given that the event itself had not been especially widely advertised and anticipation had not been built up. For example, in the West, the agreement was marked by a mixture of "yawns and praise." Indeed, a few days after the Meech Lake meeting, there was little media coverage of the event.[62]

This was certainly not the case in Quebec, where reaction was akin to spontaneous combustion. While Premier Bourassa characterized the agreement as "a giant step for Quebec," Parti québécois leader Johnson described it as "a leap backwards for Quebec."[63] He claimed that "Mr. Bourassa has sold the house of Quebec...for less than the market price set by the eager buyers,"[64] and described the agreement as "the monster of Meech Lake."[65] Members of the Parti Indépendendiste castigated Bourassa for "reduc[ing] our identity to some 'distinct society' [that] is the product of intellectual aberration."[65] Former PQ Cabinet Minister Pierre de Bellefeuille claimed that Meech Lake "is a trap for Quebec."[67] Former Premier Lévesque said that he found the agreement "neither very good nor disastrous."[68] In response to Bourassa's comment that "Mr. Mulroney showed great political leadership...coupled with his obvious skills as a negotiator,"[69] *La Presse* columnist Lysiane Gagnon observed: "Prime Minister Mulroney as a great conciliator? Really, Mulroney had nothing to conciliate; it was an open bar and each province helped itself....Quebec didn't even achieve a shadow of special status....The other provinces fought tooth and nail for the sacrosanct principle of equality. And they too will have everything Quebec asked for."[70] In general, nationalist critics of the agreement claimed that the 'distinct society' clause was ambiguous and potentially useless (and Quebec might lose in the courts), and that Quebec had not acquired a constitutional veto as all provinces had been given the same right.

After the weekend, political reaction to the agreement began to heat up in Ottawa. In question period, Prime Minister Mulroney faced concerns about the lack of aboriginal involvement at the conference, provincial veto of the creation of new provinces, and the future of a national day care programme. With regard to the last issue, Turner asked whether it "would be possible to have a national day care program guaranteeing equal treatment for all children in both have and have-not provinces." The Prime Minister replied "the answer is yes, absolutely....With regard to the spending power, I can give...the assurance that the right, obligation, and authority of the Parliament of Canada to conduct national affairs with respect to spending are uninhibited and unfettered. At all times we can act in the national interest."[71]

Over the weekend, Turner had been advised by several Liberals to 'temper his enthusiasm' for the agreement. On Monday, he continued to declare that he "welcomed the successful conclusion of a deal bringing Quebec into the fabric of the Constitution Act of 1982," but he noted that "I have the feeling that Mr. Mulroney gave away too much to achieve that deal....You can always make a deal if you're willing to give enough away....The question we ask is who was speaking for the federal interest. Who was speaking for Canada?" He concluded that the provincial veto had effectively killed the possibility of Senate reform, and NDP leader Broadbent concluded as well that reform was now "dead as a dodo."[72]

On 5 May 1987, the agreement was tabled in the Senate, and prompted the Liberals' Senate opposition leader MacEachen to observe that "it is very clear that the Meech Lake communiqué represents a significant shift of power and authority from the Government of Canada and the Parliament of Canada to the governments and legislatures of the provinces....We will have...a weaker national government and a weaker national Parliament....One is not surprised that the provincial premiers found it possible to adhere to the Meech Lake agreement, because their status and authority is enhanced."[73] MacEachen's reading of the agreement was in tune with that of Premier Bourassa who concluded that "if there is a principle to be derived from the Meech Lake agreement, it is that Canada is now a far more decentralized country than it was."[74] Rémillard stated starkly, "Centralization is over. We are going into the direction of a decentralized and asymmetrical federalism."[75]

On the same day, Manitoba Premier Pawley expressed reservations about the language of the spending power item, and stated that its wording might have to be changed at the constitutional conference that would formalize the Meech Lake agreement. "We have to be quite satisfied about the federal spending power," said Pawley, who insisted that if Ottawa's spending power was not preserved then Manitoba would not sign the Constitution. "That is the most important power to us, the small provinces." Pawley had expected the Meech Lake talks to fail, and had not been as intimately involved in the run-up process. He had felt isolated at the meeting, and had left feeling that the ingredients of the accord could be changed.[76]

On 8 May 1987, the first cracks appeared in the federal Liberal party's position on Meech Lake. Former cabinet minister Donald Johnston announced his resignation from the Liberal shadow cabinet, as he wanted the freedom to speak out against the agreement. An anglophone member from Quebec, Johnston had been recruited into federal politics by Pierre Trudeau, whose views on federalism he shared. "Mulroney has set about to change the face of Confederation by giving and giving, and eroding the powers of the central government," Johnston claimed. He was particularly worried that the 'distinct society' clause would undermine the possibility of developing a bilingual Canada.[77] His resignation symbolized the emerging split in the federal Liberals' Quebec caucus, between francophones and anglophones. Liberal MP Marcel Prud'homme declared that "Mr. Johnston is having difficulty understanding that Canada is changing. He is not changing as fast as the party. We are living through a debate that is going to lead us to a different Canada and Donald Johnston does not accept this."[78] Johnston was later vilified by André Ouellet as a "Westmount Rhodesian," a comment for which Ouellet later apologized. Liberal Jean Lapierre described Johnston's attitude as "the perception of a saleswoman from Eaton's ten years ago."[79] Johnston received some support, notably from the English language press in Montreal. Over the next weeks, divisions in the Liberal party caused by Meech Lake would overshadow the substance of the constitutional deal.[80]

On 11 May 1987, Quebec began parliamentary hearings on the Meech Lake agreement, while in Ottawa all three federal party leaders endorsed the agreement in the House of Commons. Prime Minister Mulroney moved the tabling of the Meech Lake principles, opening his comments by stating:

> On 20 May, 1980, in a referendum on its political future, Quebec said yes to the rest of Canada. Some seven years later at Meech Lake, the rest of Canada said yes to Quebec. ...The Meech Lake Agreement represents a conscious act of nation-building by all first ministers, requiring generosity of spirit and a deep understanding on all sides. By recognizing the distinctiveness Quebec brings to Canada, we affirm our identity as a nation and strengthen our sovereignty as a people.

He reviewed the principles of the agreement, taking particular care to insist that medicare could have been established under the new spending power principle; that Parliament will continue to protect minority linguistic rights; that unfinished constitutional position — like aboriginal self-government — would be pursued. He asked that "we put aside party politics at this great moment in our history."[81]

The opposition parties obliged the Prime Minister. Opposition leader Turner maintained that Liberals "raise[d] this debate above partisan considerations and...create[d] a genuine climate of mutual understanding and generosity, the impact of which has surely contributed to the success of the meeting at Meech Lake....We have steadfastly refrained from politicizing this question in the House of Commons or across Canada." Even in the absence of the final legal text, "we take a positive and constructive approach towards any constitutional proposition aimed at making Quebecers full-fledged partners in the Confederation of Canada...this is why we endorse this motion...It is indeed a good day for Canada and for Quebec." Turner outlined some reservations that he had about the agreement, including the absence of constitutional recognition of Canada's multicultural reality and the aboriginal peoples; the potential weakening of the federal government's spending power and its capacity to initiate national programs; the rigidity generated by the unanimity principle of the amending formula (which would make Senate reform impossible); and the potential weakening of the Charter of Rights and Freedoms. Despite these not insubstantial reservations, Turner endorsed the Meech Lake agreement. [82]

NDP leader Broadbent took a similar approach. He described the Meech Lake agreement as "a remarkable document" whose "purpose...is something which should be endorsed by all Canadians in all regions of our land...it seems that the Meech Lake Agreement...provide[s] the requisite opening to the Province of Quebec,... meet[s] the concerns of other provinces, and...maintain[s] a strong unifying role for the federal government." Like Turner, Broadbent agreed that "an extreme effort should be made for a non-partisan approach by us all to achieve the goals and principles which the Prime Minister addressed today." He then elaborated a series of reservations about the agreement, including the ambiguity of the phrase 'distinct society' as well as the word 'compatible' with regard to the objectives of shared cost programmes; the oversight of not placing the aboriginal issue on the constitutional agenda; the provincial veto of the creation of new provinces; and the rigidity of the amending formula ("almost irretrievably bad"). Despite these reservations, Broadbent strongly endorsed the Meech Lake agreement.[83]

At the national level of government, then, the unusual development of all-party, non-partisan support gave the Meech Lake agreement considerable political momentum, imposed party discipline on individual MPs, and seriously limited the extent to which the agreement could be scrutinized and criticized in the House of Commons.

At the same time, Quebec began hearings in the parliamentary committee on institutions. The Quebec government was the only one that offered hearings on the Meech Lake principles, before they were translated into constitutional terms at the Langevin meeting in June. The hearings were televised and were open to the public. They were nonetheless fairly constrained: they would last for but six days, five of which were devoted to hearing experts and witnesses. The government and opposition were each allowed to call three experts.[84]

The opposition Parti québécois accused the government of proceeding with far too much haste, particularly as there had not been an extensive public debate on the agreement. However, an editorial in *Le Devoir* suggested that the issue "arouses a superb lack of interest within the great majority of Québécois."[85] On 12 May at the opening of the hearings, Parti québécois leader Johnson criticized the government for holding a constitutional discussion in the absence of a final, legal text. The next day, Jean-Luc Pépin (co-chairman of the Task Force on Canadian Unity) described the agreement as "essentially Trudeauist." The sociologist Fernand Dumont described the 'distinct society' phrase as an important accomplishment, but one that risked generating confusion as it was not specified as being based on the French language. On 14 May, Jacques Parizeau claimed that the agreement signalled a 'retreat,' as the 'distinct society' phrase comprised only a 'symbol' or 'image' that amounted to little, particularly if the Canadian Charter prevailed over it. The spending power clause was seen to be a major and unacceptable shift of authority to the federal government. Rémillard responded by saying that "it is not in our interest to define the notion of a distinct society," while Bourassa stated that he would look for a safety clause on the spending power to protect Quebec's interests. On 19 May, the Quebec NDP split from the federal party. Quebec leader Harney said that the 'distinct society' clause was a "simple and vague symbol," and the constitutional process had been fundamentally undemocratic. On 20 May, the Fédération des travailleurs du Québec, the Centrale de l'enseignement du Québec and the Mouvement national du Quebec all stated their opposition to the Meech Lake agreement. On 21 May, Alliance Quebec and the Parti québécois agreed in criticizing the government for holding hearings on a non-finalized text and for planning to sign a constitutional agreement in June that nobody would have seen.[86] The hearings ended with considerable public reservation about the agreement — particularly about the 'distinct society' clause and the spending power — and tremendous dissatisfaction with the constitutional process surrounding Meech Lake.

As government officials worked to translate the Meech Lake principles into constitutional terms, various groups and individuals articulated their reservations about the agreement. On 14 May, Canadian Bar Association president Bryan Williams criticized the new provision for appointing Supreme Court justices. "What if the federal government does not agree to the provinces' lists and the provinces refuse to submit any other names...does that mean that nobody sits on the Supreme Court?"[87] On the same day, former prime minister Trudeau asked rhetorically whether the agreement makes "the Canadian government that much weaker that it will be unable to use its constitutional powers in times of economic disaster?"[88] On 19 May, Premier Bourassa admitted that officials were having difficulty translating the principles into adequate legal language,[89] but federal and provincial officials left a 20 May meeting optimistic that they could produce a final document by 2 June.[90] On the same day, Alliance Quebec (a 400,000 member association of Quebec anglophones) criticized the agreement for inade-

lature held a perfunctory debate on the Meech Lake principles, a debate that was limited to addresses by the three party leaders (NDP leader Rae spoke in favour of the agreement, while Conservative leader Grossman criticized it for its vagueness and for weakening the federal government: "Have we converted Confederation into a hotel where provincial guests check in and out at will?").[92]

In an electrifying development on 27 May, former prime minister Pierre Trudeau broke a three-year period of political silence by launching a vitriolic attack on the Meech Lake Agreement and its designers see (Inset V).In an article published simultaneously in the *Toronto Star* and *La Presse*, Trudeau asserted that "it would be difficult to imagine a more total bungle." He criticized the 'distinct society' approach, claiming that Quebec did not need special powers. The other premiers and the Prime Minister had agreed to this because "each saw in it some political advantage to themselves." Claimed Trudeau: "Those who fought for a single Canada, bilingual and multicultural, can say goodbye to that dream. We are henceforth to have two Canadas, each defined in terms of its language." Trudeau described Quebec's nationalist politicians as "snivellers" and "losers," while Prime Minister Mulroney was characterized as a "weakling" who, "with the complicity of ten provincial premiers...will render the Canadian state totally impotent."[93]

Reaction to the Trudeau intervention was swift. Premier Bourassa said that Trudeau's remarks were unfortunate, and betrayed a centralist vision of Canada that no longer reflected Canada's reality: "One does not change at his age!"[94] Prime Minister Mulroney described it as "low level comedy," PEI Premier Ghiz "profoundly disagreed" with Trudeau, while Newfoundland Premier Peckford stated that Trudeau had "had his chance and botched it."[95] Alberta Premier Getty stated that "Albertans have never shared Mr. Trudeau's view of Canada." British Columbia Premier Vander Zalm claimed that "he forgets that Canada is made up of provinces." Manitoba Premier Pawley said that "what he demonstrated is an over-obsession with federalist authority." New Brunswick Premier Hatfield insisted that "he should remember that many of the things that he finds fault with were in fact tried by him." Saskatchewan Premier Devine asked, "If he's really sincere about the process and about the country, why not be involved earlier? He knew the Premier of Quebec had all these proposals."[96] In a CBC radio interview, Trudeau later explained that "I thought there would be enough people to protest that it wouldn't happen. I saw there weren't too many, so...."[97] On 30 May, Senator Lowell Murray replied to Trudeau's article with an article of his own published in *Le Devoir* and *The Globe and Mail* (see Inset VI). In it, the Minister of Federal-Provincial Relations retorted that it was Trudeau who had bungled the constitutional process in 1981-82 by isolating Quebec; that Trudeau himself had proposed many of the Meech Lake principles; that his fear of balkanization was "inspired by an overweening centralist bias"; and that "his polemics seem more like a last hurrah."[98]

"SAY GOODBYE TO THE DREAM OF ONE CANADA"

The real question to be asked is whether the French Canadians living in Quebec need a provincial government with more powers than the other provinces.

I believe it is insulting to us to claim we do....The members of (the) new generation know that the true opportunities of the future extend the boundaries of Quebec, indeed beyond the boundaries of Canada itself. They don't suffer from any inferiority complex...they need no crutches...

Unfortunately, the politicians are the exception to the rule. And yet one would have thought that those who want to engage in politics in our province would have learned at least one lesson...Quebecers like strong governments, in Quebec and in Ottawa...They know instinctively that they cannot hope to wield more power within their province, without agreeing to wield less in our nation as a whole.

How, then, could 10 provincial premiers and a federal prime minister agree to designate Quebec as a 'distinct society'?

It's because they all, each in his own way, saw in it some political advantage to themselves.

Those who never wanted a bilingual Canada...get their wish..with recognition of "the existence of French-speaking Canada...and English-speaking Canada"...Those Canadians who fought for a single Canada, bilingual and multicultural, can say goodbye to their dream: We are henceforth to have two Canadas, each defined in terms of its language...the government of Quebec must take measures and the legislature must pass laws aimed at the uniqueness of Quebec...Thus Quebec acquires a new constitutional jurisdiction that the rest of Canada does not have: promoting the concentration of French in Quebec...

Those who never wanted a Charter of Rights entrenched in the Constitution can also claim victory...the Courts will have to interpret the Charter in a way that does not interfere with Quebec's 'distinct society' as defined by Quebec laws...

...(the) principle of withdrawl accompanied by "fair compensation" is to be applied to all "new shared-cost programs". This will allow the provinces to finish off the balkanization of languages and cultures with the balkanization of social services...what provincial politician will not insist on distributing in his own way...and to the advantage of his constituents, the money he will be getting painlessly from the federal treasury?

...From now on, the Canadian government won't be able to appoint anyone to the Supreme Court and the Senate except people designated by the provinces! ...any province that doesn't like an important constitutional amendment will have the power to either block the passage of that amendment or to opt out of it, with "reasonable compensation" as a reward!

This...gives each of the provinces a constitutional veto (and)...an absolute right of veto over Parliament, since the Senate will eventually be composed entirely of persons who owe their appointments to the provinces...Canada's highest court will eventually be composed entirely of persons put forward by the provinces.

What a magician this Mr. Mulroney is and what a sly fox! He managed to approve the call for Special Status...the call for Two Nations...the call for a Canadian Board of Directors made up of 11 first ministers...and the call for a community of communities.

He has not quite succeeded in achieving sovereignty-association, but he has put Canada on the fast track for getting there. It doesn't take a great thinker to predict that the political dynamic will draw the best people to the provincial capitals, where the real power will reside, while the federal capital will become a backwater for political and bureaucratic rejects.

What a dark day for Canada was this April 30, 1987! In addition to surrendering to the provinces important parts of its jurisdiction (the spending power, immigration), in addition to weakening the Charter of Rights, the Canadian state made subordinate to the provinces its legislative power (Senate) and its judicial power (Supreme Court); and it did this without hope of ever getting any of it back (a constitutional veto granted to each province)...

All of this was done on the pretext of "permitting Quebec to fully participate in Canada's constitutional evolution". As if Quebec had not...fully participated in Canada's constitutional evolution!..."Constitutional evolution" presupposed precisely that Canada would have its Constitution and be able to amend it. Almost invariably, it was the Quebec provincial government that blocked the process...Quebec would 'permit' Canada to Canadianize the colonial document we had instead of a Constitution, only if the rest of Canada granted Quebec a certain 'special status'...when (ever) the Canadian government tried to restart the process...it faced the roadblock of 10 provinces which all wanted their own 'special status'; inevitably, they had enrolled in the school of blackmail of which Quebec was the founder and top-ranking graduate...

The provincialist politicians, whether they sit in Ottawa or Quebec, are...perpetual losers; they don't have the stature or the vision to dominate the Canadian stage, so they need a Quebec ghetto as their lair...That bunch of snivellers should simply have been sent packing and been told to stop having tantrums like spoiled adolescents. But our current political leaders lack courage....It would be difficult to imagine a more total bungle.

Mr. Bourassa...chose to flail around on the one battlefield where the péquistes have the advantage: that of the nationalist bidding war...The péquistes will never stop demonstrating that the Meech Lake Accord enshrines the betrayal of Quebec's interests....As for Mr. Mulroney, he had inherited a winning hand...since 1982, Canada had its Constitution, including a Charter...From then on, the advantage was on the Canadian government's side; it no longer had anything very urgent to seek from the provinces; it was they who had become the supplicants...

Alas, only one eventuality hadn't been foreseen: that one day the government of Canada might fall into the hands of a weakling...the Right Honorable Brian Mulroney, PC. MP, with the complicity of 10 provincial premiers, has already entered into history as the author of a constitution which...will render the Canadian state totally impotent. That would destine it, given the dynamics of power, to eventually be governed by eunuchs.

Pierre Trudeau, Toronto Star, 27 May 1987

SENATOR LOWELL MURRAY REPLIES TO TRUDEAU

Speaking of bungling, former prime minister Trudeau would not have been able to use that term...had he not himself concluded the constitutional accord of Nov. 5, 1981...No one should ever deny what the Constitution Act, 1982 achieved for Canada...(but) we cannot overlook the less desirable results...The conference...only ended up isolating Quebec. The Quebec government alone did not sign the accord that allowed the patriation of Canada...

Practicing the art of the possible, Mr. Trudeau had to cut his losses and pay a high price for a constitutional accord which enshrined the equality of the provinces and the 'opting out' and the notwithstanding clauses, and yet without succeeding in bringing Quebec on side.

Recalling the solemn promises of renewal Mr. Trudeau repeatedly made to them at the time of the referendum, Quebecers felt betrayed. Since then, Quebec has refused to participate actively in the constitutional evolution of Canada...This is the 'winning hand' Mr. Trudeau left us when he departed from political life: a Canada legally united on paper, but in reality unreconciled.

...a constitution merely translates into legal text the shared values that men and women willingly choose, in their minds and hearts, when they decided to live together in the same country...Seen in this perspective, the recognition of Quebec's distinct society...is simply an acceptance of the country's sociological and political reality...

I do not see why an appointment method so clearly federalist in both principle and practice should damage the country...it should help Canadians accept the Supreme Court's role as the impartial arbiter and legitimate guardian of the country's

---

that "his polemics seem more like a last hurrah."[98]

The Trudeau intervention may well have strengthened the first ministers' resolve, but it created further headaches for an already-divided Liberal party. The Trudeau outburst appeared to catch Liberals by surprise, and gave encouragement to anglophone Quebec MPs like Donald Johnston and David Berger who were already speaking out against Meech Lake. Leading Liberals like Herb Gray tried to downplay Trudeau's remarks: "Mr. Trudeau was attacking Mr. Mulroney and the premiers" and not John Turner, but the party looked increasingly divided. Turner's chief lieutenant in Quebec, Raymond Garneau, claimed that it was not Meech Lake that threatened Canadian unity, but Mr. Trudeau: "I do not want to relive the October Crisis, nor the confrontations which took place in the past between anglophones and francophones." J.C. Malepart declared, "the choice of the party, if it wants to review its position [on Meech Lake]...will be to bring back David Berger and Donald Johnston and lose J.C. Malépart and R. Garneau." Liberal supporters in the ethnic communities began to criticize Turner's handling of Meech Lake. Terry Popowich, who had engineered the "Friends of John Turner" movement, declared that "a lot of grassroots Liberals do not agree

constitution...the same reasoning applies in the appointment of senators from provincial lists...

As for 'opting out' with reasonable compensation...(t)o say that the 'balkanization' of Canada will be advanced because a province refuses to give up one of its powers to Ottawa and asks not to be penalized as a result, seems to me not only exaggerated but clearly inspired by an overweening centralist bias.

Regarding the provincial veto over the reform of federal institutions...(o)nce the principle of equality was enshrined in the Constitution on Nov. 5, 1981, the only way to give Quebec a veto was to also give a veto to all the provinces...I do not see how we could decently effect major changes concerning the Supreme Court or Parliament, or decide to create a new province, without the consent of all the partners of the federation...

The Meech Lake agreement marks a first step in 'civilizing' the future use of the (federal) spending power for national shared-cost programs in areas of exclusive federal jurisdiction...Why would (Mr. Trudeau) term it catastrophic...that a province be allowed to withdraw from a new shared-cost program in an area of exclusive provincial jurisdiction, so long as the pursuit of national objectives is not itself compromised?

Mr. Trudeau reminds me of those generals who long for war during peacetime...his polemics seem...like a last hurrah. It is not everything to fight the war; it is necessary to know how to build the peace...Although perhaps less dramatic and spectacular, and certainly less confrontational than the patriation of the Constitution, the patriation of Quebec remains simply indispensable for Canada's future.

History will recognize Brian Mulroney's contribution at Meech Lake in leading Canada to the completion of this historic unfinished business left to us by Mr. Trudeau.

Globe and Mail, 30 May 1987.

with the accord. The heart and soul of the party is at stake here." Several other prominent Liberals, including Donald Macdonald, spoke out against Meech Lake and in support of Trudeau's position. For his part, Liberal leader Turner refused to allow party misgivings about the agreement to be articulated, and instead pressed the government to commit itself to open hearings on Meech Lake before the principles became law. A Liberal caucus committee headed by Robert Kaplan and Lucie Pépin prepared a draft statement demanding a more open constitutional process, and Turner was urged to release it as an open letter. Instead, he chose to use its contents as questions in the House of Commons.[99]

In the run-up to the June First Ministers' Conference, various groups continued to criticize the agreement, including women's groups, native peoples' organizations, and a loose coalition of historians and constitutional experts. Government leaders in the Yukon and the Northwest Territories stated that they would seek court action against the agreement. The Canadian Council on Social Development, the National Anti-Poverty Association, the Canadian Day Care Advocacy Association, the National Council of Welfare, the Canadian Institute of Child Health, the Canadian Council on Children and Youth, and the National Advisory Council on the Status of Women all expressed concern that the development of national social programmes would be constrained and that existing programs would be affected. Alliance Quebec asked that more time be taken, while Senator Forsey criticized various features of the agreement for being overly vague.[100]

At this stage, two premiers became identified as potential opponents of certain features of the accord. Premier Pawley declared that "I'm going to use every means within my ability to persuade other first ministers that the wording [of the agreement] does require more precision." He was particularly concerned about the meaning of the phrase 'national standards' in the shared cost clause, and the question of who would define the phrase. Pawley expressed concerned about the necessity of protecting the rights of native people and the people of the territories. He insisted on the need for public hearings and an open process: "This is a very deplorable situation, if we have a constitutional draft being circulated and then we are being advised by anyone that we create problems if we ask questions." Ontario Premier Peterson promised that Ontario would hold public hearings before Ontario ratified any constitutional deal, and urged that Ottawa hold such hearings: "I don't want any sense that this is being force-fed or shoe-horned into a preordained time frame." He said that he sensed a growing feeling that the agreement was "cooked up in a locked room somewhere."[101]

In Quebec, Premier Bourassa on 28 May rejected opposition demands that he 'take advantage of' the constitutional conference to increase Quebec's gains. This closed the door on those who had criticized Bourassa for not acquiring enough at Meech Lake to guarantee Quebec's cultural security. Bourassa expressed optimism that matters could be settled on 2 June: "We are going to ratify one of the greatest political victories of Quebec." But he noted that he would try to establish that it was the French language that made Quebec 'distinct'.[102]

On 2 June 1987, the first ministers arrived in Ottawa for a constitutional conference that would attempt to formalize in constitutional terms the principles agreed upon a month earlier. During that month, an all-party consensus, which appeared to be well-insulated against criticism, had evolved at the federal level. As a result, there were few mechanisms, short of the media, via which criticisms could be articulated. On the other hand, some of the premiers had experienced considerable political pressure. Premier Bourassa faced nationalist criticism that Quebec had 'lost' on the 'distinct society' and spending clauses. He had had to face this criticism in an open committee hearing — his was the only government that allowed public intervention of this sort. Premiers Pawley and Peterson were feeling pressure from interest groups that argued that the federal government had been weakened too much and would be incapable of developing sound social programmes. Native groups and the territories complained about the agreement, but lacked an avenue of political intervention.[103]

The eleven first ministers met in the fourth floor boardroom of the Langevin Building, which is situated across Wellington Street from Parliament Hill. They were isolated in one room, with only two 'bureaucrats' present: Norman Spector (secretary to the cabinet for federal-provincial relations) and Oryssias Lennie (an Alberta official), who represented the federal and provincial governments respectively. The bureaucratic teams were situated in an adjacent room, and each met with its government leader in small rooms along the hall. This was a highly unusual, tightly controlled arrangement. The marathon meeting began at 10 AM and did not conclude until 5:30 AM the following day. The first ministers would discuss a particular clause, which would then be drafted and typed; the leader would bring it to his delegation for discussion and response, and would then return to the private meeting. This process happened 15 to 20 times . There were two major issues to be dealt with at this meeting, since the Supreme Court, immigration, and amend-

---

■ Inset VII ■

THE LANGEVIN MEETING: A REPORTER'S VIEW

At one point during the all night vigil, there was a sense among the federal delegation that the deal could not hold together. In fact they were telling us out on the sidewalks somewhere around 4:00 in the morning that they thought it was just about over...Once again at Langevin, not a single technical advisor from the provinces was allowed in that room at any point.

Every time they broke for coffee, each premier would go to consult with his experts. Then they would go back in the room. Then all the experts would suddenly get together to try and find out what the other positions were. They tried to work out a consensus among themselves so when their guys came out the next time they could kind of massage their backs like boxers, and send them back in with the right line...There are wonderful stories of premiers...coming out and talking to their advisers and repeating texts 180 degrees from what really was on the table, mixing up clauses and numbers, not understanding the relationships. It really was very difficult....

Elly Alboim, "Inside the News Story: Meech Lake as Viewed By An Ottawa Bureau Chief", in R. Gibbins (ed), *Meech Lake and Canada: Views from the West* (Edmonton: Academic Publishing, 1988), p. 243.

---

ing formula issues were more or less settled, as was the process for the second round. One issue was the question of opting out of shared-cost programmes, which was raised by Premiers Peterson and (especially) Pawley. They were anxious to ensure that provinces would not be given financial compensation unless they met national objectives and criteria set by the federal government. Premiers Getty, Vander Zalm and Bourassa were not keen about this approach. The other issue was the 'distinct society' clause. Premier Bourassa wanted to ensure that the courts would not weaken what he hoped would be an effective source of authority for the Quebec government. Premier Peterson was concerned about the impact this clause would have on aboriginal and multicultural rights. The meeting began with a discussion of the former issue that, by lunchtime, resulted in a tentative draft. After lunch, discussion shifted to the latter issue, which took until 2 AM to settle. After 2 AM, the discussion shifted back to the spending clause, centering on a battle between Premier Bourassa and Premiers Pawley and Peterson. After this was resolved, discussion focused on a number of subsidiary issues, such as multicultural and aboriginal rights, that had not been discussed at Meech Lake. By 5:30 am, agreement was reached, and at noon on 3 June 1987 an official signing ceremony took place (see Inset VII).[104]

At the Langevin meeting, seven changes were made to the principles agreed upon at Meech Lake. At least four could be described as substantial (see Appendix I for the draft constitutional resolution). The biggest change was in the clause dealing with Quebec as a 'distinct society' (see Section 2 of the Constitution Act 1867, in Appendix I). The distinct society section was placed within the 1867 constitution itself. Two major changes ocurred at the Langevin meeting. First, the description of the 'character' of Canada was changed. In the Meech Lake agreement, Canada was described as consisting of "French-speaking Canada...and English-speaking Canada." The Langevin proposal described Canada as comprising "French-speaking Canadians...and English-speaking Canadians." The former seemed to imply the existence of 'two Canadas' while the latter suggested the existence of 'one Canada' made up of different individuals. Second, a new Section 2(4) was added, ensuring that the existing rights of Parliament and the provincial legislatures were not affected by this 'distinct society' section, particularly regarding power to regulate language rights. This was added as a guarantee to both levels of government that the constitutional division of powers had not been affected, and that each would continue to have jurisdiction over language policy.

The spending power clause was also changed significantly (see Constitution Act 1867, Section 106A(1),(2)). In what was probably the key political compromise, Premier Bourassa agreed to a change in the language of the Meech Lake principles and Premier Pawley swallowed his anxiety about this issue. NDP leader Broadbent made a secret phone call to Prime Minister Mulroney before the Langevin meeting, which laid the basis for the compromise that NDP Premier Pawley accepted. In the Meech Lake document, it had been agreed that financial compensation would be granted to opting-out provinces who initiated programs "compatible with national objectives". The discussions in the Langevin building changed this phrase ever-so-slightly: the word 'the' was added, and the compromise was sealed. Section 106A(1) would read "compatible with *the* national objectives", which, to those with apprehensions, appears far more forceful and forthright about concrete, as opposed to hazy, objectives. Moreover, the clause refers to a program "that is established by the Government of Canada" — the Meech Lake clause made no reference to anything actually established by the federal government. This clarified the spending power clause immensely, and asserted to a far greater extent the federal spending power and its role in establishing shared-cost programmes in areas of federal jurisdiction. However, as a trade-off with Premier Bourassa, a new clause 106A(2) was added, stating that this section did not extend the jurisdiction of either level of government, thus assuring Bourassa that federal spending power would be limited.

With respect to immigration, a new clause was added (see Constitution Act 1867, Section 95B(3)). There was some concern that the 95B(1) phrase that any immigration agreement would have "the force of law" put the Charter of Rights in jeopardy in this area. 95(3) insists that the Charter applies in this area.

The amending formula and proposals for the "Second Round" and constitutional conferences did not undergo any changes at this meeting (with regard to the former see Constitution Act 1982 Section 40ff; on the latter, see Constitution Act 1982, Section 50). The Supreme Court proposal underwent a minor change: a new section was added that, by implication, ensured and extended judicial independence (see Constitution Act 1867, Section 101D).

Finally, two principles that were not contained in the original Meech Lake agreement were added. There had been concern expressed that the new Section 2 'distinct society' clause would threaten certain Charter rights, particularly with regard to multiculturalism and native peoples. A new section was added (see Constitution Act 1982, Section 16) protecting these rights from the distinct society clause. A further statement in the Langevin proposal was added in response to the 'distinct society' clause. In response to a request by Alberta Premier Getty, the preamble to the 1987 Constitutional Accord and the motion for a resolution to amend the Constitution included the statement that the Constitution "would recognize the principle of equality of all of the provinces."

THE RATIFICATION PROCESS

It was moving to watch the first ministers...as they signed the agreement they had struck to win Quebec's political consent to the Constitution. Perhaps the most memorable moment was Premier Bourassa's statement that Quebec signs this statement with its head held high and with joy — and the slight hint of passion, so rare in this reserved politician, when he talked about the greatness of Canada. A day that brings such a declaration from a premier of Quebec...is one to treasure.[106]

"Today we welcome Quebec back to the Canadian constitutional family," declared Prime Minister Mulroney at the signing ceremony on 3 June 1987; "today we close one chapter in Canadian history and begin another."[107]

The signing ceremony also closed one chapter in the constitutional process and started another. For each first minister would now have to return home and have the constitutional package passed by his legislature within three years. If even *one* of the legislatures should not pass the package, then the proposed changes would not take effect.

This was not anticipated to be an overwhelming challenge. After all, each of the first ministers had made a political commitment to pass the package, and each commanded a majority in his respective legislature (the Ontario government was in a minority situation, but would be given a majority that summer). Moreover, as Premier Bourassa noted, it would be difficult for a province to act against the first ministers' unanimous will to accept Quebec's adherence to the Constitution.[108]

Indeed, Bourassa acted quickly to make it difficult for the other governments to reject or amend the agreement. On 18 June, the Quebec National Assembly began a marathon emergency debate to pass the constitutional agreement. The Parti québécois opposition was caught by surprise, and accused the government of 'undue haste.' Bourassa argued for the support of the agreement in total, and announced that the government would not consider any amendments; these would have to wait until the second round of negotiations. He described the agreement as "one of the most beautiful and strongest expressions of enlightened patriotism that we have had in this National Assembly since the beginning of our history." On 23 June 1987, after 35 hours of debate, the Quebec National Assembly passed the constitutional agreement.[109] "It was fitting that the National Assembly should pass the constitutional resolution just before St. Jean Baptiste day. After all the years when the holiday was used to promote Quebec's withdrawal from Canada, this year it signalled a drawing together of the country."[110] Considerable political momentum was created by Quebec's action; once Quebec had ratified the agreement, opposition to it would be equated with opposition to Quebec.

On the federal level, Opposition leader Turner asked the Prime Minister on 3 June whether public hearings on the agreement would be held. The Prime Minister replied that "there will be appropriate parliamentary hearing of this matter," but also stated that he would recommend that the House of Commons accept the document in its entirety.[111] Mulroney later confirmed that a parliamentary committee would be struck, but reiterated that any change or amendment would have to be approved by all 11 first ministers.[112] A special joint committee of the Senate and House of Commons was established, but the Liberal-dominated Senate decided to hold its own hearings as well. This annoyed Senator Lowell Murray, who concluded that this action was a challenge to John Turner's leadership.[113] The character of the parliamentary hearings was foreshadowed when the Conservatives rejected a motion to allow the committee to hold hearings in the Yukon and the Northwest Territories.[114] The joint committee would stay put in Ottawa (but the Senate committee would hold hearings in the North in August). The committee was co-chaired by Conservative Senator Arthur Tremblay (a constitutional expert) and Conservative MP Chris Speyer (who would later be appointed a judge of the divisional court of Ontario). The 17 members (12 MPs and 5 senators) were not an exceptional group save for Senator Tremblay, NDP MP Pauline Jewett and Liberal MP Robert Kaplan.[115] The decision to hold hearings in August was politically suspicious and controversial, as Canadians tend not to be politically active or attentive in what is a holiday month. The Senate committee did not take up its task in earnest until the autumn, after the special joint committee had issued its report.

Any idea that improvements could be initiated by the special joint committee was squelched by the Prime Minister in an interview on 22 June. "The joint committee will do its work and make its recommendations, but as far as I'm concerned, let me tell you that the Meech Lake accord is an impressive document...and that I have no hesitation in recommending it to the rest of the country as it was negotiated."[116] Throughout this process, the Prime Minister was adamant that it was an all-or-nothing deal. Mulroney basked in the warm glow of his accomplishment, and predicted that this constitutional agreement would guarantee a Conservative victory in the next election.[117] On the other hand, the Liberal party continued to reel from the internal divisions generated by the agreement. "I will...admit," declared Turner candidly, "that the past month has been a difficult one." At a Liberal party conference in Port Hope, party members approved of Turner's supporting the accord and directed him to seek improvements to it.[118]

There were rumblings of discontent with the agreement in the interval before the special joint committee hearings. Critics described the process as closed and hasty. Political activist Rosemary McCarney characterized it as "an illegitimate exercise of power. Eleven men met in the middle of the night while their limousines waited outside, with the engines running." Historian Michael Bliss described it as "smash-and-grab constitution-making."[119] Women's groups expressed concern about their rights. The Women's Legal Education and Action Fund (WLEAF) informed the Prime Minister that "we are sounding the alarm that the equality rights of women and minorities have been forgotten in the accord."[120] Asked about this by Pauline Jewett, Mulroney told the House of Commons that "there is absolutely nothing in the Meech Lake Accord that would diminish or in any way affect equality rights for women and minorities."[121] The Canadian Ethnocultural Council issued a paper titled "To the Back of the Bus," which asked that multiculturalism be given equal status to bilingualism. In response, the Prime Minister asserted that "the multicultural dimension of Canada is firmly protected and always will be in the multicultural dimension of the [accord]."[122] On 20 July, NDP candidate Audrey McLauglin won a federal by-election in the Yukon on an anti-Meech Lake campaign.[123] In late July, hearings began at the Yukon Supreme Court on the Yukon government's

WITNESSES AT THE JOINT COMMITTEE HEARINGS
ON THE MEECH LAKE ACCORD

INDIVIDUALS

For

Gerald Beaudoin
Robert Décary
Yves Fortier
Raymond Hébert
Eric Kierans
Peter Leslie
Peter Meekison
Laurent Picard
Jack Pickerskill
Gordon Robertson
Richard Simeon
Robert Stanfield
Ron Watts
Solange Chaput-Rolland

Against

Izzy Asper
David Christie
Ramsay Cook
Deborah Coyne
Timothy Danson
Eugene Forsey
Ralph Goodale
Tony Hall
Al Johnson
Wayne MacKay
Frank McKenna
Stephen Scott
Nick Taylor
John Whyte
Pierre Trudeau

ORGANIZATIONS

For

Fédération des femmes du Québec
Quebec Status of Women Council

Against

NACSW
NACWL
WLEAF
CACSW
Ad Hoc Committee of Women
Freedom of Choice Women
Canadian Day Care Advocacy Association
National Anti-Poverty
  Association
Canadian Council on Social Development
Council of Yukon Indians
Innuit Committee on National Issues
Government of NWT
Government of Yukon
Native Council of Canada
Assembly of First Nations
Metis National Council
Association of Metis and non-Status Indians of
  Saskatchewan
Canadian Bar Association
Canadian Institute on Minority Rights
Human Rights Institute of
  Canada

Fisheries Council of Canada
National Farmers Union
Public Service Alliance of Canada
National Union of Provincial
  Government Employees
United Electrical, Radio and Machine Workers
Canadian Labour Congress
Canadian Nurses Association
Canadian Federation of Students
Société franco-Manitobaine
Mouvement Québec-Francais
Canadian Parents for French
Alliance Quebec
German-Canadian Congress
Canadaian Ethnocultural Council
Chinese-Canadian National Council
National Association of
  Japanese Canadians
National Association of Canadians
  of Origins in India
Canadian Federation of Ethno-
  Businesses and Professionals
Canada West Foundation
Canadian Committee for Triple 'E' Senate

lawsuit against the accord.[124] On the election trail, Ontario Premier Peterson experienced tremendous pressure from critics, particularly women's groups, and his sympathetic responses suggested that he might consider reopening constitutional discussions.[125]

The special joint committee hearings began on 4 August. Testimony was heard from 131 groups and individuals in the dead of summer, and 301 written submissions were made. Senator Lowell Murray was the first witness and, in some ways, he could have been the last. He described the constitutional package of changes as "a seamless web and an integrated whole":

> Some critics of the accord assume the first ministers undertook to negotiate more than they did...suggestions to improve the accord and broaden its scope often are misplaced, no matter how well-intentioned they are. If any egregious errors in the amendment are identified, they can, as First Ministers agree, be amended immediately.[126]

The government's position was that there were no flaws in the agreement, that it was an all-or-nothing package, and that the committee should consider changes only to blatant or outrageous errors. Even these would have to be approved by 11 governments. Anything more would risk unravelling the process. This was a compelling position: it suggested that the existing package of changes was the only package that could generate governmental consensus. This created an asymmetrical debate between an existing, agreed-upon package and a non-existing package whose creation seemed unlikely.

The hearings had two 'tracks.' On one were academics and constitutional experts, evenly divided in their views. On the other were organized interests, more or less unanimous in criticizing the accord, albeit for different reasons (see Inset VIII). Scrutiny of the constitutional agreement focused on six major issues, which were rehearsed and re-rehearsed endlessly:

§ linguistic minority groups, women's and multicultural groups expressed concern about the impact of the 'distinct society' clause on Charter rights;

§ critics claimed that the 'distinct society' clause was either symbolic (which would lead to disillusionment in Quebec) or real (which created a two-Canada situation);

§ discrimination against the North was cited in criticizing the unanimity requirement in creating new provinces, the nomination process to the Supreme Court and the Senate, and the North's exclusion from the constitutional process itself;

§ provincial involvement in Supreme Court and Senate appointments, control over immigration, compensation for opting out, and predominance at the entrenched first ministers conferences were criticized for creating a weakened if not powerless federal government;

§ Senate reform had been made impossible as a result of the unanimity principle;

§ the constitutional process was criticized as being closed, rushed, and undemocratic.

It remained transparently clear, though, that the committee was not going to entertain any amendments. The overwhelming political reality was that this was the 'Quebec Round,' and trade-offs on non-Quebec matters would not be entertained. Symbolic of this fact was the deflecting of criticisms made at the hearings by women's groups.

The National Action Committee on the Status of Women's Louise Dulude argued that clause 16 "does present a real threat to the rights of women in Canada." "We all remember 1981," said Sylvia Gold, "when we were forgotten....There are unquestionable risks in the agreement....It would not be wise for the women of Canada to take the chance...." The Ad Hoc Committee of Women on the Constitution retained the law firm Tory, Tory, Des Lauriers and Binnington to write a legal opinion. That brief (written by Mary Eberts and John Laskin) concluded: "You cannot say that there is no risk of harm to women's rights...There is reason to believe that it could happen".[127] There was some sympathy for these claims, even amongst Conservative members of the joint committee (e.g., David Daubney and Leo Duguay).

On 18 August, the Prime Minister intervened to derail the claims of women's groups. He suggested that these groups were using rights arguments to harm the province of Quebec. He cited an article written by *La Presse* columnist Lysiane Gagnon: "A lot of people are using that as a Trojan horse, not because they're trying to protect women's rights, but because they don't want a distinct society and the Meech Lake Accord." The Prime Minister stated, "It's a very thoughtful piece, some of whose judgments I share."[128] Women's groups were outraged, and described the comments as wicked, but the damage was done. The Prime Minister had transformed a rights issue into an English-Canada-versus-French-Canada issue (this was taking place at precisely the same time that Bill C-22 was being given similar treatment; see p 84). Later, the largest women's organization in Quebec — La fédération des femmes du Québec — stated before the committee that "we do not subscribe to the unfortunate interpretation that Quebec women could see themselves deprived of their rights to equality"; the Quebec Council on the Status of Women argued that there were no legal reasons to be concerned and that Quebec had a strong record of respect for women's rights.[129] Committee Chairman Speyer found it to be "extraordinarily ironic" that legal opinion in Toronto was more concerned about the rights of women in Quebec than Quebec women were.[130] The Prime Minister took MPs Daubney and Duguay for a 'no nonsense' lunch, and the issue was no longer raised.[131]

In the last analysis, the issue had been and was Quebec. And nothing better symbolized division on this issue than the conflicting testimony of Pierre Trudeau and Solange Chaput-Rolland. The former's arguments have already been noted (see Inset V). According to Trudeau, the accord undermined the national government, which would in future be run by "a kind of remote control by the provinces." The provinces would have a veto over the national legislature (appointments to the Senate), over the national judiciary (appointments to the Supreme Court), and over Parliament as a whole (first ministers conferences), as well as over national policy and consensus (control of immigration, opting out with compensation, the unanimity formula, the 'distinct society' clause). "Of course," he concluded, "finally peace has been restored to federal-provincial relations. Yes, peace! But at what price?"[132]

The previous day, Chaput-Rolland made a telling and emotional case in favour of the agreement (see Inset IX). She maintained that Quebecers were desperately looking for a signal that Canadians wanted Quebec to remain in

---

■ Inset IX ■

A QUEBECER'S EXPLANATION OF
THE SIGNIFICANCE OF MEECH LAKE

I think none outside Quebec knew the reality of the referendum (of 1980)... English Canada could not care less one month after, and it stung me and it stung all of us who had fought so hard to remain in Canada and to find ourselves outside of Canada. You know, it was a very dramatic gesture when Lévesque put the flag of Quebec at half mast on the day you were all celebrating (the signing of the new Constitution). But our hearts were at half mast that day, because we were out of a country (in which) we had chosen to remain.

So the accord of Meech Lake brought us something *incroyable* as a gesture of friendship. Since the telephone rang at our house and a friend called me from Meech Lake to say 'it is done', I have held my head high, believing at last that I did not deceive my compatriots when, with the *non* team, we told them that there would be a place for Quebec in the Canada of tomorrow. There will be room for French-speaking Quebecers in Canada's federal institutions and the Canadian federation will be rejuvenated.

And I would really like people to know that for us Quebecers, as for all the others here and everywhere else, the Meech Lake accords are not an end, but the beginning of a grand process, I think. But I must tell you that for me it is really the first time that I have felt, YES, I won that referendum.

But surely by now you all know that if Meech is to fall, for whatever reason, there can be no more negotiations, no more justifications. If Quebec is once again to realize that it is more difficult to opt into Canada than to stay out, then surely you know that the roads of tomorrow can only lead to another form of independence....[147]

Solange Chaput-Rolland, former journalist and Quebec MNA, member of the Pépin-Roberts Commission, and recently named by Prime Minister Mulroney to the Senate

Canada. The agreement was seen as finally making concrete the 'renewed federalism' promised to Quebecers for having rejected separatism in the 1980 referendum.[134]

Less than three weeks after the conclusion of the hearings, the committee issued its report (only one of the four Liberals on the committee signed it). The report opened with the clinching argument: "The question before us...is not whether a different solution might have been reached or whether other constitutional issues might also have been added. It is quite simply whether or not the accord agreed upon should be adopted..." It concluded that the accord "represents a reasonable and workable package of constitutional reforms." The report also raised four concerns for the future: public participation in constitutional change, the relation of the Charter to other ingredients of the Constitution, the unanimity rule as applied to the creation of new provinces, and the aboriginal issue.[135]

Before the constitutional agreement was debated in the House of Commons, Saskatchewan became the second province to endorse Meech Lake. Legislative debate had first begun in July, at which time opposition parties focused their rage on the immigration provisions (which were seen as jeopardizing future population growth in the province, given the guarantee to Quebec). There were also unsuccessful calls for public hearings. Premier Devine endorsed the unanimity principle and mused "I wouldn't want to bring in a new province with 50 percent of the population and three or four provinces against it....You [the new province] would feel like an ugly sister." Although the premier was absent for the vote, the constitutional motion passed 43-3.[136]

The Constitutional Amendment, 1987 was introduced for debate in the House of Commons on 29 September 1987. It was an odd, drawn-out, shapeless, and anti-climactic affair. For peculiar scheduling reasons, it was impossible to arrange for all three leaders to speak on the opening day of debate, or even on the same day, and this undermined whatever drama the debate might have had. On opening day, the only leader to speak was John Turner; the Prime Minister and NDP leader Broadbent did not speak until 26 October. The debate took four weeks during which time 77 MPs participated. The way in which the opposition parties proceeded was of major interest. The agreement continued to be divisive for the Liberals. Senior party MP Lloyd Axworthy had become increasingly critical, maintaining that the accord discriminated against northerners and westerners. Turner was in a delicate position. He needed the support of his Quebec MPs, who were becoming increasingly annoyed with those Liberals who were critical of Meech Lake. But there was considerable extra-parliamentary pressure to avoid over-enthusiasm, so Turner agreed to submit a series of amendments.[137] During the ratification debate, Turner played the non-partisan high road, but submitted amendments dealing with aboriginal and multicultural rights, linguistic minorities, the precedence of the Charter, more constrained opting-out provisions, elimination of the unanimity formula, and a constitutional conference on aboriginal rights.[138] Eleven Liberals broke rank and voted against the constitutional agreement.

NDP leader Broadbent gave a short, dull, and lethargic presentation, highlighted by the praise he extended to the Prime Minister. He characterized the constitutional process as a "remarkably creative and productive non-partisan approach" led by first ministers who had done "a very fine job." He continued to express concern about aboriginal rights, the North, women's rights, multiculturalism and visible minorities.[139] Two NDP members broke ranks (Ian Waddell and Audrey McLaughlin).

An unanticipated feature of the last stages of the debate was a statement by Queen Elizabeth during her visit to Canada. She praised the Prime Minister and the premiers for their Meech Lake accomplishment, which she saw as "reinforc[ing]...respect for human rights and liberties in Quebec in confirming it as a 'distinct society'". Premier Bourassa was enthusiastic about this trans-Atlantic British support.[140]

When the debate was closed and the final vote was taken, the House of Commons was almost full (258 of 282 MPs voted). The vote was 242-16 in support of the constitutional agreement. Two Conservatives (Nickerson and Nowlan) broke party ranks, and independent MP Tony Roman also voted against. Four Conservatives abstained; two others left just before the vote was taken. The constitutional amendment would now proceed to the Senate, which had 180 days to deal with it. It took 178 days for it to respond.

THE MOMENTUM SHIFTS

New Brunswick

Political attention now shifted to the provincial level, and anti-accord critics began lobbying the premiers furiously.[141] What at first seemed an inexorable march toward ratification was given a resounding jolt by the election in New Brunswick. On 13 October, Liberal Frank McKenna won an astonishing electoral mandate, capturing every seat in the legislature. During the campaign, McKenna had declared that a Liberal victory would be a vote for changing the Meech Lake deal: "I'm asking the people of New Brunswick for a mandate to go in and negotiate the best possible deal...Hatfield didn't go to the people of New Brunswick and tell them whether he would sign it or not before he negotiated."[142] After the election, he continued to declare that he could not support the constitutional agreement. During the winter of 1988, Premier McKenna met with Premier Bourassa to sign an energy deal. Bourassa was unable to move McKenna from this position.[143] Prime Minister Mulroney turned the heat on as well: "It would be a very heavy responsibility for someone to veto [the accord] and thereby preclude the possibility of bringing Quebec into the constitution...But Mr. McKenna is a big boy, and the responsibilities are there." It was reported that the other provinces were exploring the possibility of constructing a 'political' agreement that would assuage McKenna's concerns by offering assurances of future constitutional change. "There is nothing formal, and nothing has been decided, but people are working on a political compromise so that McKenna doesn't lose face," said a Quebec provincial official.[144] Over and above traditional Liberal concerns about the accord's impact on rights and the federal power, McKenna wanted removal of the clause that required a constitutional conference on the fishery; he felt that this was a move towards allowing Newfoundland control over who could fish in east coast waters.[145] Before the first ministers conference in November 1987, top federal officials (Norman Spector, Mary Dawson, and Frank Iacobucci, who was later named Chief Justice of the Federal Court of Canada) travelled to New Brunswick to brief McKenna and try to persuade him to sign the accord. Premiers also exerted moral pressure on him at the conference. Lowell Murray insisted that the 'political reality' was that McKenna had six months to sign: "If after all other provinces have said yes, and New Brunswick says wait two more years...then effectively the answer is no." McKenna remained unmoved. "I'm still operating on a three-year timetable...I'm not going to be provoked on that...there's no basis for six months." He responded to his being characterized as a 'black sheep', by saying, "It doesn't bother me. I didn't get to be the premier of the province simply by going along with the crowd."[146] In May 1988, McKenna announced that public hearings would not take place until the autumn. This plan was later upset by the calling of the federal election. New Brunswick would not hold public hearings until late January 1989; these hearings would adjourn when the legislature was sitting, so they were not expected to be concluded before the spring or summer. It was thus anticipated that the New Brunswick legislature would not consider the constitutional agreement until the autumn of 1989.[147]

Manitoba

The situation in Manitoba developed to the same political effect and uncertainty. In the fall of 1987, Premier Pawley began to face anti-accord sentiment from senior members of the provincial NDP, who were canvassing support for the presentation of an anti-accord motion at the party's annual convention.[148] On 18 December, Premier Pawley announced that he was reconsidering his support of the constitutional agreement, prompted by Ottawa's decision to push ahead with the Free Trade Agreement in the absence of provincial unanimity.[149] New Brunswick's McKenna observed, "I may have a potential ally."[150] The NDP government unexpectedly fell on 9 March 1988, precipitating the calling of an election for 26 April as well as the resignation of Pawley as NDP leader. Still smarting from the CF-18 decision, Manitobans had been apprehensive about the Meech Lake agreement. An anti-Meech Lake movement grew during the winter, at the municipal level and in the rural areas. In early December, the Rural Municipality of Woodlands passed a resolution condemning the constitutional agreement for giving Quebec special privileges and for sabotaging the process of Senate reform. By early February, three dozen other municipalities had followed suit in passing a similar motion, which included the passage, "in a democratic country, no one province should be given extended powers to the detriment of others." There was also considerable concern that the immigration provisions of the agreement would solidify the dominance of central Canada (as Manitoba and other western provinces would not be able to use immigration as a source of potentially disproportionate population growth).[151] By the time the Manitoba government fell, 15 provincial NDP riding associations had passed resolutions urging the government to reject the constitutional agreement, for being flawed, unclear, imprecise, and the result of secret negotiations. At its convention in early March, the NDP had to devise a face-saving compromise resolution calling on the government to "take steps to deal with the flaws in the accord prior to having the legislature make a decision on the accord." In the provincial leadership race to replace Pawley, none of the four candidates indicated that he felt bound to the Meech Lake Agreement. More ominously for the ratification process, Manitoba Liberal leader Sharon Carstairs was a political ally of Jean Chrétien and a long-time critic of the Meech Lake deal.[152] While the pro-accord Conservative party had had a large early lead in the polls, it managed to win only 25 of the province's 57 seats. On the other hand, the Liberals won 20 seats. In a radio interview following the election, Carstairs stated that the Conservatives would have 'grave difficulty' in getting legislative approval for the agreement: "I can't imagine Mr. Filmon being that foolish. In essence, Meech Lake is dead." Premier-elect Filmon himself admitted that Meech Lake might not be a top priority: "It may well be that Meech Lake doesn't come on to the agenda for quite some time." The *Winnipeg Free Press*, under the headline, "Meech Lake Really is Dead," wrote "there is no doubt that the Liberal leader is part of a majority in the legislature which will not accept Meech Lake as it stands." A disproportionate number of NDP seats were in northern Manitoba, where there was strong native sentiment against the accord, so it could be anticipated that half or more of the NDP MLAs would not support the agreement. When the Filmon government presented its Throne Speech on 21 July 1988, the constitutional deal remained a low priority for the government, which announced that public hearings would be held in the fall. The minority government survived debates on the Throne Speech and the budget, but its position was made more precarious by the defection of Tory backbencher Gilles Roch to the Liberals (making the standings Conservatives 24, Liberals

21, NDP 12). Roch revealed that "there is tremendous federal pressure on the provincial Conservative caucus to support and pass Meech Lake." Uncertainty deepened after the federal election, as provincial NDP leader Doer declared that his party would not support the accord as it stands. "Meech Lake must be improved before it comes to a vote. We will not back down." This was the first formal indication that the NDP would not support the constitutional agreement. Its declaration of opposition was triggered by the effective confirmation during the November 1988 federal election of the Free Trade Agreement which the NDP saw as weakening federal power particularly in the area of social policy. The NDP called for amendments to the accord to ensure that the federal spending power would not be weakened, as well to guarantee minority and aboriginal rights. Carstairs was "absolutely delighted" by Doer's decision, and observed: "We may be at a pivotal point in history."[153]

Other Developments

Other events also contributed to the deceleration of the ratification process. The Senate Task Force on the Meech Lake Constitutional Accord and the Yukon and Northwest Territories issued its report on 1 March 1988. The Senate group had travelled to the territories, holding public hearings in Whitehorse, Yellowknife, and Iqaluit. Thirty-one groups and individuals gave testimony, which focused on the provincial veto of the creation of new provinces, absence of northern involvement in the appointment of senators and Supreme Court justices, and the absence of the North in the constitutional process.[154] The Task Force recommended that a number of amendments be made to the constitutional agreement:

§   the territories should be allowed to nominate senators and Supreme Court justices;

§   the territories should be allowed to participate in constitutional conferences;

§   the creation of new provinces should be a matter between the territories and the federal government;

§   aboriginal issues should be placed as a continuing item on the constitutional agenda;

§   aboriginal people should be characterized in the constitution as a distinct society. [155]

These recommendations were passed on to the Senate committee-of-the-whole, whose hearings on the constitution had been held on and off again from October through March. These hearings were not particularly non-partisan. Of the two dozen or so groups and individuals which the Senate heard, only one speaker — former Liberal cabinet minister Jack Pickersgill — was pro-Meech Lake. All the other representations were anti-accord, with the rehearsal once again of concerns about the agreement's impact on native rights, the territories' disappointments, the rights of women and linguistic minorities, the future of national social programs, multiculturalism, and the weakening of the federal government.

On 30 March 1988, Pierre Trudeau appeared before the Senate (Lowell Murray and most Conservative senators chose to be absent). The former prime minister maintained that Mulroney had given up everything while Quebec had received more than it had bargained for: "national reconciliation was able to bring temporary peace to federal-provincial relations by negotiating a sweetheart constitutional deal whereby enormous amounts of power were transferred to the provincial governments, and particularly to the premiers." He described the accord as being like the "parson's egg: it is not only bad in part, it is completely bad. I think it should be put out in the dustbin..." Reacting to this presentation, Alberta Premier Getty told the annual convention of Alberta Conservatives that "while I knew the accord was very good, after Mr. Trudeau's intervention I'm certain it's one hell of a deal."[156]

The Senate hearings ended on 31 March, and on 18 April the Senate sent the constitutional bill back to the House of Commons with nine amendments. These were more or less the same ones as those proposed by Liberal leader Turner in the House of Commons the previous October (see p. 272). The amendments were characterized by Lowell Murray as being "killer amendments" that, if accepted, would scuttle the constitutional deal. He exploited the Liberal party's split on the issue, as comprising "two visions of Canada warring within the bosom of a single political party."[157]

During the winter, labour opposition to the Meech Lake agreement surfaced. The labour movement had been rather circumspect in its reaction to Meech Lake. It did not want to embarrass the federal NDP, which had at a very early stage endorsed the agreement with enthusiasm. In its submission to the special joint committee, the Canadian Labour Congress had castigated the constitutional process for being 'authoritarian' and 'paternalistic,' and had criticized the opting out and unanimity provisions of the agreement. The Canadian Union of Public Employees (CUPE) passed a resolution at its January convention, describing the agreement as "flawed, inadequate, and unacceptable." At a convention in early March, the National Union of Provincial Government Employees (Canada's second-largest union) passed a resolution condemning the agreement for the vagueness of its language, the absence of public debate, and the threat to social programs created by the opting out provisions.[158]

On 4 April, the ratification process suffered another (indirect) blow, when Saskatchewan introduced its language law. The Supreme Court had ruled in February that all of Saskatchewan's laws since 1905 were invalid — because they had been written only in English. The Saskatchewan government faced two options. It could translate all of its laws since 1905 into French, or it could pass a law retroactively legalizing all of the legislation that had been enacted. It chose the second option. While the new law would allow French to be spoken in the legislature, there would be no French Hansard and only some bills would be translated into French at some future time. Some court services would be available in French. The Saskatchewan action split the federal Conservative caucus, and led Prime Minister Mulroney to declare that he was 'disappointed' in the Saskatchewan action. For many observers, New Brunswick Premier McKenna included, this action appeared to underscore the weak protection given to minority language rights in the Meech Lake Agreement. [159] In early July, the Alberta government passed similar language legislation. Bill 60 (two pages long, eight sections) declared Alberta to be bilingual on the floor of the legislature and in the courts, but unilingual everywhere else. This was characterized as "Saying No to Bilingualism."[160]

As the momentum toward ratification of the constitutional agreement seemed to weaken, Prime Minister Mulroney tried to go on a counterattack. Talking to reporters on 7 March, he dared opponents of the accord to stop hiding, and played his 'Quebec card': "Let those who oppose Meech Lake say so squarely....Those who want to send a message to Quebec and Canada that they are against the accord, let them stand up and stop hiding behind other people. We'll see what Canadians and Quebecers have to say about that." He went on to claim that Alliance Quebec (the organization of the minority of English-speaking Quebecers) had endorsed the agreement. However, Alliance Quebec had opposed the agreement on four public occasions: the May 1987 Quebec hearings, the August 1987 special joint committee hearings, in the Senate on 2 December 1987, and at the Ontario hearings on 24 February 1988.[161] To make matters worse for the Prime Minister, La fédération des francophones hors Québec (which spoke for one million francophones outside of Quebec) sent him a surprise letter. The letter stated that the constitutional agreement was "incomplete and unacceptable" and a threat to minority rights.[162]

During March, a fierce debate took place in the Nova Scotia legislature, that left unresolved and uncertain the fate of the Meech Lake agreement in that province — which had an election looming on the horizon. The opposition Liberals and NDP staged a mini-filibuster over the agreement, that consumed the first two weeks of the legislative session. Opposition concerns centred on the opting-out provisions of shared-cost programmes (decentralization was seen as a threat to weaker provinces such as Nova Scotia), gender rights, an elected Senate, and the bilingual/multicultural character of Canada. The government refused the call for a select committee study. The fiercest debate centred on the issue of placing the fisheries on the constitutional agenda. Liberal leader MacLean introduced a motion asking that jurisdictional responsibilities for fisheries not be changed without the prior agreement of all four Atlantic provinces. He claimed that Nova Scotia was the only province that had given something up as the price of getting Newfoundland Premier Peckford to sign the agreement. "Perhaps the premier did not realize the significance at the time....He might have been tired after that 19 hours, so he might have inadvertently thought the wording...did not affect the interests of Nova Scotia." There was widespread speculation that the Prime Minister had asked the premier to pass the constitutional agreement before the expected spring provincial election, for fear that the Conservative government in Nova Scotia would not be re-elected. After 11 March, debate was suspended on this issue, and was not pursued again until the end of the session in late May.[163]

The constitutional agreement continued to be divisive for the Liberal party and, as it conducted its in-fighting in public, negative scrutiny of the accord was sustained. After an extended period of silence, ex-Liberal cabinet member and leadership candidate Jean Chrétien spoke out against the deal. He urged Ontario Premier Peterson to insist on an amendment that would protect Charter rights. "I know that some lawyers argue that the Charter will not be overridden, but I also know that some lawyers can be wrong. We cannot as a country afford to take that chance." He complained about "a leadership vacuum in Ottawa....Who will speak for Canada?" He criticized the accord's backers for saying that, "anybody who speaks out, it's because he's anti-Quebec...Nobody would be able to say I'm anti-Quebec".[164] (Anti-Meech Lake forces in the Liberal party were strengthened in the 1988 election. Only 12 MPs were returned from Quebec, and 75-85 percent of the Liberal caucus appeared to be anti-accord. These members were immediately vocal in their criticism of Meech Lake.)

The situation for the Liberal party in Ontario was not much better. At its annual meeting, a motion was introduced to seek three amendments to the accord, dealing with Charter preeminence, tougher opting-out provisions, and an easier amending formula for the creation of new provinces. The motion was only narrowly defeated, 259-246. In an informal interview on 12 May, Premier Peterson said that he was now willing to consider amendments to the agreement: "There are lots of discussions going on. But nobody's got any specifics...I'm not saying absolutely there can't be an amendment somewhere. But that's not for me to say. We're reasonable." After alarm bells began to ring in the first ministers' offices across the country, the next day Peterson retracted this statement, and asserted that no amendments would be made at this time.[165]

One year after the Meech Lake meeting, the ratification process appeared to have stalled. Only three provincial legislatures had approved the agreement. Opinion polls in early April indicated that only one in four Canadians supported the accord, down 50 percent from the previous year. Moreover, the Saskatchewan language controversy, the criticism by francophone groups outside of Quebec, the New Brunswick and Manitoba elections, Trudeau's performance before the Senate, the Senate amendments, court challenges by the territories, and the agreement's rough treatment in the Nova Scotia legislature amounted to a huge political weight against the ratification process. On top of all this, three of Canada's cleverest lawyers were taking the agreement to court. They were acting on behalf of the Canadian Coalition on the Constitution, a loose coalition of academics, lawyers, and interest groups such as the National Anti-Poverty Coalition, the Canadian Day Care Advocacy Association, the Canadian Institute for Child Health, the Canadian Mental Health Association, the Canadian Ethnocultural Association, and the Women's Legal Educational and Action Fund. Edward Greenspan, Morris Manning, and Timothy Danson argued to the court that the agreement was unconstitutional because it amounted to an illegal transfer of powers from the federal to the provincial governments; the distinct society clause was so vague as to be destructive; and the Charter's preeminence should be established.[166]

THE MOMENTUM SHIFTS BACK

Despite this litany of apparent roadblocks and setbacks, the ratification process moved right along, and the momentum seemed to swing back again. Because the Senate had passed amendments to the constitutional agreement, the House of Commons had to pass the original constitutional act again. The legislation was re-introduced in the House of Commons on 19 May (with speeches by Hnatyshyn, Jewett, and Kaplan), and the debate ended on 14 June (with speeches from the three party leaders). As was to be expected, the debate was a bit lethargic and without surprises. Hnatyshyn urged that the opposition parties not introduce amendments, as "such proposals could only encourage their provincial cousins."[167] While Kaplan asserted that "the government has made a terrible mistake in tactics in insisting that the Meech Lake accord is a seamless web," the NDP's Pauline Jewett declared that "Meech is stronger than we ever dreamed, and better, and more effective."[168] Prime Minister Mulroney admitted that "the Meech Lake Accord is not perfect," but declared that the 1982 constitutional deal had "depriv[ed] the federal government of the flexibility inherent in a comprehensive negotiation."[169] With less than half his caucus present, beleaguered Liberal leader John Turner gave an oddly formal and academic review of Canadian constitutional history, before re-introducing the same amendments he had proposed the previous fall. NDP leader Broadbent's presentation was even more supportive than his fall 1987 talk, and his criticisms were more muted.[170] On 23 June 1988, the House of Commons voted 200 to 7 to override the Senate amendments. Only four Liberals voted against (Caccia, Penner, Berger, Finestone), while eight were absent and two abstained. Two NDP members abstained (McCurdy, Robinson) and one voted against (Audrey McLaughlin). Conservative David Nickerson also voted against.

On 7 December 1987, Alberta became the third province to ratify the constitutional agreement. The NDP had asked for public hearings to be held, but the Conservative government declined the request. The NDP then sponsored its own hearings, and in mid-September held meetings in Grande Prairie, Edmonton, Red Deer, Calgary, Lethbridge, and Medicine Hat. One hundred and fifty submissions were made, all but one of which expressed deep concern about the accord. The media ignored the hearings. A snap vote ended legislative debate and surprised the Opposition, whose members were in another part of the building. As a result, the constitutional agreement was passed unanimously.[171]

An eerie quiet descended on the provincial legislative level over the rest of the winter, creating the impression that the ratification process was stalled. But through the spring and early summer, five provinces ratified the constitutional agreement. On 13 May, Prince Edward Island became the fourth province, and the first Atlantic province, to approve the accord. PEI was also only the second province to hold public hearings (over five days in April and May). The constitutional committee recommended that the agrement be approved by the legislature, with outstanding concerns and issues to be pursued in the next constitutional round. Only one member — a Liberal — voted against the agreement.[172]

On 25 May 1988, Nova Scotia became the fifth province to affirm the constitutional agreement. After two weeks of fierce and inconclusive debate in March, the government waited until the last two days of the legislative session to resume and quickly end debate. The Opposition balked at the rushed process of approving the constitutional deal. Opposition leader Vince MacLean argued that "it locks Nova Scotia into a position of supporting Newfoundland's request for the fishery, and I say why give that away at the moment." The Opposition tried unsuccessfully to adjourn debate until public hearings were held. Eventually, the agreement was passed 35 to 7. The six Liberal members voted against, and three NDP members abstained. Premier Buchanan was absent from almost all of the debate. An election was held in Nova Scotia during the summer. Liberal leader MacLean declared that he held the same views as Manitoba's Sharon Carstairs and promised, if elected, to try to convince the other premiers to change the agreement. In the event, Premier Buchanan was returned to office (albeit with a reduced majority), so another threat to the constitutional agreement was eliminated. [173]

In late June, the Ontario committee on the constitution issued its report. Ontario had been one of only two provinces to hold public hearings on the constitutional package to this stage of the ratification process. However, Premier Peterson had made it clear that he wouldn't change his mind about the accord, and that women's groups, natives, and northerners would have to wait until the next round of constitutional talks. The committee gave unanimous but "reluctant" support to the agreement. Its reservations were neutralized by the prospect of the agreement's ending Quebec's constitutional isolation. The committee issued two companion resolutions, one asking that a broader conceptualization of Canada's fundamental characteristics be developed, and the other asking that aboriginal rights be placed on the constitutional agenda. It also recommended that a standing committee on the constitution be established. On 29 June 1988, Ontario became the sixth province to approve the constitutional package, by a vote of 112 to 8. During the voting, proceedings were disrupted by a group of 20 women, members of the Ad Hoc Committee of Women on the Constitution, singing, "We are gentle angry people, and we are singing, singing for our rights."[174]

Later that day, British Columbia became the seventh province to pass the constitutional agreement. Of all the provinces, BC's ratification of the Meech Lake Agreement produced the least amount of fanfare (Alberta was a close second). The constitutional motion was presented on 28 June 1988, but its thunder was stolen by the events surrounding Attorney-General Smith's resignation. The legislation was given perfunctory treatment in a quick debate, and was passed on 29 June by a vote of 42 to 5 (the five members were from the NDP). Opposition NDP leader Harcourt expressed some concerns, which were assuaged in the anticipation of Quebec's signing the Constitution.[175]

On 7 July 1988, Newfoundland became the eighth province to ratify the accord. Premier Peckford introduced a motion in mid-March, and the Liberal opposition carried out a filibuster of sorts. Opposition Liberal leader Clyde Wells criticized the accord for weakening the federal spending power as well as the Charter, and for creating a rigid amending formula. The ratification motion passed 28 to 10, with two NDP members and former Liberal Leo Barry joining 25 Conservatives in support of the motion. Ten Liberals voted against. Fourteen members were absent for the vote, including Premier Peckford.[176]

A number of judicial decisions knocked away some constraints on the ratification process. In mid-February, the Yukon and Northwest Territories went to the Supreme Court, seeking to appeal two earlier court of appeal decisions that ruled that the federal government had no obligation to consult the territories before signing the constitutional agreement. The territories were represented by soon-to-be Supreme Court Justice John

Sopinka, who argued that political convention and common law requires the federal government to consult citizens before making constitutional changes that affect those citizens' rights. During the summer, the Supreme Court rejected the territories' appeal that the Meech Lake agreement was unconstitutional. The court accepted the federal argument that territorial governments do not exist in legal terms, so cannot bring a court case.[177] In September 1988, a second attempt by the Canadian Coalition on the Constitution to challenge the constitutionality of the Meech Lake accord was thrown out of the court. Mr. Justice Bud Cullen of the Federal Court of Canada ruled that the accord is only a 'tentative agreement' that cannot be disputed in the courts.[178]

FEDERAL ELECTION 1988

Almost two years after the Meech Lake meeting, the ratification process was still unfolding. Ratification had gone relatively smoothly at the federal level, where all-party agreement insulated an already tightly controlled process. In most provincial situations, the process was similar. Majority governments easily overcame opposition criticism and ratified the accord. Critics of the agreement found themselves very much on the outside of a process in which only governments themselves had real power. However, electoral changes in New Brunswick and Manitoba resulted in the rapid deceleration of the ratification process. Uncertainty in these provinces created an opening for opponents of the accord, political parties and interest groups alike. At the halfway point in the ratification period, the provincial leaders in New Brunswick and Manitoba awaited the results of the November 1988 federal election, to see whether this would affect the process one way or the other.

The 1988 election was essentially a one-issue campaign, dominated by the free trade issue. There was little to no campaign discussion of the Meech Lake deal at the national level. It is likely that this would have been the case even in the absence of the free trade issue, as the three major parties had acted in a way that made the constitutional development a non-partisan matter. Moreover, each party eyed Quebec as an electoral prize that required its fidelity to Meech Lake. The Conservatives emerged as the big electoral winner nationally, but also and particularly in Quebec, where they won 60 of 75 seats. For both the Liberals and the NDP, this was a disheartening result, since they had swallowed certain traditions and principles in supporting Meech Lake in hope of expanding their electoral success in Quebec.

After the election, Prime Minister Mulroney tried to present his national electoral victory and his electoral dominance of Quebec as signifying popular approval of the Meech Lake deal. At a press conference on 22 November, he declared that Manitoba and New Brunswick were now 'obliged' to pass the constitutional agreement. Manitoba Liberal leader Carstairs immediately criticized the Prime Minister's comments as being "absolutely ludicrous....The Canadian public did not vote on Meech Lake. It was not a federal issue. I mentioned it in my campaign. He [Mulroney] didn't, except when he went into Quebec."[179] The next day, Manitoba NDP leader Doer announced that his party would not support the deal as it stood. Liberal Robert Kaplan - who had engineered Liberal Party support of Meech Lake in 1987–88 — declared that Meech Lake was "doomed": "We've reached a roadblock and it's not going to go through." [180] On 7 December the Prime Minister issued a caution to Meech Lake opponents: "It will be important for the Liberal Party and the NDP — not just for months but for decades — as to how this matter is handled." New Brunswick remained unmoved and Premier McKenna issued a warning of his own: "The harsher rhetoric coming from the government is tending to harden the resolve of those people who disagree with Meech Lake." [181]

UNANTICIPATED DEVELOPMENTS

As 1988 drew to a close, the fate of the Meech Lake Accord was by no means settled but it could be envisioned that it would eventually be ratified by the remaining provinces. Then, an unanticipated development generated a series of events which threatened to block the ratification process.

On 15 December 1988 the Supreme Court struck down certain provisions of Quebec's language law. Bill 101 had aimed at protecting the French language in Quebec by insisting that signs in Quebec be exclusively in French. The Court ruled that "it has not been demonstrated that the prohibition of the use of any language other than French...is necessary to the defence and enhancement of the status of the French language in Quebec, or that it is proportionate to that legislative purpose." Its decision was 5–0, and endorsed earlier verdicts by the Quebec Superior Court in 1984 and the Quebec Court of Appeal in 1986. In an agonizing decision, Premier Bourassa then introduced Bill 178, a compromise law, which proposed to allow bilingual signs inside buildings but insisted on unilingual French signs outside buildings. In the process, Bourassa invoked section 33 of the Charter, the notwithstanding clause, to overturn the Supreme Court decision and to protect the Quebec government from legal attack on this bill for the next five years. This action provoked both the resignation of three (of four) of Bourassa's English cabinet ministers and the wrath of Quebec nationalists who supported Bill 101 and the language status quo. [182]

Outside of Quebec, there was widespread criticism of Bourassa's actions. While Prime Minister Mulroney appeared prepared to accept the idea of French-only signs in Quebec, he pleaded with Bourassa not to use the notwithstanding clause, for fear of an anti-Quebec backlash in the rest of Canada which would hurt the ratification chances of the Meech Lake Accord. However, Quebec house leader Michel Gratton noted that "...every lawyer we consulted told us that unless we used the notwithstanding clause we would be back in court by January." [183] While the federal government condemned Bill 178 for undermining minority rights in Quebec, it blamed the previous Liberal government for constructing a constitution containing a notwithstanding clause. [184]

The Prime Minister's fears were confirmed almost immediately in Manitoba. Premier Filmon had introduced the Meech Lake legislation in the legislature on 16 December, characterizing the agreement as "too narrow a foundation upon which to build" but concluded that it was "a necessary first step." He proposed to devise a companion resolution (as Ontario had done) to register Manitoba's concerns. Then on 19 December, Filmon suspended debate on Meech Lake, in light of Quebec's introduction of Bill 178 and its use of the notwithstanding clause. Quebec's action was a "national tragedy to which we had no option but to respond...We could not stand idly by and let our principles of justice and fair play be compromised." Bill 178 was seen to "violate the spirit of Meech Lake", and further debate on the accord "may invite a very negative anti-Quebec backlash and...could cause deep dissension." He urged Mulroney to call a First Ministers' Conference "on an urgent basis." [185]

Filmon and other Manitobans (and Canadians) were concerned not only about the use of the notwithstanding clause but also about Premier Bourassa's claim that, had the Meech Lake Accord been ratified, he would have used the distinct society clause to justify Bill 178. This confirmed the fears of New Brunswick's Frank McKenna, who demanded federal initiatives: "It's again time to say the government of Canada has a role to play in promoting and protecting the role of minorites. That has been one of the additions we wanted to see to Meech Lake." [186]

Lowell Murray criticized Filmon for his "hasty" action "taken in the heat of the moment. It is a decision much to be regretted." Prime Minister Mulroney declared that Filmon was wrong to link Quebec's language initiatives with Meech Lake and declined to summon a special meeting of the first ministers. A meeting in early 1989 was already set but, as Senator Murray noted, "any changes in the Accord would astonish me." The Prime Minister remained optimistic: "I believe we shall surmount these difficulties...The Meech Lake Accord will be ratified as is." [187]

Early in the new year, Filmon asked the federal government to resolve the controversy by sending the distinct society clause to the Supreme Court for a court reference. "Eight provinces have said the distinct society clause is nothing but a recognition of the reality that exists in Quebec. But at the same time...you have...Premier Bourassa indicating that the distinct society clause would have given them the power to implement their [language] bill without the use of the notwithstanding clause." Filmon's view was that it was better to have a court ruling than to re-write the clause.[188]

DISCUSSION

The terms of the Meech Lake constitutional agreement assigned to the provinces (really, the premiers) increased political power and authority. The agreement proposed to increase the provincial role in national institutions (Senate and Supreme Court), to generate increased provincial responsibility in certain policy areas (immigration, shared cost programmes), and to institutionalize a new layer of government which the provinces would dominate (yearly constitutional conferences with the principle of provincial unanimity in crucial areas). Quebec was to be considered a distinct society in a constitutional sense. In short, the Meech Lake deal promised to decentralize political power and authority in Canada. Of course the agreement — at the time of writing — had not yet been ratified and looks increasingly unlikely to be ratified. In the real worlds of Canadian politics almost anything can happen however, and it may be that eleventh hour changes or parallel motions will be effected to assuage the concerns of New Brunswick and Manitoba. But even if this, or something more dramatic occurs, it is inconceivable that the decentralizing tendency will suddenly change course. The reality of Canadian political life is that the provinces will play an increasingly critical role at the national level of government.

Of all the myriad worlds of Canadian politics, the world of amending the constitution is perhaps the most closed and elitist. It is governments that shape and alter the constitution in Canada. Citizens and groups watch this process, and perhaps complain. But they have little power and authority, and no formal avenues of intervention into the constitutional amendment process. For some observers, this is not a particularly upsetting observation, as they cannot imagine how a participatory approach to constitutional amendment might be devised. After all, the challenge of getting 11 governments to agree on something is immense, particularly with regard to issues and concerns where significant disagreement exists. For others, this closed world reflects the nature of Canada's deferential political culture, which has encouraged Canadian citizens to invest considerable authority in their elected (and non-elected) leaders to construct the political structures, processes, and policies that shape those citizen's lives. But others see this closed world as smacking of a paternalistic and elitist process inherited from an earlier, pre-democratic era.

How one sees the Meech Lake process depends on two fundamental variables: one's view of how politics ought to work, and whether the results appear to be acceptable. With regard to the latter, the Meech Lake case is a classic example of how the symbols of politics dominate both political substance and process. In the last analysis, the Meech Lake case was a Quebec issue. It was characterized by the first ministers as the 'Quebec Round' — even though it was a round in which all the provinces gained as much as Quebec. Every pro-Meech Lake presentation by a political leader or 'expert' began with the 'bottom line' first: Quebec was finally signing the Canadian Constitution. A 'flaw' was being repaired, the 'family' was all together again, the 'wounds' were being healed, a political 'embarrassment' was being remedied. Presentations then went on to outline the 'imperfections' of Meech Lake that raised 'serious concerns.' Women, natives, northerners, and linguistic minorities were told that their anxieties were, more or less, legitimate — but that the first order of business was to deal with the Quebec situation. These other concerns would be dealt with at a later constitutional stage. No one bragged about a consitutional process that allowed, at most, 'discussion' and 'scrutiny.' But regardless of these and other issues, the case was made to support the accord, because Quebec would sign the Constitution, and this would allow the pursuit of these other issues.

This is not to deny the importance or seriousness of this accomplishment. Quebec *was* dealt with shabbily in 1981-82. Moreover, the absence of its signature from the Constitution could hardly be allowed to become a permanent state of affairs. Nor is it meant to exaggerate Quebec's constitutional accomplishments, which were relatively modest and commonsensical relative to the demands and expectations of the previous two decades.[189] The Parti québécois and other nationalist groups in fact accused the Quebec government of 'selling out.' Quebec's gains were, more or less, accomplished by the other provinces as well. The point is that this is but one accomplishment amongst an infinite series of potential political accomplishments and values — and it had the capacity to override all the rest in the minds of the key political actors and a series of observers and experts. Moreover, the accomplishment comprised only one package of ingredients amongst an infinite series of packages, but these possibilities were not debated or taken seriously. They were smothered by Quebec's signature.

The Meech Lake Agreement also had content and significance beyond the Quebec issue. It is hard to imagine that the other nine premiers would have signed the agreement otherwise. Indeed, Meech Lake was a classic political trade. The nine provinces had a variety of constitutional issues that they wanted to pursue but the constitutional process was dead as long as Quebec refused to participate in it. It was in the nine provinces' direct self-interest to go along with Quebec's five conditions. On the other hand, what Quebec wanted was in the hands of the other nine premiers, any one of whom could have blocked the realization of these conditions. They did go along — but on condition that they received, more or less, everything that Quebec did. The playing out of the Quebec issue had the effect, as Roger Gibbins suggests, of universalizing 'special status.'[190]

The hinge on which the deal swung was, getting Quebec to sign. This one ingredient cooled the antagonistic positions of Alberta, British Columbia, and Nova Scotia, who were vehemently opposed to special status. It more or less forced John Turner to be uncritical of the agreement, lest he lose his Quebec caucus and electoral support, and forced the Liberal party to swallow some of its traditional principles and positions in order to avoid appearing 'anti-Quebec.' It led the normally centralist, nationally oriented NDP to be fairly uncritical and mute about the accord's decentralizing implications. And it neutralized the substantial concerns raised by various interest groups and commentators. For example, women's groups were incapable of creating the political momentum they had generated in 1981 for Charter Section 28. While there was a great deal of concern in the special joint committee hearings over the impact of the 'distinct society' clause on women's (and others') equality rights, this concern was given the kiss of death when commentators in Quebec and the Prime Minister himself characterized these concerns as being a cover for an 'anti- Quebec' position. When Quebec women's groups testified that they were not worried about how the 'distinct society' clause might affect women's equality rights, the battle was over. The relationship between various clauses and the Charter was a highly complex one that caused divisions amongst Canada's leading constitutional experts. The Quebec card essentially brushed these complexities aside and simplified the issue. To the extent to which observers valued Quebec's signing as the highest constitutional priority, concerns about the other features and the process of Meech Lake were more or less put to the side. The ratification debate, then, was distinctly asymmetrical because opposition to the accord was made to look 'selfish' in light of the noble accomplishment of Quebec's return to the constitutional family.

Supporters of the constitutional package saw Meech Lake as an historic opportunity to complete the constitutional circle, and a tremendous accomplishment in the face of the challenges involved in getting 11 leaders to agree. The construction of this all-province constitutional consensus also assuaged criticisms that the process had been 'rushed' and 'closed.' There was little to no public participation in the Meech Lake constitutional process. None of the 11 first ministers was elected on a platform of creating such a constitutional package. At most, two leaders had made some sort of electoral commitment, but only Quebec Premier Bourassa had been elected after specifying a constitutional package or set of principles. Prime Minister Mulroney had made vague promises to convince Quebec to sign the Constitution, but this was not presented as a political priority and no strategic criteria or principles were presented. The governments themselves represented only a small proportion of the Canadian population, as they each received only a fraction of popular support. The run-up to Meech Lake was tightly controlled and almost invisible, and was played out amongst bureaucratic officials. These discussions were not made public, and no documents were issued for public discussion and debate. Various drafts and trial positions were circulated, but were kept secret. The federal government never formulated a position that was made public. Indeed, it is still not known whether it had a position, other than the goal of realizing an agreement. The sessions at Meech Lake and in the Langevin Building were restricted to the first ministers and a few non-elected advisers. After the Meech Lake meeting, only one of the provinces (Quebec) conducted public hearings on the accord in anticipation of the next first ministers' meeting, and it did not have ratification hearings. In the ratification process that has followed the Langevin meeting, only two provinces, Ontario and PEI, have had public hearings (New Brunswick and Manitoba plan to have them), and both public hearing processes were constrained by government assertions that the accord could not be changed. Quebec's Premier Bourassa refused , as he put it, to subject Quebecers to another divisive debate. In the other six provinces, debate was either perfunctory and lethargic (Alberta, British Columbia, Saskatchewan) or divisive, impotent, and frustrating (Newfoundland, Nova Scotia, Quebec). At the national level, there were public hearings at a joint special committee. However, these hearings were compressed into one month in the middle of the summer, and with the clear understanding that no amendments to the agreement would be taken seriously. Within the House of Commons, criticism and scrutiny of the accord was inhibited by party discipline and the decision of the opposition parties to make Meech Lake a non-partisan issue. As a result, there was little political 'play' at the national level.

Of course, the federal government had consciously designed this process to minimize squabbles and disagreements and maximize the probability of success. Hence, the process made tremendous political sense. Moreover, it was very much in equilibrium with what it was accomplishing. By and large, Meech Lake was a deal amongst *governments*, and the substance of the agreement dealt primarily with relationships between the two levels of governments. The federal government set out to convince the Quebec government, not the Quebec people, that it ought to sign the Canadian Constitution. As a result of the constitutional deal, the federal government in effect 'gave,' or proposed to share, political power with the provincial governments. This deal was made at first ministers conferences, at which heads of governments made the deal amongst themselves. These heads of governments then returned home to have their legislatures ratify what they had already decided. Citizens, legislatures, political parties, even cabinets took a back seat to the first ministers and *their* institutional turf — the first ministers' conference.

Banting and Simeon maintain that constitutional processes "are important because they are not neutral. Different institutions weigh different interests differently, giving fuller expression to some and minimizing others."[191] Indeed, Alan Cairns has demonstrated this brilliantly in the case of the 1981 constitutional talks.[192] As in 1981, the Meech Lake process saw the interests of the provincial governments predominate in the closed, exclusive first ministers' meetings at Meech Lake and the Langevin Building — in which they outnumbered the federal government ten to one. In the ratification process, though, these provincial issues and concerns all but disappeared, pushed to the side as new players finally entered the process and articulated a bewildering and eclectic array of issues: women's rights, multiculturalism, national social programs, native rights, the status of the territories, language issues, the efficacy of the federal government, and so on. These issues and concerns were not given many opportunities for airing, as so few public hearings were held, and these did not offer the promise of change. Moreover, the Quebec issue prevailed against much of what came on to the agenda, particularly as there was no obvious way, or institutional mechanism, via which all of these other issues could be made to fit together in a constitutional consensus.

There was, however, an odd asymmetry in the process. While the first ministers' meetings and discussions were one-day affairs, the ratification process was potentially three years long. (Some controversy arose even about the ratification timetable, as it was argued that the wrong section of the constitution has been invoked to set the deadline and that Premiers McKenna and Filmon were not bound by the three year schedule set at Meech Lake as they had not been party to that agreement). [193] Since 3 June 1987, the Canadian public has been given four opportunities to be democratically active in a direct sense — at election time. On 13 October 1987 and 26 April 1988, Canadians in New Brunswick and Manitoba used the electoral process to vote out of office two governments that were party to the Meech Lake deal. In so doing, the ratification process was 'opened up' considerably, as the government of New Brunswick is now anti-accord and the minority Manitoba Conservative government faces an anti-accord majority.

The Meech Lake agreement may nor may not pass, or there may be a last minute compromise that encourages New Brunswick and Manitoba to approve it. Regardless of where the story ends, it reflects two different visions of what the constitutional process is all about. In a reflective and insightful presentation at the Senate's Meech Lake hearings, Alan Cairns explained how Canada's constitutional experience had become a contradictory and incoherent one. On the one hand, politicians (particularly first ministers) see the Constitution as 'theirs' — as a "governments' constitution." On the other hand, the constitutional exercise in 1981, and the advent of the Charter have produced an alternative view of a "citizens' constitution". Various social groups — women, multicultural groups, natives — actively secured a 'presence' in the Constitution which led them to feel that the Constitution was 'theirs.' From this has come two different visions of what a Constitution is and how it should be changed. Governments see it as a primarily a regulator of governmental relations, with governments alone to be involved in its amending. Certain citizen's groups see the Constitution as regulating relations between governments and citizens, with the latter having a role in its amending. The Meech Lake process, said Cairns, saw the first ministers limiting the constitutional agenda to federalism and the constitutional process to themselves. This has frustrated and alienated Canadian citizens who had other priorities and wanted to be involved in the process. [194] This clash of visions — embodied in the tension between a government-based amending formula and a citizen-based Charter — is surely one of the most substantial issues that must be dealt with in Canada in the future.

The Meech Lake deal illustrated other of the many worlds of Canadian politics. For John Turner, the Meech Lake deal turned out to be a bad dream. It divided his party on linguistic grounds, and highlighted the extent to which his leadership would continue in the shadows cast by his predecessor, Pierre Trudeau, and his potential challenger, Jean Chrétien. He may have weathered the storm, but the costs were high. The Liberals' dismal electoral showing in Quebec in the federal election made Turner's Meech Lake strategy look politically costly and ineffective. One can expect further bloodletting in the Liberal party as pro- and anti-Meech Lake forces fight it out. The same can be said for the NDP, whose expensive Quebec campaign reaped no fruit but did produce alienation from its Quebec wing and a certain degree of rebellion from the western provincial parties.

For other leaders, like Mulroney and Bourassa, Meech Lake has appeared until recently to be a triumph. Both leaders were politically exposed, in the sense that each had actually promised that Quebec would sign the constitution. But each would gain tremendous political advantages if a deal could be struck. From their perspectives, Meech Lake demonstrated the power that the chief executives have in setting the agenda and controlling the political process.It also showed the potential for change and accomplishment that skillful leadership offers. If Meech Lake is eventually ratified, it will be as significant an ideological accomplishment for Mulroney as anything he has achieved on the economic front. The decentralizing vision of the agreement reflects an ideological reaction against a centralist, big state. In conjunction with the Free Trade Agreement, Meech Lake comprises a substantial transformation of what Canada is and how it will function as a nation. Mulroney's federal election victory and his electoral dominance of Quebec appear to have solidified this vision. For Bourassa, Meech Lake's early success reflected considerable political skill. The timing of the Supreme Court ruling on Bill 101 was unfortunate for him, but he had laid a political foundation for using the notwithstanding clause by not interfering in Saskatchewan and Albertan language politics in the previous year. Ratification of the Meech Lake Accord would represent a significant political accomplishment for Bourassa.

The Meech Lake story once again illustrates the incredible importance the courts will assume in Canadian political life in the future. While testimony at public hearings and speeches in legislatures exhibited a wide array of views on Meech Lake, there was agreement on one point: it would be left to the courts to sort out many of the controversial issues generated by the new constitutional package. For example, the courts would ultimately be asked to determine the effective meaning of the 'distinct society' clause, and particularly its relationship to the various articles in the Charter. Indeed in the wake of Quebec's Bill 178, Manitoba Premier Filmon asked for a Supreme Court ruling on the meaning of the distinct society clause *before* the ratification of the Meech Lake Accord. The Meech Lake case demonstrated that a critical issue in the future would be the determination of the relationship between the Charter and the other parts of the Canadian constitution. And this fundamental issue is one that the courts will decide.

Finally, the Meech Lake story shows starkly how many different visions of Canada exist in our society. Canada is simultaneously a country of regions, provinces, groups with rights, sexes, cultures, different languages, and national spirit and goals. Meech Lake demonstrated the extent to which political leaders and the policy process must be in tune with and informed by each of these visions. A fascinating political development in Canada is how the articulators of these visions want these visions articulated within the constitution. Canada seems now to face the prospect of changing the Constitution every other month. In the real worlds of Canadian politics, the political challenge is how to simultaneously make real these myriad and conflicting constitutional visions, in order to minimize political alienation and maximize national unity.

DISCUSSION QUESTIONS

1) What role did legislatures play in the process leading up to Meech Lake and in the ratification process? Could this role have been more substantial?

2) Discuss the role of political parties, and their relationships, during the ratification process. Were the positions of national and provincial parties in tune with each other?

3) Why did the opposition parties in Ottawa decide to make Meech Lake a non-partisan matter? What impact did this have on the politics of constitutional change? What impact did this have on the opposition parties themselves?

4) Why was Meech Lake so divisive for the Liberal party? Could Liberal leader Turner have done anything different to positive effect?

5) Why were interest groups and organizations so ineffective in realizing their goals in the ratification process?

6) To what extent did the first ministers represent 'the people' in the Meech Lake process?

7) Should the newly elected governments in Manitoba and New Brunswick feel bound by their predecessors' agreement to ratify the accord?

8) Has the first ministers' conference replaced Parliament as Canada's highest political authority?

9) Discuss Cairns' distinction between a governments' constitution and a citizens' one. Where do your sympathies lie?

10) What does this case suggest about the role of the Charter in Canadian politics in the future?

11) Is Canada's amending process more or less democratic than other democratic countries? To what extent should the people be directly involved in constitutional change? Should amendments be subject to a national referendum?

12) What is the relationship between how a government is elected and what it then proceeds to do? Should a government be allowed to do things that it did not talk about during the election campaign?

13) Imagine you are New Brunswick premier Frank McKenna. What issues and concerns would you be considering as June 1990 approaches?

CHRONOLOGY

20 May 1980	Quebec Referendum.
5 November 1981	Ottawa and nine provinces agree on constitutional package.
17 April 1982	New constitution formally signed, without Quebec.
6 August 1984	Mulroney's Sept-Iles nomination speech: pledges to bring Quebec into constitution.
4 September 1984	Conservatives win landslide election victory.
February 1985	Quebec Liberal party position paper *Mastering Our Future*; the five conditions.
2 December 1985	Liberal party wins Quebec election.
9 May 1986	Mont Gabriel Conference: Quebec reiterates its five conditions.
13 June 1986	*Le Devoir* interview with Liberal leader John Turner: supports Quebec's conditions.
July 1986	Quebec 'sells' its package to other provinces.
10–12 August 1986	27th Annual Premiers Conference: Edmonton Declaration puts Quebec on agenda.

November 1986	Vancouver first ministers' conference: agreement to pursue constitutional settlement.
November 1986	Federal Liberals debate Quebec proposals at convention.
January 1987	NDP debates Quebec proposals at convention (and in March 1987).
March 1987	Quebec does not attend constitutional conference on aboriginal rights.
5–6 March 1987	Multilateral meeting of federal and provincial officials regarding Quebec's proposals.
mid-April 1987	Mulroney sends premiers a letter outlining Ottawa's response to Quebec's proposals.
30 April 1987	Agreement reached at Meech Lake.
8 May 1987	Donald Johnston resigns from Liberal shadow cabinet.
11 May 1987	All three Ottawa party leaders endorse the constitutional accord.
12 May 1987	Quebec begins hearings on the accord (only province or government to do so).
27 May 1987	Trudeau slams accord in *La Presse* and *Toronto Star*.
2–3 June 1987	Langevin Block meeting: agreement reached.
5 June 1987	Mulroney (on TV) promises committee hearings.
11 June 1987	Senate refers accord to committee of the whole.
12 June 1987	Mazankowski proposes a joint House of Commons/Senate committee to study the accord.
16 June 1987	House of Commons endorses joint committee.
17 June 1987	Senate endorses joint committee.

18 June 1987	Quebec begins debate on accord.
23 June 1987	Quebec National Assembly passes the accord (first province to do so).
4 August 1987	Joint committee hearings begin.
5 August 1987	Senator Murray announces government will amend only 'egregious' errors.
13 August 1987	Senate establishes a task force on the accord and the Yukon and Northwest Territories.
27 August 1987	Trudeau appears before the joint committee.
2 September 1987	Joint committee hearings end.
16–29 September	Provincial NDP holds its own 'public hearings' in Alberta.
21 September 1987	Joint committee issues report.
23 September 1987	Saskatchewan approves accord (second province; debated 17, 21, 22, 23 September).
29 September 1987	House of Commons begins debate (continues on 30 September; 1, 2, 5, 6, 8, 19, 21, 22 October).
22–3 October 1987	Queen Elizabeth speaks in favour of accord.
13 October 1987	Liberals win election in New Brunswick; Premier Frank McKenna anti-accord.
26 October	House of Commons passes accord.
24 Oct.–2 Nov. 1987	Senate Task Force in Whitehorse, Yellowknife and Iqaluit.
4 November	Senate committee of the whole hearings begin in earnest (continue 18 November; 2, 9 , 16 December; 27 January; 2, 3, 10, 11 February; 1, 2, 16, 23, 30, 31 March).
7 November 1987	Jean Chrétien speaks out against accord.

November 1987	New Brunswick election: Liberal Frank McKenna elected premier.
7 December 1987	Alberta approves accord (third province; debated on 23, 25, 30 November, 2, 3, 4, 7 December).
2 February 1988	Ontario public hearings begin (to June; report issued 23 June).
1 March 1988	Nova Scotia ratification debate begins (continues 3, 4,7, 8, 10, 11 March).
1 March 1988	Senate Task Force on Yukon and NWT issues report.
9 March 1988	Manitoba government falls.
9–10 March 1988	La féderation des francophones hors Quebec speaks out against accord.
30 March 1988	Trudeau appears before Senate committee.
31 March 1988	Senate hearings end.
4 April 1988	Saskatchewan language controversy.
21 April 1988	Senate amends the accord.
25 April 1988	PEI public hearings begin (continue on 27 April, 2,5,10 May).
26 April 1988	Manitoba election: minority government.
3 May 1988	Court challenge launched by Canadian Coalition on the Constitution.
13 May 1988	PEI ratifies accord (fourth province).
19 May 1988	House of Commons debates Senate amendments. New Brunswick announces that committee hearings will begin in the autumn.
25 May 1988	Nova Scotia ratifies accord (fifth province) (continuation of March debate on 24, 25 May).

2 June 1988	Supreme Court rejects NWT/Yukon court challenge.
22 June 1988	House of Commons passes accord for second time.
29 June 1988	Ontario approves accord (sixth province). British Columbia approves accord (seventh province).
7 July 1988	Newfoundland approves accord (eighth province).
15 December 1988	Supreme Court strikes down Quebec's Bill 101.
16 December 1988	Meech Lake debate begins in Manitoba.
18 December 1988	Quebec introduces Bill 178 and uses notwithstanding clause.
19 December 1988	Manitoba legislature suspends Meech Lake debate.
June 1990	accord deadline; Ottawa and all provincial governments must sign by this date for the constitutional changes to come into effect

Constitution Act, 1867

1.   The Constitution Act, 1867 is amended by adding thereto, immediately after section 1 thereof, the following section:

Interpretation

"2.   (1)   The Constitution of Canada shall be interpreted in a manner consistent with

(a)   the recognition that the existence of French–speaking Canadians, centred in Quebec but also present elsewhere in Canada, and English–speaking Canadians, concentrated outside Quebec but also present in Quebec, constitutes a fundamental characteristic of Canada; and

(b)   the recognition that Quebec constitutes within Canada a distinct society.

Role of Parliament and legislatures

(2)   The role of the Parliament of Canada and the provincial legislatures to preserve the fundamental characteristic of Canada referred to in paragraph (1) (a) is affirmed.

Role of legislature and Government of Quebec

(3)   The role of the legislature and Government of Quebec to preserve and promote the distinct identity of Quebec referred to in paragraph (1) (b) is affirmed.

Rights of legislatures and governments preserved

(4)   Nothing in this section derogates from the powers, rights or privileges of Parliament or the Government of Canada, or of the legislatures or governments of the provinces, including any powers, rights or privileges relating to language."

2. The said Act is further amended by adding thereto, immediately after section 24 thereof, the following section:

Names to be submitted

"25. (1) Where a vacancy occurs in the Senate, the government of the province to which the vacancy relates may, in relation to that vacancy, submit to the Queen's Privy Council for Canada the names of persons who may be summoned to the Senate.

Choice of Senators from names submitted

(2) Until an amendment to the Constitution of Canada is made in relation to the Senate pursuant to section 41 of the Constitution Act, 1982, the person summoned to fill a vacancy in the Senate shall be chosen from among persons whose names have been submitted under subsection (1) by the government of the province to which the vacancy relates and must be acceptable to the Queen's Privy Council for Canada."

3. The said Act is further amended by adding thereto, immediately after section 95 thereof, the following heading and sections:

"Agreements on Immigration and Aliens

Commitment to negotiate

95A. The Government of Canada shall, at the request of the government of any province, negotiate with the government of that province for the purpose of concluding an agreement relating to immigration or the temporary admission of aliens into that province that is appropriate to the needs and circumstances of that province.

Agreements

95B. (1) Any agreement concluded between Canada and a province in relation to immigration or the temporary admission of aliens into that province has the force of law from the time it is declared to do so in accordance with subsection 95C(1) and shall from that time have effect notwithstanding class 25 of section 91 or section 95.

Limitation

(2)   An agreement that has the force of law under subsection (1) shall have effect only so long and so far as it is not repugnant to any provision of an Act of the Parliament of Canada that sets national standards and objectives relating to immigration or aliens, including any provision that establishes general classes of immigrants or relates to levels of immigration for Canada or that prescribes classes of individuals who are inadmissible into Canada.

Application of Charter

(3)   The <u>Canadian Charter of Rights and Freedoms</u> applies in respect of any agreement that has the force of law under subsection (1) and in respect of anything done by the Parliament or Government of Canada, or the legislature or government of a province, pursuant to any such agreement.

Proclamation relating to agreements

95C.   (1)   A declaration that an agreement referred to in subsection 95B(1) has the force of law may be made by proclamation issued by the Governor General under the Great Seal of Canada only where so authorized by resolutions of the Senate and House of Commons and of the legislative assembly of the province that is a party to the agreement.

Amendment of agreements

(2)   An amendment to an agreement referred to in subsection 95B(1) may be made by proclamation issued by the Governor General under the Great Seal of Canada only where so authorized

(a)   by resolutions of the Senate and House of Commons and of the legislative assembly of the province that is a party to the agreement; or

(b)   in such other manner as is set out in the agreement.

95D. Sections 46 to 48 of the <u>Constitution Act, 1982</u> apply, with such modifications as the circumstances require, in respect of any declaration made pursuant to subsection 95C(1), any amendment to an agreement made pursuant to subsection 95C(2) or any amendment made pursuant to section 95E.

95E. An amendment to sections 95A to 95D or this section may be made in accordance with the procedure set out in subsection 38(1) of the <u>Constitution Act, 1982</u>, but only if the amendment is authorized by resolutions of the legislative assemblies of all the provinces that are, at the time of the amendment, parties to an agreement that has the force of law under subsection 95B(1)."

4. The said Act is further amended by adding thereto, immediately preceding section 96 thereof, the following heading:

<u>"General"</u>

5. The said Act is further amended by adding thereto, immediately preceding section 101 thereof, the following heading:

<u>"Courts Established by the Parliament of Canada"</u>

6. The said Act is further amended by adding thereto, immediately after section 101 thereof, the following heading and sections:

<u>"Supreme Court of Canada</u>

101A. (1) The court existing under the name of the Supreme Court of Canada is hereby continued as the general court of appeal for Canada, and as an additional court for the better administration of the laws of Canada, and shall continue to be a superior court of record.

Constitution of Court	(2) The Supreme Court of Canada shall consist of a chief justice to be called the Chief Justice of Canada and eight other judges, who shall be appointed by the Governor General in Council by letters patent under the Great Seal.
Who may be appointed judges	101B. (1) Any person may be appointed a judge of the Supreme Court of Canada who, after having been admitted to the bar of any province or territory, has, for a total of at least ten years, been a judge of any courts in Canada or a member of the bar of any province or territory.
Three judges from Quebec	(2) At least three judges of the Supreme Court of Canada shall be appointed from among persons who, after having been admitted to the bar of Quebec, have, for a total of at least ten years, been judges of any court of Quebec or of any court established by the Parliament of Canada, or members of the bar of Quebec.
Names may be submitted	101C. (1) Where a vacancy occurs in the Supreme Court of Canada, the government of each province may, in relation to that vacancy, submit to the Minister of Justice of Canada the names of any of the persons who have been admitted to the bar of that province and are qualified under section 101B for appointment to that court.
Appointment from names submitted	(2) Where an appointment is made to the Supreme Court of Canada, the Governor General in Council shall, except where the Chief Justice is appointed from among members of the Court, appoint a person whose name has been submitted under subsection (1) and who is acceptable to the Queen's Privy Council for Canada.

Appointment from Quebec

(3) Where an appointment is made in accordance with subsection (2) of any of the three judges necessary to meet the requirement set out in subsection 101B(2), the Governor General in Council shall appoint a person whose name has been submitted by the Government of Quebec.

Appointment from other provinces

(4) Where an appointment is made in accordance with subsection (2) otherwise than as required under subsection (3), the Governor General in Council shall appoint a person whose name has been submitted by the government of a province other than Quebec.

Tenure, salaries, etc. of judges

101D. Sections 99 and 100 apply in respect of the judges of the Supreme Court of Canada.

Relationship to section 101

101E. (1) Sections 101A to 101D shall not be construed as abrogating or derogating from the powers of the Parliament of Canada to make laws under section 101 except to the extent that such laws are inconsistent with those sections.

References to the Supreme Court of Canada

(2) For greater certainty, section 101A shall not be construed as abrogating or derogating from the powers of the Parliament of Canada to make laws relating to the reference of questions of law or fact, or any other matters, to the Supreme Court of Canada."

7. The said Act is further amended by adding thereto, immediately after section 106 thereof, the following section:

Shared–cost program

"106A. (1) The Government of Canada shall provide reasonable compensation to the government of a province that chooses not to participate in a national shared–cost program that is established by the Government of Canada after the coming into force of this section in an area of exclusive provincial jurisdiction, if the province carries on a program or initiative that is compatible with the national objectives.

Legislative power not extended

(2)   Nothing in this section extends the legislative powers of the Parliament of Canada or of the legislatures of the provinces."

8.   The said Act is further amended by adding thereto the following heading and sections:

"XII — Conferences on the Economy and Other Matters

Conferences on the economy and other matters

148.   A conference composed of the Prime Minister of Canada and the first ministers of the provinces shall be convened by the Prime Minister of Canada at least once each year to discuss the state of the Canadian economy and such other matters as may be appropriate.

XIII — References

Reference includes amendments

149.   A reference to this Act shall be deemed to include a reference to any amendments thereto."

Constitution Act, 1982

9.   Sections 40 to 42 of the Constitution Act, 1982 are repealed and the following substituted therefor:

Compensation

"40.   Where an amendment is made under subsection 38(1) that transfers legislative powers from provincial legislatures to Parliament, Canada shall provide reasonable compensation to any province to which the amendment does not apply.

Amendment by unanimous consent

41.   An amendment to the Constitution of Canada in relation to the following matters may be made by proclamation issued by the Governor General under the Great Seal of Canada only where authorized by resolutions

of the Senate and House of Commons and of the legislative assembly of each province:

    (a)   the office of the Queen, the Governor General and the Lieutenant Governor of a province;

    (b)   the powers of the Senate and the method of selecting Senators;

    (c)   the number of members by which a province is entitled to be represented in the Senate and the residence qualifications of Senators;

    (d)   the right of a province to a number of members in the House of Commons not less than the number of Senators by which the province was entitled to be represented on April 17, 1982;

    (e)   the principle of proportionate representation of the provinces in the House of Commons prescribed by the Constitutiion of Canada;

    (f)   subject to section 43, the use of the English or the French language;

    (g)   the Supreme Court of Canada;

    (h)   the extension of existing provinces into the territories;

    (i)   notwithstanding any other law or practice, the establishment of new provinces; and

    (j)   an amendment to this Part."

10.   Section 44 of the said Act is repealed and the following substituted therefor:

Amendments by Parliament

"44.   Subject to section 41, Parliament may exclusively make laws amending the Constitution of Canada in relation to the executive government of Canada or the Senate and House of Commons."

11.   Subsection 46(1) of the said Act is repealed and the following substituted therefor:

Initiation of amendment procedures

"46.(1)   The procedures for amendment under sections 38, 41 and 43 may be initiated either by the Senate or the House of Commons or by the legislative assembly of a province."

12.   Subsection 47(1) of the said Act is repealed and the following substituted therefor:

Amendments without Senate resolution

"47.(1)   An amendment to the Constitution of Canada made by proclamation under section 38, 41 or 43 may be made without a resolution of the Senate authorizing the issue of the proclamation if, within one hundred and eighty days after the adoption by the House of Commonts of a resolution authorizing its issue, the Senate has not adopted such a resolution and if, at any time after the expiration of that period, the House of Commons again adopts the resolution."

13.   Part VI of the said Act is repealed and the following substituted therefor:

"Part VI

Constitutional Conferences

Constitutional conference

50.   (1)   A constitutional conference composed of the Prime Minister of Canada and the first ministers of the provinces shall be convened by the Prime Minister of Canada at least once each year, commencing in 1988.

Agenda

(2)   The conferences convened under subsection (1) shall have included on their agenda the following matters:

(a)   Senate reform, including the role and functions of the Senate, its powers, the method of selecting Senators and representation in the Senate;

(b) roles and responsibilities in relation to fisheries; and

(c) such other matters as are agreed upon."

14. Subsection 52(2) of the said Act is amended by striking out the word "and" at the end of paragraph (b) thereof, by adding the word "and" at the end of paragraph (c) thereof and by adding thereto the following paragraph:

"(d) any other amendment to the Constitution of Canada."

15. Section 61 of the said Act is repealed and the following substituted therefor:

References

"61. A reference to the Constitution Act 1982, or a reference to the Constitution Acts 1867 to 1982, shall be deemed to include a reference to any amendments thereto."

General

Multi-cultural heritage and aboriginal peoples

16. Nothing in section 2 of the Constitution Act, 1867 affects section 25 or 27 of the Canadian Charter of Rights and Freedoms, section 35 of the Constitution Act, 1982 or class 24 of section 91 of the Constitution Act, 1867.

CITATION

Citation

17. This amendment may be cited as the Constitution Amendment, 1987.

NOTES

1. Constitution-making "can dramatically cast into relief some of the basic characteristics of the political system and of the power of different groups within it, in ways which are sometimes hidden in the play of day-to-day politics. Constitution-making may thus be especially revealing precisely because it is not a normal process." K. Banting and R. Simeon, (eds.), *Redesigning the State: The Politics of Constitutional Change in Industrial Nations* (Toronto: University of Toronto Press, 1985), 3.

2. A. Lijphart, *Democracies* (New Haven: Yale University Press, 1984), 187–97.

3. K. von Beyme, *The Political System of the Federal Republic of Germany* (Aldershot: Gower Publishing Co., 1983), 13.

4. Pointed out by A. Cairns, in Banting and Simeon, 124–26, 135–36.

5. R. Graham, *One-Eyed Kings* (Toronto: Totem Books, 1986), 404.

6. *Canadian Annual Review*, 1983, 71.

7. Ibid., 1984, 41; *Montreal Gazette*, 7 August 1984; *Le Devoir*, 7 August 1984.

8. *Le Devoir*, 7 August 1984. Here and elsewhere translation from the French by the authors.

9. House of Commons, *Debates*, 5 November 1984, 5,6 (emphasis added).

10. Ibid., 3 December 1984, 822-23.

11. *Le Devoir*, 2 February 1985.

12. Quebec Liberal Party, *Mastering our Future* (February 1985). *Le Devoir*, 6 February 1985. With regard to the veto, the Liberals were prepared to accept, as a minimum condition, a veto limited to Article 42 (viz., national institutions), conditional on the acceptance of the principle of opting-out with full financial compensation for all other matters dealing with the sharing of power. With regard to the spending power, the Liberals argued for two features: that something akin to the amending formula be applicable to any proposed federal initiative involving conditional subsidies, and that 'conditions' be limited to general 'norms' of communal application and not have the effect of regulating the management of these programs.

13 K.. McRoberts, *Quebec: Social Change and Political Crisis*(Toronto: McClelland and Stewart, 1988), 334ff.

14. *Le Devoir*, 20 August 1985.

15. Ibid., 5 October 1985.

16. *Globe and Mail*, 8 March 1986.

17. Ibid., 14 April 1986.

18. Ibid., 9 May 1986; 10 May 1986; 12 May 1986; *Le Devoir*, 9 May 1986.

19. *Le Devoir*, 10 May 1986; *Globe and Mail*, 12 May 1986.

20. *Le Devoir*, 10 May 1986.

21. House of Commons, *Debates*, 20 May 1986, 13,410–11.

22. *Le Devoir*, 13 June 1986; see also *Globe and Mail*, 14 June 1986.

23. *Globe and Mail*, 4 June 1986.

24. Ibid., 5 July 1986.

25. Ibid., 9 August 1986.

26. Ibid., 8 July 1986; 30 July 1986.

27. Ibid., 8 July 1986.

28. Ibid., 9 August 1986.

29. Ibid., 11 August 1986.

30. Ibid., 13 August 1986.

31. *Le Devoir*, 12 August 1986.

32. Ibid., 13 August 1986.

33. *Globe and Mail*, 13 August 1986.

34. *Le Devoir*, 13 August 1986; *Alberta Report*, 1 September 1986, 10–11.

35. *Globe and Mail*, 14 August 1986.

36. Ibid., 22 September 1986.

37. Ibid., 25 September 1986.

38. House of Commons, *Debates*, 1 October 1986, 11–12.

39. Ibid., 3 October 1986, 45.

40. *Le Devoir*, 3 November 1986.

41. Ibid., 10 January 1987; 12 January 1987.

42. Ibid., 16 March 1987.

43. *Globe and Mail*, 13 March 1987; 28 March 1987.

44. House of Commons, *Debates*, 17 March 1987, 4255–56

45. *Globe and Mail*, 18 March 1987.

46. Ibid., 23 March 1987.

47. Ibid., 17 April 1987.

48. *Maclean's*, 11 May, 1987, 8ff.; House of Commons, *Debates*, 27 April 1987, 5235.

49. House of Commons, *Debates*, 27 April 1987, 5228–29.

50. *Globe and Mail*, 25 April 1987.

51. *Maclean's*, 11 May 1987, 9. See also D. Taras, "Meech Lake and Television News" and L. Felske, "Fractured Mirror: The Importance of Region and Personalities in English Language Newspaper Coverage of Meech Lake," in R. Gibbins, (ed.), *Meech Lake and Canada: Perspectives From the West* (Calgary: Academic Publishing, 1988).

52. *Le Devoir*, 30 April 1987.

53. *Maclean's*, 11 May, 1987, 81ff.; 16 August, 1987, 8ff.

54. Elly Alboim, "Inside the News Story: Meech Lake as Viewed by an Ottawa Bureau Chief," in Gibbins, 239.

55. *Macleans's,* 11 May, 1987, 8–9; *Globe and Mail*, 1 May 1987.

56. House of Commons, *Debates*, 1 May 1987, 5628–29.

57. Ibid., 5629–30.

58. Ibid., 5630.

59. Ibid., 5629.

60. *Globe and Mail*, 2 May 1987.

61. Ibid., 4 May 1987.

62. Ibid., 2 May 1987; see also Taras, op. cit.

63. *Le Devoir*, 1 May 1987.

64. Ibid., 2 May 1987.

65. Ibid., 4 May 1987.

66. Ibid., 2 May 1987.

67. *Maclean's*, 17 August 1987, 13.

68. *Le Devoir*, 4 May 1987.

69. *Maclean's*, 11 May 1987, 13.

70. *La Presse*, 2 May 1987.

71. House of Commons, *Debates*, 4 May 1987, 5684, 5688.

72. *Globe and Mail*, 5 May 1987.

73. Senate, *Debates*, 5 May 1987, 932.

74. *Globe and Mail*, 4 May 1987.

75. *Le Devoir*, 5 May 1987.

76. *Globe and Mail*, 6 May 1987; see also G. Friesen, "Manitoba and the Meech Lake Accord," in Gibbins, op. cit.

77. *Globe and Mail*, 12 May 1987.

78. *Le Devoir*, 9 May 1987.

79. Ibid., 12 May 1987; *Globe and Mail*, 12 May 1987.

80. *Montreal Gazette*, 12 May 1987.

81. House of Commons, *Debates*, 11 May 1987, 5930–33.

82. Ibid., 5333–38

83. Ibid., 5938–42.

84. *Le Devoir*, 8 May 1987.

85. Ibid., 9 May 1987.

86. *Le Devoir*, 13 May 1987; 14 May 1987; 15 May 1987; 20 May 1987; 22 May 1987.

87. *Globe and Mail*, 15 May 1987.

88. Ibid.

89. Ibid., 20 May 1987.

90. Ibid., 21 May 1987.

91. Ibid.

92. Ibid., 27 May 1987; *Toronto Star*, 27 May 1987.

93. *Toronto Star*, 27 May 1987.

94. *Le Devoir*, 28 May 1987.

95. *Maclean's*, 8 June 1987, 11.

96. *Globe and Mail*, 28 May 1987.

97. Ibid., 29 May 1987.

98. Ibid., 30 May 1987.

99. Ibid., 28 May 1987; 29 May 1987; 30 May 1987; 1 June 1987; 2 June 1987; *Le Devoir*, 30 May 1987.

100. *Globe and Mail*, 29 May 1987; 30 May 1987; 1 June 1987.

101. Ibid., 2 June 1987.

102. *Le Devoir*, 29 May 1987; 1 June 1987; 2 June 1987; 3 June 1987.

103. *Globe and Mail*, 1 June 1987; 2 June 1987.

104. Ibid., 3 June 1987; 4 June 1987; *Maclean's*, 15 June 1987, 8–10, 15–16.

105. Elly Alboim, "Inside the News Story: Meech Lake as Viewed By An Ottawa Bureau Chief," in Gibbins, op. cit., 243.

106. *Montreal Gazette*, 4 June 1987.

107. *Globe and Mail*, 4 June 1987.

108. *Le Devoir*, 4 June 1987; 5 June 1987; 8 June 1987.

109. *Le Devoir*, 10 June 1987; *Canadian Parliamentary Review*, Autumn 1987, 20,21. Bourassa said: "It must be stressed that the whole Constitution, including the Charter, will be interpreted and applied in light of the section on our distinct identity. This has a bearing on the exercise of legislative authority, and it will enable us to consolidate what has already been achieved and to gain more ground." *Le Devoir*, 19 June 1987.

110. *Montreal Gazette*, 25 June 1987.

111. House of Commons, *Debates*, 3 June 1987, 6674–75.

112. *Globe and Mail*, 5 June 1987.

113. Senate, *Debates*, 9 June 1987, 1179–85; 10 June, 1198–1206; 11 June, 1215–58; 16 June, 1233–41; *Globe and Mail*, 12 June 1987; 18 June 1987.

114. *Globe and Mail*, 17 June 1987.

115. The Committee comprised 14 members. The Senators were Arthur Tremblay, Derek Lewis, Raymond Perreault, Brenda Robertson and Yvette Rousseau. The MPs were Suzanne Blais-Grenier, Albert Cooper, David Daubney, Leo Duguay, Benno Friesen, Charles Hamelin, Pauline Jewett, Robert Kaplan, Lorne Nystrom, Laurence O'Neill and André Ouellet.

116. *Globe and Mail*, 23 June 1987; see also House of Commons, *Debates*, 25 June 1987, 7611.

117. *Globe and Mail*, 15 June 1987.

118. Ibid., 22 June 1987.

119. Ibid, 4 June 1987; 6 June 1987.

120. Ibid., 24 June 1987.

121. House of Commons, *Debates*, 26 June 1987, 7679

122. *Globe and Mail*, 7 July 1987.

123. Ibid., 22 July 1987.

124. Ibid., 29 July 1987.

125. *Globe and Mail*, 5 August 1987; 10 August 1987.

126. Senate, House of Commons, *Minutes and Proceedings of the Special Joint Committee of the Senate and the House of Commons on the 1987 Constitutional Accord* (Ottawa, 1987), 2: 10,11,14,17. Hereafter referred to as special joint committee.

127. Ibid., 13:24; *Globe and Mail*, 11 August 1987; 12 August 1987; Special Joint Committee, 15: 127,129.

128. *Toronto Star*, 19 August 1987; House of Commons, *Debates*, 20 August 1987, 8248–49

129. *Toronto Star*, 19 August 1987; 1 September 1987.

130. *Globe and Mail*, 27 August 1987.

131. Ibid.

132. Special joint committee, 14: 116–123

134. Ibid., 13: 139–46.

135. Special joint committee, *Report*, 137,138, 141–42; *Le Devoir*, 22 September 1987.

136. *Globe and Mail*, 10 July 1987; *Le Devoir*, 8 July 1987; Saskatchewan, Legislative Assembly, *Debates*, 17,21,22,23 September; *Regina Leader-Post*, 18 September; 23 September; 24 September; *Globe and Mail*, 23 September 1987.

137. *Le Devoir*, 10 September 1987; *Globe and Mail*, 11 September 1987.

138. House of Commons, *Debates*, 29 September 1987, 9428-32.

139. House of Commons, *Debates*, 21 October 1987, 10240–44.

140. *Toronto Star*, 25 October 1982.

141. *Globe and Mail*, 10 October 1987.

142. *Globe and Mail*, 28 September 1987.

143. *Toronto Star*, ibid., 18 March 1988; *Le Devoir*, 18 March 1988.

144. *Globe and Mail*, 19 March 1988; *Le Devoir*, 23 March 1988.

145. *Maclean's*, 11 April 1988, 8,10; *Globe and Mail*, 16 May 1988; 19 May 1988.

146. *Toronto Star*, 23 November 1987.

147. Ibid.

148. Ibid., 3 October 1988; 25 November 1988.

149. Ibid., 19 December 1987.

150. Ibid., 20 December 1987.

151. *Alberta Report*, 8 February 1988, 8-9; *Globe and Mail*, 22 January, 1988; 1 March 1988.

152. *Globe and Mail*, 9 March 1988; 11 March 1988; *Toronto Star*, 6 March 1988.

153. *Globe and Mail*, 28 April 1988; 30 July 1988; 9 September 1988; *Financial Post*, 2 May 1988; *Winnipeg Free Press*, 1 May 1988; *Globe and Mail*, 3 October 1988; 25 November 1988; 24 November 1988.

154. *Toronto Star*, 25 October 1987; *Globe and Mail*, 26 October 1987; *Maclean's*, 1 November 1987, 12.

155. Senate, *Proceedings of the Senate Task Force on the Meech Lake Constitutional Accord and on the Yukon and the Northwest Territories*, Chapter 8.

156. Senate, *Debates*, 30 March 1988, 2982, 2984, 2985, 2995–97; *Calgary Herald*, 10 April 1988.

157. *Peterborough Examiner*, 21 April 1988.

158. *Toronto Star*, 10 March 1988.

159. *Globe and Mail*, 6 April 1988; 7 April 1988; 8 April 1988; 9 April 1988. *Maclean's*, 25 April 1988, 12–15.

160. *Alberta Report*, 4 July 1988, cover story.

161. *Globe and Mail*, 8 March 1988.

162. Ibid., 10 March 1988.

163. Nova Scotia, Legislative Assembly, *Debates*, 1 March 1988, 177–203; 3 March 1988, 329–64; 4 March 1988, 383–416; 7 March 1988, 439–70; 8 March 1988, 512–39; 10 March 1988, 680–97; 11 March 1988, 727–56; *Halifax Chronicle Herald*, 2 March 1988; 5 March 1988; 21 March 1988; 24 March, 1988; *Globe and Mail*, 23 March 1988.

164. *Toronto Star*, 26 November 1987.

165. *Toronto Star*, 8 May 1988; *Globe and Mail*, 13 May 1988; 14 May 1988.

166. *Globe and Mail*, 3 May 1988; 1 June 1988.

167. House of Commons, *Debates*, 19 May 1988, 15,633–36.

168. *Globe and Mail*, 20 May 1988.

169. House of Commons, *Debates*, 14 June 1988, 16,406–08.

170. Ibid., 16,413–17.

171. Alberta, *Legislative Assembly*, 23 November 1987, 2001ff; 25 November, 1987, 2046ff; 30 November 1987, 2093ff; 2 December 1987, 2161ff; 3 December 1987, 2197ff; 4 December 1987, 2227ff; 7 December 1987, 2244ff; *Calgary Herald*, 22 November 1987; 24 November 1987; 3 December 1987; 8 December, 1987; *Globe and Mail*, 9 December 1987.

H. Palmer, "The Flaws of the Meech Lake Accord: An Alberta Perspective," in Gibbins, op. cit.

172. *Globe and Mail*, 14 May 1988.

173. Ibid., 18 May 1988; 26 May 1988; *Halifax Chronicle-Herald*, 25 May 1988; *Toronto Star*, 26 May 1988; *Globe and Mail*, 26 January 1988; 6 June 1988; *Toronto Star*, 31 July 1988; *Maclean's*, 15 August 1988, 10-1.

174. *Globe and Mail*, 24 June 1988; 30 June 1988.

175. *Vancouver Sun*, 28 June 1988; 30 June 1988.

176. *St. John's Evening Telegram*, 30 June 1988; 8 July 1988.

177. *Globe and Mail* 17 February 1988. See also 29 July 1987; 17 August 1987; 30 January 1988.

178. Ibid., 27 September 1988.

179. Ibid., 23 November 1988.

180. *Globe and Mail*, 8 December, 1988.

181. Ibid., 9 December, 1988.

182. Ibid., 16 December, 1988; 19 December, 1988.

183. *Maclean's*, 2 January, 1989, 39.

184. See Lowell Murray, *Globe and Mail*, 5 January, 1989.

185. Ibid, 20 December, 1988.

186. Ibid, 21 December, 1988.

187. Ibid, 21 and 28 December, 1988; *Toronto Star*, 1 January, 1989.

188. *Globe and Mail*, 12 January, 1989.

189. K. McRoberts, *Quebec: Social Change and Political Crisis* (Toronto: McClelland and Stewart, 1988), 394–404.

190. Gibbins, op. cit., 120.

191. Banting and Simeon, op. cit., 18.

192. Cairns in ibid., 121–27.

193. *Globe and Mail*, 13 January, 1989; *Toronto Star*, 15 January, 1989.

194. Cairns in Senate, *Debates*, 10 February 1988, 2739–42; see also A. Cairns, "Citizens (Outsiders) and Governments (Insiders) in Constitution-Making: The Case of Meech Lake", in *Canadian Public Policy*, XIV Supplement, September 1988, 121–45.

A BIG DEAL?

FORGING THE CANADA–US FREE TRADE AGREEMENT

The Canada–US Free Trade Agreement, signed just minutes before the midnight deadline on 3 October 1987, was possibly the most contentious and complex policy initiative ever undertaken by a Canadian government. Initially about removing tariffs and other trade barriers between the two economies, the agreement quickly became the focus of a debate about the very nature of Canada. Over the two years it took to negotiate, and the additional year it took to be made law, it became the centre of several "worlds" of Canadian politics. It was debated by the provinces and the regions, and raised questions about the nature of economic development in the country as well as the provincial role in international trade negotiations. It was a catalyst for business-government relations, since Ottawa needed advice from industry experts on everything from auto parts to hog marketing. It dominated Canada's relations with the United States, and became the central focus of bilateral affairs for three years. It agitated virtually every constituency in the country, from women, pensioners, and economists, to wine growers, auto workers, and poets. Finally, it became the only serious campaign issue in the 21 November 1988 federal election. Now that it has taken effect, it will alter Canada's economic destiny. Few cases could provide such a rich and panoramic view of the variety and vigour of Canadian politics and policy making.

"Let the people decide!" With this battle cry, John Turner, leader of the federal Liberal party, hurled his grappling hook across the chasm of despair and unpopularity that had almost swallowed his party by the summer of 1988. A month later the numbers looked even worse: the Conservatives, who only a year before had had the lowest popularity ratings of any Canadian government in polling history, suddenly had the support of 40 percent of decided voters. Worse, the New Democrats under Ed Broadbent were ready to capture second place. The Liberals, Canada's "natural governing party" for most of the postwar period, seemed about to plunge into a defeat even worse than their humiliation in 1984 (when they lost the government and held on to only 40 seats).

On 1 October, Prime Minister Mulroney finally called the election for 21 November 1988. Mulroney's private polls predicted a Tory majority. No single issue seemed to divide the electorate, though there was an undertow of anxiety about the future. Unemployment and inflation were down, the Tories had kept their noses clean over the summer, and the party was united. Mulroney's advisors thus found their strategy: keep the Prime Minister (who was still personally disliked by many voters) cocooned from the media, and avoid issues. The Tory campaign slogan epitomized blandness: "Managing Change." Happily for them, the Liberal campaign began to fly apart within days: Turner's leadership was attacked, announcements were bungled, organization collapsed. Media pundits began to measure Turner's political coffin, and even Ed Broadbent mused about Canada's emerging "two party system" — minus the Liberals. John Turner needed an issue, some political stiletto to stab through the complacency that was rapidly suffocating the campaign. He found it in the Conservative's Free Trade Agreement (FTA), and for a few short weeks before the campaign ended he sunk its sharp, hard blade repeatedly into the Tory's exposed underbelly: the fear that a Mulroney government was dismantling, through the deal, Canada's social programmes and ultimately, its sovereignty.

The strategy made desperate sense. The FTA had only been initialled by Mulroney and President Reagan on 2 January 1988. The Commons debate in the summer had been vituperative, but the Tories had used their crushing majority to ram it through. Turner and Allan MacEachen (Liberal majority Senate leader) announced in July that the Senate would not pass the deal without an election. While the pro- and anti-FTA forces had been quiet for most of the year, Turner knew that he had the populists on his side: FTA support was concentrated in the business community, while opponents spanned the union movement, many cultural organizations (and prominent Canadians such as Margaret Atwood), and farmers. Turner also knew his history: Canadians had rejected versions of free trade with the United States in 1891 and 1911. In both of those elections, ironically, free trade had been championed by the Liberal Party, and in both the anti-free trade party (the Conservatives) had won. The last serious attempt to negotiate even a limited trade deal with the United States came in 1965, when Simon Reisman helped draft the *Agreement Concerning Automotive Products between the Government of Canada and the Government of the United States* (the Auto Pact). That had also been pushed by a Liberal government, and at the time had been quite unpopular. Since then Canadian governments had see-sawed between "industrial strategies" (forcefully assisting domestic Canadian industrial growth) and "third options" (trying to diversify trade ties to Europe). Behind all these flawed attempts was the hard and disturbing reality of

Canadian economic bondage to the United States: by 1987, over 76 percent of Canadian exports went to the US, and about 70 percent of our imports originated there. And behind that reality was an even more politically fundamental one: the lesson of Canadian history was that Canadians, if given a clear choice between intimate ties with the United States or nationalism, would ultimately decide in favour of nationalism, of sovereignty, of maintaining and preserving Canada's culture and its way of life. John Turner hoped that Brian Mulroney would stumble over this almost Newtonian law of Canadian elections.

He was wrong. On 21 November 1988, in what turned out to be the most volatile election in Canadian history, the Tories won 170 seats to the Liberals' 82 and the New Democrats' 43. The Tories had an absolute majority (the first time back-to-back majorities had been won since the 1950s, and the first consecutive Tory majorities since John A. Macdonald) with national representation, even from "anti-free trade" Ontario. The FTA would go through. The people had decided.

The free trade debate from 1985 to 1988 (and it is far from over in many respects) is a garish collage of contrasts and reversals, coiling its way through every conceivable issue of Canadian politics and entwining the opposing sides in an unwilling and ungainly duet. Traditionally, the Liberals had been the party of free trade in Canada; in 1988 John Turner proclaimed his opposition to the deal as "the fight of my life." In 1983 Brian Mulroney opposed free trade with the United States; in 1985 he authorized negotiations. Ontario, the province that benefitted most from trade with the United States (especially the Auto Pact), proved to be the centre of resistance to the deal. Quebec, historically Ontario's partner in demanding tariff protection for central Canadian industry, and the centre of Canadian concerns about cultural sovereignty, strongly supported the deal. The deal itself, hundreds of pages and clauses long, heralded as the single most extensive trade agreement in history, was hammered out literally hours before the deadline over buckets of cold chicken in a Washington office.

The politics of the FTA oozed into every pore of Canadian political life. It inflamed regionalism, touched on federal-provincial jurisdictional battles, involved the Quebec question, the place of women, the viability of culture, and the influence of the United States. It drilled directly into the nerve of Canada–United States trade policy, and since it held implications for international trade negotiations (through the General Agreement on Tariffs and Trade), Canada was the subject of discussion in Geneva, Bonn, and Tokyo. Cultural icons — Margaret Atwood, Pierre Berton, Adrienne Clarkson, Mordecai Richler, Harold Town, Morley Callaghan — weighed in for one side or the other. The election campaign was marked by unprecedented "third party" (that is, non-political party) advertising for or against the deal. In the final days of the campaign, numbed Canadian voters could stare at more than half a dozen party and FTA ads in the morning paper.

The free trade story evolved in two phases. The first was the negotiations themselves, beginning in 1985 and continuing through 1986–87. This phase yielded a deal and a ferocious debate among the Canadian intelligentsia. Curiously, the Canadian public was never as aroused over the deal as were the intellectuals, and so the legislation to implement the FTA limped through Parliament and Congress in the dog days of August 1988. Opposition parties would, of course, muster outrage, but their parliamentary numbers precluded any successful blockage. When the Liberals decided to use their Senate majority to prevent passage in August, Mulroney waited a month before announcing the election. At that point, as noted earlier, the electorate seemed in a perfect, dozy mood to re-elect the government. The campaign drove the second phase. Antennae twitching to Turner's nationalist rhetoric, the electorate reared up and away from the Tories in an historic reversal of support. Brian Mulroney had jumped into the election with the parachute of "Managing Change"; half way down, he found himself lashed to the anvil of free trade.

This chapter focuses on the two phases, and develops three themes or perspectives on the real worlds of Canadian politics. The first is the political world of international and bilateral negotiations. The following section on the negotiations shows how matters of great national and international importance can be embarked upon with only fuzzy ideas and watery conviction. The second theme is the difficulty of coherently debating a deal as complex as the FTA. A review of the arguments on both sides, in the election and before it, shows the weight of political symbols in questions even as apparently arcane as economic trading arrangements. Finally, the chapter throws light on how political actors — parties, interest groups, the media — manoeuvre around an issue as large and strategic as the FTA. This is not a story of "normal politics." It was all or nothing, and personal, party, and ultimately national fortunes rode in the balance.

THE NEGOTIATIONS

Taking the Plunge: 1985

Arm in arm, President Ronald Reagan and Prime Minister Brian Mulroney crooned "When Irish Eyes Are Smiling" to the assembled audience at the gala put on for Reagan's visit to Quebec City on 17 March 1985, St. Patrick's Day. Dubbed the "Shamrock Summit," it was a meeting of two men united by more than Irish blood. Reagan thanked God for Canada in one of his speeches, and Mulroney praised the President as personifying the "success and accomplishment of today's America."[1] They were men who obviously liked one another, who shared a vision of Canada and the United States amicably living in close and intimate relation on the North American continent. They also shared a belief, though in different measure, in the efficacy of market systems and the need to minimize, where possible and appropriate, the role of government in everyday life. In the 1984 general election the closest thing Brian Mulroney had to a coherent foreign policy was to pledge to improve relations with the US.

Rumours had been leaked before the summit that one of its specific achievements would be a statement on trade. In the end, no one mentioned free trade or comprehensive trade, phrases sure to ring alarms in both countries, but the two leaders pledged to "halt protectionism." President Reagan went further and acceded to Mulroney's request that he go to bat for Canada against protectionist measures being considered in the American Congress. The 18 March 1985 statement appointed James Kelleher (Canada's minister for international trade) and William Brock (the US trade representative) to "chart all possible ways to reduce and eliminate existing barriers to trade."[2] They were to report in six months. Meanwhile, action would be taken to resolve specific impediments to trade between the two countries, such as government procurement programmes, regulations, reduction of tariff barriers, and easier entry of business persons into the two countries. While officials preferred to call all of this a move to "freer trade" rather than "free trade," the implications were clear.

They were clear because these initiatives did not originate with either Brian Mulroney or Ronald Reagan. As earlier noted, enhanced trade with the US has been on the Canadian policy agenda since Confederation, and had been mooted at various times through the 1970s. Even the Liberal government of Prime Minister Pierre Trudeau, not noted for its warm relations with Reagan's America, had decided in 1983–84 that some form of freer trade with the US would be worth pursuing. The Department of External Affairs reviewed the question in several discussion papers,[3] and in 1984 Gerald Regan, the Liberal minister of international trade, agreed to cooperate with William Brock on studies of the possibilities for freer trade in four areas: steel, farm equipment, urban mass transit equipment, and computer services. After the 1984 election, the Tories discovered that the Americans were no longer interested in this "sectoral approach." The rising American trade deficit had generated demands for protection, not free trade. The Tory government therefore decided to change tactics but keep the broader strategy the same: it would still try for better trade and assured export markets, but would be prepared to negotiate trade-offs *between* industries, so that losses in one might be offset by gains in another. This was the only way to attract American interest.[4] A Tory government discussion paper on trade policy made it clear that a "comprehensive agreement" on trade with the US was the preferred route, and that no option, even the status quo, was without risks.[5]

The Shamrock Summit had raised free trade as a "definite maybe," and consequently threw the issue into the public arena without, however, providing any real indication of what Ottawa might do, how it might pursue negotiations, and what sorts of trade-offs it would be willing to contemplate. Thus the summer of 1985 was a season of fretting and fuming, of contradictory claims by various ministers, and of what to many seemed an ominous silence across the border. Shortly after the summit, Brock was nominated for secretary of labour: the position of US trade representative went vacant for a time. President Reagan was preoccupied with other matters, and so no one in Washington paid much attention to free trade with Canada. A US International Trade Commission report was leaked shortly after the summit, indicating that American industry would have little to fear from a deal with Canada, but the study was commissioned before the leaders had met and so had a narrow focus.[6] That left the debate to Canadians.

Despite the fact that at this point no one knew what the terms of a negotiated deal might be, the pro- and anti-free trade sides of the issue congealed rapidly, and hardened that summer. Over the next two years, no matter what course the negotiations took or what was thought to be on the table, virtually no prominent spokespersons from either side ever changed their minds (Premier Bourassa of Quebec was a notable exception). Once committed to support or to oppose, people stayed committed. In some ways this made the Canadian debate over free trade predictable and tiresome, but it also gave it a hard and sometimes bitter edge.

Supporters emerged early. Premier Peter Lougheed of Alberta, who had been a proponent of free trade for some years, immediately began to urge the government to go ahead and strike a deal before the opportunity (which he gauged would last no more than six months in the US, after which protectionist forces would carry the day) was lost. The Canadian Chamber of Commerce, a broadly representative business lobby, presented a brief to the government in April urging negotiations on a comprehensive deal, but if that were not possible, then on a sectoral basis.[7] On 15 May, for the first time, the western premiers agreed to set aside their personal reservations and jointly proposed that Canada enter into free trade negotiations with Washington.[8] Even the NDP premier of Manitoba, Howard Pawley, agreed to send a telex to Ottawa, though he wanted safeguards such as a long and gradual implementation of any deal, and government assistance to workers and industries adversely affected by it.[9] Provincial support gathered momentum, and at the August 1985 premier's meeting in St. John's, all the provinces except Ontario were asking for immediate free trade negotiations.[10] Canadian business was also largely in favour of negotiations.[11]

Opponents emerged early as well. Labour unions took only a few weeks to announce that free trade would be an economic disaster for the country. The Canadian Labour Congress (CLC) in May presented a brief to International Trade Minister Kelleher claiming that free trade with the US would cost 1 million Canadian jobs. Dick Martin, executive vice-president of the

CLC, said, "If we went down the road of free trade, many of the manufacturing plants now located in Canada would simply move to the United States because they could have access to both markets."[12] A month later, CLC president Dennis McDermott added, "We will all be bloody Americans within the decade if this comes off."[13] Bob White, director of the Canadian Auto Workers (in 1985 it was still the Canadian branch of the United Auto Workers), echoed this sentiment by arguing that free trade would make Canadians less secure, cost jobs, and endanger sovereignty.[14]

Industrial sectors that guessed they would lose under a free trade deal also voiced criticisms early on. The textile industry, located in Quebec and Ontario, has enjoyed protection (against cheap, third-world products) that enables it to compete domestically. Industry spokespersons therefore had reservations about a deal with the US that might erode this protection.[15] In August, farmers represented by the Canadian Federation of Agriculture expressed their opposition to comprehensive free trade, since they felt that it would undermine Canada's system of marketing boards, supply management, and tariff protection for horticulture.[16] The Motor Vehicle Manufacturers Association and the Automotive Parts Manufacturers Association, together representing companies that account for 35 percent of Canada–US trade, were distinctly unenthusiastic about free trade as well.[17]

The final core of early opposition to a deal was the Ontario government. Premier David Peterson, heading a Liberal minority government at the time, had good reason to be concerned. As a senior Ontario trade official told a special provincial committee commissioned in the summer to review bilateral trade, "Ontario would suffer considerably" under free trade.[18] As the country's industrial heartland, heavily dependent on the auto trade, and with 90 percent of its exports already going to the US, Ontario did not obviously stand to benefit from reduced tariffs. Premier Peterson took his reservations to St. John's for the premier's meeting, but failed to convince his colleagues.

In Ottawa, the government kept its head down and tried to decide on a policy. Kelleher's report on trade options to cabinet in June showed some strong support for free trade across the country, but drew back from recommending negotiations.[19] By late summer, however, it was clear that the Royal Commission on the Economic Union and Development Prospects for Canada, appointed by Pierre Trudeau in 1983, would recommend a free trade deal with the US. Donald Macdonald, the chief commissioner, had proclaimed himself in favour of free trade almost a year earlier, causing an uproar within the commission. For most of its life, the commission had been ridiculed as a patronage boondoggle and a make-work scheme for the country's academic economists, but now its report promised to change the tenor of the free trade debate considerably. As a former Liberal minister of finance, Donald Macdonald would provide bi-partisan credibility to the idea.[20]

The commission finally released its report on 5 September 1985. The report touched on virtually every aspect of Canadian public policy, but its centerpiece, as had been anticipated, was a recommendation in favour of free trade.[21] The commission rejected the sectoral approach, and while it supported a comprehensive trade deal with the US, Macdonald acknowledged that the issues were so complex, even after years of study, that this support required a "leap of faith." The report did not suggest immediate free trade without conditions, however. Any deal would have to be phased in over ten years, have protections for culture, ensure that both countries could maintain separate tax and customs regimes (with respect to third countries), cover non-tariff barriers, and have a binding dispute resolution mechanism. It also suggested binational panels of arbitrators, as well as rules of origin to ensure that goods from third countries would not be diverted through either Canada or the United States, and enter the other country under low or no duty.

For the first time since the Shamrock Summit in March, there was something concrete to discuss. For months, the Prime Minister had helped to confuse the issue by referring to his preference for "free trade," "freer trade," and "comprehensive trade." The Royal Commission report injected some clarity into the debate, and had dozens of volumes of research to back up its recommendations. The Tories saw their chance and took it. Four days after the report was made public, Brian Mulroney rose in the House of Commons to answer a question on when he would make up his mind on free trade. He and President Reagan had given themselves six months, to September 17, to take action, and Mulroney said that the Canadian government had decided to negotiate and would inform Washington within a week.[22] That was in fact done on 26 September 1985, when Mulroney called the President and told him that Canada wanted to negotiate "the broadest possible package of mutually beneficial reductions in tariff and non-tariff barriers between our two countries."[23] The Canadian government had already made some preliminary preparations in giving External Affairs Minister Joe Clark ultimate responsibility for the talks,[24] and in appointing a permanent advisory committee headed by Walter Light, former chief of the Canadian electronics multinational Northern Telecom.[25]

These decisions being finally announced, there followed several weeks of bobbing and weaving by Canadian officials on what the negotiations would actually entail. This was in part because Canadian officials, with the exception of the Canada–US desk in External Affairs, were cool to the idea of free trade. The politicians were forcing the issue, and had to carry the bureaucrats along with them.[26] It was also in part because of the different approaches the two countries could be seen to be taking to the talks. American spokespersons consistently urged the widest possible scope; Clayton Yeutter, the newly appointed US trade representative, remarked that "almost everything ought to be discussed" in the negotiations.[27] The US ambassador to Canada, Thomas Niles, was quoted shortly after as hoping that there could be a dispassionate discussion of such things as broadcasting, book publishing, magazines, cable television, and films.[28] The Canadian government was fuzzy about what it wanted from a deal, and moreover petrified at the thought of setting off opponents by not standing firm for all that was sacredly Canadian, from auto parts to the CBC. It had to assure Canadians that the negotiations would not compromise culture, sovereignty, or popular economic programmes, while it simultaneously assured Americans that it was prepared to bargain in good faith. So, one day Joe Clark admitted that some cultural industries, like book publishing, "might" be on the table,[29] and a few days later the Prime Minister asserted that cultural industries were not to be included in the negotiations.[30] Their assurances were undermined by continued American statements that the talks would have to be wide open and include the Auto Pact, agriculture, social programmes, and subsidies.[31]

A further complication that fall was the Canada–US softwood lumber dispute. It heated up in mid-year, around the time of Clayton Yeutter's nomination hearings as US trade representative, but extended back at least two years. Canadian lumber exports had grown steadily in the 1980s until they accounted for 31 percent of the American domestic market. Lumber producers in the northwest American states, under pressure, had already forced one review of Canadian pricing practices by the US Commerce Department's International Trade Administration (which found no special subsidies on Canadian lumber) in 1983. Pressure on Congress to limit Canadian lumber imports had, however, continued. In October 1985 the US Trade Commission released a study of the Canadian lumber industry that was widely interpreted in the US as showing that Canadian stumpage fees (the fee that lumber producers pay to provincial governments for cutting timber) were too low and constituted an unfair subsidy. Congress was thus in a belligerent mood, which did not bode well for an FTA. On the Canadian side, complaints about lumber imports were seen as proof that the Americans were not serious about real free trade, and would never allow Canada to compete in American markets. The lumber dispute continued to irritate Canada–US relations well into the next year.

Meanwhile, preparations on the Canadian side continued on two critical issues: who would head negotiations and what would the role of the provinces be? On 8 November the Prime Minister announced that Simon Reisman would be Canada's ambassador for the US trade talks.[32] Reisman, a barrel-shaped, squat man with the looks and gravelly voice of a contender on All Star Wrestling, was a shrewd choice. He had had a distinguished career as a civil servant, notably as the chief negotiator in 1965 of the Canada–US Auto Pact and, later, the deputy minister of finance. He had left government in the mid-1970s to take up private consulting. Reisman was given *carte blanche* by the government to pick his team from the ranks of the very best and brightest civil servants in Ottawa. In a matter of days, the Trade Negotiations Office (TNO) became the place to be in official Ottawa.

The other issue was the role of the provinces. Provincial pressure had pushed Ottawa's free trade decision along, and Brian Mulroney had fought the 1984 election on a platform of better federal-provincial relations. Moreover, it was widely assumed that any free trade deal would necessarily touch upon provincial powers, and certainly on provincial interests. Ontario continued to express reservations about the talks, and needed to be mollified. But would the provinces only be "consulted," or would they be right there at the table with Reisman? At the First Ministers' Conference in Halifax in late November, Mulroney agreed to the "principle of full provincial participation" but refused to say what that meant.[33] The provinces preferred to interpret it liberally, and claimed that the TNO would take its instructions from the first ministers and that Ottawa and the provinces had an equal say in determining the tone and direction of negotiations. A week later, Joe Clark questioned that view and directly challenged Premier David Peterson, its principal exponent.[34] Clark claimed that the Halifax agreement had only applied to the "preparatory phase" of the negotiations, that is, for the next three months. After that, the Government of Canada would be in charge. The issue remained unresolved by year's end.

In all this time, since the Canadian request for trade talks, there had not been any official response from Washington. This was in part because of congressional testiness over lumber. Finally, however, on 10 December Reagan sent a letter to two key congressional committees asking for authority to negotiate a deal with Canada. The committees had 60 working days to respond, and there was no reason to assume clear sailing, since at least one committee (the Senate Finance Committee, chaired by Robert Packwood of Oregon) had strong representation from northern lumber states.

Thus were the negotiations born. The birth was far from auspicious, however. The federal government had agonized for six months before committing itself, and even then seemed unsure of what precisely would be on the table. The main lines of criticism of free trade with the US were firmly sketched out by December 1985. Their point was two fold. Living next to the American elephant, Canadian culture had thrived only by virtue of special subsidies and special protection. The "Canadian way of life" was reflected in our choice of more costly and comprehensive social programmes. Free trade could mean an end to our subsidies, and pressures to dismantle our social safety net. While the talks were broadly supported by business, especially large exporting sectors, the array of opponents was formidable: the NDP, the Liberals, most labour unions, the National Action Committee on the Status of Women, the newly formed Council of Canadians headed by Mel Hurtig, and the provinces of Ontario and Quebec (Premier Robert Bourassa defeated the Parti québécois in December, and expressed strong reservations about free trade). The CLC had refused to join the government's advisory committee on free trade.[35] Congressional sentiment, when it thought of Canada at all, was decidedly negative, and there were strong American lobbies (e.g., lumber, grain producers, steel, paper) that were prepared to oppose a deal with Canada. All of this had its effect on Canadian public opinion. Whereas in June 65 percent of Canadians had favoured free trade with the US, at year's end support had dropped to 58 percent, and was strongest in the West and weakest in Ontario.[36] Free trade was shaping up as the most regionally and ideologically divisive issue in postwar Canadian history.

The Long Grind, 1986-87

In one sense, the agenda was now set: organize and negotiate. Simon Reisman met at the first opportunity in the new year with provincial trade officials, to try to determine the role of the provinces in the coming negotiations.[37] No information was released after the meeting, though it was clear that some provinces still held to the view that the Prime Minister had agreed to full provincial partnership in the talks. It was just as clear that Reisman was not going to operate this way, and so the issue of provincial participation continued to fester until June.

Reisman's other task was to get his TNO together and operating. One part of this involved the industrial sector committees, with members from the private sector to advise the negotiating team. On 9 January 1986, the government announced another 38 appointees to the Advisory Committee chaired by Walter Light. The committee was to report directly to the international trade minister, but would work with Reisman to give him a sense of private sector sentiments. Despite the boycott by the CLC, the government managed to appoint one labour representative: James McCambly, head of the 220,000-member Canadian Federation of Labour, the only labour union organization prepared to consider free trade. Still to come in April was the appointment of 14 industry committees to provide specific advice, sector by sector.

The other part of Reisman's task was to build his own team of negotiators in the TNO. Reisman was in an enviable position. In contrast to the American team, which came to be headed by a mid-level official reporting to the US trade representative, Reisman had the direct support of the Prime Minister. Moreover, he knew the Ottawa ropes, had substantial prestige within the federal bureaucracy, and was permitted to skim the cream of the mandarinate for the TNO. The TNO was the sole negotiating body, and so did not have to deal with other departments and agencies trying to protect their own mandates. Reisman even succeeded in having Sylvia Ostry, ambassador for multilateral trade, report to him.[38] This was important, since there were several departments in the federal government that were skeptical of the trade talks. External Affairs was miffed that its key role in matters of this type had been usurped, and the Department of Regional Industrial Expansion was also unhappy because it felt that free trade might undermine regional development programmes. The TNO was to have been a lean, tight operation, but as senior people were recruited by Reisman, they brought some of their own with them, and the organization soon grew to over 100 people.

While Reisman prepared, the government also took some action. International Trade Minister Kelleher revealed a new aggressiveness in the government's attitude to its critics: he noted that the Tories had decided early in the game to turn the other cheek, but that this had not noticeably muted the criticisms coming from labour or the Ontario government. Free trade opponents were noisy, emotional, and wrong, said Kelleher.[39] This was followed only days later by what was now becoming a ritual of denials that certain things were on the bargaining table. External Affairs Minister Joe Clark told the House of Commons that agricultural marketing boards would not be up for discussion.[40] (Marketing boards set quotas in the production of things like eggs and chickens, thereby raising prices to consumers and ensuring a return to producers.) As part of the new strategy to win support, the government adopted a publicity plan in early February that involved circulating thousands of copies of a glossy, 100-page book on free trade, as well as sending Cabinet ministers on speaking tours.[41] And in an effort to diffuse claims that an FTA would leave thousands of workers unemployed, the Prime Minister promised on open-line radio in Montreal that any deal would be accompanied by re-training programmes for unemployed workers.[42]

By March the Prime Minister had to turn his attention to the US; if Congress turned down the President's request to negotiate a free trade deal, the whole initiative would die on the vine. The President had requested congressional approval for a "fast track" process, whereby any deal signed between Canada and the United States would be voted upon as a whole by the Congress, not clause by clause. This was critical, since it would increase the odds of clean passage through the complex congressional system. Such requests to Congress have a 60-day limit; if the Senate and House committees did not grant the President's request to proceed on a fast track, then the whole issue would have to go before legislative committees for hearings. Reagan and Mulroney both wanted to avoid this, but the Congress, having the whip hand now, was pressuring the administration for action on Canada–US trade irritants such as lumber, before acceding to free trade talks. The 60-day limit expired on 21 April. Mulroney visited Washington in March, and lobbied hard with congressional leaders and the President — though he avoided a joint address to Congress, on advice that the situation was too delicate and easily inflamed.

Mulroney had no success in turning the tide, in part because trade issues had tied Washington into knots for the last year. Congressional elections were scheduled for the fall of 1986, and so American legislators were extremely sensitive to protectionist pressures coming from all quarters in the face of a mounting US trade deficit. The Reagan administration was committed to free markets and philosophically opposed to protection through higher tariffs or other measures. This put Reagan at odds with Congress. Moveover, there had been some tensions within the administration on how to handle free trade talks with Canada. The chief American negotiator, Peter Murphy, had not been appointed until mid-February, and came as something of a surprise to observers. Only 37 years old and facing a much more experienced Reisman, Murphy's credentials came essentially from negotiating textile agreements in Geneva.[43] Murphy did not have Reisman's latitude or his seniority: he reported to Clayton Yeutter, US trade representative, and had to borrow staff on a temporary basis from other government departments. To complicate matters further, the US Treasury Department had less than complete trust in Murphy, and insisted that it handle banking and financial negotiations itself.[44] The Americans were united on one thing, however: if negotiations were to proceed, they would not exempt anything at the outset, be it culture or agriculture. This had been a consistent posture over the previous months. As well, any hopes that a deal would include an exemption for Canada from US countervails were discouraged.[45]

These American tensions blew up forcefully and surprisingly when, less than two weeks before the deadline, ten members of the Senate Finance Committee said that they would vote against opening talks with Canada.[46] The committee members were less irritated with Canada than with the President, who had rejected calls for protectionist trade legislation. The core of the opposition came from senators representing lumber states, but the trade deal provided a convenient excuse to roast the administration for its trade policies. Canada began a lobbying campaign, but the key efforts would have to be made by the US administration. On 14 April several members of Reagan's cabinet met to discuss options, and Clayton Yeutter and his staff began to contact senators. The Canadian ambassador to Washington, Allan Gotlieb, dispatched his embassy officials. Several American industry associations (e.g., National Association of Manufacturers, the US Chamber of Commerce, and the National Foreign Trade Council) began to lobby in favour of a deal as well.[47] Tension increased as the administration seemed unable to change senators' minds before the crucial vote on 17 April. At the eleventh hour, the administration did succeed in having the vote postponed by a week, in order to have more time to lobby.[48] At this point, as many as 14 of the 20 senators seemed opposed to the talks. The President began to contact senators directly, and his intervention seemed to shift the balance sufficiently that on the eve of the vote of 21 April, there were some optimistic signs that the committee might approve the talks. Reagan's phone calls were backed by a letter wherein he stated that he would consult the senators during the talks, and most importantly, try to resolve the lumber dispute with

Canada.[49] Reagan also made it clear that if the Senate Finance Committee voted down a deal, he would simply submit another request.[50] In a torturous cliff-hanger, the vote was postponed again until 23 April, the last possible day for a committee decision. At the last moment Senator Sparky Matsunaga of Hawaii switched his vote to favour talks, resulting in a 10–10 vote on 23 April. American Senate rules state that a tie is as good as a win, and so the fast track option was approved.

Reagan had expended some political capital to gain this victory. He had promised action on the lumber issue, and was forced to send a letter to the Senate committee outlining what he hoped would come from the negotiations. This letter could then be cited by the committee when a final agreement finally came forward. Reagan's "wish list" outlined what would in effect become the instructions to Peter Murphy: (1) no special exemption for Canada under US trade remedy legislation, (2) a deal on government procurement, (3) access to Canadian service markets, (4) comparable treatment of intellectual property rights and investment, and (5) guarantees that provinces would abide by an agreement.[51] Peter Murphy followed some weeks later by reiterating that the Americans wanted to throw everything open to discussion, including the Auto Pact, medicare, and unemployment insurance, and that any trade deal would have to contain concessions from the provinces.[52]

The Canadian side moved quickly as well, once the Senate had cleared the way for negotiations. Within several days, International Trade Minister Kelleher had named the heads of the 14 Sectoral Advisory Groups on International Trade (SAGITs) to assist Reisman. The SAGITs gave the TNO some crucial insights into key business sectors, but also expressed the symbiotic relationship that had grown up between the free trade negotiators and Canadian business. (Interestingly, the SAGITs were modelled on American committees that had been established in the 1970s to advise the US government on trade matters.) Canadian labour had been against the FTA from the very beginning, and now was frozen out of the institutions established to negotiate a deal. In large part, of course, this occurred because labour unions did not wish to participate, but it was nonetheless extraordinary that such an important policy initiative would be undertaken with virtually no support whatsoever from the organized union movement (with the exception of the Canadian Federation of Labour).

If unions deliberately remained outside the negotiating process, the provinces wanted desperately to be part of it. In this case, however, Ottawa wanted to minimize participation, in part because the Tory government was coming to the view that any deal it struck should fall as completely within its own jurisdiction as possible. This view was based on the constitutional ambiguity of international agreements: if Ottawa accepted terms that required provincial participation and cooperation, it could be held hostage by recalcitrant premiers. As well, if provincial interests were to be part of the bargaining, then it would be difficult to resist demands to have provincial representatives right at the table with Reisman. But in matters like this, fragmenting the leadership of the TNO could be disastrous. So, as early as January, the Prime Minister made it clear that only federal negotiators would be across the table from the Americans.[53] The provinces kept up their original November 1985 Halifax demands to be jointly responsible, with Ottawa, for the talks,[54] but External Affairs Minister Joe Clark told the House of Commons flatly that the federal government would control the negotiations.[55] The dispute simmered all February, and raised strong doubts about the kind of deal that Ottawa could realistically pursue. Critics pointed out that if the provinces were not included and agreeable, Canada could never hope to negotiate a comprehensive deal that would, for instance, cover non-tariff barriers. Finally, in March nine of the provinces (excepting Ontario) presented a proposal to the Prime Minister. They wanted to be regularly briefed by Reisman, and have access to data and sensitive strategic plans and the right to advise on issues of provincial jurisdiction.[56] There was no official response to the proposal, though Joe Clark visited provincial capitals in late March to gather information for a first ministers' meeting on the question.[57] When the American Senate Finance Committee narrowly passed President Reagan's request for fast-track negotiations, Mulroney could no longer waffle on the problem of provincial participation. The talks would have to go ahead now, and the provincial role would have to be clarified. Reisman and Murphy were scheduled to meet formally for the first time in June; Mulroney finally indicated that he would try to resolve the question. On June 2 at a private buffet dinner in the centre block of the House of Commons, Mulroney and the premiers met to determine how the power would be shared.

It was a difficult meeting for Mulroney. The premiers' support for the FTA had been shaken in previous months by Ottawa's refusal to consider the power-sharing issue, but most fundamentally by American trade actions. The lumber dispute had been boiling in the background through the Senate committee deliberations, and the President had promised some action on Canadian imports in order to mollify the senators from lumber-producing states. He took action in late May by slapping a 35 percent duty on imports of Canadian shakes and shingles.[58] Almost simultaneously, the House of Representatives passed an omnibus trade bill that would define Canadian timber pricing practices as subsidies. The US East Coast fishing industry succeeded in getting tariff protection against Canadian fish, and American officials began to prepare an appeal under the GATT of provincial liquor policies.[59] Canada's currency was trading at 30 percent below the US dollar, giving Canadian exporters an advantage in US markets. A mood of protectionism and resentment against Canada was becoming evident, ironically just on the eve of the free trade talks. To the government's supporters, this was proof that an FTA needed to be signed immediately; for critics, it showed that Ottawa was not in control of its agenda, and that it was being softened up for concessions.

The 2 June meeting with the premiers resulted in the Prime Minister's agreeing to meet with the provinces once every three months to review progress in the trade talks, and to give the provinces a role in directing Reisman. However, the provinces agreed that Ottawa would have to call the shots in the end, and even Premier Peterson acceded to this point.[60]

With the provinces now in line, Mulroney moved to shore up political support among the populace. Opposition to the trade talks had not changed its character or any of its arguments, but it had intensified considerably over the year and had improved its organization. The Council of Canadians was formed explicitly to fight the free trade deal (many of its members were from the former Committee for an Independent Canada, formed in the 1970s to attack foreign/American ownership of the Canadian economy). A Toronto Coalition Against Free Trade was formed with membership from the United Church, the Canadian Council of Churches for Global Economic Justice, the National Action Committee for the Status of Women, the Canadian Confederation on the Arts, and several labour unions. Some prominent public figures also lent their names to this group at a 17 March rally against free trade at Massey Hall in Toronto: Pierre Berton (author), Bishop Remi de Roo (head of the Canadian Conference of Catholic Bishops), David Suzuki (broadcaster), Bob White (leader of the Canadian Auto Workers), and Bruce Cockburn (singer). The union movement kept up its opposition as well. The Auto Workers handed out kits on free trade to their 14,000 members in February, and the Ontario Federation of Labour launched a province-wide campaign against free trade in the same month. The CLC followed with a national campaign at the end of April. In the face of this, and polls that showed that support for free trade among the general population was soft to begin with, Mulroney took to the airwaves. On 16 June, the evening before the negotiators sat down in Washington to start formal talks, Mulroney made a televised address to the nation. This was the first such address since his election in 1984. He spoke for 15 minutes, conceding that the talks would "not be easy or without risk," but maintaining that, if successful, the FTA would "provide jobs and greater prosperity for the country."[61]

The talks thus began in Washington under far less auspicious circumstances than one might have predicted even six months earlier. The US Senate had shown itself to be irascible and touchy on trade questions, and in a definite protectionist frame of mind in the face of elections due later in the year. The President had only two years left before the end of his term, and the extraordinary efforts he had expended simply to extract a tie vote from the Senate Finance Committee cast doubt on his ability to later carry the FTA through Congress. Opposition to the deal in Canada had not declined. It had grown in strength and visibility, to the point where virtually no organized sector except big and medium-sized business supported it wholeheartedly. Ontario still had strong reservations, and even the western premiers had groused about their role in the negotiations. Finally, Simon Reisman's personal style irritated almost everyone. In a curious reversal of stereotypes, Peter Murphy, the quiet, youthful, and soft-spoken American negotiator, seemed more "Canadian" than the cigar-chomping, tough-talking, and touchy Reisman. As one commentator put it, Reisman was the best Canadian to negotiate with the Americans, but not the best to deal with Canadians.

The first formal negotiating session of the two teams was on 17 June 1986. (There had been a preliminary meeting of Reisman and Murphy in Ottawa on 21 May, but that was simply to get acquainted and to plan the bargaining sessions.) Once again, American officials made it clear that they viewed the talks as wide open: anything could and should be brought up, from medicare to the CBC, and nothing should be exempted at the outset. Peter Murphy continued to insist that the Auto Pact and social programmes might be on the agenda for the talks,[62] even while the Prime Minister was defending himself in the Commons for not once having used the phrase "free trade" in his address to the nation.[63] In talking to reporters after their meetings, Murphy and Reisman gave widely different interpretations of what was on the table. At one point, to emphasize that social programmes and the Auto Pact were *not* the agenda, Reisman turned directly to Murphy to ask if he was listening.[64]

The teams met a total of seven times in 1986, discussing different issues at each meeting. Their third meeting (29–31 July) focused on agriculture and US trade protection law. The fourth meeting (9–11 September) treated government procurement. The fifth (24–26 September) marked the end of "exploratory sessions" where the two teams simply raised issues for discussion and review. Subsequent meetings were to involve real negotiations, but discussion went more slowly than anticipated. The sixth meeting that year was on 12–14 November. It consisted of a review of the previous five meetings and of the work undertaken by ten working groups and two fact-finding committees established in earlier talks.[65] The seventh and final meeting took place in Washington on 16–18 December.

The 1986 meetings were largely exploratory, and since they were secret, there was no indication of any progress on negotiating an FTA. There were several broad developments in the talks and around them, however, that suggested that they might eventually founder by the October 1987 deadline.

First, the Americans seemed less than completely committed, serious or sensitive about the talks. This had been shown in various ways, from the difficulties encountered in the Senate Finance Committee to the appointment of Peter Murphy, a junior official, to conduct the talks. Moreover, there had been the shakes and shingles episode, and threats to impose a tariff on lumber. Reisman had a larger staff, more authority, and better analytical back-up than Murphy, also indicating differing priorities on the two sides.

Second, there were continuing disputes about what actually was on the table and what the negotiations were about. The Prime Minister shied away from describing his goal as "free trade," and Reisman shifted ground several times on whether or not the talks actually included social programmes and the Auto Pact. After several months of insisting that the Auto Pact would not be open for negotiation, Reisman changed his mind in November and said if it were raised by the US, then it would be reviewed.[66]

Third, there were emerging tensions on the Canadian side between Reisman and other senior officials. Pat Carney had replaced James Kelleher as international trade minister in the summer, and proceeded to centralize political authority for the trade talks in her hands. Carney cut Reisman's direct route to the Prime Minister and had him report to her. Sylvia Ostry, Canada's ambassador to GATT, chaffed at having Reisman as her boss. Reisman, in turn, resented the fishbowl within which he had to operate. His career in trade had been forged in the 1960s, when it was possible for officials to negotiate among themselves without much political interference or overview. The free trade talks were irritating because the media were circling like piranhas for any slips, the provinces wanted constant consultations, and interest groups across the country were pouncing on every shred of evidence to show that Reisman was selling Canada down the river.[67]

A fourth pessimistic factor was the softwood lumber dispute that erupted in October. A decision on Canadian pricing practices had been pending for some months, but few people expected the American government to slap on a 15 percent duty on imports of Canadian lumber. Canada's lumber exports to the US amounted to $4 billion annually, and some analysts predicted that the duty would cut up to 5,000 Canadian jobs and reduce imports by $500 million.[68] Pat Carney vowed to "fight this all the way," and the Prime Minister promised "strong and vigorous action." Both, however, continued to support the trade talks as a mechanism for arriving at a deal that would avoid such disputes in the future. The essence of the American case was that provincial pricing policies, and particularly stumpage fees, were artificially low and thus constituted a subsidy for Canadian producers as compared to their competitors in the domestic American market. Ottawa had anticipated this decision in September, and with the provinces had offered a deal to the Americans whereby stumpage fees would increase, but by less than 15 percent. Canada made repeated offers to raise its own domestic taxes (and thereby achieve the same effect as a duty, while keeping the increased tax revenues in Canada), but the dispute was unresolved by year's end.

Virtually none of the news was good for free trade proponents in 1986. The Economic Council of Canada released a study in October claiming that a free trade deal with the US would create 370,000 jobs in Canada, but the methodology was suspect and the conclusions were in any case overshadowed by the grim war of words over lumber.[69] Congressional elections in November brought Democratic majorities to both the House of Representatives and the Senate, promising to complicate the President's efforts to push trade liberalization policies through. (The Democratic party is traditionally more protectionist than the Republican party.) The federal Tories had reeled from trade crisis to trade crisis, the Prime Minister had failed to sell the message, and Simon Reisman had appeared to get nowhere with his boyish counterpart, Peter Murphy. With the deadline less than a year away, the odds seemed heavily stacked against a deal.

The first six months of 1987 cast further doubts on the eventual success of talks. Postures and positions on both sides of the border, if anything, became more brittle and predictable as the winter passed. The softwood lumber dispute was resolved by Canada's agreeing to tax itself in the amount of the proposed duty, but the President retained the right to retaliate if Canada reneged. This resolution did nothing to improve the public's confidence that the government could negotiate a good deal with the United States, and so Pat Carney launched a $12 million publicity programme in January to trumpet the benefits of an FTA with the US.[70] Further doubts were raised when Peter Murphy, contradicting the US ambassador to Canada's assurances, claimed once again that the Auto Pact was on the negotiating agenda. Simon Reisman called Murphy's remarks "mischievous,"[71] while Premier Peterson of Ontario immediately announced that the Auto Pact was untouchable, and hinted that he would fight a provincial election on the issue.[72] Peterson was not the only premier to claim some ultimate right of approval over the FTA: a month later, Premier Bourassa of Quebec reminded the federal government that some sort of "ratification formula" for the FTA should be worked out, one that would be similar to a constitutional ratification formula in giving Quebec a veto.[73]

The Canadian free trade debate continued to obey the demarcations set the previous year. One development was an attempt to rally pro-free trade opinion in the form of the Canadian Alliance for Trade and Job Opportunities, founded by former Alberta premier Peter Lougheed and former royal commission chief Donald Macdonald. Others behind the scheme included Thomas d'Aquino (president of the Business Council on National Issues), Darcy McKeough (former Treasurer of Ontario and businessman), and David Culver (chairman of the Business Council on National Issues and president of Alcan Aluminum Ltd.).[74] The group's founders betrayed once again that the core support for free trade with the US was coming from Canada's business class. In contrast, the Pro-Canada Network, formed in April by the now ubiquitous Mel Hurtig, was an umbrella for over 25 anti-free trade groups and organizations, including the National Federation of Nurses Unions, the Canadian Teachers Federation, the National Farmers Union, the Canadian Auto Workers, the CLC, and the Association for Native Development in the Performing Arts.[75] In May, the Pro-Canada Network's sister organization, the Council of Canadians, published a full-page ad proclaiming "Free Trade Isn't Free. It Costs Your Independence," and asking readers whether they would "stand on guard for Canada."[76]

The federal government was clearly sensitive to the strength of this extra-parliamentary opposition. It increased its own propaganda budget, and the Prime Minister, during a January visit to Washington, tried to goad the Americans into taking the talks more seriously. In March, he finally gave a specific list of things Canada wanted from a deal. An FTA with the US must have a method for dealing with trade remedy legislation such as countervails and anti-dumping provisions, must gradually reduce tariffs, and must address non-tariff barriers (NTBs). Any deal would have to exempt the regional development policies characteristic of Canada but unfamiliar in the US. [77] This announcement was coupled with a motion introduced in the House of Commons by the government to support bilateral trade talks with the US, which passed 160–58 on 17 March. Both opposition parties voted against the motion, which called for talks as "part of the government's multilateral trade policy, while protecting our political sovereignty, social programs, auto industry, agricultural marketing systems, and unique cultural identity."[78]

The negotiations proceeded under these somewhat strained circumstances. They got off to a rough start with the dispute over whether the Auto Pact was to be included in the deal, and sank into a murk of working groups and "fact finding" through the early winter, to resurface for public attention in April. By this point Canada's main objectives had emerged, in part because of the lumber dispute and in part because of the omnibus trade legislation that was working its way through Congress. Canada wanted "national treatment" (firms and goods from each country would, in the other country, be treated no differently than firms and goods originating in the other country). Canada also wanted a binding dispute resolution system (in the form of a joint panel to adjudicate disputes) that would protect it from American trade remedy legislation. Canada wanted protection for cultural industries. Finally, and this was something that Simon Reisman pushed for, Canada wanted to develop a subsidies code, that is, a register of those government actions that could be considered "subsidies" to firms, and some procedures for deciding on the fair application of subsidies. On the US side, a key demand now was some exemption from or relaxation of Canadian investment laws that restricted foreign ownership.[79] As Reisman put it, these were "big rocks to move," particularly since investment had not originally been on the table, and Pat Carney had not given Reisman a mandate to negotiate the issue. But the Americans could use the investment chip to bargain against Canadian demands for some sort of dispute resolution mechanism.[80] By the end of May, the talks had reached a log jam, with the Canadians unwilling to give anything on investment without something from the Americans on dispute settlement; and the Americans demanding wide-open talks on investment before they considered anything else.[81]

Canadian frustrations with the talks led the Prime Minister to go up a level and lobby the President directly in early June at the world economic summit in Venice.[82] The President platitudinously praised the benefits of free trade, but it was clear that while Ronald Reagan supported the general concept of an FTA with Canada, he had hardly staked his political career on a deal. Prime Minister Mulroney had. It was already widely accepted that the next federal election would be on free trade, and that Ottawa saw a deal with the US as the capstone for its domestic economic policy. Canada had gone into the negotiations vaguely wanting better access to American markets and some protection from American trade remedies. Now, with barely four months to go and with Tory credibility completely entwined with the FTA, the Americans were beginning to demand concessions in areas that cut very close to nationalist interests: investment, finance, services, and the Auto Pact. The negotiators dealt with some of these issues in the June meeting, but were far from resolving them. A new note crept into the talks at this point, one in which the Canadian side began to seem a bit more eager and a bit more optimistic than the American side. Insofar as this reflected negotiating postures, it showed the Americans as having the advantage. Canada needed a deal more than they did; as well, Murphy could constantly harp on the political difficulties he would face in Congress in selling a deal that wasn't satisfactory from an American point of view.[83]

Despite being assured of getting a deal through the House of Commons because of his majority, Mulroney had his own difficulties with the provinces. On July 7 the premiers and the Prime Minister met to hear Reisman go through a preliminary version of what the deal might include.[84] The premiers, in particular Bourassa of Quebec, Pawley of Manitoba, and Peterson of Ontario, were concerned about the short time remaining to hammer out a deal (less than 90 days) and the lack of information about what a deal might entail.[85] The premiers emerged from their seven-hour meeting united in support of Ottawa's demand that the deal include a binding settlement mechanism, though they remained sceptical and worried about the likelihood of getting a deal before the deadline.[86] On hearing of this, American senators John Danforth (Rep., Missouri) and Lloyd Bentsen (Dem., Texas), both key members of the Senate Finance Committee, said that such a dispute mechanism would never get through the Congress. The US would never give up its sovereignty over trade remedy legislation to some quasi-judicial administrative body.[87] Administration officials later supported this view, and so the dispute settlement mechanism quickly emerged as a major impediment to any deal.

The talks were deteriorating. The teams met in Ottawa on 19 July for what was supposed to be three days of discussion. Murphy left after half a day. It was difficult to gauge the tension, since at this stage both of the key negotiators said virtually nothing to the press. After several more short meetings, the teams decided to get together for a week-long marathon session to try to merge drafts of a deal. About 20 Canadians and 50 Americans went to a government training centre in Cornwall, Ontario, each with a draft version of an agreement about 100 pages long. They expected to work hard, but virtually every key issue — government procurement, investment restrictions, services, transportation, subsidies, and dispute resolution — was approached differently in each of the drafts.[88] The results were disappointing: while both Reisman and Murphy claimed they were a bit closer to a deal at the end of the week, Reisman mused that perhaps, in the end, it would require a meeting of the President and the Prime Minister to resolve the outstanding issues.[89]

Eight months of negotiations had done nothing but clarify where the sides disagreed. In the beginning, it seemed that the Canadian team would run circles around the smaller and less-experienced American one. By August, Murphy looked cool and noncommittal; Reisman had acquired the image of an irritable and frustrated bulldog, straining at the Prime Minister's leash. Moreover, the Americans had placed a whole set of completely unanticipated issues on the table. The Canadian team had set its sights so high, with demands for a dispute resolution mechanism and a subsidies code, that only major concessions could even begin to attract American interest. Public support for the talks was sliding, despite millions of PR dollars spent by Ottawa, and the deadline was only six weeks away.

Crisis and Decision:
September—October 1987

The Canadian government knew that the talks would collapse without some high-level interventions from the administration. That had been the rationale behind Mulroney's earlier visit to Washington, and the meeting with President Reagan in Venice in June. In September the Tories decided to focus the efforts of two senior ministers, Joe Clark (external affairs) and Michael Wilson (finance) on the powerful Economic Policy Council, a cabinet-level committee that gave Peter Murphy his orders.[90] The council was chaired by Secretary of the Treasury James Baker, whom Wilson would see in Washington during meetings of the International Monetary Fund. The Americans were reluctant to politicize the negotiations, holding to their view that any deal would have to stand on its commercial merits. Nonetheless, Ambassador Gotlieb and his people began to make the rounds in Washington to line up support for the talks. Trade Minister Carney was effectively invisible in all of this, indicating that the Prime Minister had lost confidence in her ability to shepherd the deal along. Mulroney had even taken over from Carney the chairmanship of the cabinet committee to which Reisman reported.

These efforts at political interventions signalled desperate pessimism on the Canadian side. The first ministers met on 14 September, and Mulroney admitted that while a deal was possible, "Canadian concerns have not been, in our judgment, appropriately addressed in some important areas."[91] Provincial scepticism had increased (though Premier Bourassa had become a strong supporter of a deal). A sign that the pressure was beginning to wear on Ottawa's resolve was the cabinet's decision to offer the Americans a compromise on investment provisions. Reisman was allowed to offer a scheme of "grandfathering" current investment provisions (exempting current laws from the deal), giving new American investments national treatment, and raising the threshold for government review. The Canadian team would also, for the first time, discuss the Auto Pact.[92] Despite this new brief to make some progress on key issues, the sides remained far apart on the major ones of investment (the Americans wanting free entry without restrictions) and disputes (the Canadians wanting a binding tribunal).

The "make-or-break" meeting came a few weeks later in Washington, on 21 September. So crucial was this meeting, with only two weeks to go before the deadline, that Michael Wilson and Derek Burney (the Prime Minister's principal secretary) flew to Washington to join Allan Gotlieb and James Baker, US secretary of the Treasury. The meeting was a purely political one, designed to take stock of the negotiations and determine what the consequences of failure would be. This intervention was to be secret, and showed again the Canadian penchant for applying political muscle to the bargaining process.[93] But the political indications were that the Americans would never accept a "binding" dispute-resolution mechanism, that is, a system whereby some joint panel would make final and binding decisions about the propriety of countervails or anti-dumping actions. Something 'softer' would have to be proposed if the deal were to be saved.[94]

Reisman and his team went to Washington, then, to argue a weak case. They had already made some compromise proposals on investment; they now had to deal with the auto trade, and they might have to retreat on the dispute resolution mechanism. This gave Murphy all the room he needed. After three days of bargaining, Reisman was obviously strained and tense. At one point, on the third day, he blew up with the press, saying that it did not have "any respect for the truth."[95] The next morning Reisman stunned those same reporters by calling off the talks. His prepared statement said that he was "suspending" the talks, but in answering questions later, he was more blunt: "As far as I am concerned, it's over." Negotiations would only begin again if the Americans "were to come and belly up to the bar and do what they need to do to give us a good agreement for Canada."[96] The main impediment had been the dispute resolution mechanism, which by now had become the key Canadian requirement for a deal. The American counterproposal had retained the supremacy of American trade law, precisely the point that troubled the Canadian side.

As Reisman briefed the cabinet on returning from Washington that evening, the country was buzzing with speculation about what it all meant. Had

Simon been outmanoeuvred and outfoxed, and simply given up in exasperation? Had he arrived at a careful judgment that the Americans were not serious about negotiating? Had the whole thing been a charade to capture attention in Washington, force a political confrontation, and perhaps lay the groundwork for a face-saving termination of the talks by Ottawa?

The talks were suspended on Wednesday, 23 September. The next day there were "high-level" communications to work around the suspension. The were no concrete results, but the Americans appeared to show a more conciliatory attitude. Certainly Reisman's walk-out had captured attention at the highest levels. Secretary Baker and Trade Representative Yeutter briefed the President on the problems, and the Canadian insistence that the deal include rules on dumping, countervails, and subsidies as well as an effective dispute resolution machinery.[97] But time was slipping away. On Friday evening, Baker called the Prime Minister's Office to explore ways of getting back to the table. The Americans wanted to get back first, before putting anything new on the table. The Canadian response was that the ball was in their court, and that there was no point in going back until there was some evidence of movement on the US side.

Calls continued frantically over the weekend, and by Sunday morning a deal had been worked out to call a meeting in Washington between Michael Wilson, Pat Carney, and Derek Burney for the Canadian side, and James Baker and Clayton Yeutter on the American side. The Canadian delegation arrived on Monday afternoon, 28 September, only one week before the deadline for the talks at midnight, 3 October. The Canadian view was that this was not a resumption of negotiations, but simply an exploration to see if negotiations should be resumed.[98] The meeting had been scheduled to last two hours, but stretched to over seven. While some progress was made on the dispute mechanism issue, more problems arose later over the question of defining subsidies.[99] Nonetheless, after a full day of cabinet meetings, Pat Carney announced on Tuesday, 29 September, that it was worth consulting further on re-opening talks.

The long distance bills mounted as the two sides continued to talk by phone. Finally, Clayton Yeutter, alarmed at the approaching deadline, asked for more face-to-face talks. On Thursday, 1 October, Wilson, Carney, and Burney flew back to Washington. Technically, these were not "trade talks" but only political negotiations preliminary to any talks between Reisman and Murphy; but everyone knew that this was the level at which a deal would be made or broken. The delegation went and returned the same day without having made progress. The talks seemed finally and irrevocably finished. Then, another phone call. Washington was finally proposing to accept the principle of a binational panel to resolve disputes, and on Friday, 2 October the Prime Minister and cabinet decided to gamble and re-open the talks. Mulroney met with the premiers that same day, and received their blessing to try to strike a deal.[100]

Reisman and his staff flew back to Washington for the start of a complicated and risky bargaining marathon. Negotiations on the political level were still underway, with Wilson and Baker addressing the permissible political trade-offs, and passing along compromises to the teams of officials for technical drafting. At the same time, Administration officials kept in touch with key Senate players to ensure that any compromises could fly by the congressional committees. By Saturday night, only hours from the midnight deadline, 90 percent of the outstanding issues had been resolved, but the question of a dispute resolution mechanism was still open. The American proposal was turned down by the cabinet, and the Canadian delegation began to pack its bags. Over fried chicken in James Baker's office, senior Canadian officials expressed sadness at having come so close and failed. Pat Carney claims that Baker studied the American proposal and the Canadian one, walked out of his office and down the hall, and told his lawyers to be creative. "That was the moment. They finally understood we were not going to sign the agreement and then they improved their offer."[101] In exchange for his concessions on the dispute mechanism, Baker won Canadian concessions on investment and financial services, and an unexpected clause on energy (see Appendix I for details). At 11:40, a mere 20 minutes from the deadline, the deal was initialled by both sides. The most comprehensive bilateral trade agreement in history had come in just under the wire.

The next few days were ones of confused and sometimes bitter reactions. Few had seen the text of the deal, and in any case there were some inconsistencies between the American version and the Canadian one. Moreover, the agreement initialled on October 3 had no legal status; it needed to be put into more precise legal language. Predictably, the opposition parties, without having seen the text of the agreement, complained that it had put Canadian sovereignty on the line.[102] Representatives of the cultural industries expressed concerns about the deal, and some surprise as well that it seemed to exempt them from at least the investment provisions. Bob White of the Canadian Auto Workers said that the deal destroyed the heart of the Auto Pact, and Ontario premier Peterson warned that it would take a lot of persuading to bring him on side. (A surprising aspect of the FTA was that it did not require provincial approval. The only section that directly affected provincial jurisdiction pertained to wine, and the FTA's provisions were not much different from the GATT's.)

There is little point in reviewing here the disputes and debates that erupted over the FTA (the main lines of disagreement are reviewed in the next section). The next few months were marked by both the comedic and the absurd, as though Canadians, in forcing themselves to be serious about an issue as big and as risky as the FTA, had to let loose a burst of silliness to break the tension. Three days after the deal was signed, the Prime Minister intoned that it would be supplemented by a "massive" retraining programme to help dislocated workers. The next day, the minister of finance remarked that he saw no need for any significant programmes of readjustment. Remarkably, in light of the massive efforts of the previous weeks and the constant priority of the talks in the newspapers over the last year, the Canadian public remained on the whole serenely disinterested in the issue, and among those who knew anything about it at all, support had been sagging steadily.[103] Perhaps this was why the government decided to have a Commons committee hold hearings across the country on the deal and report to the House before the text of the deal itself was available. These lighter moments were marred by the rising bitterness of the emerging debate over the FTA. Bob White and his Auto Workers took out full page ads decrying the "sale of Canada," and Simon Reisman replied by charging that FTA opponents were using Nazi "Big Lie" techniques to brainwash the Canadian public.[104] In testimony to the Commons committee, Margaret Atwood, an opponent of the deal, argued that "our national animal is the beaver, noted for its industrious habits and its cooperative spirit. In medieval bestiaries it is also noted for its habit, when frightened, of biting off its own testicles and offering them to its pursuer. I hope we are not succumbing to some form of that impulse."[105]

The final text of the agreement was still to be negotiated, and so Reisman and Murphy started meeting again in mid-October, shooting for a November deadline. Things got sticky almost immediately, since the haste of the original agreement had left large gray areas in the deal. Unsurprisingly, the dispute settlement mechanism raised problems from the start, once negotiators tried to figure out whether the binational panel should be the only route of appeal in countervail cases.[106] The American shipping industry was lobbying for an exemption from the deal, and there were questions about the revisions to the Auto Pact. Reisman refused to be hurried, saying that he was not going to "leave any nickels on the table." The negotiations stretched through November and past the first ministers' meeting to consider the FTA. The Prime Minister and premiers therefore had to discuss the FTA without seeing the final text. The late November meeting saw three premiers reject the agreement: Peterson (Ontario), Pawley (Manitoba), and Ghiz (PEI). Brian Mulroney, arguing that the country could not be run by committee, pledged to move forward with the FTA as soon as a final text became available.

The negotiators met again on 1 December, and continued to wrangle over shipping and auto trade.[107] The next day they had a gruelling 14 hour meeting, but in a replay of their September talks, both negotiators grimly emerged to say that they had hit an impasse. Good will was rapidly evaporating as each side blamed the other for holding up a final agreement. The talks broke off and were scheduled again for the next week. Pressures mounted on the American administration to exempt shipping from the deal, since the US shipping industry feared that Canadian vessels were more competitive.[108] Finally, after two days of almost non-stop bargaining, the teams completed the final text of the FTA on 7 December.

Changes were made from the original agreement in October.[109] The final text excluded any reference to transportation, thus satisfying the concerns of the American shipping lobby. The binational panel would be the final appeal for countervail cases, but the US succeeded in having only three of the five members, rather than all of the panel, drawn from the legal profession. Canada retained preferential postal rates for Canadian publications, and won a provision that allowed shares from the privatization of a crown corporation to be restricted to Canadians. The final draft of the FTA also gave more explicit recognition to Canadian agricultural supply management boards. The FTA was initialled by President Reagan and Prime Minister Mulroney separately, quietly, and without ceremony, on 2 January 1988.

Both sides then prepared to draft legislation that would enact the FTA in their respective countries. Congress, of course, had to either pass or reject the agreement as a whole, without amendments, as a result of the 'fast-track' process. This improved considerably the prospects of passage, and while there was some congressional grumbling, the FTA encountered surprisingly little opposition. On the Canadian side, because of the Tory majority, the legislative process would also be straight-forward, though much more acrimonious due to the sworn enmity between the opposition parties. John Crosbie, appointed minister of international trade in April 1988, did not soothe FTA opponents when he described them as "CBC-type snivellers, the Toronto literati, the alarm-spreaders, and the encyclopedia-peddlers."[110] It was Crosbie's responsibility to introduce the enabling legislation (which he did in May 1988), and to pilot it through the House.

21 NOVEMBER 1988: THE 'FREE TRADE ELECTION'

The progress of the FTA, though punctuated from time to time with dramatic reversals and interventions, had been agonizingly slow. The deal was announced in the wee hours of 4 October 1987, a legal text only became available on 7 December, and the agreement was not signed until 2 January 1988. From then, however, the legislative pace picked up on both sides of the border. On the American side there was an attempt by various anti-trade lobbyists to halt the deal, but this was ignored by the Administration, and the US Senate Finance committee began consideration of the FTA on 17 March 1988. In keeping with the low profile that the deal had had in the United States, there were few voices of protest or criticism, and the bill encountered no difficulties on the American side. The House of Representatives passed it on 9 August, the Senate passed it on 19 September, and President Reagan signed it on 28 September.

The Canadian enabling legislation had more difficulty and became the key issue in the November 1988 election campaign. Bill C–130 was introduced for first reading in the Commons on 24 May 1988. During second reading debate, the opposition parties made it clear once again that they were against the deal. John Turner claimed that if the deal went through and he were subsequently elected prime minister, he would tear it up. The New Democratic Party was unyielding in its opposition as well. In committee, the Liberals and New Democrats proposed over 50 amendments to the bill, many of which would have changed the agreement substantially through the addition of new conditions and institutions, and others which sought to clarify and entrench the exemptions for the whole range of Canadian social and regulatory programmes. In an unexpected development, both opposition parties demanded amendments to ensure that there would be no inter-basin water exports from Canada to the United States, claiming that the FTA allowed them and indeed that they were part of the deal.[111] In response to this pressure, International Trade Minister John Crosbie allowed an amendment to the bill stating that "for greater certainty, nothing in this act or the agreement except article 401, applies to water." The only other major amendment to the bill in committee was the removal of the clause that had stated that Bill C–130 overrode any other federal legislation that happened to be inconsistent with it. The bill was passed with these amendments on 4 August and sent back for third and final reading in the Commons.

John Turner introduced an even greater complication in late July. Fearing that he might be outflanked in his opposition to the deal by the New Democrats, he announced that he had asked the Liberal majority in the Senate to block the trade bill until a general election. Turner knew that nothing he or the New Democrats could do in the House would stop the bill. Ultimately, the crushing Conservative majority would prevail and the bill would be passed. But the majority of members in the Senate had been appointed by Liberal governments, and the trade bill could not become law until it passed there too. His strategy was to claim that this use of appointed senators was a supremely democratic act, since it would allow Canadians a chance to vote on a momentous piece of legislation that had never been part of the 1984 Tory campaign. The New Democrats, momentarily surprised, soon announced that they did not support this manoeuvre, since it was a deliberate attempt to thwart the will of Parliament. Turner then announced an alternative trade platform that focused on multilateral negotiations in the GATT and sectoral free trade with the United States in industries such as steel and chemicals.

The opposition parties were prepared to use virtually every means at their disposal to delay the bill. On 15 August they sent a letter to Deputy Government House Leader Douglas Lewis saying that they thought they would need 350 days to debate the bill, the equivalent of one and a half years of parliamentary time. Lewis was outraged, as was Crosbie. The Speaker of the House had ruled by this time that 77 opposition amendments were in order and could be debated and voted upon. On 16 August the government introduced a time allocation request that limited debate to less than a week.[112] The Tory majority passed it easily.

On 16 August 1988, John Turner met with Quebec Premier Robert Bourassa to iron out their differences on free trade. It was not a successful meeting. Premier Bourassa maintained his position that the Quebec government and Quebec Liberal party would be neutral in the coming federal election, and that party members could work for and vote for anyone they pleased. He said that he would continue to defend the Mulroney free trade deal and speak out to correct the record.

It was hot and muggy that summer in Ottawa. Accusations sizzled on the hot griddle of nationalist rhetoric, "experts" mud-wrestled over the deal's finer points, and everyone watched the clock, waiting for the election. John Turner had demanded that the "people decide." At first, when he and his Liberal senators froze Bill C–130, it seemed that the Prime Minister might declare a constitutional crisis and call the election. Labour Day came and went, and September slipped by uneventfully. The Tories kept cool, waiting for their polling to haul in a harvest of opinion indicators. The data showed surprising satisfaction; even Brian Mulroney, once the most unpopular prime minister in Canadian polling history, had respectable numbers. Above all, no one seemed to care about free trade. The Tory strategy was set: wait a while so that memories of John Turner's Senate manoeuvre might fade, smear some comforting salve on the electorate's general anxieties, keep the Prime Minister away from the press, and, above all, keep away from specific issues. On 1 October, Mulroney finally announced the election, to be held on 21 November 1988. What at first looked like a cake-walk turned into a razor-slashing fight for political survival.

The NDP strategy was to focus on its key asset, the personal popularity of Ed Broadbent. Posters and commercials in the early campaign displayed his beaming visage, urging voters to do it for Ed. The Liberals did not have the luxury of a popular leader: over the previous four years, John Turner had had to fight off attacks from within his own party, a party that was still in debt and disorganized. Within days Turner had to face the embarrassment of being attacked on an open-line show by one of his own riding presidents. That was followed by a bungled announcement on child care. In the second week, voters watched a Quebec Liberal meeting break out in shouts and turmoil as angry Grits protested against what they claimed was backroom meddling in the nomination process. Frank McKenna, the Liberal premier of New Brunswick, joined the Liberal premier of Quebec in supporting the FTA. Ed Broadbent openly remarked that the Liberals might be headed for oblivion in favour of a two-party (Tory v. NDP) system. The polls showed the Liberals in third place, and on 19 October the CBC reported that there had been serious consideration in senior Liberal ranks to dump Turner and select a new leader, *in the middle of the campaign.*

Then came the debates. Never in Canadian political history has a campaign turned around so quickly, on such a thin dime. Two three-hour debates were held on consecutive evenings (24 and 25 October). The French debate produced no overwhelming winner, and after the first two hours of the English debate the three leaders were still even. Then, for several minutes, the tube imploded in a white-hot exchange between Turner and Mulroney. The issue? The same one that John Turner had nailed his colours to that summer — free trade. Turner's attack was emotional and scattered, but in the close boundaries of TV he hit a nerve: Canada would lose its sovereignty with the FTA. Mulroney, who had succeeded in remaining aloof through the first part of the debate, was goaded into an equally emotional response, but his was defensive while Turner had the advantage peculiar to the medium: he was jabbing with clear and calculated precision on a single, powerful point. TV news lives for "sound bites," a segment (usually 20 seconds) that purports to represent an event, and the more dramatic the better. Turner and Mulroney had provided *the* sound bite. While Turner's performance through the evening had been mediocre, he peaked in those 20 seconds, the 20 seconds that were played over and over on news broadcasts from Victoria to St. John's. The effect had pundits slack-jawed. The conventional wisdom that debates do not change voting intentions was now laughable: the Liberals went from last to first place in three days.

A new and completely different campaign dominated the last three weeks. Mulroney emerged from his cocoon, became more partisan, and sparred with hecklers and even met with them to defend the FTA. There was only one issue: free trade. The NDP tried to catch up, but John Turner and the Liberals had made it their issue, and clearly it was getting a response across the country. In retrospect, the Tory strategy was carefully calibrated to first knock Turner down, attack his credibility, and then shift attention to Liberal weaknesses. Tory cabinet ministers fanned out to defend the deal and attack the man. Finance Minister Michael Wilson called Turner a liar on national TV. John Crosbie captured headlines in a brutal shouting match with students. Turner kept hammering home his theme that free trade would undermine social programmes, lose jobs, and eventually cost the country its sovereignty, but within a week it began to sound shrill. While Mulroney's cabinet ministers broke all the normal rules of campaign propriety in questioning Turner's credibility, the Prime Minister himself tried to focus on the difference between the "experienced Tory team" and the Liberal "Rat Pack" (a reference to the small, loud group of Liberals that had captured media attention in 1984–85 with their parliamentary gutter-fighting). The Tories also found a fat target in Liberal election promises: Turner refused initially to say where the billions of dollars needed to pay for them would come from, and the Conservatives hammered at this contrast between their "good management" and the disarray and fiscal profligacy of their opponents.

Still, free trade was the theme, and even if Liberal efforts were losing their focus, other groups were stoking the fires. To a degree unprecedented in modern Canadian elections, third parties (that is, non-political party groups) advertised and agitated either for or against the deal. The lead opponents were the Pro-Canada Network, with strong connections to the union movement and, in particular, the Canadian Auto Workers. They, along with other groups like the Canadian Union of Public Employees, ran ads and produced booklets lambasting the deal and the government. The counterattack came from the Canadian Alliance for Trade and Job Opportunities, largely a business lobby, and individual businesses or producer associations. In the last days of the campaign, the papers were choked with pro- and anti-FTA ads run by third-party groups. For example, the *Globe and Mail* of 19 November ran two ads from "cultural producers." The first read: "The Mulroney-Reagan Trade Deal is a hastily concluded agreement that was made for political reasons, and not for the welfare of our country. It will irrevocably damage the Canada that we care about." It had 39 signatures, including those of Margaret Atwood, Pierre Berton, Adrienne Clarkson, Timothy Findlay, Margot Kidder, and Gordon Pinsent. Five pages later, a group calling itself "Artists & Writers for Free Trade" ran the following ad: "We, the undersigned artists and writers, want the people of Canada to know that we are in favour of the Canada–United States Free Trade Agreement. There is no threat to our national identity anywhere in the agreement. Nor is there a threat to any form of Canadian cultural expression. As artists and writers, we reject the suggestion that our ability to create depends upon the denial of economic opportunities to our fellow citizens. What we make is to be seen and read by the whole world. The spirit of protectionism is the enemy of art and thought." This ad had 63 signatories, including Alex Colville, Ken Danby, George Jonas, W.P. Kinsella, Mordecai Richler, and Harold Town.[113] Emmett Hall, often called the "father of Canadian medicare," fired a shot in the last weeks of the campaign by publicly denying that the FTA would undermine Canadian social programmes.

The polls began to turn around in the last week of the campaign. But even on election eve, few pundits were prepared to give firm predictions, and most guessed gingerly at either a Tory minority or slim majority government. The TV networks began their election coverage at 8 PM; by 8:40 (EST), computers chattering away, they all predicted a Tory majority. The magnitude of that victory was completely unanticipated: Tories 170; Liberals 82; NDP 43. Perhaps most surprisingly, the Tories were able to increase their support in Quebec (from 58 seats and 49.6 percent of the vote in 1984, to 63 seats and 53 percent of the vote), and hold their own in allegedly anti-free trade Ontario (47 seats and 38 percent v. 42 seats and 39 percent for the Liberals).

The following day, both John Turner and Ed Broadbent conceded that democratic politics had to be respected: they had fought almost exclusively on free trade and had been beaten. The "people had decided." The deal would go through.

DISCUSSION

The Free Trade Debate: What Was it About?

There are few if any issues in recent Canadian history that have engendered as much fierce and fiery debate as free trade. Provincial premiers, federal politicians, artists, writers, economists, industry associations, women's organizations, churches...the list is endless. Not only was the debate extraordinarily wide-ranging, it was bound up with the most central issues of any polity: sovereignty, culture, survival. The free trade debate was about more than economics: it was about the nature of the country. Ordinarily, it would be difficult if not impossible to summarize a debate of this scope, but the main lines of demarcation were set surprisingly early, and only slightly revised when the deal itself was released in December 1987. It is worth asking why this could be, given the complexity of the issues and the length and complexity of the FTA.

Complexity is in itself part of the answer. Few people have the time or the inclination to master the intricacies of international trade law, but the FTA relies heavily on understandings that flow from the GATT and other obligations. The FTA covers virtually every aspect of Canadian and American economic life, is studded with incomprehensible terms and arcane language, and is almost mystically ineffable in its implications. It relies on certain assumptions about the nature of economic growth, on the effects of trade liberalization, on the responsiveness of entrepreneurs, and on the good will of governments. The FTA is a hard shell surrounding a core of vaporous promises by the two parties to be civil to each other. It is easy to worry about an agreement that depends so much on being nice. In the face of these uncertainties and complexities, it is entirely understandable that people operated on cues and signals, on their intellectual shorthand about the way the world operates and the directions in which it should go. This is not the same as saying that people responded emotionally to the issue. There was nothing easier in the free trade debate than impugning the motives or the intellect of one's opponents, since so much of both sides of the debate depended on judgment. Judgment is not sheer, unbridled emotion; it is rational guesswork in the face of complexity and imperfect information.

On what were the judgments about free trade, both pro and con, based? The brief history of negotiations and the reactions to them suggest the following. At one level, perhaps the deepest if not necessarily the most crucial, the issue was about the nature of America and Americans. Is the United States of America best symbolized by Rambo or Thoreau, by Nixon or Nader, by bombs or baseball, by its crime rates or its Constitution? No country, certainly not one as vast and complex as the United States, can be conveniently encapsulated in a single image, but most people have a visceral sense of the Americans, not necessarily as purely good or purely bad, but tending to one or the other. This provided important clues to the debate. The FTA, everyone agrees, binds Canada closer to the American economy. But is the American economy healthy or sick? Is it a vibrant home of innovation, wealth, and opportunity, or a final bastion of tottering capitalism reliant on racism and sweatshops? It seems almost absurd to say that one's view of the FTA depended to a degree on whether one liked America or not, but a recurring theme in anti-free trade arguments was that the agreement was a pipeline that would pollute Canadian cultural and social life with American influences.

The other cue in the debate was one's view of state and market. Those who held that free, open capitalist markets with a reasonable minimum of state intervention are the best creators of wealth were inclined to support the deal. Those who held otherwise were sceptical. To the later group, capitalist economies only work well (i.e., provide reasonable incomes and benefits) if there is a substantial degree of state intervention. The FTA operates on the logic that removal of state intervention, in this case in the tariff fields, will ultimately benefit everyone.

Political arguments can never be reduced to assumptions. They consist of claims and counterclaims , of assertions and statements of fact, and most importantly, of *causal* connections. The pro-FTA argument was that the deal would create jobs, enhance economic efficiency, and shield Canada from American protectionism, without affecting social programmes and culture. The anti-FTA argument was that the deal would de-industrialize the economy, lose jobs, fail to protect us, and create pressures that would ultimately bury everything from medicare to CanLit. In one sense, these technical arguments were entirely the plaything of experts and elites, like ancient scholastics debating arcane matters of doctrine while the peasants laboured, oblivious, outside the abbey walls. The *political* debate among the parties, the leaders, and the interest groups was less precise, but drew its inspiration from and found its footing within the more deliberate engagement of the experts. The expert debate did not determine the election, but the language of the election debate cannot be understood without a grasp of how and why the experts disagreed. The disagreements clustered around four issues: 1) energy, (2) manufacturing and industrial development, (3) the dispute resolution mechanism, and (4) the likely economic and social consequences. There were many other issues, of course, such as the scale of tariff reductions, the effects on agriculture, the Auto Pact, the wine industry, and the inclusion of services, but these four captured the public's attention.

(1) Energy

The debate over the energy provisions of the FTA hinged on older ones about the National Energy Program (NEP) of 1980. Those who disliked the NEP liked the FTA because under it, nothing like that programme could happen again. Those who liked the NEP, disliked the FTA for the same reason that their opponents liked it. Simon Reisman was especially proud of the energy provisions: "The energy chapter is, in my judgment, the best chapter in the agreement."[114] An opponent of the provisions, quite naturally, argued that "the deal will make permanent policies already initiated by the Mulroney government for deregulation and continental integration of Canada's energy sector."[115] Critics pointed to the way that the energy chapter makes some traditional Canadian policies difficult if not impossible: export restrictions of some resources, two price systems to favour domestic industries, and perhaps attempts to increase resource rents and use them for development (e.g., the Alberta Heritage Savings Trust Fund). There are also several gray areas: do the prohibitions against a government *charging* more for energy in export markets apply to Crown corporations? This is an important issue for hydro electrical utilities.[116] FTA 904 allows restrictions of energy exports from one party to another for reasons of shortage and conservation, as long as the restriction does not reduce the other party's *proportion* of the total supply made available as measured over the last three years, does not involve the deliberate imposition of a higher export price than what prevails domestically, and does not disrupt normal channels of supply to the other party. The proportionality requirement might make it impossible, in the case of a severe shortage, for a provincial government to phase out exports entirely. This may mean permanent US access to supplies that we have traditionally assumed to be simply surplus to our needs.[117] A particularly bizarre scenario is no less possible: a provincial government might cut its exports (which it has the right to do under the FTA), thereby forcing the federal government to meet its export commitment to the United States either by reducing domestic consumption somehow, or by *importing* oil to re-ship south of the border. None of this troubles supporters of the agreement. Since energy trade is largely free now as it is, the FTA provisions provide a basis for sound growth in the future, particularly for the uranium sector, which was a big winner in the deal because of the lifting of American import restrictions. Otherwise, the energy chapter in the FTA "represents nothing more than an extension and clarification of Canada's existing rights and obligations under the GATT."[118]

(2) Manufacturing and Industrial Development

The key provisions on manufacturing in the deal include lowered tariffs, government procurement, and revisions to the Auto Pact. For opponents, no "one really knows how many Canadian firms are poised to take advantage of lower tariffs."[119] The chapter on government procurement was criticized because with it, "the Canadian government has signed away to a North American common market its decision-making authority over a Canadian tool of economic policy. In the process, it restricts future governments from using their large volume purchases to promote a wide range of domestic goals, including regional development, local sourcing, special support of particular industries, research and development, and affirmative action."[120] The chapter on automotive trade was attacked because of the change in safeguards (from 60 per cent Canadian content rule to 50 per cent North American content) and the elimination of duty remissions and waivers. The rules of origin now mean that companies will get the benefits of the Auto Pact without having to meet the old safeguards.[121] The Auto Pact still exists, but is now restricted to present members. In essence, the Pact has been "frozen," and the stick that the Canadian government could formerly use to enhance production in this country has been whittled down somewhat so that it applies with less force than before.

Proponents of the deal saw tariff reduction as good in itself, at least in the Canadian context with its reasonably flexible economy. The government procurement provisions were not seen by proponents as preventing or limiting key policy instruments, because those provisions apply only to a specific list of government entities, a specific list of goods, and only for amounts above a given threshold. Moreover, there are exceptions for small businesses. Simon Reisman had in fact hoped for a more ambitious chapter; even so, he estimated that as much as $4 billion in US contracts was now opened to Canadian bids, while $650 million in Canadian contracts was opened to Americans.[122] Finally, on auto trade, proponents tended to focus on the rising concerns in the United States in the last few years over Canada's use of waivers and remissions, and its extension of Auto Pact status beyond the Big Three to overseas competitors. In their view, the Auto Pact was due for revision if not abrogation, and "the automotive clauses in the FTA are about as good as could be expected."[123]

(3) The Dispute Resolution Mechanism

The dispute resolution mechanism was a major component of the deal, and predictably generated completely different assessments from the two sides in the debate. Critics argued that Canada did not get what it set out to get from the trade deal — exemption from US trade remedy laws. All that the deal provides is a referee system that replaces the final tier of judicial review. Canada is still subject to "process protectionism," the American system whereby companies can take competitors through a process that amounts to trade harassment. No such thing is available to Canadian companies.[124] On countervails and anti-dumping, the two countries have only agreed to continue negotiating, and the panels reviewing trade determinations will only have the power to decide if those determinations conform to existing law. This led critics to suggest that, in effect, Canadians will be helping Americans apply their own law against Canadian products and companies. Finally, the FTA calls for an extraordinary amount of notification and consultation that in principle will be done under the aegis of the new Trade Commission, but the deal is far from clear on how much scope and budget the commission will have to do its job.[125] As well, all this notifying and consulting will lead to a centralization of the Canadian political system, in that it will force the provinces to accept constant federal monitoring. The existing degree of centralization, both federal and parliamentary, in Canada will ensure quicker compliance with commission decisions, and so the Americans will have an advantage in being able to stall because of the need to clear everything with various authorities. One observer concluded that the commission will be in the impossible position of having extraordinarily wide responsibilities without any power to back up its decisions. The consequence will be to "push Canada's political integration in a US-controlled North America to levels barely thought possible before the Mulroney era dawned in 1984."[126]

Simon Reisman saw the dispute resolution mechanism differently: "In effect, we have established a watchdog to ensure that the laws are interpreted fairly and applied properly and that there is no arbitrariness in the application of those laws."[127] Donald Macdonald had hoped for an agreement on subsidies, but thought that the panel system would ensure greater fairness and would have changed the outcome of the softwood lumber case.[128] To him, the general dispute settlement procedure for disagreements that fall within the scope of the agreement was of "long-range significance." The advantages are: a specific forum in the commission for consultation and mediation; a defined timetable set for stages of dispute settlement procedure; if the parties are not satisfied by the commission's decision, they can retaliate with "equivalent effects"; the process will be quicker than GATT's; and there will develop a body of "jurisprudence" on Canadian-American trade within the commission.[129] The pro-deal commentary on the dispute resolution mechanisms seemed to concentrate on the long term benefits of developing formal institutional structures to deal with bilateral trade issues, while recognizing the limitations of the deal's specific provisions.

(4) Economic and Social Consequences

While part of the rationale behind a trade agreement from the Canadian point of view, was to escape the wrath of American protectionism, the other, larger point was to stimulate the Canadian economy and to provide the basis for increased jobs and income. Everything in the deal is from the Canadian perspective aimed at these goals. A major part of the domestic debate over free trade focused on what the deal's economic consequences were likely to be, and perhaps even more importantly, on the deal's political and social consequences. These are two very separate planes of discussion, and they may be incongruent. For example, it might be entirely logical to concede that the deal will generate jobs and income while claiming that it will undermine Canada's sovereignty to an intolerable degree. In practice, critics of the deal claimed that the economic payoff will be minimal and perhaps even negative, and the political and social costs will be far too high. The deal's defenders argued that it will produce modest but real short-term economic gains, has the potential to generate larger gains in the future, and will not unduly constrain Canada's sovereignty or undermine its culture.

On the economic question, it is virtually impossible to arrive at any confident conclusions. Even supporters of the FTA agreed that the deal is likely to have limited impact on job creation.[130] Indeed, some economists were prepared to argue that the point of the FTA is not to increase employment, "but rather to increase efficiency, labour productivity, and income. Moreover, like technological change, the FTA will make the Canadian economy more competitive, and thus increase its ability to create high-productivity, high-income jobs in the future."[131] This was hardly a ringing endorsement, and provided a backdrop for other, more pessimistic scenarios wherein the FTA, because of its provisions on services, a sector dominated by female labour, will disproportionately affect women.[132] Job losses in some sectors such as agriculture could be firmly predicted, but "winners" were much harder to identify.

Identifying winners depends on how firms will respond to the new reality of the FTA. This in turn involves making predictions about entrepreneurship, or business creativity. Almost by definition, this is an elusive quality. Proponents of the deal tended to be optimistic about the *elan vital* of Canadian capitalists, both large and small, and argued that they will be able to avail themselves of opportunities south of the border. A related issue was whether Canadian firms would remain in Canada, or move south in pursuit of lower wages and market proximity. If they left, Canada would be "exporting jobs." The deal's critics assumed that Canadian tariffs have both protected indigenous firms and forced US companies to locate here in order to avoid high duties. With tariffs gone, firms are exposed to competition from the US, and have no need to be here in the first place. Of those subsidiaries that remain, some will be prohibited from exporting to the US by their American parents, who do not want competition in the home market with their own subsidiaries. As one critic put it, "the rationalization on a North American basis that is compelled by free trade could provide the excuse for phasing out, or down-sizing, Canadian plants and jobs."[133]

Ironically, the FTA's economic consequences turned out to be far less important in the election debate than its impact on Canadian social, cultural, and political life. The deal does exempt cultural industries, and would not appear to directly affect key social programmes such as family allowances, pensions, health care, education, unemployment insurance, or child care. The deal's critics pointed instead to four broad and insidious mechanisms whereby American values and practices will infect Canada. We may call the first "internal mutation"; it assumes that as American goods, services, and companies begin to operate more freely in Canada, they will bring the American economic style with them, a style often characterized by critics as depending on low wages, union busting, and dangerous cost-cutting. In an unregulated private market, this will place pressures on indigenous Canadian firms to compete or die.

The second and third mechanisms depend less on the commercial than on the political responses to competition of firms on either side of the border. US firms, facing competition from Canadian companies who pay less for their employees' health benefits because of medicare, or less for their pension benefits because of Old Age Security, may launch countervails claiming that these public programmes are unfair subsidies. It is doubtful that such action would have any basis in the FTA, since these programmes are national in scope, but they would have tremendous nuisance value, so much so that they might inhibit policy makers from launching new programmes, and slowly corrode the political will that sustains the existing ones. On the Canadian side, firms may feel that their tax rates or employer contributions to programmes like unemployment insurance (which are more generous and hence more costly in Canada than in the United States) put them at a disadvantage in competing with US firms in the American market. Canadian-based firms selling to the US will still have to meet Canadian standards in wages and benefits, but will sell their products in markets where their competitors have met lower and less expensive standards. This would create pressures within the Canadian business community to either roll back or at least freeze some key Canadian social policies.

The fourth and most general mechanism of importing American values into Canada is found within the very philosophy of the FTA. In fact, this is less a mechanism than a mood, one that colours both the deal and its language, so that without even knowing it, Canadians adopt an individualistic, competitive, market-oriented — in a word, American — world view. For example, the FTA accepts the American definition of culture as "business", and speaks of cultural industries.[134] Gerald Caplan, chair of a recent task force report on Canadian broadcasting and a prominent member of the New Democratic Party, put the point directly:

Precisely the issue that I underline is the choice between a market-driven economy and an interventionist economy. And precisely the point I made is that we will be more closely tied to the US economy and to the US political economy, which frowns on interventionism and on the kind of tripartitism which, it seems to me, holds out a reasonable future for Canada. Although I'm not at all convinced it can happen, the kind of deal proposed will make that kind of interventionism less possible. It's not a matter of exposing our kids to Miami Vice, it's not a matter of 5 percent tariff changes; it's a matter of the organic change. And because of that, I think the agreement should be defeated.

I believe that many of the spokespersons for free trade are trying to peddle an American individualism; a set of values, in my view, that is inappropriate for Canada. I find them inappropriate and frightening. It is all about how tough we have to get and how we have to be tough to compete in the tough international market place.[136]

This perspective necessarily leads to an uncompromisingly harsh view of the agreement. One nationalist concluded that "Canada's ability to establish public goals is set into a new North American framework."[136] Another went further in foreseeing that when implemented, "the Free-Trade Agreement becomes, by virtue of its scope and regulatory importance, the new national policy for Canada. All other federal and provincial policies will have to conform to its framework and goals."[137] The FTA, in short, is the end of Canada.

Free Trade and the Canadian Political Process

There are, in every nation's history, events that shape an epoch or define the profile of a decade. Canada has had some of these: World War II and its conscription crisis, the Quebec 1980 referendum, the battle over the Constitution. The FTA is of the same magnitude and significance, not necessarily because of the economic changes it brings in its wake (some economists claim that the changes may be minor, at best) but because of the passions it aroused. The debate it engendered reached far deeper into the collective Canadian psyche than perhaps anything else in the previous 20 years. It had that magical and terrifying power of great public issues to arouse, crystallize, and intensify a myriad of feelings and beliefs about the nature of the country.

All the more surprising, then, that the government practically stumbled onto it in 1985. Brian Mulroney had in 1983 rejected free trade as an economic policy option because he thought it would tie Canada too closely to the United States. His change of heart had something to do with the developments cited earlier: the 1983 Liberal government initiatives, the climate of protectionism in the United States, the American disinterest in sectoral trade, and the question of where Canada would go in a world dominated by trading blocs. But other factors were in play, because Canadian policy might have simply continued on the multilateral track, with ginger overtures to the Americans on specific issues. Canada's job-creation record was good enough that the Prime Minister could have hoped for continued, modest growth over the first term of his government. It must be understood that Brian Mulroney was the key man behind the deal: he decided to pursue it, he put his own people (Burney and Wilson) in the field when the game got rough, and he personally chaired the cabinet committee that oversaw the negotiations. As he once put it, his neck was on the line. And yet he took the risk. Why?

No one but Brian Mulroney himself knows the answer, but there are several signs of what was in his mind during those fateful days in September 1985, as he weighed his options. First, Mulroney *liked* Americans. He had been raised in a small Quebec town whose prime industry was owned by Americans. Some cheap shots were taken on this theme during the campaign, implying that Mulroney had already sold his soul to the US as a boy, and now he wanted to sell the country. But the real significance of his background goes deeper: Mulroney could never see America as some evil empire, wholly different from Canada in its aspirations and destiny. This psychological orientation lay behind his commitment, made in the first days of his leadership of the Progressive Conservatives, to improve relations with the United States.

Another factor was his obsession with economic growth and jobs. Mulroney had fought the 1984 election on a platform of "jobs, jobs, jobs." It is arguable that he had no deep vision of where he wanted to lead the country, besides away from some of the excesses of the Trudeau years. His one overriding mission seemed to be to give the country prosperity, and his other initiatives were subordinated to that. The FTA was ultimately irresistible from this perspective: if a good deal could be pulled off with the Americans, then the economy would get a huge boost, one moreover that might help the regions more than the centre.

A final psychological factor that might have pushed the Prime Minister over the brink of decision was his own fuzzy ideological leanings. One should never make too much of the ideological commitments of politicians, but the FTA clearly appealed to Mulroney's indistinct ideas of state and society. At the outset of the negotiations, before it could be confidently predicted that a deal could be struck that left culture and social programmes untouched, it was reasonable to assume that the FTA would undermine the role of the state in Canadian economic life. It would clearly do that with respect to tariffs, but the whole idea of 'free trade' rested on an assumption that free markets do things better than governments do. The FTA had sex appeal for a Tory Prime Minister sceptical of the traditional instruments of interventionist state power.

While it may seem frightening that a decision as momentous as the one to embark on talks was taken largely because of these background psychological factors, it helps explain the Canadian side's total confusion over what it wanted. Only Simon Reisman, free trade warrior that he was, knew the game and the prize: he wanted as wide open a deal as possible. The cabinet was less sure, and the Prime Minister entirely muddled at first. For a while, Canada's overtures to the US were like the love that dares not speak its name. No one wanted to say "free trade" or comprehensive trade, in part out of fear, in part from confusion about what the outcomes would be. Brian Mulroney and his cabinet were not clear-eyed, right-wing valiants, smiling with grim confidence as they waded into the enemy of "snivellers and CBC types.". They had gut instincts about what they thought might come from an FTA, but they were not trying to tear down the entire edifice of Canadian social and cultural life in a bid for more trade. That is why they seemed so hopelessly evasive in the early stages of the talks: they did not want culture, social programmes, the Auto Pact, or any thing else quintessentially Canadian, on the table. On the other hand, if they could get a big advantage from a small concession on any of these, they were interested. The Tory soul was cleft in two.

The real world of the FTA negotiations was even messier than this honest confusion would imply. First, there was the problem of the provinces. Mulroney had nailed his colours to the mast of federal-provincial relations early in 1984: cooperation and compromise and sweetness and light would reign again once he assumed the chair vacated by Trudeau. The premiers, especially the western ones, had supported the FTA, but Mulroney had to walk a thin and wavering line throughout the talks. The provinces, with the exception of Ontario, seemed interested in a deal with the US, but did not want to give Ottawa *carte blanche*. Ottawa knew that it could not negotiate effectively with ten governments at its elbow, but it also knew that it could not sell a deal to the US without being able to guarantee provincial cooperation. Mulroney's initial strategy was to give assurances of cooperation and participation while refusing to specify what that meant for the talks. Once the talks were underway, he managed to wrest a commitment from the provinces to give Ottawa negotiating power in exchange for provincial ratification. Squabbles continued over the ratification formula, but Reisman quietly worked at a deal that could be implemented completely within the federal domain. The reality of the negotiating process and of federal-provincial relations had forced Ottawa to bargain for a specific kind of deal, ironically one that attenuated federal powers much more than it did provincial ones. Fearing provincial power to negate a deal, Mulroney allowed a deal that further eroded federal powers.

A second complicating factor was the talks themselves. International negotiations, depending on the issues at hand, are at best gruelling, at worst a kind of political hardball where the only rule is to try to win the best deal you can for your country. Bilateral economic talks can be especially difficult, and require preparation, determination, and willpower to see them through. Simon Reisman probably was the best man for the job: he knew the area, and he was tough. He also had some of the best minds in Ottawa behind him. But he went into the negotiations from a weak position, and in negotiations, like war, position is everything. Canada had made the first move on the FTA by asking for talks. Moreover, Canada's interest lay in *avoiding* American trade measures such as the omnibus trade bill and countervails. In any negotiation, the supplicant is always in the weaker position, particularly if the point of the negotiation is to win protection from the power of the other party. Canada's position was undermined in the next year, when various American authorities, without coordinated intent, slapped trade remedies on Canadian imports. Canada's stake in the talks was greater than America's, and in order to avoid throwing it all away, Canada did not react vigorously to the US trade actions. Peter Murphy no doubt smiled as he read the signs. Moreover, Canada eventually set its hopes impossibly high with the demand for a binding dispute resolution mechanism and a deal on subsidies. The realities of American politics would never permit either a Canadian exemption from American trade law or a quasi-judicial body that would override American law.

All this came to a head when Canadian authorities fought for a deal in September 1987. Reisman gave up the talks in good faith; he had had enough, and Murphy was not budging on the dispute resolution issue. But the politicians had gone too far now, too much had been invested in the talks. It is wrong to think that the Tories "conceded" on investment, services, finances, or the Auto Pact. The Tories had never liked the investment controls of the Foreign Investment Review Agency or the baroque interventions of the National Energy Program: giving in on these issues was easy. And the Auto Pact was under pressure anyway, since it was now operating in a way that encouraged non–North American car manufacturers to set up plants in Canada to export to the US. American authorities were going to pull the plug one way or another. Financial services were being de-regulated by Ottawa already, and so this did not represent a concession in the government's mind. Nonetheless, Michael Wilson and Derek Burney finally gave the Americans what they wanted, and got a dispute resolution mechanism in return.

This was not the way that many Canadians saw it, of course. The Tories had not conceded much if anything from *their* agenda, but they had compromised some key policy traditions extending back to the early 1960s, traditions built by Liberal governments at the goading of the NDP. These policies, in investment, tariff protection, energy, and social policy, had been symbols of central power and national will. The social programmes had always been piecemeal and inadequate, but they had been steps along the road to what many saw as a more just and humane society. The FTA became such a potent political symbol precisely because it could be seen as a frontal attack on this tradition. Despite its safeguards, exemptions, exceptions, and escape clauses, the FTA was rooted in soil quite different from that which had nourished much of Canadian federal public policy since the mid-1960s. It still allows the same goals to be pursued as before, but it constrains that pursuit by limiting the permissible policy instruments.

The FTA, like previous attempts to forge a free trade deal with the US, became a quivering lightning rod for all the electric storms of nationalism and identity that have beset the country's history. That is one reason why the debate was never monopolized by experts and elites. Salvo after salvo was fired from both camps in the form of studies, reports, commentaries, debates, analyses, and projections, using all the sophisticated weaponry of modern public policy discourse. The government did try to sell the deal to the public, but the millions it spent on advertising were little more than glossy propaganda. The public simply did not respond. Had the election campaign been held to three weeks and the vote called for October 21 instead of November 21, the Tories might have won without making much fuss at all about free trade. John Turner's intervention, desperate and perhaps even calculated, nonetheless finally dragged the issue forcibly onto centre stage. In the arc light glare of the election campaign, the debate moved to a different plane than the one it had occupied for the experts. It became more emotional, more a matter of symbols and vision than of sections and clauses. But like a game of three-dimensional chess, the moves on this different plane were related to strategies developed on the other. Opposing politicians girded their rhetoric with references to studies done by opposing experts. The references were often elusive and fleeting, but vital, since the FTA could not be discussed *entirely* in symbolic terms. The experts did not determine the debate, or even succeed in setting its boundaries, but they provided ammunition for the war of words about the FTA's contents and consequences.

More than experts were involved in the fray. Interest groups, as noted earlier, entered the debate and the campaign with unprecedented vigour. In this case, the only clear and consistent support for the FTA came from business, especially big business already operating in the North American market. Opposition came from unions, farmers, cultural elites, and social policy advocates. It is rare to find such a clear line (though of course there were exceptions on each side) between the business agenda and the agenda of what might loosely be called the "popular sector." The business agenda won, but not through the exercise of business pressure on government. Voters across the country made a choice to support the party that in turn supported the FTA. But institutional factors made the victory seem more decisive than it really was. Canada's parliamentary system elects MPs on a plurality basis, so that in most cases Tories were elected with less than 50 percent of the votes; nationally, the Conservatives had the support of only

43 percent of voters. In so far as both the Liberals and the NDP opposed the FTA, it might be said that the majority of Canadians, in fact, *voted against free trade*. But the system operates on the basis of seats in the Commons, not votes in the hustings. The Tories, with 170 seats, have a clear majority. Moreover, the Liberal strategy of making free trade *the* issue of the campaign backfired to a degree, since by winning a majority, the Tories could claim an undisputed mandate to implement the deal.

In some respects, the 1988 election was Canadian democracy's finest hour. There was a real issue, a real debate, and stakes so high that many voters entered polling booths on the final day, after seven weeks of intense debate, still undecided about their choice and the country's destiny. Rare is the election where voters might consider a simple pencil tick the end of a nation. Equally rare, however, is an issue that resolves itself cleanly, especially one as large and as complex as the FTA. The deal was passed and went into effect on schedule, but the debate was far from over. The new challenge will be to reconcile the benefits that flow from the FTA with the aspirations that flowered from opposing it.

DISCUSSION QUESTIONS

1) Discuss the FTA's symbolic content. In what ways could it be seen to express Canada's best aspirations as well as its ultimate doom?

2) Review the cultural arguments against the FTA. In what ways was the FTA expected to undermine Canadian culture?

3) Business was about the only sector of Canadian society to support the FTA consistently. Discuss the significance of this.

4) In terms of what eventually emerged in the FTA, why was it logical for the western provincial governments to support the deal and for Ontario to oppose it?

5) How did the differences between the Canadian and American political systems affect the negotiations and their outcome?

6) The opposition to the FTA came from what some have called the "popular sector": trade unions, women's organizations, social action groups. What ideological assumptions would unite such a disparate sector?

7) A major part of the free trade debate involved predicting consequences. But no one, not even the experts, was terribly confident of what the consequences of such a huge policy initiative would be. Discuss the problems this poses for the making of public policy.

8) What could the "political negotiations" deal with that the "technical discussions" between Reisman and Murphy could not?

9) Review the terms of the FTA as outlined in this chapter. Would they prevent a publicly funded, nation-wide system of child care centres?

10) The Liberal party had a more difficult time with the FTA than the NDP did. Discuss why this would be so, in terms of the party's traditional ideology, its regional basis, and its policy legacy when it formed the federal government under Trudeau.

CHRONOLOGY

1854	First free trade agreement between Canada and US signed; welcomed in US as step towards annexation of Canada; helped triple Canadian exports within a decade.
1866	Abrogation of reciprocity treaty (encouraged by US fishing and lumber industries; US moved to protective tariffs).
1879	National Policy — a reaction to the ending of tariff reciprocity; tariffs ranged from 25 to 40 percent.
1911	Free trade election; Laurier's Liberal government and his free-trade platform defeated.
1947	Aborted US-Canada free trade agreement.
1953	Idea of free trade agreement raised between Eisenhower and St-Laurent; later dropped.
1965	Negotiation of Auto Pact (Canadian side led by Simon Reisman).
1982	Macdonald commission (Royal Commission on the Economic Union and Development Prospects for Canada) established.
1985	
January	Council of Canadians founded by Mel Hurtig.
February 15	First ministers' meeting; PM says he will proceed with FTA idea as premiers clearly approve (particularly Lougheed).
March 17-18	Quebec Conference ("Shamrock Summit") between Reagan and Mulroney.

March 18	Reagan and Mulroney announce that USTR Brock and MINT Kelleher are to look at "all possible ways to reduce and eliminate existing barriers to trade" and report back in six months.
late March	Brock given new position as secretary of labour; Yeutter provisionally appointed as new USTR (appointment to be approved by Congress).
July	Special Committee on Economic Affairs of Government of Ontario appointed to hold hearings on free trade. Committee, composed of 11 members from all parties, has 14-week schedule of hearings.
Summer to August 8	Special Joint Parliamentary Committee on Canada's International Relations travels to six cities across Canada to gather views on free trade and Strategic Defence Initiative.
August 22	Premier's conference in St. John's; FTA negotiations recommended by all premiers with exception of Ontario.
September 5	Macdonald report released; strongly in favour of free trade.
September 9	PM announces in House of Commons that he will pursue a free trade agreement with US.
September 17	Reports of Canada and US officials on whether to proceed with free trade (commissioned at Shamrock Summit) given to Reagan and Mulroney.
September 26	Mulroney calls Reagan, asking for FTA talks; assures House of Commons that he told Reagan cultural industries were not to be on bargaining table.
October 2	Reagan responds favourably to Mulroney proposal but makes no mention of cultural industries being exempted from FTA discussions.
November 8	PM picks Simon Reisman to lead Canadian side of FTA negotiations.

November 28-29	Halifax first ministers' meeting; PM and premiers establish 90-day period, beginning in mid-December, to work towards common ground on (1) a joint federal/provincial data base for FTA talks, (2) outlining of objectives, (3) obstacles to objectives, and (4) definition of full provincial participation.
December 10	Reagan formally notifies Congress of the Administration's intent to enter into FTA negotiations with Canada; Congress has 60 working days to either veto idea or, by remaining silent, to allow the talks to proceed.

1986

January 7	Reisman has first meeting with provincial bureaucrats (objective is to negotiate role of provinces in FTA talks).
January 9	International Trade Advisory Committee members named.
January 20-21	International Trade Advisory Committee meets for the first time in Ottawa.
February 3-4	Closed meeting of provincial trade ministers in Toronto during which protests are made about Ottawa's failure, so far, to allow full provincial participation in FTA talks.
March 18-20	("Shamrock Summit II") Mulroney visits Washington, DC; advised not to address Congress because of fears of protectionist backlash at FTA.
April 11	Ten out of twenty Senate Finance Committee members vow to vote against FTA talks request on April 17.
April 17	After intense lobbying, Senate Finance Committee vote postponed to April 22.
April 18	President Reagan announces he will send letter of appeal to Senate Finance Committee members opposing FTA (letter later turns into phone call).

April 22	Senate Finance Committee vote postponed to April 23, last possible day before "fast-track" option expires.
April 23	Senate Finance Committee passes request to begin FTA negotiations on 10–10 vote just before expiry of 60-day period; Congress has option of telling President to proceed, or holding off until a legislative committee can hold hearings on FTA.
April 25	Chairman of sectoral advisory groups on international trade (SAGITs) announced.
May 21-22	Canada-US FTA talks open with Reisman and Murphy concentrating on administrative details, described by Ottawa as "exploratory talks."
June 2	PM meets with premiers at private dinner to discuss power-sharing arrangements in FTA talks (six months after 90-day deadline set in November 1985); consultations every three months agreed upon.
June 16	PM goes on television prime time to make speech in favour of free trade negotiations.
June 17	Second session of FTA talks, continuing "issue exploration."
July 29-31	Third session of FTA talks, covering specific issues of agriculture and US trade laws.
September 9-11	Fourth round of preliminary FTA talks.
September 17	PM meets with premiers in Ottawa.
late September	Fifth preliminary FTA talks take place in Washington; objective is to complete preliminaries in this round.
November 4	Mid-term congressional elections; Democrats win Senate majority.
November 12	Sixth FTA negotiating session in Ottawa.

| December 16-18 | Seventh FTA negotiating session in Washington, DC. |

1987

January	Working groups established.
late January	More than half of US Congress sponsors omnibus trade bill.
March 11	First ministers' conference in Ottawa — discussions over formal ratification of FTA by provinces (inconclusive); premiers agree to allow at least another three months of negotiations with US.
March 16	Special debate in House of Commons on FTA begins; motion calls for support for bilateral trade agreement that would include protection for auto pact, cultural heritage, and agriculture.
March 16	FTA talks; subject is agriculture.
March 17	Motion to support free trade passes in Commons 160–58.
March 19	Alliance for Trade and Job Opportunities (pro-FTA) formed.
April 4	Pro-Canada Network formed in Ottawa.
April 5-6	Reagan/Mulroney Summit; Reagan makes speech to Parliament in support of FTA.
May 19-21	FTA talks — Ottawa.
May 19	Working party on investment issues formed.
May 25	FTA talks "log jammed" because of disagreements over investment.
June 11	Economic Summit in Venice (PM bring up FTA with President Reagan).
June 15-22	FTA talks — Washington, DC.

June 22	First ministers' conference scheduled (postponed to early July because of blockages in FTA negotiations).
July 7	First ministers conference — premiers complain about lack of information available, particularly in view of short time before deadline.
July 13-14	FTA talks — Washington, DC.
July 20	FTA talks — Ottawa; completed in half a day instead of scheduled two days; Murphy flies to Washington, DC.
August 20	Negotiating teams exchange 100-page drafts of FTA.
August 24-28	"Mammoth" FTA session in Cornwall (20 Canadians and 50 Americans participating).
August 27	Premiers' conference, which expresses concern at US protectionism.
September 10	Ontario election — Peterson wins majority.
Sept. 10-11	FTA talks — Washington, DC.
September 10	Meeting of Economic Policy Council, Washington.
September 14	First ministers' meeting — Peterson learns Auto Pact is on FTA table (castigated 18 September by Carney for giving press confidential details of FTA).
September 16	USTR Yeutter and Murphy meet with industry group that offers advice to US government on FTA negotiations.
September 19	"Secret" consultations involving PM, Wilson, Burney before 21 September official negotiations.
Sept. 21-23	FTA session — Washington, DC.
September 23	Canada suspends FTA negotiations.
September 24	US/Canada telephone discussions of FTA at political level with PM involved.

September 26	US sends two-page proposal exploring ways to restart negotiations to Burney in Prime Minister's Office.
September 27	US letter rejected because it does not meet Canadian demands.
September 28	"High-level" meeting (Wilson, Carney, Burney, Gotlieb, Campbell, Baker, Yeutter) in Washington, DC. Meeting proposed by Burney in letter to Baker (letter drafted by group including Reisman but under Burney's direction) that reiterated five bottom-line Canadian conditions.
September 29	Canadian government sends Washington document on definition of subsidies.
September 30	Washington responds to document; some "shifting of ground" on dispute settlement.
October 1	Wilson/Carney/Burney fly to Washington to attempt to smooth ground for restarting of discussions (2 1/2-hour meeting); "bargaining has shifted to the political level." Team returns to Ottawa in evening having made "no apparent progress."
October 2	Emergency meeting of premiers in Ottawa; no details of FTA provided.
October 2	Negotiating team sent back to Washington, DC.
October 3	Negotiations continue; deal struck at 11:40 PM and announced 1:15 AM Sunday morning.
October 4	First version of FTA released to media.
October 5	Second version (with reference to Bill C–22 removed) tabled in Parliament.
October 6	PM meets with premiers to review FTA, even though full agreement not yet available.
October 7	PM announces "massive" retraining programme to help workers adjust to economic upheaval.

October 8	Referring to PM's statement of October 7, Finance Minister Wilson says, "We do not expect that there will be a need for any significant programmes of adjustment."
November 1	Commons Committee on External Affairs and International Trade begins hearings on FTA (even though final text of FTA probably not ready under end of November).
November 16	Commons resumes sitting.
November 23	Commons Committee travels to conduct hearings on FTA, starting with Vancouver.
Nov. 26-27	First Ministers' Conference on the Economy — Toronto; PM says that advisory council to deal with job adjustment will be formed.
November 30	Negotiations on legal wording of FTA text resume.
December 1	Murphy/Reisman continue haggling and negotiating over legal wording of FTA text.
December 2	Trade negotiators finish 14-hour meeting; in two-hour meeting with PM and Cabinet Executive Trade Committee afterwards, Reisman admits final legal wording of text still not completed.
December 3	House of Representatives Committee writes to Administration asking that shipping issues be taken out of FTA.
December 5-6	Work on legal text continues through weekend.
December 7	Final text agreed on.
December 10	Final round of negotiations completed and final text initialled.
December 11	Final text released to House of Commons at noon; explained to reporters in "controlled environment."
December 17	First ministers' conference in Ottawa — will go

through final text of FTA.

1988

January 2	FTA signed by PM Mulroney and President Reagan independently, without great ceremony.
February 18	US Administration announces schedule for congressional consideration of FTA; promises vote to be scheduled by October 8, by August 12 if possible (when Congress recesses).
March 17	US Senate Finance Committee begins consideration of FTA.
April 1	John Crosbie appointed Minister for International Trade.
May 24	Bill C–130, the legislation to implement the deal, introduced to the House of Commons.
August 9	US House of Representatives passes Free Trade Bill
August 31	Bill C–130 passed in the House of Commons. Opposition MPs sing the American anthem, wave the Canadian flag, and are joined by derisive hooting from the public galleries.
September 19	US Senate passes Free Trade Bill
September 28	President Reagan signs the American Free Trade Bill
October 1	The Prime Minister calls the election for 21 November 1988.
November 21	Election held with following results: Tories 170 seats; Liberals 82 seats; NDP 43 seats.
December 31	Canadian Free Trade legislation passed and signed into law, to go into effect January 1, 1989.

Appendix I: The Free Trade Agreement:

A Summary

The agreement took various forms, each more elaborate than the last, over the period October 1987 to fall 1988. First came the Principles of Agreement signed on 3 October 1987. The text of the FTA that was then based on these principles was 305 pages, counting various interpretive annexes, but not counting tariff schedules. Bill C–130 was 127 pages long, contained 153 clauses, and amended 27 federal statutes. On top of that, there was the American version of the agreement, with American explanatory notes.

The discussion will use the following reference system when citing the FTA: articles of the agreement will be cited as "FTA 301," clauses of articles will be cited as "FTA 301.4," and annexes will be cited as "FTA Annex 301."

1. OBJECTIVES AND SCOPE

The FTA is divided into eight parts. Part 1 deals with objectives and scope; Part 2 with trade in goods (containing the key chapters on rules of origin, measures, national treatment, technical standards, agriculture, wine and distilled spirits, energy, automotive goods, and various exceptions for emergencies and under GATT rules); Part 3 deals with government procurement; Part 4 with services (including investment); Part 5 with financial services; Part 6 with institutional provisions regarding dispute resolution; Parts 7 and 8 with miscellaneous issues. Each of the parts contains chapters, and the articles within the chapters are keyed so that, for instance, all articles in chapter 19 begin with the number 19. FTA 1901 is thus the first article in chapter 19.

The FTA must be read as a whole, since many of chapters and provisions overlap. At the most general level, the FTA is quite straightforward. It begins by establishing a free trade area, that is, an area comprising Canada and the United States, in which there will be no tariffs on goods traded between the partners, and national treatment of both goods and companies of one country by the other. The chapters on trade in goods set out the rules pertaining to most of the key sectors, along with some exceptions. The parts dealing with government procurement, services, and financial services liberalize trade in these areas. The third pillar of the agreement is the mechanism for dealing with disputes and disagreements, and is followed by some specific provisions for special cases like cultural industries.

Chapter 1 of the FTA states as objectives of the agreement the intent to "eliminate barriers to trade in goods and services," "facilitate conditions of fair competition," "liberalize significantly conditions for investment," and "establish effective procedures for the joint administration of this Agreement"(FTA 102). A central question, of course, is the degree to which the FTA overrides other laws, or might constrain Canada's ability to make nationalistic policies. The agreement is somewhat unclear on this. For example, the preamble states that one of the guiding principles of the deal is "to reduce government-created trade distortions while preserving the parties' flexibility to safeguard the public welfare." FTA 103, however, states that the parties to "this agreement shall ensure that all necessary measures are taken in order to give effect to its provisions, including their observance, except as otherwise provided in this agreement, by state, provincial, and local governments." FTA 104.2 says that the provisions of the FTA prevail over other bilateral *and multilateral* agreements to which they are both a party, unless specifically provided for otherwise by the agreement.

The heart of the agreement is in FTA 105, which states that "each party shall, to the extent provided in this agreement, accord national treatment with respect to investment and to trade in goods and services." National treatment means just that: no discriminatory taxes or other barriers that disproportionately disadvantage the goods or services produced by one of the parties in the other party's territory.

2. TRADE IN GOODS

Tariffs: Part 2 of the FTA opens with a chapter on rules of origin. This is crucial, since a free trade area allows the partners to maintain separate tariff regimes against third countries, and the agreement is to apply only to trade in goods and services produced in Canada or the United States or both. Neither country wants to allow "trans-shipments," whereby goods made outside the free trade area are shipped to one of the partners, perhaps with heavy domestic duties, and then simply re-shipped to the other partner. Chapter 3 of the FTA deals with rules of origin. The basic principle is in FTA 301, which says that goods originate if they are "wholly obtained or produced" in the territory or either territory (FTA 301.1), or if they come from outside but have been "transformed" so as to be subject to a change in tariff classification. The classification system will be the International Convention on the Harmonized Commodity Description and Coding System, approved by the Customs Cooperation Council, an international body, in 1983. Goods that have merely been packaged, combined, or diluted with water or some other substance do not count (FTA 301.3), though spare parts, tools, and accessories that come with equipment/machinery will be allowed (FTA 301.4). The FTA will allow partners to produce goods in their territory but ship them through a third country as long as there is no handling apart from what is necessary purely for transportation in the third country (FTA 302). This was included to prevent goods produced in the United States from being shipped to Mexico for further processing and then re-entering the United States for duty-free export to Canada. FTA Annex 301.2, subsection 4(a), clarifies the notion of origin further, by stating that a good will be considered to come from one of the parties if 50 percent of cost of production (materials plus cost of assembly) is accounted for by either or both parties. There is a saving clause for the apparel industry, so that it can continue to import raw materials (fabric) to a certain limit and still have goods counted as originating in the parties' territory.

The crux of the section on trade in goods is the reduction of tariffs. Tariffs are reduced according to three formulae over ten years, depending on the sector's ability to compete. For some sectors (e.g., computers, whiskey, and skis), tariffs were completely eliminated on January 1, 1989. For other sectors (e.g., subway cars, explosives, and furniture), tariffs will be eliminated in equal steps over five years (20 per cent per year). All other tariffs will be eliminated in equal steps over 10 years (10 per cent per year). If both countries agree, the staging can be accelerated (FTA 401.5). After the agreement comes into effect, neither country may increase any of its tariffs, unless specified by the agreement itself (FTA 401.1). FTA 403 ensures that special customs user fees applied by the United States, whereby importers pay for the American customs services they require, will gradually be eliminated.

The rest of the chapter contains several articles that limit the use of the tariff for industrial policy purposes. FTA 404, with certain minor exceptions, prohibits the use of what are called "duty drawbacks," whereby a manufacturer gets back the duty he might have paid on an imported product, as long as that product is incorporated into another product that is subsequently exported. Duty drawbacks have been used by Canadian governments to encourage export by domestic manufacturers. This article goes into effect on 1 January 1994. FTA 405 prohibits the introduction of any new "customs waiver" programmes that are conditional on performance requirements, and calls for the elimination of all existing programmes (except for automotive trade) by 1 January 1998. Customs waivers of this type exempt a manufacturer from paying duty on imported items as long as that manufacturer meets certain requirements set by the government, such as minimum levels of export or minimum levels of domestic purchasing of parts. If either party to the agreement can show that such a programme adversely affects its interests, the other party must either discontinue it or make it generally available to any importer. FTA 407 disallows quantitative restrictions, as well as minimum export and minimum import price requirements. These provisions affirm GATT obligations. FTA 407 allows either party to impose import or export restrictions on goods to or from a third country, even if they flow through the territory of the other party. FTA 408 prohibits export taxes unless such taxes are applied on the same goods destined for domestic consumption. So, for example, Canada could not, as it did in the 1970s, apply an export tax on oil going to the United States, thus keeping domestic prices lower than the Americans' prices.

Chapter 4 of the FTA seeks to eliminate tariffs and other measures such as duty drawbacks, waivers, quotas, and export taxes that restrict trade. But the FTA recognizes that in some cases, countries will need to limit trade in goods. The agreement does this by incorporating existing GATT provisions. These provisions allow import and export control measures for such reasons as protection of public morals (e.g., prohibitions on trade in pornographic materials), human, animal or plant life, and national treasures. These exemptions are specifically listed in Chapter 12 of the FTA, but they are governed by FTA 409, which deals with GATT allowances for impositions of export controls on items in short supply, conservation schemes, and domestic price stabilization schemes. The article says that such restrictions may not include price increases due to special levies, and that the proportion of exports remain the same (as measured by the level in the last three years). This article is identical to FTA 904 in the energy chapter, and so pertains specifically to energy exports. The point of the article is to ensure that any quantitative restrictions in energy exports are not disruptive to the other party.

The FTA also allows exceptions to the open trade in goods for emergency purposes. These are addressed in Chapter 11 of the agreement, which places restrictions on the powers of either party to limit imports. FTA 1101 allows either party to temporarily raise duties on imports if those imports have caused injury to domestic interests. Such measures may only last for a maximum of three years, and in any case will not be allowed after 31 December 1998. The other party must be notified and consulted if such action is taken, and has the right to demand trade concessions in another area that cancel out the negative effects of the restrictions. If such compensation is not forthcoming, the offended party may apply countervailing tariff action with trade effects "substantially equivalent" to the action taken by the other party (FTA 1101.4). As well, global actions taken by either party to limit imports will normally exempt the other party, unless imports from that party are "substantial" (from five to ten percent of total imports).

National Treatment : Chapter 5 is only one page long, but is central to the agreement. FTA 501 says that each party "shall accord national treatment to the goods of the other party" in accordance with GATT rules, especially GATT Article III. FTA 502 extends the national treatment provision to the provinces and states.

Taken together, these articles mean that Canadian governments, both federal and provincial, cannot treat American goods any differently than they treat domestic goods with respect to taxation, regulations for sale, transportation, distribution or production. American governments cannot discriminate against Canadian goods. Each country may still, of course, apply taxes and regulations as it sees fit; the difference under the FTA is that they may no longer apply them differently depending on the origin of the good. The incorporation of the GATT rules is important as well, since GATT Article III, for example, exempts government procurement programmes and subsidies paid exclusively to domestic producers.

Technical Standards : Chapter 6 deals with technical standards, other than for agriculture, food, and beverages. FTA 601.02 exempts the provinces and states from the subsequent provisions, so that they apply only to national standards. FTA 603 states that no standards are to be set up to act as barriers to trade. FTA 604 aims at compatibility of standards between the two countries, but since many technical standards are set by private bodies, such as the Canadian Standards Association, FTA 605 provides that the two countries will essentially recognize the accreditation systems operating in each of their territories with respect to testing facilities, inspection agencies and certification bodies. FTA 609 defines "make compatible" to mean mutual recognition of differing standards as being technically identical or equivalent in practice.

Agriculture : Chapter 7 deals with agriculture. It is one of the longest and most complicated of any in the agreement, and while in many respects it leaves traditional policy structures in place, it does liberalize some sectors of Canadian-US agricultural trade. FTA 701 addresses agricultural subsidies. It affirms that the parties have as their goal, on a global basis, the eventual "elimination of all subsidies which distort agricultural trade." Neither party shall "introduce or maintain any export subsidy on any agricultural goods" in bilateral trade (FTA 701.2). The agreement defines an agricultural subsidy as one that is "conditional upon the exportation of agricultural goods" (FTA 711). While these subsidy provisions go beyond existing obligations of the parties under the GATT, export subsidies are not widely used by either country, so the bulk of "real" subsidy programmes remain unaffected by FTA 701.2.

FTA 702 is the so-called "snapback" provision that provides an escape clause from FTA 401 and its gradual elimination of most tariffs on agricultural products over a ten year period. Either party is allowed to temporarily apply duties on imported fresh fruits or vegetables if the price of those imports falls below 90 percent of the average import price for five consecutive days. The article places limits on the amount of the duty that may be levied, the products against which it may be levied, and its duration. FTA 704.1 provides for free trade in beef and veal, but FTA 704.2 allows quantitative restrictions of imports from either party if those restrictions are deemed necessary to give effect to restrictions of imports from other countries. What this means is that if Canada wished to restrict imports of Argentinian beef to protect the domestic market, it could place restrictions on US beef imports as well, if it thought such imports were frustrating its goals. FTA 705 is a provision on licence requirements for imports of grains. If the level of US government support for wheat, oats, and barley becomes equal to or less than that provided in Canada, Canada will eliminate import permit requirements for these products originating in the United States.

FTA 706 establishes floors for import levels of chickens and chicken products, turkey and turkey products, and eggs and egg products. This article limits Canada's practice of putting quantitative import restrictions on these products. The floor for imports of chickens and chicken products is 7.5. percent of the previous year's chicken production in Canada; the floor for imports of turkeys and turkey products is 3.5 percent of current year's Canadian domestic turkey production quota; and the floor for eggs and egg products varies from 1.647 percent for shell eggs, to 0.714 percent for frozen, liquid, and further processed eggs, to 0.627 percent for powdered eggs.

FTA 708 deals with technical regulations and standards for agricultural, food, beverage, and related products. It is an important article, since many restrictions on agricultural trade are buried in precisely these sorts of rules. The article states that the parties "shall seek an open border policy with respect to trade in agricultural, food, beverage, and certain related goods." It then goes on to list several principles that shall guide the regulation of such goods. The parties will "harmonize their respective technical regulatory requirements and inspection procedures" (the FTA defines "harmonization" for the purposes of this article as "making identical"), apply quarantine restrictions on a regional rather than national basis, and establish equivalent accreditation procedures for inspection systems and inspectors. The rest of the article establishes requirements for notification and consultation, as well as for working groups to implement the provisions of the article.

It is important, in the case of agriculture, to note what the FTA *does not* include. It does not directly modify Canada's system of marketing boards or stabilization programmes.

Wine, Spirits, and Beer: Wine and distilled spirits qualify for a separate chapter in the agreement. This is because of the complicated marketing and production arrangements by which they are governed, especially in Canada.

Each province controls the sale of wines and spirits, and is given the exclusive power, under the federal *Importation of Intoxicating Liquors Act*, to import intoxicating liquors into the province from anywhere, including other provinces. Though practices vary, all provinces have as the core of their system a government monopoly over distribution, and this allows special pricing and listing policies to favour domestic producers. On 2 February 1988, a preliminary GATT ruling was made of practices whereby Canadian provincial liquor authorities discriminated against foreign products. Those practices were found to be in violation of the GATT rules.

Chapter 8 removes discriminatory provincial pricing and listing policies. FTA 802 stipulates that procedures for the listing of wines and spirits be "transparent" and based on normal commercial considerations. An exception is made for British Columbia estate wineries producing less than 30,000 gallons of wine annually: they are entitled to automatic listing. FTA 803 deals with pricing policies. Prices for imported products may still be higher than for equivalent domestic products, as long as the differential reflects higher costs of marketing and distribution. Apart from that, any existing price differentials must be gradually phased out by 1 January 1995 (FTA 803.2). FTA 804 provides that there should be no discrimination in the distribution of imported and domestic products, with the exception of on-premise sales by wineries and distilleries, and private wine store outlets in British Columbia and Ontario. Quebec is also allowed to maintain its requirement that any wine sold in Quebec grocery stores be bottled in Quebec. FTA 805 removes the Canadian requirement that any bulk imports of distilled spirits had to be blended with Canadian spirits, but under FTA 806 bourbon and Canadian whiskey are protected as distinctive products of the respective countries that have to be made there.

Beer and malt beverages are explicitly excluded from the provisions of the agreement. Chapter 12, which deals with exceptions, grandfathers all measures pertaining to the internal sale and distribution of these products.

Energy: Despite its prominence in debates over the FTA, Chapter 9 on energy is quite short. For the purposes of the agreement energy products include coal, oil, natural gas, electricity, and fissionable materials. The existing provisions under GATT allow various exceptions in free trade of energy products, principally for reasons having to do with conservation, shortages and national security. Also, both Canada and the United States are signatories to the 1974 *Agreement on an International Energy Programme*, which calls for energy sharing among members in case of specified supply disruptions.

The principal importance of Chapter 9 is that it restricts the use of some of the key policy instruments that defined federal energy, especially petroleum and natural gas, policy in the 1970s through to the National Energy Program of 1980. FTA 903 is a carbon copy of FTA 408, and prohibits special taxes on the export of energy goods unless those taxes are also levied on energy goods destined for domestic consumption. FTA 904 copies FTA 409, and allows restrictions of energy exports from one party to another for reasons of shortage and conservation, as long as the restriction does not reduce the other party's *proportion* of the total supply made available as measured over the last three years, does not involve the deliberate imposition of a higher export price than what prevails domestically, and does not disrupt normal channels of supply to the other party. If, for example, Canada wished to reduce exports of natural gas or oil, it could only do so by reducing domestic supply as well, since the proportion of exports to the United States must remain stable.

If one of the parties feels that the other has undertaken discriminatory energy regulatory actions, that party may initiate direct consultations. FTA 906 allows existing or future incentives for oil and gas exploration, development, and related activities. FTA 907 narrows the definition of national security as a basis for export or import restrictions, and applies mostly to the United States, which has relied disproportionately on this rationale.

Automotive Products: The Auto Pact was negotiated in 1965 and came into effect in 1966. It created a system of duty-free trade between Canada and the United States in automotive parts and new automobiles, and incidentally provided a huge boost to the Ontario economy. The Auto Pact provisions that created this duty-free system differed. On the US side, a rule of origin was applied so that duties were waived as long as 50 percent of the value of a new car was created in North America. Parts were treated as "Canadian" and therefore duty free if imported by bona fide American car manufacturers. On the Canadian side, two performance criteria were used. First, manufacturers had to produce as many cars in Canada as they sold in Canada. Second, manufacturers had to ensure that 60 percent of the value of their production was Canadian in origin. If they met these performance criteria, they were allowed to import automotive parts from anywhere in the world. Originally, when the only automotive manufacturers located in Canada were the Big Three, this presented no problems, since they would import parts from the United States. Later, however, as manufacturers from other countries located in Canada, they were granted duty remissions on the same terms as those applied in the Auto Pact, so that they could receive "Auto Pact status." This was a singular advantage, since it allowed them to export products to the United States duty free. The Canadian performance criteria came to be called "safeguards," since they ensured that a fixed proportion of production would be undertaken in Canada. If a company failed to meet the criteria, duties would be slapped on its parts imports, thus raising the price of its cars and putting it at a disadvantage against its competitors.

Chapter 10 of the FTA must be seen against this backdrop and that of Chapters 3 and 4, dealing with rules of origin and general tariff provisions. Chapter 3 of the FTA imposes a new 50 percent North American value rule of origin, one that is calculated more narrowly than the old US rule. Chapter 4 stipulates that aftermarket automotive parts will carry no tariff as of 1994; production parts will have their duties reduced over ten years (though of course in practice most of these parts move duty free within the North American market). What does Chapter 10 say specifically about trade in automotive goods? In effect, its one key article limits the use of duty waivers or remissions by the Canadian government. FTA 1002.1 limits duty waivers to existing qualified Canadian manufacturers (listed in FTA Annex 1002.1). Export based duty waivers shall be calculated, after 1 January 1989, by excluding exports to the territory of the other party (FTA 1002.2). They will terminate on or before 1 January 1998. Furthermore, duty remissions granted to a limited list of companies (e.g., Honda, Hyundai, and Toyota) on the basis of performance requirements will terminate no later than 1 January 1996.

In a sense, these articles may be seen as a "freezing" of the Auto Pact. Canada may still engage in remissions and duty waivers, and may do so on the basis of traditional safeguards, but it can extend these breaks only to companies that currently operate in Canada and meet the requirements. As well, since trade in North American automotive parts will be free eventually, these remissions and waivers will ultimately only apply to the import of non–North American parts, estimated to be worth about $300 million annually. Canada cannot offer this deal to new manufacturers locating here, nor can it offer breaks to companies who will use Canada as a base for exports to the United States.

Finally, FTA 1003 states that Canada will eliminate its import restrictions on used cars over a five year period.

Exceptions: Many of the key exceptions to free trade in goods have already been cited. Chapter 11 deals with exceptions that come under the rubric of emergency actions. FTA 1101 allows temporary action against imports whose reduced tariffs under Chapter 4 substantially harm a domestic industry. Tariff reductions may be halted, and tariffs even increased to some degree, as long as the party taking action notifies and consults the other party, and the action is limited in duration. FTA 1101.4 gives a right of compensation for such actions, and where such compensation cannot be agreed upon, the right to take tariff action having equivalent tariff effects.

Chapter 12 incorporates the allowable exemptions under GATT Article

XX. FTA 1203 has miscellaneous exceptions that remove logs and un-processed fish from the terms of the FTA.

3. GOVERNMENT PROCUREMENT

Governments in modern industrial states are huge buyers of everything from paper clips to guided missiles. Many governments typically develop "procurement" policies, which use the purchasing power of the state for wider purposes. Governments may insist that the paper clips they buy be produced domestically, even if they pay higher prices as a consequence. The point of the procurement policy is not simply to get the cheapest item, but to stimulate domestic industry, or in other cases to protect domestic sovereignty. This is not restricted to socialist or nationalist governments: the United States, both at the federal and the state level, has a multitude of "Buy America" programmes. Canada has also favoured domestic suppliers.

This was recognized by GATT members as early as 1973, in the Tokyo Round, and the GATT has had a procurement code since 1981, though it is quite limited since it covers goods only over a specific amount, excludes most services, and does not apply to sub-national levels or to defence spending. The FTA incorporates this existing GATT code, and all its subsequent changes. The FTA obligations merely lower the threshold of bids to US$25,000, and apply only to procurements between this amount and the GATT floor of US$171,000 (FTA 1304.1). FTA 1305 and 1306 expand the procedural and information exchange obligations of the two countries with respect to government procurement. FTA 1305 stipulates that all competitors be treated equally in terms of providing information and in being able to tender and make bids. FTA 1306 says that the parties will cooperate in monitoring the implementation and enforcement of obligations under the chapter, and will exchange needed information. The FTA Annex 1304.3 lists the government departments and agencies of both parties that are covered by the chapter. On the Canadian side, small business is exempted, while on the US side some defence items and small and minority businesses are exempted.

Simon Reisman estimated that the FTA chapter on government procurement opens about $650 million in Canadian contracts to US bids, and $4 billion in US contracts to Canadian bids.

4. SERVICES, ENTRY AND INVESTMENT

Services : Services trade has emerged as an issue because of recent technological developments that for the first time allow international competition in services that once would have been provided almost exclusively at the local level. Global service industries have developed, and the FTA breaks new ground in international trading agreements by incorporating several provisions on their treatment.

The FTA covers services in Chapter 14, and lists the covered services in FTA Annex 1408 (for illustrative purposes only; the official list is based on the standard industrial classification numbers applicable in each country). Transportation, day care, basic telecommunications, and government provided services such as education, health, and social services are not covered. Management of some health and social services is covered, however, as are computer services. FTA 1402.1 ensures national treatment for service providers, and FTA 1402.2 stipulates that sub-national governments must provide treatment "no less favourable than the most favourable treatment" they provide to their own service providers. This means that even if a province or state discriminates against another province or state within its own country, it must give American or Canadian nationals the most favourable treatment. FTA 1402.3 lists exceptions to this, so that different treatment is allowed for "prudential, fiduciary, health and safety, or consumer protection reasons." FTA 1402.5 makes it clear that all existing discriminatory provisions are grandfathered, though future changes should not make these provisions *more* discriminatory, and of course all new provisions should be consistent with the agreement. FTA 1402.9 exempts government procurement or subsidies from the chapter. FTA 1403 encourages the mutual recognition of licensing and certification requirements for the provision of covered services by nationals of the other party. Finally, FTA 1406.1 denies chapter's benefits to services that can be shown to have been indirectly provided by persons in a third party.

Temporary Entry for Business Persons : Chapter 15 of the FTA seeks to simplify the temporary entry of business persons into the two countries. It establishes the general principle that the parties shall provide temporary entry to business persons who otherwise qualify under applicable laws relating to public health and safety and national security. It also stipulates rights of consultation and appeal of decisions.

The system will create four categories of entrants: business visitors (e.g., those involved in research and design, marketing, sales), traders and investors, professionals, and intra-company transferees. Both countries will minimize their approval procedures, eliminating, for example, petitions and labour certification tests.

Investment : Chapter 16, which deals with investment, is one of the most contentious in the entire agreement. Canada has, since the late 1950s, had strong reservations about foreign, especially American, investment. Since the late 1960s, it has used various policy instruments to either curtail foreign investments, review their impact and ensure that they accord with the national interest, or excluded them entirely. The FTA limits the use of some of these instruments.

FTA 1601 stipulates that the chapter applies to all investments except financial services, government procurement, and services other than those covered under chapter 14. Each party is to extend national treatment to investors from the other party with respect to new investments, takeovers, the conduct of business, and sales of enterprises (FTA 1602.1). Neither party can impose minimum equity participation in firms by its own nationals (FTA 1602.2), or require an investor of the other party to sell its investment by reason of its nationality (FTA 1602.3). The requirement of favourable treatment applies to the sub-national governments as well (FTA 1602.4). Interestingly, the key article of the chapter, FTA 1602, includes several exemptions that apply with particular force to Canada. FTA 1602.5 allows Canada to introduce "any new measure" in respect of federal or provincial Crown corporations, even if it is inconsistent with the chapter. However, once such a measure is in place, it may not be made more inconsistent with the chapter (FTA 1602.6). Other exemptions follow ones cited previously concerning differences in treatment due to "prudential, fiduciary, health and safety, or consumer protection reasons" (FTA 1602.8).

The chapter goes on to place some limits on traditional policy devices to curtail foreign investment. FTA 1603 prohibits the imposition on an investor of the other party of performance requirements such as minimum exports or domestic content. FTA 1605 prohibits nationalization or expropriation of investments by investors of the other party except for a "public purpose," "in accordance with due process of law," on a "non-discriminatory basis," and "upon payment of prompt, adequate, and effective compensation at fair market value." FTA 1606 limits either party from preventing investors transferring profits, royalties, or other proceeds of their investment, unless such prevention is made in an equitable and non-discriminatory way.

Existing legislation is grandfathered, though Canada agreed to raise its threshold for the review of direct acquisitions in four steps to $150 million. The current threshold is $5 million, meaning that any investment above this amount will be reviewed by Investment Canada. Raising the threshold will remove many American investments from the review process. Canada also agreed to discontinue its review of indirect investments (investments made in Canada by American-owned subsidiaries) by 1992. By grandfathering existing provisions this way, Canada maintains its legislation controlling investment in such sensitive areas as oil, gas, uranium mining, cultural industries, and financial (other than insurance) and transportation services.

5. FINANCIAL SERVICES

The FTA gave financial services its own section consisting of one small chapter. The United States, under FTA 1701, undertook largely to exempt Canadian financial institutions from future changes in American law that would discriminate on the basis of national origin. Canada, on the other hand, made commitments that required several changes in existing federal legislation. First, Canada agreed to exempt Americans from foreign ownership provisions that currently prohibit non-Canadians from owning financial institutions (FTA 1703.1). However, Americans will still be restricted by the general provision of the Bank Act that no person may own more than 10 percent of a bank. Second, United States-controlled Canadian bank subsidiaries are exempted from limitations on the total domestic assets of foreign bank subsidiaries in Canada (FTA 1703.2). Finally, Canada agreed not to use its foreign investment review powers to unduly impede the entry of American financial institutions into the domestic Canadian market (FTA 1703.3).

6. INSTITITIONAL PROVISIONS

The FTA is shot through with requirements for notification, consultation, compensation, and further negotiation. There are large areas that are unclear, others that will invite dispute, and still others in which the agreement calls for continued review and negotiation. All of these demand some institutional mechanism to manage the agreement and to deal with disputes. The FTA splits the problem of disputes/consultation/negotiation into two parts. The first deals with explicit provisions of the FTA itself. This is a matter of how to manage those terms upon which the parties were able to agree. The second deals with the thorny problem of trade remedy legislation, which the parties *were not* able to resolve. Trade remedies consist of such measures as countervailing duties and anti-dumping measures, whereby a country explicitly erects protective tariffs or other measures against what it considers to be unfair competition by importers.

Managing the FTA : Chapter 18 of the FTA establishes a Canada–United States Trade Commission to deal with "the avoidance or settlement of all disputes regarding the interpretation or application of this agreement or whenever a party considers that an actual or proposed measure of the other party is or would be inconsistent with the obligations of this agreement" (FTA 1801). The commission will have power in all matters except those dealing with financial services (FTA Chapter 17) and trade remedy cases involving anti-dumping and countervailing duties.

The commission will not only resolve disputes but will supervise the implementation of the FTA and its subsequent elaborations. It will be composed of representatives of both countries, the principle representatives being the cabinet level officer or minister primarily responsible for international trade. The commission will convene at least once a year, with meetings being held alternately in the two countries. It will develop its own rules and procedures, though all its decisions must be taken by consensus. It will also have the power to establish and delegate responsibilities to ad hoc or standing committees and working groups (FTA 1802).

The FTA assumes that the two countries will notify each other and consult with respect to any possible measures each is considering that might affect the agreement. So, if the United States were considering legislation that might affect Canada's interests under the agreement, it would be obligated to inform Canada as early as possible, in writing, before the measure was implemented. If this were impossible, then immediate notification after implementation is required (FTA 1803.2). Even if the United States were convinced that any measure it was considering would not affect Canada, Canada would still have the right of consultation (FTA 1804). If these consultations did not resolve a matter within 30 days, either party may request a meeting of the commission, and unless otherwise agreed that meeting must take place within 10 days (FTA 1805.1). The commission has 30 days to try to resolve disputes; if it cannot, it must refer the dispute to binding arbitration of a specially appointed panel. If a party fails to implement the decision of such a panel, and the parties are unable to agree to compensation or remedial action, then the other party has the right to take action that will remove "equivalent benefits" from the non-complying party (FTA 1806). What this means is that if a panel found against the United States, but the Americans refused to implement the decision, then Canada could raise a tariff or take some other action whose economic effect would cancel out the gain sought through the disputed measure.

The panels are the heart of the dispute resolution system. They will consist of five members, appointed from a roster kept by the commission. Two will be Canadian, two American, and the commission will appoint a chairperson. If either party fails to appoint its panelists within 15 days, they shall be selected by lot from those of its citizens on the roster. If the commission fails to appoint a chair within 15 days, then at the request of either party, the panelists have 15 days to appoint one. If they in turn fail, the chair will be selected by lot from the roster (FTA 1807.3). Once established, the panels may set their own procedures, as long as they involve at least one hearing and the opportunity to submit both written and oral arguments (1807.4). Their proceedings will be confidential, and unless otherwise agreed, they will base their decision on the submissions and arguments of the parties.

Within three months of the chairperson's appointment, the panel must submit a preliminary report with its findings of fact and recommendations

(FTA 1807.5). Panelists may submit separate opinions. Parties have 14 days to respond to the initial report, and the panel then has another 16 days to revise and reconsider its initial report, if necessary (FTA 1807.6). The final report of the panel is to be published, along with "any separate opinions, and any written views that either party desires to be published" (FTA 1807.7), and will go to the commission, which normally will resolve the dispute in such a way as to conform with the recommendation of the panel (FTA 1807.8). Whenever possible, the resolution of the dispute will be the *non-implementation* of the offending measure that caused the panel to convene in the first place. Alternatively, the measure could go through but the other party would have to be compensated (FTA 1807.8). If the commission cannot reach agreement within 30 days of receiving the panel's final report, and a party considers that its interests under the agreement will be impaired, that party has the right to suspend "benefits of equivalent effect" to the other party until some satisfactory resolution can be achieved (FTA 1807.9).

Anti-dumping and Countervailing Duties : As noted earlier, much of the original impetus for the free trade negotiations, from the Canadian side at least, was the concern over rising American protectionism. This protectionism took the form of capricious application of anti-dumping and countervailing duties. The first pertains to goods that are sold at prices lower than in their domestic market. The second is conceptually different, though the effect is the same. In countervail cases, a government may decide that manufacturers of imports have been unfairly subsidized in some way by their domestic governments, giving their products an unfair advantage. A countervailing duty is a special tariff set, theoretically, to make up the difference of the subsidy. In the early days of the free trade negotiations, it was hoped that Canada would be able to escape such actions entirely. The best that the FTA could achieve, however, was a complicated review process that leaves intact both the domestic law-making powers of both countries, and their judicial mechanisms for dealing with anti-dumping and countervail applications. A working group is to be established that, over five to seven years, is to develop a new subsidies code (FTA 1906 and 1907).

Each party "reserves the right to apply its anti-dumping law and countervailing duty law to goods imported from the territory of the other party" (FTA 1902.1). Each party may also modify these laws, but such modifications will apply to the other party only if it is explicitly named. The other party must be notified and consulted, and such amendments must not offend the spirit of the GATT and must be consistent with the general purposes of the FTA to liberalize trade (FTA 1902.2). But the real issue, at least for the short term, is not the laws themselves, but the decisions that are made with respect to anti-dumping and countervails, based on these laws. The FTA does not affect the powers of either party to make such determinations; all it does is substitute a quasi-judicial review process to determine whether such a decision was in accordance with the party's anti-dumping or countervailing duty law (defined as "relevant statutes, legislative history, regulations, administrative practice, and judicial precedents"). The FTA establishes special expert panels to replace the final judicial review functions of the Federal Court (Canada) and the Court of International Trade (US).

Panelists are to be drawn from a roster consisting of 50 people, 25 from each country. The parties are to consult, and propose candidates of "good character, high standing and repute," who show qualities of "objectivity, reliability, sound judgment, and general familiarity with international law" (FTA Annex 1902.2(1)). Because of the panel's quasi-judicial functions the majority of members on each panel must be lawyers. Like the arbitration panels under chapter 18, these panels will also have five members. Each party will initially propose two panelists, and each party has up to four peremptory challenges it may make of the other's panelists. Both parties have to agree on the appointment of the fifth panelist. In the event of disagreement or inability to appoint the first two panelists and the fifth panelist, the same type of procedures apply as in the case of arbitration panels under chapter 18, though the time limits are somewhat longer (FTA Annex 1901.2(3)). The chair, who must be one of the lawyers on the panel, will then be elected by majority vote. In the absence of a majority, the chair will be chosen by lot (again, from the lawyers on the panel). All panelists will be governed by a code of conduct to be established by the parties (FTA 1910).

Either party may request panel review of an anti-dumping or countervailing duty determination made by the other. The parties have 30 days from the publication or notification of such a determination to make their written request for a panel review (FTA 1904.4). While the parties have to design rules of procedure for the review panels, these rules will be based on prevailing judicial ones pertaining to appellate courts. The procedural rules will be designed in a way that ensures final panel decisions will be submitted no later than 315 days after the request for the panel was made (FTA 1904.14).

A close reading of Chapter 19 shows that it contemplates two types of panels and two types of determinations. The first is covered by FTA 1903, and pertains to the review of statutory amendments. In this case, a panel can only issue an opinion as to whether an amendment to an anti-dumping or countervailing duty statute does not conform to the GATT or to the spirit of the FTA. If it does recommend modifications to the statute, the parties have to consult to seek a resolution within 90 days. If they fail, and if nothing has been done within nine months of the end of this consultation period, the offended party may take comparable legislative action, or may terminate the FTA with 60 days' notice (FTA 1903.3).

The second type of panel reviews final anti-dumping and countervailing duty determinations. These panels may uphold the determination (i.e., decide that it is consistent with the law) or remand it, and its decisions are final and binding on the parties (FTA 1904.9 and 1904.10). Remanding means that the original authority that issued the order must amend it in a way consistent with the panel's ruling. There is a time limit on this, which, while it varies, will not exceed the time allowed for the authority to make its determinations in the first place.

7. OTHER PROVISIONS

Part 7 of the FTA includes miscellaneous matters, but several are of critical importance. FTA 2001 exempts the treatment of taxation from the FTA, upholding rights and obligations under the 1980 Convention between Canada and the United States of America with Respect to Taxes on Income and on Capital. FTA 2002 allows various restrictions to be applied by either party, within limits, with regard to balance of payments issues. There are provisions on national security, intellectual property, softwood lumber, and plywood standards. On the whole these are relatively minor aspects of the FTA, but several articles are of more direct interest.

FTA 2005 explicitly exempts cultural industries from the agreement. Cultural industries are defined as enterprises engaged in the publication, distribution, sale and exhibition (if this applies) of books, magazines, and newspapers; film or video recordings; audio or video music recordings; printed music; and radio, television, cable broadcasting, satellite programming, and broadcast network services (FTA 2012). The exemption is not complete, however. The tariff provisions of the FTA apply (FTA 401), as does the specific provision that if Canada demands the divestiture of a business in the cultural industry because of its indirect purchase by an American firm, Canada will offer to buy the business at a fair price (FTA 1607.4). Also, FTA 2006 stipulates that Canadian cable broadcasters will have to pay a royalty for the retransmission of American TV programmes by 1 January 1990. Up to now, cable operators have been able to pluck American signals from the ether for free, and simply retransmit them to Canadian viewers for a fee. The general right that each of the parties has to invoke consultation and dispute settlement procedures on any measure they deem will nullify or impair any benefit reasonably expected to flow from the agreement, does not apply to cultural industries (FTA 2011.2).

FTA 2005.2 reads: "Notwithstanding any other provision of this agreement, a party may take measures of equivalent commercial effect in response to actions that would have been inconsistent with the agreement but for paragraph 1." Since cultural industries are not covered by the FTA, Canada may pass laws in the field that contravene the agreement, for example, laws prohibiting the importation of American non-pornographic films or magazines in order to protect the domestic market. FTA 2005.2 allows the United States to completely circumvent the procedures in Chapter 18 on dispute resolution, and take action as it sees fit (but not inconsistent with the FTA) to exact equivalent commercial effect. The nature of this effect is not discussed in the FTA, and it need not be in the cultural area. Canadian actions against American videos could be met with American actions against Canadian fish.

Finally, there are provisions on the establishment of "monopolies" or state enterprises. FTA 2010.1 says that nothing in the agreement "shall prevent a party from maintaining or designating a monopoly." If the establishment of a monopoly might affect the interests of persons of the other party, there are requirements of prior notification and consultation, as well as an obligation by the offending party to minimize any impairment of benefits under the agreement for the other party (FTA 2010.2). A monopoly, once established, may not discriminate in its sales against persons or goods of the other party, or use its monopoly power in other markets (through, for example, subsidiaries) to compete unfairly (FTA 2010.3).

Appendix II:

International Trade Terms

General Agreement on Tariffs and Trade: Usually referred to as the GATT. Founded in 1948 (the agreement itself was signed in 1947) with a membership of 23 countries that has grown to almost 100. The GATT headquarters are located in Geneva. The agreement contains rules which govern trade, negotiations over trade, and grievances among signatories. Negotiations over the GATT occur in "rounds" every seven years, usually named after the place in which they are centred. The current (1988) negotiations are called the Uruguay Round.

Tariffs: Also called duties, these are a tax levied on imports. They serve various purposes, from revenue raising (very important for Canada in the early years after Confederation) to the protection of domestic industries. In principle, a tariff is an added cost that the importer passes on to consumers, raising the price of the product. If a domestic industry has trouble competing with imports, tariffs can make those imports less attractive to consumers. The tariff can thus be used to "protect" domestic industries, with the consequence that domestic prices might be higher.

Non-Tariff Barriers: Also known as NTB's, these are means of protecting domestic industries from imports in the absence of tariffs. Special administrative requirements (e.g., processing fees, landing in selected ports, extra paperwork, demands that imports meet unreasonably high or unusual standards) can block supplies of imports just as well as tariffs.

Protectionism: A general policy stance taken by a government to reduce imports and protect the domestic market. Distinct from mere use of tariffs. Implies a broad trade strategy, usually with respect to a given sector (e.g., manufacturing, agriculture).

Government Procurement: The purchases governments make, from paper clips to space satellites. In modern economies the government is the single largest buyer of goods and services, and so most governments develop policies to make most of those purchases in the domestic market.

Trade Deficit: In simple terms, when a country buys more from abroad than it sells. This usually means that domestic producers are facing stiff import competition, and that the deficit is being funded through foreign borrowings. Borrowing cannot go on indefinitely, and so substantial and sustained trade deficits usually lead countries to consider ways to increase exports and decrease imports. Protectionist measures can address the latter problem. The US trade deficit in the late 1980s was therefore linked to calls in Congress to pass protectionist trade laws.

Comprehensive v. Sectoral Trade Deal: The former refers to an agreement that covers virtually the entire economy. The latter is restricted to selected sectors of the economy, for example, steel, automotive products, or electronic goods.

Countervailing Duties: Also referred to as "countervails". Most countries have some regulatory mechanism to review imports and judge whether they are coming in "fairly" or not. One type of unfairness is known as "dumping", whereby a foreign competitor saturates a market with products sold at less than market prices (this might be done to get rid of excess stocks or to capture new markets). Domestic producers can take their complaints to the domestic regulatory agency, which may then apply a countervailing duty (a special tarrif) to make up the difference between the import price and the "proper" price. This may also be done in cases where domestic producers claim that competitors have been unfairly subsidized in some way by their host government (e.g., tax breaks, special export incentives). The point to note is that most countervails are unpredictable, since they are *special* measures (part of a panoply of "trade remedies") that exist alongside a country's normal trade laws.

Appendix III

Cast of Characters in the Free Trade Debate

Government

Prime Minister Brian Mulroney

James Kelleher
Pat Carney   Ministers of International Trade
John Crosbie

Members Of Canadian Negotiating Team

Simon Reisman, Ambassador for International Trade Negotiations
Gordon Ritchie, Ambassador and Deputy Chief Negotiator
Alan Nymark, Assistant Chief Negotiator, Federal-Provincial Relations
Charles Stedman, Assistant Chief Negotiator, Liaison with Private Industry and SAGITs
Andrei Sulzenko, Chief of Staff
Bill Dymond, in charge of position preparation on government purchasing practices
Michael Hart, in charge of position preparation on U.S. protectionism
Bruce Macdonald, Reisman spokesman

External Affairs Officers Involved With FTA

Derek Burney, Chief of Staff to Prime Minister
Bruce Phillips, Director of Communications, Prime Minister's Office
Donald Campbell, Assistant Deputy Minister, United States Branch
Peter Lloyd, Director-General, Communications, Trade Section

John Buchanan (Cons. Nova Scotia) in favour
David Peterson (Lib. Ontario) opposed
Joseph Ghiz, (Lib. P.E.I.) opposed
Howard Pawley, (NDP Manitoba)opposed
Grant Devine, (Cons. Saskatchewan) strongly in favour
Brian Peckford, (Cons. Newfoundland) in favour
Robert Bourassa, (Lib. Quebec) strongly in favour
Bill Vander Zalm, (Social Credit B.C.) strongly in favour
Don Getty, Alberta (Cons. Alberta) strongly in favour
Frank McKenna, (Lib. New Brunswick) in favour

Sectoral Advisory Groups On International Trade (SAGITs), and their Chairpersons

(10-15 members per committee)
1. Agriculture, Food and Beverages
   Benoit Lavigne, Agricultural Consultant, Montreal
2. Fish and Fish Products
   Victor Young, Chairman, Fishery Products International, St. John's
3. Mineral and Metals
   William James, Chairman, Falconbridge Ltd., Toronto
4. Energy Products and Services
   Robert Pierce, President, Nova Corp, Calgary
5. Chemicals and Petrochemicals
   Firman Bentley, V.P., Polysar Ltd., Sarnia
6. Forest Products
   Raymond Smith, President, MacMillan Bloedel Ltd., Vancouver
7. Industrial, Marine and Rail Equipment
   Guy Champagne, President, Exeltor Ltd., Bedford, Quebec.
8. Automotive and Aerospace
   Jack Ripley, Chairman, Allied Signal Canada Ltd., Mississauga
9. Textiles, Footwear and Leather
   Sandy Archibald, Chairman, Britex Ltd., Bridgetown, Nova Scotia
10. Apparel and Fur
    Peter Nygard, Chairman, Nygard International, Winnipeg
11. Consumer and Household Products
    Pierre Lortie, President, Provigo, Montreal
12. Computer Equipment and Services
    Alex Curran, Chairman, SED Services Inc., Saskatoon
13. Financial Services
    Jalynn Bennett, V.P., Manufacturers Life Insurance Co., Toronto

14. General Services
   Gail Cook, V.P., Bennecon Ltd., Toronto

International Trade Advisory Committee

Walter Light, Chairman (Chairman, Northern Telecom)
Laurent Beaudoin (Chairman, Bombardier)
David Culver (President, Alcan)
Bruce Howe (B.C. Resources Investment Corp.)
Maureen Prendiville (Prendiville Sawmills Ltd.)
James McCambly (Canadian Federation of Labour)
Sally Hall (Consumers Association of Canada)
Wendy Dobson (Executive Director, C.D. Howe Institute)

Interest Groups

1. Opposed to FTA

Council of Canadians

— includes Margaret Atwood, Maude Barlow, Pierre Berton, Grace Hartman, Jacques Hébert, Mel Hurtig, Norman Jewison, Eric Kierans, Hugh MacLennan, Farley Mowat, Alphonse Ouimet, Peter Pollen, David Suzuki, Charles Taylor, John Fryer

Pro-Canada Network (offshoot of *Council of Canadians*)

Maude Barlow, Chairman
Mel Hurtig
National Federal of Nurses Unions (Kathleen Connors)
Canadian Teachers Federation (Frank Garrity)
Centrale de l'enseignement du Quebec
Association for Native Development in the Performing Arts (Lenore
   Keeship-Tobias)
Canadian Labour Congress (Shirley Carr)
Canadian Auto Workers (Bob White)
Louis Laberge
Yvon Charbonneau
Gerald Larose

Toronto Coalition Against Free Trade (formed February 1986, later
   drops"Toronto" from the name)
— includes Nancy White, Bishop Remi de Roo, Pierre Berton, David
Suzuki, Bob White, Bruce Cockburn, United Church of Canada, Canadian
Churches for Global Economic Justice, National Action Committee for the
Status of Women , National Farmers Union, Council of Canadians, Canadian
Conference on the Arts (Curtis Barlow)

Quebec Coalition Against Free Trade (formed July 1987)
— includes four trade unions: CEQ, UPA, CSN and FTQ
Ontario Federation of Labour (Cliff Pilkey, President)

Business Council for Fair Trade (established 16 December 1987)
— includes James Conrad, Executive Director, Comcheq Payroll
Services Ltd. (William Loewen),   Preston Manufacturing Company Ltd.
(Tom Taylor)

2. In favour of FTA

Canadian Alliance for Trade and Job Opportunities
(described as non-government funded, non-partisan)
— includes Peter Lougheed, Joint Chairman, Donald Macdonald, Joint
Chairman, David Culver, President, Alcan, and Chairman, Business Council
on National Issues (BCNI), Thomas d'Aquino, President, BCNI, Darcy Mc-
Keough, former Treasurer of Ontario, Michel Bélanger, Chairman, National Bank of Canada, Canadian Manufacturers Association (Laurent Thibault,
President), Canadian Chamber of Commerce (Roger Hamel, President),
Canadian Federal of Independent Business (John Bulloch, President),
Aerospace Industries Association, Pharmaceutical Manufacturers Associa-
tion of Canada, Western Canadian Wheat Growers

Consumers Association of Canada (Sally Hall, President)

National Association of Manufacturers (Alexander Trowbridge,
   President)

Canadian Exporters Association (Frank Petrie, President)

Council of Forest Industries of British Columbia (President, Michael
   Apsey)

NOTES

1 *Globe and Mail*, 19 March 1985.

2 *Globe and Mail*, 19 March 1985.

3 Two in particular, both released in 1983, were important: *Canadian Trade Policy for the 1980s* and *A Review of Canadian Trade Policy*.

4 *Globe and Mail*, 21 January 1985.

5 *Globe and Mail*, 30 January 1985.

6 *Globe and Mail*, 23 March 1985. The report studied only 35 industry groups, and looked only at tariff barriers.

7 *Globe and Mail*, 25 April 1985.

8 *Globe and Mail*, 16 May 1985.

9 *Winnipeg Free Press*, 17 May 1985.

10 *Globe and Mail*, 23 August 1985.

11 *Globe and Mail*, 9 May 1985; 26 June 1985. See also the submissions by business organizations to the Macdonald commission, particularly the pro-free trade stance by the Canadian Manufacturers' Association, an organization with a long history of support for tariff barriers.

12 *Toronto Star*, 28 May 1985.

13 *Toronto Star*, 28 June 1985.

14 *Toronto Star*, 27 July 1985. Both the American and Canadian branches of the United Steelworkers also opposed free trade; *Globe and Mail*, 4 June 1985.

15 *Globe and Mail*, 2 May 1985; 18 July 1985.

16 *Toronto Star*, 3 August 1985.

17 *Toronto Star*, 9 August 1985.

18 *Globe and Mail*, 24 July 1985.

19 *Globe and Mail*, 26 June 1985.

20 *Globe and Mail*, 27 July 1985.

21 Royal Commission on the Economic Union and Development Prospects for Canada, *Report*, 3 vols. (Ottawa: Minister of Supply and Services, 1985).

22 *Montreal Gazette*, 10 September 1985.

23 *Globe and Mail*, 27 September 1985.

24 *Globe and Mail*, 25 September 1985.

25 *Globe and Mail*, 18 September 1985.

26 Interview, Ottawa, August 1988.

27 *Globe and Mail*, 28 September 1985.

28 *Globe and Mail*, 30 September 1985.

29 *Globe and Mail*, 1 October 1985.

30 *Toronto Star*, 4 October 1985.

31 These remarks were made variously by William Merkin (deputy assistant US trade representative) on 7 October and by William Brock (US secretary of labour) on 23 October.

32 *Globe and Mail*, 9 November 1985.

33 *Globe and Mail*, 30 November 1985.

34 *Globe and Mail*, 4 December 1985.

35 *Toronto Star*, 11 October 1988.

36 *Globe and Mail*, 23 December 1985. These figures are from an Environics and CROP poll conducted from 18 November to 11 December on 2,036 Canadians.

37 *Globe and Mail*, 8 January 1986.

38 *Globe and Mail*, 11 January 1986.

39 *Globe and Mail*, 23 January 1986.

40 *Globe and Mail*, 24 January 1986.

41 *Globe and Mail*, 6 February 1986.

42 *Globe and Mail*, 8 February 1986.

43 *Globe and Mail*, 18 February 1986.

44 *Globe and Mail*, 22 March 1986.

45 *Globe and Mail*, 28 February 1986.

46 *Globe and Mail*, 12 April 1986.

47 *Globe and Mail*, 15 April 1986.

48 *Globe and Mail*, 18 April 1986.

49 *Globe and Mail*, 22 April 1986.

50 *Globe and Mail*, 23 April 1986.

51 *Globe and Mail*, 29 April 1986.

52 *Globe and Mail*, 16 April 1986.

53 *Toronto Star*, 27 January 1986.

54 *Globe and Mail*, 4 February 1986.

55 *Globe and Mail*, 5 February 1986.

56 *Globe and Mail*, 5 March 1986.

57 *Globe and Mail*, 28 March 1986.

58 Canada's somewhat curious response was to slap a tariff on US books and periodicals.

59 *Globe and Mail*, 27 May 1986.

60 *Globe and Mail*, 3 June 1986.

61 *Globe and Mail*, 17 June 1986.

62 *Toronto Star*, 19 June 1986.

63 *Globe and Mail*, 18 June 1986.

64 *Globe and Mail*, 19 June 1986.

65 *Globe and Mail*, 12 November 1986.

66 *Globe and Mail*, 13 November 1986.

67 *Globe and Mail*, 13 September 1986.

68 *Globe and Mail*, 17 OCtober 1986.

69 *Globe and Mail*, 20 October 1986.

70 *Globe and Mail*, 19 January 1987.

71 *Globe and Mail*, 16 January 1987.

72 *Globe and Mail*, 10 January 1987.

73 *Globe and Mail*, 20 February 1987.

74 *Globe and Mail*, 19 March 1987.

75 *Globe and Mail*, 6 April 1987.

76 *Toronto Star*, 7 May 1987.

77 *Globe and Mail*, 13 March 1987.

78 *Globe and Mail*, 18 March 1987.

79 *Globe and Mail*, 27 April 1987.

80 *Globe and Mail*, 21 May 1987.,

81 *Globe and Mail*, 25 May 1987.

82 *Globe and Mail*, 10 June 1987.

83 *Globe and Mail*, 17 June 1987.

84 *Globe and Mail*, 7 July 1987.

85 *Globe and Mail*, 8 July 1987.

86 *Globe and Mail*, 9 July 1987.

87 *Globe and Mail*, 9 July 1987.

88 *Globe and Mail*, 24 August 1987.

89 *Globe and Mail*, 29 August 1987.

90 *Globe and Mail*, 10 September 1987.

91 *Globe and Mail*, 15 September 1987.

92 *Globe and Mail*, 16 September 1987.

93 *Globe and Mail*, 21 September 1987.

94 *Globe and Mail*, 23 September 1987.

95 *Globe and Mail*, 23 September 1987.

96 *Globe and Mail*, 24 September 1987.

97 *Globe and Mail*, 25 September 1987.

98 *Toronto Star*, 28 September 1987.

99 *Globe and Mail*, 30 September 1987.

100 *Globe and Mail*, 3 October 1987.

101 *Globe and Mail*, 5 October 1987.

102 *Globe and Mail*, 5 October 1987.

103 *Globe and Mail*, 28 October 1987.

104 *Toronto Star*, 31 October 1987.

105 *Toronto Star*, 5 November 1987.

106 *Globe and Mail*, 17 November 1987.

107 *Globe and Mail*, 2 December 1987.

108 *Globe and Mail*, 4 December 1987.

109 *Globe and Mail*, 8 December 1987.

110 *Globe and Mail*, 12 April 1988.

111 *Globe and Mail*, 2 August 1988.

112 *Globe and Mail*, 16 August 1988.

113 *Globe and Mail*, 19 November 1988.

114 Simon Reisman, in *Assessing the Canada–US Free Trade Agreement*, ed. Murray G. Smith and Frank Stone (Ottawa: IRPP, 1987), 46.

115 John Dillon, "Continental Energy Policy," in *The Free Trade Deal*, ed. Duncan Cameron

(Toronto: James Lorimer, 1988), 104.

116 Andrew Jackson, "The Trade Deal and the Resource Sector," in *The Free Trade Deal*, 98.

117 Ibid., 101.

118 Edward A. Carmichael, "Energy," in *Free Trade: The Real Story*, ed. John Crispo (Toronto: Gage, 1988), 68.

119 Duncan Cameron and Hugh Mackenzie, "Manufacturing," in *The Free Trade Deal*, 118.

120 John Calvert, "Government Procurement," in *The Free Trade Deal*, 136.

121 Hugh Mackenzie, "Free Trade and the Auto Industry," in *The Free Trade Deal*, 127.

122 Reisman, op. cit., 44.

123 Ronald J. Wonnacott, "Labour Market Adjustments," in *Free Trade: The Real Story*, 63.

124 Duncan Cameron, Stephen Clarkson, and Mel Watkins, "Market Access," in *The Free Trade Deal*, 52.

125 Stephen Clarkson, "The Canada–United States Trade Commission," in *The Free Trade Deal*, 29. The following articles of the FTA, for example, call for the commission to be notified of any actions: 1102.2, 1102.3, 1402.3, 1602.8, 1803. There is a blanket provision for consultation in FTA 1804, as well as specific provisions.

126 Ibid., 45.

127 Reisman, op. cit., 44.

128 Donald Macdonald in *Assessing the Canada–US Free Trade Agreement*, 26.

129 Ibid., 27-28.

130 Richard G. Harris, "Employment Effects," in *Free Trade: The Real Story*, 107.

131 Wonnacott, op. cit., 132.

132 Lane, "The Impact of the Free Trade Deal on Work," 218.

133 Watkins, "Investment," 89.

134 Susan Crean, "Reading Between the Lines: Culture and the Free-Trade Agreement," in *The Free Trade Deal*, 230.

135 Gerald Caplan in *Assessing the Canada–US Free Trade Agreement*, passages from 260, 231 respectively.

136 Cameron, "Introduction," *The Free Trade Deal*, vii.

137 Daniel Drache, "North American Integration," in *The Free Trade Deal*, 73.

INDEX

167-68; Conservative government approach to, 128, 151; Customs regulations and, 133-35, 136-37, 142, 154; definition of, 111; difference between hard and soft core, 108; difficulties in legislating for, 151-53; early approach of Canadian courts, 114-15; effects of technology on availability, 114-15; general role of courts in, 154; judicial decisions regarding, 113-14, 114-15, 118-19, 121, 123, 132-33, 135, 154-55; legislative attempts under Conservatives, 130-4; legislative attempts under Liberals, 119-30; regulation by provinces, 117, 123, 126. *See also* Hicklin test; obscenity; Bill C-38; Bill C-53; Bill C-54; Bill C-58; Bill C-111; Bill C-114; Bill C-207

Pornography, feminist position on, 110-12, 120, 122-24, 125, 128-29, 132, 155-56

Pro-Canada Network, 333, 345

Prohibited Importation Unit (pornography), 134

Provinces and Policy-making, 65-66, 78, 96-97, 117, 324, 328-29, 330, 333, 338, 340, 353. *See also* Federalism, executive federalism

Prud'homme, Marcel, 254

Public opinion, 135, 142, 187, 192, 203, 280, 325, 343

Rae, Bob, 257

Ralliement créditiste, 174, 176

Reagan, Ronald, 68, 74, 130, 203, 316, 318-19, 320, 322, 324, 335, 341; persuading Congress, 326, 327-28

Red Hot Video, 124, 125

Red Paper (pharmaceuticals), 67

Regan, Gerald, 319

Regionalism, in Canadian politics, 24, 35-39, 41-42, 46-47, 96-97; and Policy-making, 21, 23, 24, 26, 31. *See also* Provinces

Reisman, Simon, 82, 316, 324, 325-26, 328, 329, 331, 333, 334, 336, 337, 340, 348, 349, 350, 355; professional background, 323

Rémillard, Gil, 238-40, 241, 253, 256

Restrictive Trades Practices Commission, 58, 94; Report of, 60

Richler, Mordecai, 317, 345

Riis, Nelson, 84

Roberts, John, 68

Robinson, Svend, 145, 148

Roch, Gilles, 275-76

Roe v. Wade (U.S., 1973), 185, 199, 203, 223

Rowe, Ken, 27

Roy, Bernard, 244

Royal Commission on Health Services (Hall Commission), 60

Royal Commission on the Economic Union and Development Prospects for Canada, 321-22

Royal Commission on Patents, Copyrights and Industrial Designs (Ilsley Commission), 60

Royal Commission on the Revision of the Criminal Code (1949), 114

Royal Commission on the Status of Women, 180

Schroeder, Vic, 31

Schumiatcher, Morris, 188, 190

Scott, Robert, 191, 193, 194, 195, 196

Section 251 (abortion). *See* Abortion

Senate, 55, 81, 342; as political institution, 95-96; committees of, 82-84, 87-88, 89-90, 114, 266-67; legislative process in, 82-83, 87-89, 90-92; reform of, 55, 81, 83-84, 85-86, 91, 241, 245, 252, 253

Simeon, Richard, 289

Sinclair Committee, 87-88; report of, 89-90

Smoling, Leslie, 191, 192, 193, 194, 195

Spar Aerospace Ltd., 23

Speaker of the Houise of Commons, *See* John Fraser

Special Committee on Pornography and Prostitution (Fraser Committee), 126, 129-30, 131-32, 138, 139, 143, 144, 146, 147, 152

Spector, Norman, 241, 244, 263, 274

Speyer, Chris, 267, 270

Stevens, Sinclair, 25

Student Union for Peace Action, 180

Supreme Court of Canada, 165-66; decision on Bill 101, 284; decision in Morgentaler case, 197-200, 204; and *Lady Chatterly's Lover*, 121; and patriation of the Constitution, 232; and Saskatchewan language legislation, 278

Suzuki, David, 330

Technology transfer, 28, 29, 33, 35, 37, 44

Thatcher, Margaret, 130, 203

Toronto Coalition Against Free Trade, 330

Town, Harold, 317, 345

Tremblay, Arthur, 244, 267

Trudeau, Pierre Elliot, 22, 24, 42, 63, 68, 82, 87, 108, 174, 175, 234, 235, 236, 242, 254,

256, 258-59, 271, 291, 319, 321, 354, 355;
appearance before Senate on Meech Lake
Accord, 277; attack on Meech Lake Accord, 257, 258-59
Turner, John, 66, 70, 73-74, 78, 84, 85-86, 89,
127, 175, 251-52, 253, 254-55, 260-61, 266,
288, 272, 277, 280, 291, 315, 316, 317, 342,
343-44, 345, 357; and Bill C-190 (pharmaceuticals), 59-62

Ultramar Canada Ltd., closing of refinery, 25
Unions, *See* Labour
United Auto Workers, 321
United Senior Citizens of Ontario, 78

Vancouver Women's Caucus, 180
Vander Zalm, William, 31, 37, 203, 257, 263
Vatican Council (1962-65), 178
Vennat, Manon, 26, 28
Vézina, Monique, 28, 29-30, 43

Waddell, Ian, 273
Wahn, Ian, 174-75
Wallis, Skip, 66, 69, 70
Weiner, Gerry, 27
White, Bob, 321, 330, 339, 340
White, Brian, 34
Wilson, Justice, 133, 198-99, 200, 205
Wilson, Michael, 89, 336, 337, 338-39, 344,
354, 356
Wimmin's Fire Brigade, 124-25

Yeutter, Clayton, 74, 322, 323, 327, 338
Young Socialists, 180, 192

Printed in Canada